ALLIED
DUNBAR
PREMIERSHIP

PLAYFAIR
RUGBY UNION
ANNUAL 1998-99

3rd edition

Ed.

HEADLINE

Typeset by
Letterpart Limited, Reigate, Surrey

Printed in England by
Clays Ltd, St Ives plc

HEADLINE BOOK PUBLISHING
A division of Hodder Headline PLC
338 Euston Road
London NW1 3BH

Contents

Editorial Preface

The war of words continued unabated last season and an overpowering sense of mistrust and rancour hangs over British rugby, particularly in England. Everybody concerned, however, must put that aside this season or the game in the four home Unions could slip into terminal decline. Playing numbers are down 20 per cent and the public are increasingly becoming bored and angry with the never-ending politics. Their patience has been stretched to breaking point. As we start the build-up towards the 1999 World Cup, the British authorities have one final chance to put their house in order and act like reasonable human beings rather than pathetic adolescent gangs in the schoolyard. Too many egos have been running wild and need to be checked. This will be the last, best chance to sell the game and everything that revolves around the sport. Mess it up this time and we can all go home.

There were occasional rays of hope last season. Newcastle were worthy Allied Dunbar Premiership champions and have worked hard to sell the game to the 'Geordie' public, while Tetley's Bitter Cup holders Saracens played attractive rugby and achieved the near-impossible by uprooting to Watford and filling the 20,000-capacity Vicarage Road. The Premiership might have been dominated by Newcastle and Saracens but it was also competitive and entertaining throughout, though it still falls some way short of the Super 12s. Elsewhere Richmond had the courage of their convictions and always attempted to play constructive running rugby despite discouraging mid-season results, Sale likewise. Bedford were pre-eminent in League Two and in Jewson One Worcester and Leeds were dominant and look fully geared up to flourish in the top flight.

The third Heineken European Cup was marred in the pool stages by ugly scenes of violence, on and off the field, and latterly by doubts over its very future – England's top clubs eventually confirmed in January that they will not be competing this season. Shame. In essence it is a wonderful competition that has added sparkle to the northern hemisphere rugby calendar and provides a welcome break from familiar and slightly jaded routines. But in many ways the competition has been ill-starred. It probably arrived three years too early, before the new professional domestic Leagues had been allowed to develop and become self-financing. Nor can it be seen as the basis of the European season – there is simply no evidence that fans will travel except for finals and semi-finals. In addition it should probably be a straightforward Cup with fewer ties – not a hybrid Cup/League, which makes too many demands in an already crowded season. Big European games should be something special, contests to be anticipated. Too many matches last season were mundane, predictable, lacking support and atmosphere.

Internationally the season merely underlined the massive gulf between the northern and southern hemispheres, bigger now even than in the days of shamateurism. To witness the sheer athleticism and physicality of the stars from Australia, New Zealand and South Africa is to wonder what our extremely well-paid full-time professionals do all week. Many of our players still look unfit and overweight – many also seem to lack basic skills such as passing and catching, at least when put under pressure.

Much more serious thought must be given to planning tours in future. England's southern hemisphere odyssey would probably have been a debacle even with a full squad, so onerous and ill-conceived was the itinerary. Clive Woodward was the recipient of the biggest hospital pass in history and only just survived.

England, however, received much unwarranted flak over their summer tour. After contributing over 20 players to the victorious Lions squad in 1997 and playing eight internationals in the winter it was quite obvious that there would be injuries and withdrawals last summer. Only three of the 17 absentees – Phil de Glanville, Paul Grayson and Jeremy Guscott – were excused on domestic grounds. Everybody else had bona fide sick notes. Wales had over 20 absentees in South Africa, Scotland rested a raft of top players in Australia, yet both countries escaped serious censure. One of the most unpalatable aspects of the season was how some interested parties, seemingly losing the argument at home, tried to enlist the international rugby community to castigate English rugby.

Domestically the season ended with the Mayfair agreement which confirmed two Premiership divisions and the English clubs' absence from Europe, as well as putting the clubs' relationship with England on a more formal basis. The agreement falls well short of perfection but agreement of any kind is preferable to a state of constant internal bickering.

The last three years of turmoil have been the biggest turn-off in the sport's history. The qualities that made it great – loyalty, honesty, flexibility and a sense of humour – seem to have been forgotten. Nobody is blameless. Some clubs are greedy and want to brush convention aside; too many players of average ability are paid too much; historically the respective Unions have been too slow to react, likewise the International Board. Both have then compensated for their previous negligence by over-reacting. Individuals with their own agendas have been given too many column inches and too much credibility. It is undeniably a mess. Yet you only have to watch a game like England's 26-26 draw with New Zealand or a Premiership encounter such as Newcastle's visit to Gloucester or Saracens' floodlit game at Kingston Park to know that rugby can still have an incredible future.

Acknowledgements

We are indebted to officials of the RFU, SRU, IRU and WRU for their assistance, Peter McMullen and Michelle Tracey at the International Rugby Board and Annmarie Freeney at Slattery PR in Dublin. Much thanks also to our patient editor Lorraine Jerram and industrious typesetter Chris Leggett. Others to provide much needed help when called upon were Andrew Harley, Bill McMurtrie, Westgate Sports Agency, David Llewellyn, John Harding, Richard Hart, Paul Beken, Nicola Goodwin, Mary Gallagher and Janet Berry.

Brendan Gallagher
Stuart Farmer
July 1998

Guide to Allied Dunbar Premiership Club Section

The following is a guide to the clubs and players in the two divisions of the Allied Dunbar Premiership. The biographies start with an individual's birth, height, weight and career. Then follows information concerning their playing career. For example, Matt Dawson (14, WS95, 4t, 1c, 1pg-28pts) indicates that at the start of the 1998-99 season Matt Dawson had won 14 full England caps, having made his debut against Western Samoa in 1995. It also indicates he has scored 28 points, consisting of 4 tries, 1 conversion and 1 penalty goal. Details are then given of his career at A/B level: A/B (11, Fr93, 7t-35pts) shows that Dawson has made 11 appearances at this level, his first being against France in 1993. In that time he has scored 7 tries.

Abbreviations for various countries are standard:

ARG	(Argentina)	NZ	(New Zealand)
AUS	(Australia)	ROM	(Romania)
CAN	(Canada)	SA	(South Africa)
ENG	(England)	SC	(Scotland)
FIJ	(Fiji)	SP	(Spain)
FR	(France)	TON	(Tonga)
IRE	(Ireland)	USA	(USA)
IT	(Italy)	WAL	(Wales)
JAP	(Japan)	WS	(Western Samoa)
NAM	(Namibia)	ZIM	(Zimbabwe)

Records of A/B appearances also include tour games against such opposition as B Col (British Columbia), S Aus (South Australia), Vic (Victoria), Nat (Natal). International records for this season's book end with England's Test against South Africa in Cape Town.

Barbarians (94) indicates that Dawson made his Barbarians debut in 1994. ADPR: 90, 23t, 6c, 16pg, 1dg-177pts indicates that in the Allied Dunbar Premiership, Dawson has made 90 appearances, scored 1 four-point try and 22 five-point tries while he has kicked 6 conversions, 16 penalties and 1 dropped goal. Where a player has scored points for more than one league club, his points total is given by club. After a player's ADPR there follow details about him, his playing career, his interests, etc. Where details of birth, height, weight etc are not given this is because we have been unable to track down such information.

ALLIED DUNBAR PREMIERSHIP

Premiership One

BATH

Formation of club: 1865
Ground: The Recreation Ground, Bath BA2 6PW
Capacity: 8,200 (Seated 2,500)
Colours: Blue, white and black
Honours: Cup Winners (10) – 1984, 1985, 1986, 1987, 1989, 1990, 1992, 1994, 1995, 1996. League Champions (6) – 1988-89, 1990-91, 1991-92, 1992-93, 1993-94, 1995-96.
Last season: ADP1 – 3rd. Heineken European Cup – Champions. Tetley's Bitter Cup – 5th round (lost 17-29 to Richmond)
Owner: Andrew Brownsword (Greetings card magnate)
Head coach: Andy Robinson. Assistant: Jon Callard
Captain: TBC

ADEBAYO, Adedayo Adeyemi (Wing)
Born Ibadan, Nigeria, 30.11.70. 5′9″, 14st 7lb. **Rep hons:** England (6, It96, 2-10pts), A (17, Sp91, 8t-38pts), Barbarians (96). **ADPR:** Bath (1989-98, 90, 43t-209pts). Frustrating season for Adedayo who did well on England's tour of Argentina in May 1997 but returned with a leg injury and made a slow start. Appeared twice for Clive Woodward's England team but by the end of the season had dropped out of the reckoning totally. Has overcome a serious knee injury (1991) to gradually fulfil the potential he first displayed at Kelly College and Swansea University. Toured Canada with an England XV in 1993 and South Africa with England in 1994. Was a valuable member of the England World Cup Sevens winning team in 1993 and represented England in Hong Kong in March 1996 and in the RWC Sevens in 1997. One of 17 children, the progeny of a major in the Nigerian Army.

BALSHAW, Iain Robert (Full-back)
Born 14.04.79. 6′1″, 13st 2lb. **ADPR:** Bath (1997-98, 8, 1t, 1c-7pts). Long-striding former Stonyhurst schoolboy who made a big impression on the England Schools tour to Australia in 1997. England U21 cap. Spent last summer resting a back injury.

BRYAN, Richard Michael (Flanker)
Born Bristol, 21.01.77. 6′3″, 16st. **ADPR:** Bath (1997-98, 13). Member of the Bath Academy who did well when deputising for injured colleagues last season.

BUTLAND, Richard de Villiers (Fly-half)
Born Cape Town, S Africa, 05.11.71. 5′11″, 13st. **Rep hons:** England A (2, NZ97, 3pg-9pts). **ADPR:** Bath (1994-98, 32, 6t, 13c, 18pg-110pts). Richard's progress continues to be frustrated by Mike Catt's presence at fly-half, so much so that at one stage last season he asked to be placed on the transfer list. Grandfather played for Natal, but Richard is of Anglo/South African stock and his family returned to England eleven years ago. Educated at Wellington College (Berks), he initially joined Harlequins but moved to Bath in 1994. Graduate of Mechanical Engineering at Bath University.

CALLARD, Jonathan Edward Brookes (Full-back)
Born Leicester, 01.01.66. 5'11", 12st 10lb. **Rep hons:** England (5, NZ93, 3c, 21pg-69pts), A (3, Sp89, 1t, 2c, 5pg-23pts), Barbarians (94-95). **ADPR:** Bath (1989-98, 102, 24t, 167c, 193pg-1027pts). Showed during Bath's memorable 19-18 Heineken European Cup victory over Brive that he is still the man for the big occasion, but Jon is now keen to develop his role as assistant coach and would be delighted if Bath could find a reliable goal-kicker. Made his senior debut for Newport against Bath before moving to the Rec and opting for England. Scored a try in Bath's 1990 Pilkington Cup triumph over Gloucester but then struggled to secure a First XV place as Jon Webb rediscovered his best form. Returned in style in 1993-94 season, making a victorious England debut against New Zealand and securing a dramatic victory over Scotland.

CATT, Michael John (Fly-half/centre)
Born Pt Elizabeth, S Africa, 17.09.71. 5'10", 13st 8lb. **Rep hons:** England (29, Wal94, 4t, 14c, 20pg, 2dg-114pts), A (1, NZ93). **ADPR:** Bath (1992-98, 76, 20t, 31c, 15pg, 5dg-222pts). Mike will be hoping to bounce back from a miserable season that included two nasty concussions, niggling hamstring problems and finally an ankle operation which forced him off England's summer tour. Versatile enough to have now played for England in four positions behind the scrum, he finally needs to decide at which position he wants to challenge for a place in England's World Cup squad. Mike was educated at Grey School, Port Elizabeth, and played for Eastern Province U21 before moving to England and almost immediately winning selection for the England U21 squad to Australia (1993). Made his full England debut against Wales as a replacement in 1994.

DE GLANVILLE, Phillip Ranulph (Centre)
Born Loughborough, 01.10.68. 5'11", 13st 6lb. **Rep hons:** England (30, SA92, 5t-25pts), A (13, It89, 3t-12pts), Barbarians (93-94). **ADPR:** Bath (1990-98, 111, 24t-116pts). Missed out on England's summer tour because of domestic reasons, but Phil remains as reliable as ever for club and country at centre. Educated at Bryanston and Durham University before winning a Blue from St Catherine's College, Oxford. Represented England, and scored two tries, in their inaugural U21 international against Romania (1989). Made his full debut, as a replacement, against South Africa in 1992. Loyal squad man Phil sat on the England bench 21 times before cementing his place in the team. First captained Bath in the 1995 Pilkington Cup final when he deputised for the injured John Hall.

EARNSHAW, Russell Dean (Flanker)
Born Billingham, 08.07.75. 6'4", 15st 3lb. **ADPR:** West Hartlepool (1995-97, 9, 3t-15pts), Bath (1997-98, 17, 5t-25pts). Rapidly developing flanker who was one of Bath's better performers in a difficult season. Educated at Red House School, Norton, and Yarm School before studying for a BA in Economics at St John's, Cambridge where he won two Blues. A keen tennis player, he is also Tim Rodber's second cousin.

EVANS, Ieuan Cennydd (Wing)
Born Capel Dewi, 21.03.64. 5'10", 13st 4lb. **Rep hons:** Wales (72, Fr87, 33t-157pts), Barbarians (85-86). **ADPR:** Bath (1997-98, 17, 8t-40pts). Record Welsh try-scorer who moved from Llanelli at the beginning of last season. Initially plagued by a groin injury sustained with the 1997 Lions, Ieuan was looking sharp again in the second half of the season and will be looking for an injury-free run this season. Has stepped down from international rugby after a record 72 caps.

FALLON, James Anthony (Wing)
Born Devon, 27.03.65. 6'1", 14st 4lb. **Rep hons:** A (6, Fr90, 3t-12pts), Barbarians (90-91). **ADPR:** Richmond (1988-90, 9, 8t-32pts), Bath (1990-92, 17, 8t-32pts),

Richmond (1996-98, 29, 25t-125pts). Returns for a second spell at Bath. May have lost some pace but still a powerful figure on the wing. Jim returned from a four-year spell with Leeds RL with the proud boast of being the only player to appear in both a Pilkington Cup final at Twickenham, with Bath, and a Silk Cut Challenge Cup final at Wembley, with Leeds in 1995.

GUSCOTT, Jeremy Clayton (Centre)
Born Bath, 07.07.65. 6'1", 13st 10lb. **Rep hons:** England (52, Rom89, 18t, 2dg-83pts), A (3, Aus88), Barbarians (89-90). **ADPR:** Bath (1987-98, 109, 53t, 8c, 1dg-263pts). Approaches the new season fresh after a summer's rest and a light workload last season, after being sidelined until after Christmas having broken his arm playing for the British Lions in South Africa and then requiring surgery on a back injury. Educated at Ralph Allen Comp, a soccer school, Jerry learned his rugby with Bath's Mini and Junior sides. Scored three tries on his England debut against Romania in Bucharest and was then called up by the 89 Lions to replace the injured Will Carling. A key member of England's Grand Slam sides in 1991, 1992 and 1995 and RWC91 and 95 squads, he missed the 94 season with a serious pelvic/groin injury. A member of the successful 1997 British Lions tour party. Blossoming TV and modelling career which included the *Body Heat Show* and, more improbably, a children's series on opera. Keen golfer.

HAAG, Stephen Martin (Lock)
Born Chelmsford, 28.07.65. 6'5", 16st 7lb. **Rep hons:** England (2, Arg97), A (6, Sp92, 1t-4pts), Barbarians (94). **ADPR:** Bath (1988-98, 107, 8t-38pts). An underrated lock and sevens specialist, Martin's consistency and competitive instincts were belatedly rewarded when he earned selection for England's tour of Argentina in 1997, when he was capped in both Tests. Was educated at Penwith College and was ever-present for England Schools in 1986 before joining Bath.

HATLEY, Steve (Scrum-half)
Born South Africa, 16.08.72. **ADPR:** Bath (1997-98, 5). Former Western Province scrum-half who played against the 1997 Lions.

HILTON, David Ivor Walter (Prop)
Born Bristol, 03.04.70. 5'10", 16st 4lb. **Rep hons:** Scotland (28, Can95, 1t-5pts), A (2, SA94), Barbarians (94). **ADPR:** Bristol (1990-92, 16), Bath (1992-98, 55, 3t-15pts). Remains a strong scrummager – his presence helped thwart Brive in that incredible series of seven scrums on the Bath line in the European Cup final – but his relative lack of mobility has seen him struggle on occasions for Scotland. David qualifies for Scotland by virtue of his Edinburgh-born grandfather Walter. Educated at Ashton Park, Bristol, David joined Bath from Bristol in 1992 and soon established himself as Chilcott's successor. Made his Scotland debut in 1995 when coming on as a replacement for former Bristol colleague Alan Sharp.

HORSMAN, Christopher Leslie (Prop)
Born 02.02.77. 6'2", 17st 7lb. **ADPR:** Bath (1996-98, 7). Has made a brave recovery from testicular cancer and shows every sign of picking up where he left off before his illness, as one of England's most promising young props.

JONES, Deiniol Llyr (Lock)
Born Carmarthen, 18.11.77. 6'5", 16st 12lb. **ADPR:** Bath (1997-98, 5). Promising former Welsh Schools lock.

LONG, Andrew Edward (Hooker)
Born Poole, 02.09.77. 5'11", 15st 8lb. **Rep hons:** England (1, Aus97). **ADPR:** Bath (1996-98, 14). Called into the full England team to play against Australia in November 1997 and despite being unceremoniously dropped, recovered to enjoy a

season captaining the England U21 squad. Educated at St Peter's School, Bournemouth, Andy joined the Bath Academy in 1996 before returning to the Bournemouth club for a short spell on loan. Captained England U21 in Australia in 1997. Has played Minor Counties cricket, as a seam bowler, for Dorset.

LYLE, Daniel Joseph (No 8)
Born San Diego, USA, 28.09.70. 6'5", 17st 12lb. **Rep hons:** US (18, Ire94, 3t-15pts), Barbarians (97-98). **ADPR:** Bath (1996-98, 19, 7t-35pts). His anterior cruciate ligament injury was a serious blow to Bath in March and his full return to fitness is important if they are to challenge for honours this season. Possesses superb ball handling skills, great pace and athleticism. Made his international debut against Ireland in 1994 and was appointed USA captain in the summer of 1996. Has always enjoyed sevens and captained the USA to victory in the Plate competition of the 1997 RWC Sevens. Back in 1992 he was an All-American gridiron representative and was trying out for the Washington Redskins when he switched to rugby.

MALLETT, John Anthony H. (Prop)
Born Lincoln, 28.05.70. 6'1", 16st. **Rep hons:** England (1, WS95), A (8, Ire94). **ADPR:** Bath (1991-98, 53, 2t-9pts). Plagued by recurring back problems last season, John needs a long injury-free run to re-establish himself for Bath and England. A product of Millfield School and West London Institute, John finally won a full cap as a replacement against Western Samoa in RWC95 after touring South Africa the previous year with England.

NICOL, Andrew Douglas (Scrum-half)
Born Dundee, 12.03.71. 5'11", 13st 4lb. **Rep hons:** Scotland (10, Eng92, 1t-4pts), A (6, Fr91, 3t-15pts), Barbarians (91-92). **ADPR:** Bath (1995-98, 43, 20t, 1c, 1dg-105pts). A difficult season for Andy finished in downbeat fashion when a recurrence of his old hamstring trouble against Newcastle led to his withdrawal from the Scottish tour party of Australia and Fiji. Powerful scrum-half who was educated at Dundee HS and played for Dundee HSFP before joining Bath. A career-threatening cruciate knee ligament injury delayed his Bath debut but Andy is now displaying the form that he showed for Scotland in his debut season of 1992-93.

PELLOW, Ricky (Centre)
Born 19.02.78. 5'8", 11st 7lb. **ADPR:** Bath (1997-98, 5). Won England Schools caps while at Colston's School.

PERRY, Matt Brendan (Centre/wing/full-back)
Born Bath, 21.01.77. 6'1", 13st 7lb. **Rep hons:** England (11, Aus97, 1t-5pts), A (1, Qld96). **ADPR:** Bath (1996-98, 32, 7t-35pts). Voted the RFU young player of the season for 1997-98, Matt enjoyed a fine season for Bath and England, his versatility and attacking skills hinting at a bright future. Capped by England Colts at fly-half, he played centre for Woodward's U21 team in Australia in 1997 but then made his full England debut at full-back against Australia last November. One of England's few successes on their southern hemisphere odyssey last summer. Educated at Millfield School – before turning professional he worked as a waiter and male model to fund his sporting career.

PETERS, Eric William (Backrow)
Born Glasgow, 28.01.69. 6'5", 16st 6lb. **Rep hons:** Scotland (24, Can95, 5t-25pts), A (6, WS95, 2t-10pts), Barbarians (92-93). **ADPR:** Bath (1993-98, 44, 11t-55pts). Possibly Bath's outstanding forward last season despite struggling to secure a first-team place before Christmas. Intensive sprint training with Margot Wells gradually paid off, never more so than when he scored three tries in eight minutes as a replacement against Gloucester. Played his early rugby for Brentwood School and Loughborough University, where he studied Economics, and captained Cambridge

University. Played for Saracens before joining Bath in 1993 and opting for Scotland. Made his Scotland debut against Canada in 1995. Impressed during RWC95 and Scotland's tour of New Zealand in 1997.

PRITCHARD, Jonathan Andrew (Centre)
Born Bristol, 20.03.78. 6′, 14st. **ADPR:** Bath (1997-98, 4). Former captain of the immensely successful Colston's Collegiate side, John has also represented England at Schools and Colts level.

REDMAN, Nigel Charles (Lock)
Born Cardiff, 16.08.64. 6′4″, 17st 2lb. **Rep hons:** England (20, Aus84, 1t-4pts), A (17, It86, 1t-4pts), Barbarians (85-86). **ADPR:** Bath (1987-98, 128, 10t-46pts). 'Ollie' showed little discernible dip in form during his testimonial season, again emerging as one of Bath's key forwards. In the summer of 1997 he answered emergency calls from both England and British Lions and let neither side down. Educated at Priory Comprehensive School and South West Bristol Technical College, 'Ollie' made his England debut at 19 against Australia in 1984 – unfortunately much of his career has coincided with the emergence of Paul Ackford, Wade Dooley, Martin Bayfield and Martin Johnson, to name just four world-class English locks. Has made a record nine winning appearances with Bath in the Pilkington Cup final and helped the club to six Courage League titles.

REGAN, Mark Peter (Hooker)
Born Bristol, 28.01.72. 5′11″, 16st 2lb. **Rep hons:** England (15, SA95), A (9, Ire95, 2t-10pts). **ADPR:** Bristol (1991-97, 69, 4t-20pts) Bath (1997-98, 19, 1t-5pts). Enjoyed mixed fortunes last season after moving from his home-town club of Bristol. Struggled to cement a first-team place with both Bath and England though there were heartening signs of a return to his best form in the latter stages. Educated at St Brendan's, Bristol and a product of the England age-group system.

STURNHAM, Ben (Flanker)
Born St Albans, 06.03.74. 6′5″, 18st 5lb. **Rep hons:** England (3, Aus 98), A (1, Ire98, 1t-5pts). **ADPR:** Saracens (1997-98, 12, 2t-10pts). Moved to the Recreation Ground in July when Bath made him an offer he could not refuse. Voted the Premiership's young player of the season last year. The latest in Saracens' legendary line of backrow discoveries that includes Dean Ryan, Ben Clarke, Eric Peters, Richard Hill and Tony Diprose. Seized the opportunity of first-team rugby offered by Hill's back injury last season and made such an impression with his power and pace that he started England's summer tour at blindside flanker against Australia in Brisbane. Joined Saracens from the St Albans club.

THOMAS, Nathan (Flanker)
Born Bridgend, 22.01.76. 6′3″, 15st 7lb. **Rep hons:** Wales (9, SA96), A (3, Sc97). **ADPR:** Bath (1996-98, 27, 3t-15pts). Started last season by being sent off against Newcastle for raking Tim Stimpson but finished strongly, proving a stalwart in an injury-ravaged pack. Rapidly developing flanker who joined Bath from Bridgend. Represented Wales in the 1996 World Students Cup before being capped at senior level.

TINDALL, Michael James (Centre)
Born 18.10.78. 6′2″, 14st 7lb. **ADPR:** Bath (1997-98, 2). Promising Academy player who starred at centre, alongside Jonny Wilkinson, during England Schools' successful tour of Australia in 1997.

UBOGU, Victor Eriakpo (Prop)
Born Lagos, Nigeria, 08.09.64. 5′9″, 17st. **Rep hons:** England (21, Can92, 1t-5pts), A (13, Aus90, 5t-21pts). **ADPR:** Richmond (1987-88, 3), Bath (1988-98, 101, 13t-61pts).

Showed occasional signs of his old dynamic form but failed to attract the eye of the England selectors. Victor has lived in England since he was 13 and was educated at West Buckland School, Devon, Birmingham University and Oxford. Numbers Richmond and Moseley among his previous clubs and made his senior England debut against Canada at Wembley in 1992.

WEBSTER, Richard Edward (Flanker)
Born Morriston, 09.07.67. 6'2", 17st. **Rep hons:** Wales (13, Aus87, 1t-4pts), A (1, SA96), Barbarians (90-91). **ADPR:** Bath (1996-98, 22, 6t-30pts). Bedevilled by yet another knee injury late in the season, Richard remains an effective flanker when fully fit. First attracted attention as an outstanding Wales Youth international in 1985-86, winning six caps, and was enjoying a summer playing club rugby in Australia the following year when he was dramatically called into the Wales team for their RWC87 play-off game against Australia in Rotorua. On his return, Richard was plagued by the first in a long series of knee injuries but earned another 'cap' against the Barbarians (1990), and produced solid performances in RWC91 against Argentina and Australia. Turned pro with Salford RL in 1993.

YATES, Kevin Peter (Prop)
Born Medicine Hat, Canada, 06.11.72. 5'11", 17st. **Rep hons:** England (2, Arg97), A (8, Vic95, 1t-5pts), Barbarians (94). **ADPR:** Bath (1993-98, 35, 5t-25pts). His 1997-98 season was totally marred by the ear-biting incident involving London Scottish flanker Simon Fenn, for which he received a six-month ban. Kevin still strenuously denies any involvement but will now be keen to put the entire episode behind him and continue a promising career. His form the previous season had earned selection for the England tour party of Argentina, where he made his international debut in the first Test in Buenos Aires. Educated at John Bentley School, Calne, before learning his rugby at Chippenham and joining Bath. Toured Australia and Fiji with England A (1995).

REVIEW

Bath tailed off disappointingly in the final two months of the season, just when they seemed poised to challenge Saracens and Newcastle for the Premiership. Injuries did not help but Bath also played without pattern and commitment in many of their late-season games. All of which contrasted with their marvellous efforts in the Heineken European Cup, which ultimately resulted in a 19-18 win over Brive in the final at Bordeaux. Bath must learn to move cautiously in the transfer market – Rugby League stars Henry Paul and Jason Robinson did not make the expected impact, neither did Argentinians Federico Mendez and German Llanes, who have both left the club.

BATH in Premiership One 1997-98

Aug 23	H	Newcastle	Lost	13 20	M.Perry(T) M.Catt(C, 2P)
30	A	Harlequins	Won	27 20	R.Butland(T, C, 5P) Penalty(T)
Oct 18	H	Bristol	Won	44 15	J.Sleightholme(T) P.De Glanville(T) A.Adebayo(T) A.Nicol(T) R.Earnshaw(T) J.Callard(T, 2C, P) E.Peters(T) M.Catt(C)
25	A	Leicester	Lost	22 33	R.Webster(T) J.Callard(C, 5P)

Nov 1	H	Richmond	Won	47	31	I.Evans(2T) P.De Glanville(T) A.Nicol(T) N.Redman(T) N.Thomas(T) K.Tsimba(T) J.Callard(2C, 2P) I.Balshaw(C)
Dec 14	A	Saracens	Lost	23	50	R.Butland(T) M.Regan(T) J.Callard(2C, 3P)
27	A	Sale	Won	13	11	R.Butland(T) M.Catt(C, 2P)
30	H	Northampton	Won	26	3	R.Earnshaw(T) A.Nicol(T) J.Callard(2C, 4P)
Feb 11	H	Gloucester	Won	47	3	E.Peters(3T) A.Adebayo(T) P.De Glanville(T) R.Earnshaw(T) J.Callard(4C, 3P)
14	H	Wasps	Won	43	27	P.De Glanville(T) I.Evans(T) J.Guscott(T) D.Lyle(T) Penalty(T) J.Callard(3C, 4P)
28	H	Harlequins	Won	39	13	M.Catt(T) R.Earnshaw(T) I.Evans(T) A.Nicol(T) E.Peters(T) V.Ubogu(T) J.Callard(3C, P)
Mar 8	A	Bristol	Won	22	16	A.Nicol(T) M.Perry(T) V.Ubogu(T) J.Callard(2C, P)
14	H	Leicester	Won	16	5	J.Guscott(T) R.Butland(C, 3P)
28	A	London Irish	Won	49	35	I.Evans(2T) A.Nicol(2T) J.Guscott(T) Penalty(T) E.Peters(T) J.Callard(4C, P) R.Butland(P)
Apr 10	H	Saracens	Lost	13	29	A.Adebayo(T) J.Callard(C, 2P)
13	A	Richmond	Lost	14	32	I.Balshaw(T) J.Callard(3P)
18	A	Gloucester	Lost	17	27	R.Earnshaw(T) E.Peters(T) R.Butland(2C, P)
25	H	Sale	Lost	19	29	R.Butland(T, 3P) J.Guscott(T)
28	H	London Irish	Won	20	3	R.Butland(T) I.Evans(T) A.Nicol(T) J.Callard(C, P)
May 2	A	Northampton	Lost	15	16	A.Adebayo(T) A.Nicol(T) J.Callard(C, P)
11	A	Newcastle	Lost	15	20	J.Callard(5P)
17	A	Wasps	Won	31	17	I.Evans(T) J.Guscott(T) A.Adebayo(T) E.Peters(T) J.Callard(4C, P)

Summary of Premiership scorers:

183 – J.Callard (T, 32C, 38P); 72 – R.Butland (5T, 4C, 13P); 47 – A.Nicol (9T, C); 40 – E.Peters (8T), I.Evans (8T); 25 – J.Guscott (5T), R.Earnshaw (5T), A.Adebayo (5T); 23 – M.Catt (T, 3C, 4P); 20 – P.De Glanville (4T); 15 – M.Wood (3T), C.Harrison (3T), J.Ewens (3T); 10 – Penalty (2T), V.Ubogu (2T), J.Sleightholme (2T), M.Perry (2T); 7 – I.Balshaw (T, C); 5 – R.Webster (T), K.Tsimba (T), N.Thomas (T), N.Redman (T), M.Regan (T), D.Lyle (T), G.French (T).

13

Summary of Premiership appearances:

22 – V.Ubogu (+2); 21   M.Perry (+3); 20 – E.Peters (+4); 19 – N.Redman, M.Regan (+6), P.De Glanville, J.Callard (+5); 18 – A.Nicol, D.Hilton (+3), A.Adebayo; 17 – J.Sleightholme (+1), I.Evans, R.Earnshaw (+1); 16 – M.Haag; 14 – R.Butland (+4); 13 – J.Mallett (+9), A.Long (+7), C.Harrison (+1), R.Bryan (+3); 12 – M.Wood; 11 – N.Thomas (+2), J.Guscott, M.Catt; 10 – G.French (+2); 8 – D.Lyle, J.Ewens (+1), I.Balshaw (+5); 7 – R.Webster; 6 – K.Yates (+1); 5 – R.Pellow (+5), F.Mendez (+3), D.Jones (+2), S.Hatley (+3), B.Cusack (+3); 4 – J.Pritchard (+2), G.Llanes, C.Horsman (+4), M.Kayson (+3); 2 – K.Tsimba (+2), M.Tindall (+1), B.Roche; 1 – D.John.

BEDFORD

Formation of club: 1886
Ground: Goldington Road, Bedford MK42 3DN
Capacity: 5,800 (Seated 800)
Colours: Oxford and Cambridge blue hoops
Honours: Cup Winners (1) – 1974-75. Division Three Champions – 1994-95
Best League finish: 12th in Division One 1989-90
Last season: ADP2 – Champions. Tetley's Bitter Cup – 4th round (lost 26-31 to Northampton). Cheltenham & Gloucester Cup – losing finalists
Owner: Frank Warren (boxing promoter)
Chief Executive/Director of Rugby: Geoff Cooke
Director of Coaching: Paul Turner
Captain: TBC

ASHFORTH, Robert William (Fly-half/centre)
Born Dewsbury, 01.05.76. 6′, 13st 7lb. **ADPR:** Rotherham (1996-98, 8, 5c, 2pg-16pts). Summer signing from Rotherham. England Schools and U21 fly-half who should be available on a regular basis, having just completed a degree course in Land Economy at Peterhouse College, Cambridge University. Educated at Bradford GS, Robert has also played for Cleckheaton and Wakefield.

BOYD, Clement Thomas (Prop)
Born Belfast, 08.11.73. 6′1″, 18st 7lb. **Rep hons:** Ireland A (1, Can97). **ADPR:** Bedford (1996-98, 26, 2t-10pts). Ireland A prop who has played for Instonians and the Currie club in Scotland while a student at Edinburgh University.

COCKLE, James Christian (Flanker)
Born Clifton, 29.10.76. 6′3″, 16st 6lb. **ADPR:** Moseley (1996-98, 28, 2t-10pts). Joins from Moseley. Outstanding prospect who has already represented England Schools and England U21. Initially signed on for Bath but got lost among the embarrassment of backrow riches at the Recreation Ground.

CRABB, Simon John (Scrum-half)
Born Hamilton, New Zealand, 04.04.69. 5′6″, 12st 10lb. **ADPR:** Bedford (1997-98, 7, 3t-15pts). Voted New Zealand's most promising player in 1993, Simon was badly hindered by injury last season. Educated at Waikato University and a qualified accountant, Simon is a former New Zealand U21 and New Zealand B representative who has played Super 12 rugby for Waikato Chiefs. Sparkled towards the end of the season, in the knockout stages of the Cheltenham and Gloucester Cup.

DEANS, Matthew Willis (Flanker)
Born Zimbabwe, 27.05.71. 6′3″, 18st. **ADPR:** Bedford (1992-98, 57, 8t-40pts). A
long-serving club stalwart, Matt is a strong-running, tough-tackling powerhouse in
the pack, and takes a 20″ shirt collar. Educated at King's School, Ely, and De
Montfort University, he played for London U21 and numbers Cambridge City
among his previous clubs. His hobbies include cricket and golf and his father played
local rugby.

EWENS, Joseph A. (Centre)
Born Bristol, 16.12.77. 6′, 13st. **Rep hons:** England A (2, Arg96). **ADPR:** Bath
(1996-98, 2), Bedford (1997-98, 7, 3t-15pts). Played on loan from Bath last season.
Won nine England 18 Group caps, captaining the side in 1995-96. Also helped
Colston's Collegiate win two consecutive Daily Mail U18 Cup titles. An England U21
cap who toured with the U21s in South Africa this summer, playing in the prestigious
Six Nations tournament.

FORSTER, Jason (Flanker)
Born Derby, 25.02.71. 6′, 15st 4lb. **ADPR:** Bedford (1997-98, 21, 14t-70pts). Welsh-
qualified flanker who scored 14 League tries last season, including seven in two
games against Fylde. Formerly with Cross Keys, Swansea and Bridgend.

HARTLAND, Virgil (Prop)
Born Cinderford, 23.04.77. 5′10″, 15st 12lb. **ADPR:** West Hartlepool (1996-98, 11),
Coventry (1997-98, 8). New arrival at Bedford from Coventry. England U21 prop
who joined Coventry last season from West Hartlepool after allegations of ear-biting.
A member of the England U21 squad that contested the Six Nations tournament in
South Africa in July 1998.

HATLEY, Neal (Prop)
Born Chorley, 23.12.69. 6′, 19st 2lb. **ADPR:** Bedford (1997-98, 17, 2t-10pts). Former
South African Students representative who has also played for Natal and Western
Province.

HOWARD, Sam (Fly-half)
Born Gravesend, 31.07.74. 6′, 13st 7lb. **ADPR:** Blackheath (1993-97, 56, 6t, 31c,
75pg, 9dg-344pts), Bedford (1997-98, 2, 1t-5pts). Talented former England Students
and England U21 fly-half who transferred to Bedford, where he is seen largely as
full-back cover. One of his two League appearances last season was when he
masterminded a 72-31 victory over old club Blackheath.

KARDOONI, Aadel (Scrum-half)
Born Tehran, Iran, 17.05.68. 5′8″, 12st 0lb. **Rep hons:** England A (6, NOtago92,
1t-4pts). **ADPR:** Wasps (1987-88, 1), Leicester (1988-97, 97, 18t-84pts), Bedford
(1997-98, 17). Joined Bedford from Leicester last season, having lost his first-team
place at Welford Road to Austin Healey – but is still an experienced and reliable
performer. Educated at Sherborne, Aadel was ever-present in the 1986 England
Schools team and played one League game for Wasps before joining Leicester, where
he became a Tigers stalwart. Toured New Zealand with England B (1992), playing in
both 'Tests'.

MURDOCH, Alistair Richard (Centre)
Born Sydney, Australia, 09.05.67. 6′1″, 14st 6lb. **Rep hons:** Australia (2, Fr93),
1t-5pts). **ADPR:** Bedford (1997-98, 15, 7t-35pts). Underrated former Australia centre
who also holds an English passport. Spent six years in the New South Wales side and
had a tremendous influence at Bedford, though his season was prematurely ended by
a nasty finger break.

MURRAY, Scott (Lock)
Born Musselburgh, 15.01.76. 6'6", 16st 7lb. **Rep hons:** Scotland (6, Aus97, 1t-5pts), A (8, It96), Barbarians (95-96). **ADPR:** Bedford (1996-98, 39, 7t-35pts). Athletic lock who survived a traumatic international debut against Australia in November 1997, when he scored Scotland's only try in a 37-8 defeat, to bounce back, recovering his form in time to make the Scotland tour party for Fiji and Australia. Former Scotland captain David Sole was a major coaching influence on his progress at Edinburgh Accies. He enjoyed a spell playing rugby in Perth, Western Australia, and is a former Scottish Schools basketball international. Educated at Morgan Academy in Dundee and a former animal technician before turning professional. Learned his rugby with Preston Lodge before moving to Edinburgh Accies.

O'MAHONY, Darragh William (Wing)
Born Cork, 18.08.72. 5'9", 11st. **Rep hons:** Ireland (3, It95, 1t-5pts), A (7, Eng95, 3t-15pts). **ADPR:** Moseley (1996-98, 33, 32t-160pts). Ireland international wing with a priceless try-scoring touch, claiming 17 in 20 League games for Moseley last season. Finished so strongly that Ireland wanted him to fly out to South Africa as a replacement when James Topping got injured, but an untimely injury meant he had to decline the invitation. Formerly with the Lansdowne club. A member of Ireland's 1995 World Cup squad, playing in the semi-final against France.

PARAMORE, Peter Junior (No 8/flanker)
Born Apia,Western Samoa, 18.11.68. 6'3", 17st. **Rep hons:** Western Samoa. **ADPR:** Bedford (1996-98, 35, 13t-65pts). Bedford's player of the year 1996-97 and voted the Division Two player of last season, Paramore is a class act, so much so that he even deputised at centre for Bedford last season. A Western Samoan international, with the superb handling skills you always associate with their sevens experts. Fiercely competitive in the tackle, Junior played his early rugby with Manurewa in New Zealand and after RWC95 turned professional with Castleford RL and Hunter Mariners RL.

RAYER, Michael Anthony (Full-back)
Born Cardiff, 21.07.65. 5'10", 13st 3lb. **Rep hons:** Wales (21, WS91, 4t, 1pg-23pts), A (3, Fr89, 1t-5pts), Barbarians (87-88). **ADPR:** Bedford (1996-98, 44, 13t, 133c, 68pg-535pts). Still Wales' best full-back by a long way, Mike was voted player of the season by the local fans as he garnered 289 League points. Joined Bedford September 96. The first player to command a transfer fee for a switch between rugby union clubs when he joined Bedford for £5,000 after a lengthy wrangle. Spent much of the summer in contractual dispute with Bedford. His turbulent career has also been marred by serious injury and ill-luck: knee problems flared in 1991; he was robbed of a British Lions tour chance when dropped by Wales in 1993; played in two World Cup play-off qualifiers against Romania and Italy before breaking his leg for Cardiff and missing RWC95. Shared top Five Nations try-scoring honours in 1994 with Nigel Walker and Philippe Saint-Andre. A former sheet-metal worker, salesman and public relations officer, he played for Llandaff North, his father Alec's old club, before joining Cardiff. Lists leisure activities as golf and babysitting!

RICHARDS, Jimmy (Hooker)
Born Pembrokeshire, 11.09.75. 5'9", 15st 3lb. **ADPR:** Bedford (1997-98, 8). Has failed to secure a first-team place but did well against Northampton in the Tetley's Bitter Cup when called upon.

SIMMONDS, Paul (Hooker)
Born Luton, 26.06.71. 5'11", 15st. **ADPR:** Harlequins (1993-95, 5), Bedford (1995-98, 26, 1t-5pts). Member of Harlequins from 90-95 but left to join Bedford after acrimonious exchanges with coaching staff. Educated at Bedford Modern School,

Paul played for England Schools and Colts before representing London U21. Worked in the City as a bond broker before turning professional.

STRAEULI, Rudolph August Wilkens (Flanker/No 8)
Born Pretoria, South Africa, 20.08.63. 6'3", 17st 4lb. **Rep hons:** South Africa (10, NZ94, 4t-20pts), Barbarians (95-96). **ADPR:** Bedford (1996-98, 16, 1t-5pts). Joined Bedford in January 1997 and made an immediate impact before rupturing an Achilles in March 1997. Returned to full fitness midway through last season and remains as strong and competitive as ever. Scored a try on international debut against the All Blacks at Dunedin in July 1994 and further tries in three of his next four matches against Argentina, Scotland and Wales. He launched his provincial rugby career with Northern Transvaal in 1986 and, a product of the Tukkies club in Pretoria, he became their 612th player to be capped by SA. Played for the Transvaal side that beat England at Johannesburg in May 1994, and scored tries on the Boks' 94 British tour against Wales A, Swansea and Combined Scottish Districts, as well as captaining them to wins over Cardiff and Combined Irish Provinces. Played in three of SA RWC95 wins, including the final when he subbed for Mark Andrews.

UNDERWOOD, Rory (Wing)
Born Middlesbrough, 19.06.63. 5'9", 13st 8lb. **Rep hons:** England (85, Ire84, 49t-210pts), A (1, Ire82), Barbarians (83-84). **ADPR:** Leicester (1987-97, 100, 43t-192pts), Bedford (1997-98, 21, 7t-35pts). Determined to enjoy one more season in the top flight after joining Bedford from Leicester at the beginning of last season. England's most-capped player and record try-scorer with 49, he was educated at Barnard Castle School along with Rob Andrew, first coming to prominence with England Colts in 1983 and winning his first senior cap against Ireland the following year. He opened his scoring account against France in Paris in his second game, was involved in England's Grand Slam triumphs in 1991, 1992 and 1995 and all three World Cup campaigns. Winner of six Lions caps, Rory scored a memorable try against New Zealand in the second Test in 1993, and equalled Dan Lambert's England record of 1907 by scoring five tries against Fiji at Twickenham in 1989.

WHETSTONE, Benjamin Marcus (Centre/wing)
Born Holbeach, 29.06.70. 5'11", 14st 7lb. **ADPR:** Bedford (1992-98, 94, 47t, 1dg-238pts). With a phenomenal try-scoring record of 47 in 94 League games, including 17 last season, Ben continues to be a source of excellence at wing or centre and Bedford supporters remain mystified at his lack of representative honours. Ben converted from soccer to rugby at 18 and joined Ely, for whom he played from 1988-91. Spent summer 1994 playing for the Belfast club in Christchurch, New Zealand.

WINTERS, Roy (Backrow)
Born Cuckfield, 13.12.75. 6'4", 16st. **Rep hons:** England A (3, NZ97). **ADPR:** Bedford (1996-98, 42, 5t-25pts). Superb all-purpose back five forward who played for England A against the All Blacks last season. Educated at Haywards Heath and Loughborough University, Roy also won England Schools and Colts caps and was the outstanding forward for England U21 in Australia in the summer of 1997.

YAPP, Anthony (Fly-half)
Born Ludlow, 26.07.77. 5'10", 12st 6lb. **Rep hons:** England U21. **ADPR:** Worcester (1996-97, 2, 1dg-3pts), Bedford (1997-98, 15, 2t, 1dg-13pts). Educated at Ludlow School, Tony learned much of his rugby at Worcester and also spent a season in Australia before joining Bedford, where he worked closely with Paul Turner. Sister Jo has emerged as a star scrum-half for the England Women's side.

ZALTZMAN, Danny (Lock)
Born Hendon, 26.12.75. 6'6". **ADPR:** Saracens (1994-97, 7), Coventry (1997-98, 12).
Former England Schools lock who failed to make the expected impact at Coventry
last season.

REVIEW

Encountered little or no opposition last season, losing just two League games – to
Rotherham and West Hartlepool when the championship was long won. The
challenge now is to again lift themselves, attract new fans and sponsors and compete
with the elite. The first priority is to replace the peerless Paul Turner at fly-half – the
promising Tony Yapp might be the answer, or Bedford might go into the transfer
market. Turner stays on as coach and his partnership with the canny Geoff Cooke
should ensure Bedford are always properly prepared. There are also obvious deficiencies in the pack, which needs to be strengthened to meet the demands of Premiership
One rugby.

Bedford in Premiership Two 1997-98

Aug 30	H	Rotherham	Won	18	11	M.Rayer(6P)
Sep 13	A	Exeter	Won	32	17	A.Murdoch(T) Penalty(T) B.Whetstone(T) T.Yapp(T) M.Rayer(3C, 2P)
20	H	London Scottish	Won	45	33	B.Whetstone(2T) A.Murdoch(T) R.O'Neill(T) M.Oliver(T) P.Turner(T) M.Rayer(3C, 3P)
27	A	Coventry	Won	22	15	B.Whetstone(T) M.Rayer(C, 4P) T.Yapp(D)
Oct 4	H	Waterloo	Won	34	21	R.Underwood(2T) A.Murdoch(T) H.Pflugler(2C, 5P)
11	A	Moseley	Won	35	16	J.Forster(2T) C.Boyd(T) T.Yapp(T) M.Rayer(3C, 3P)
18	H	West Hartlepool	Won	22	9	Penalty(T) M.Rayer(C, 5P)
25	A	London Scottish	Won	22	15	M.Rayer(T, C, 5P)
Nov 8	H	Coventry	Won	77	3	B.Whetstone(3T) M.Rayer(2T, 8C, 2P) M.Deans(T) J.Forster(T) A.Murdoch(T) M.Pechey(T) P.Turner(T) R.Underwood(T)
Dec 13	A	Waterloo	Won	28	14	S.Crabb(T) D.Hinkins(T) R.Kirke(T) B.Whetstone(T) M.Rayer(4C)
20	H	Moseley	Won	32	16	M.Rayer(2T, 2C, P) A.Murdoch(2T) J.Forster(T)
27	A	Fylde	Won	67	7	J.Forster(3T) B.Whetstone(2T) M.Deans(T) A.Murdoch(T) S.Murray(T) Penalty(T) M.Rayer(8C, 2P)
Jan 17	H	Fylde	Won	50	14	J.Forster(4T) N.Hatley(T) S.Murray(T) S.Platford(T) R.Underwood(T) M.Rayer(5C)

31	H	Orrell	Won	47	22	P.Turner(2T) B.Whetstone(2T) R.Stone(T) R.Underwood(T) M.Rayer(4C, 3P)
Feb 14	A	Wakefield	Won	24	13	J.Paramore(T) J.Wells(T) B.Whetstone(T) R.Winters(T) M.Rayer(2C)
Mar 7	A	Blackheath	Won	37	13	S.Crabb(T) J.Forster(T) R.Underwood(T) B.Whetstone(T) D.Whiston(T) M.Rayer(3C, 2P)
14	H	Wakefield	Won	36	10	S.Crabb(T) J.Ewens(T) Penalty(T) D.Whiston(T) R.Winters(T) M.Rayer(4C, P)
28	A	Orrell	Won	29	16	M.Deans(T) J.Forster(T) J.Paramore(T) B.Whetstone(T) R.Winters(T) M.Rayer(2C)
Apr 11	A	Rotherham	Lost	17	18	Penalty(T) B.Whetstone(T) M.Rayer(2C, P)
18	H	Exeter	Won	16	3	M.Rayer(T, 2P) B.Whetstone(T)
25	H	Blackheath	Won	72	31	R.Stone(3T) S.Brading(T) J.Ewens(T) J.Forster(T) N.Hatley(T) S.Howard(T) S.Murray(T) J.Paramore(T) R.Underwood(T) M.Rayer(7C, P)
May 2	A	West Hartlepool	Lost	29	48	S.Brown(T) J.Ewens(T) J.Paramore(T) R.Straeuli(T) R.Winters(T) M.Rayer(2C)

Summary of League scorers:

289 – M.Rayer (6T, 65C, 43P); 85 – B.Whetstone (17T); 70 – J.Forster (14T); 35 – R.Underwood (7T), A.Murdoch (7T); 25 – Penalty (5T); 20 – R.Winters (4T), P.Turner (4T), R.Stone (4T), J.Paramore (4T); 19 – H.Pflugler (2C, 5P); 15 – S.Murray (3T), J.Ewens (3T), M.Deans (3T), S.Crabb (3T); 13 – T.Yapp (2T, D); 10 – D.Whiston (2T), N.Hatley (2T); 5 – J.Wells (T), R.Straeuli (T), S.Platford (T), M.Pechey (T), R.O'Neill (T), M.Oliver (T), R.Kirke (T), S.Howard (T), D.Hinkins (T), S.Brading (T), S.Brown (T), C.Boyd (T).

Summary of League appearances:

21 – R.Underwood, M.Rayer, S.Murray, J.Forster (+1); 20 – R.Winters (+2); 19 – B.Whetstone; 18 – C.Boyd (+3); 17 – A.Kardooni (+3), N.Hatley (+2); 15 – T.Yapp (+3), P.Turner (+6), S.Platford (+3), J.Paramore, A.Murdoch (+1); 13 – M.Deans (+10), J.Cullen (+4); 12 – R.Kirke (+1), D.Hinkins (+1); 11 – P.Simmonds (+7); 8 – R.Straeuli (+2), J.Richards (+1); 7 – J.Wells (+1), R.Stone (+3), H.Pflugler (+1), J.Ewens, S.Crabb (+3); 6 – M.Pechey (+1); 5 – P.Hewitt (+2), S.Brading (+2), S.Brown (+3); 4 – P.Anglesea (+2); 2 – D.Whiston, R.Thompson, J.Probyn (+1), R.O'Neill, M.Oliver (+1), S.Howard (+1), N.Hadley, A.Davis (+2); 1 – S.McCurrie (+1), J.Hinkins (+1).

GLOUCESTER

Formation of club: 1873
Ground: Kingsholm, Kingsholm Road, Gloucester GL1 3AX
Capacity: 10,500 (Seated 1,250)
Colours: Cherry and white
Honours: Cup Winners (3) – 1972, 1978, 1982
Best League finish: 2nd in Division One, 1988-89 and 1989-90
Last season: ADP1 – 7th. Heineken European Cup – Q/F (lost 22-53 to Stade Francais). Tetley's Bitter Cup – 5th round (lost 11-30 to Northampton). Cheltenham & Gloucester Cup – Winners
Owner: Tom Walkinshaw (Arrows F1 owner)
Director of Rugby: Richard Hill. Assistants: John Brain, Dave Pointon
Captain: Dave Sims

BECK, Laurie John Henry (Scrum-half)
Born Cheltenham, 02.01.71. 5'10", 13st 2lb. **ADPR:** Gloucester (1990-98, 21). Reliable scrum-half who joined Gloucester from Cheltenham. Represented South West Juniors at water polo.

BENTON, Scott (Scrum-half)
Born Bradford, 08.09.74. 5'11", 13st 11lb. **Rep hons:** England (1, Aus98), A (3, Otago97, 2t-10pts), Barbarians (97-98). **ADPR:** Morley (1992-96, 23, 6t-30pts), Gloucester (1995-98, 42, 6t-30pts). Dramatically called into the England side to play Australia in June 1998 after the withdrawal, through injury, of captain Matt Dawson and showed real spirit and bravery throughout a difficult tour. Educated at Morley HS, Scott transferred to Gloucester from Morley at the beginning of the 1995-96 season. The former England Colts captain came to national prominence last season when he scored a try for England A against the All Blacks at Leicester and served as a bench replacement in the Five Nations internationals against Scotland and Ireland.

CARTER, Nathan Edwin (Flanker)
Born Gloucester, 22.06.72. 6', 15st. **ADPR:** Gloucester (1996-98, 2t-10pts). Vastly underrated openside flanker who learned his trade so well at local side Gordon League that Gloucester felt able to part with Scotland wing forward Ian Smith.

CATLING, Christopher Edward (Full-back)
Born Coulsdon, Surrey, 17.06.76. 6'2", 14st 2lb. **Rep hons:** England A (5, SA96). **ADPR:** Exeter (1995-96, 6, 1t-5pts), Gloucester (1996-98, 39, 4t, 1dg-23pts). Having narrowly missed out on an England tour place in the summer, Chris is one of the most exciting counter-attacking full-backs around but needs to add consistency to his defensive game. Educated at Whitgift School in Croydon, Chris was ever-present in the England Schools Grand Slam side of 1994, captained by Gloucester's Phil Greening, before moving to Exeter University. Signed from the Exeter RFC in the summer of 1996, Chris was a member of England's World Students Cup squad in South Africa in 1996 and a tourist with England U21 in Australia the following year.

CORNWELL, Mark John (Lock)
Born Gloucester, 22.02.73. 6'7", 17st. **Rep hons:** England A (1, Ire98). **ADPR:** Gloucester (1994-98, 22, 1t-5pts). Promising lock who joined from Old Richians. Mark has benefited from time spent with the Hamilton's club in South Africa and developed well last winter.

DEACON, Andrew (Prop)
Born Gloucester, 31.07.65. 6'2", 17st 9lb. **ADPR:** Gloucester (1991-98, 76, 5t-25pts). Experienced former Gloucester captain who joined the club from Longlevens. One of the most underrated props in the country.

DEVEREUX, Simon (No 8/Lock)
Born Gloucester, 20.10.68. 6'3", 17st. **ADPR:** Gloucester (1992-98, 57, 2t-10pts). Stalwart former Spartans backrow forward, rarely far away from the fiercest action. Hit the headlines in 1995 when he received a nine-month prison sentence after being found guilty of assault in a second-team match against Rosslyn Park, when he broke an opponent's jaw with a punch.

EMMERSON, Craig Anthony (Centre)
Born Halifax, 14.09.71. 6', 13st 1lb. **ADPR:** West Hartlepool (1991-92, 1), Morley (1992-96, 37, 5t-25pts), Gloucester (1996-98, 13). Underrated former Morley centre, Craig was the first player Gloucester paid a transfer fee for. Made his League debut against Saracens in September 1996 and proved a useful squad member last season.

FANOLUA, Terry Laauli (Centre)
Born Motoutua,W Samoa, 03.07.74. 6', 13st 9lb. **Rep hons:** W Samoa. **ADPR:** Gloucester (1997-98, 22, 7t-35pts). One of the players of the Premiership season, the former Western Samoan sevens captain proved a major force in Gloucester's revamped backline, showing great strength in the tackle and real pace on the outside. Will miss the opening month of the season as Western Samoa prepare for their World Cup qualifying tournament in Australia.

FIDLER, Robert John (Lock)
Born Cheltenham, 21.09.74. 6'5", 16st 8lb. **Rep hons:** England (2, NZ98), A (6, SA96, 1t-5pts). **ADPR:** Gloucester (1994-98, 52, 6t-30pts). Along with David Sims, forms one of the strongest second-row pairings in the Premiership. Played for the ERP XV against New Zealand at Ashton Gate last season and toured the southern hemisphere with England in the summer, winning Test caps alongside Dave Sims against New Zealand and South Africa. Son of former Gloucester and England lock John Fidler. Educated at Cheltenham College.

FORTEY, Christopher Paul (Hooker)
Born Gloucester, 25.08.75. 6', 16st 8lb. **ADPR:** Gloucester (1996-98, 16, 1t-5pts). Promising young hooker who rose to the occasion during Phil Greening's absences. Twin brother Lee is a former England U21 prop now playing for Moseley.

GLANVILLE, Peter Neil (Flanker)
Born Gloucester, 10.06.71. 6'2", 15st 6lb. **ADPR:** Gloucester (1992-98, 68, 3t-15pts). Underrated blindside flanker who battled on bravely as club captain last season despite a painful groin injury that eventually required a double hernia operation. Having started with Longlevens, Peter came to prominence playing for the South West in the CIS Divisional championship in 1995. Formerly a sales manager for his father's tyre firm before turning professional.

GREENING, Philip Bradley Thomas (Hooker)
Born Gloucester, 03.10.75. 6', 16st 13lb. **Rep hons:** England (5, It96), A (4, WS95, 1t-5pts). **ADPR:** Gloucester (1994-98, 37, 2t-10pts). Struggled with injury and a loss of form for much of last winter, but looked back to his dynamic best by the end of the season and travelled with England to Australia, New Zealand and South Africa. Made his international debut as a replacement against Italy and started the first Test against Argentina in 1997. Captained England Schools and Colts and earned England A selection during his first season of senior rugby in 1995-96. Educated at Kingsholm Junior, Chosen Hill and Gloucester College. Joined Gloucester from Spartans.

JEWELL, Robert James (Wing)
Born Bromsgrove, 11.10.78. **ADPR:** Gloucester (1997-98, 5, 1t-5pts). Promising wing who joined from Gordon League, Rob was capped by England Colts last season and made his senior debut against Fylde in December 1997.

JOHNSON, Brian Gareth William (Wing)
Born Wegberg, W Germany, 27.07.72. 5'11", 12st 6lb. **Rep hons:** England A (4, SA96), Barbarians (96-97). **ADPR:** Newbury (1996-98, 20, 35t-175pts), Gloucester (1997-98, 13, 5t-25pts). An important signing from Newbury, Brian has real pace and will surely profit from Gloucester's new attacking style. An army captain, he is studying at RMCS Shrivenham.

LUMSDEN, Audley Emmanuel (Wing/full-back)
Born London, 06.06.67. 6', 14st 3lb. **Rep hons:** England A (1, Fr89, 1t-4pts). **ADPR:** Bath (1987-96, 45, 18t-86pts), Gloucester (1996-98, 23, 7t-35pts). Evergreen former Bath utility back who may have lost the blazing pace of his youth but remains an accomplished performer at full-back and on the wing. A graduate of both Bath and Oxford Universities, where he won a Blue in 1992, Audley is now a physics teacher at Millfield School. Remarkably he has continued at the top level despite suffering a serious broken neck in 1989.

McCARTHY, Neil (Hooker)
Born Slough, 29.11.74. 5'10", 16st. **Rep hons:** Barbarians (96-97). **ADPR:** Bath (1996-97, 2), Bedford (1996-97, 7), Gloucester (1997-98, 10, 1t-5pts). Joined from great rivals Bath having spent much of the 1996-97 season on loan to Bedford. Represented England Colts for a record three years at prop, captaining the side in his last season, but has switched to hooker with success.

MANNIX, Simon James (Fly-half)
Born Lower Hutt, New Zealand, 10.08.71. 5'9", 13st. **Rep hons:** New Zealand (1, Fr94), Barbarians (96-97). **ADPR:** Sale (1996-98, 22, 8t, 25c, 35pg, 1dg-198pts). Superb playmaker at outside half who fell out spectacularly with Sale midway through last season and was reduced to a touchline spectator thereafter. Will complete three years residency in November 1998 and has declared his intention of challenging for an England Test spot. Played for the Petone club in New Zealand and also spent two seasons with Tarvisium in Italy.

MAPLETOFT, Mark Sterland (Fly-half)
Born Mansfield, 25.12.71. 5'7", 13st 1lb. **Rep hons:** England (1, Arg97, 1pg-3pts), A (7, SA96, 2t, 8c, 12pg, 1dg-65pts). **ADPR:** Rugby (1989-94, 41, 7t, 14c, 45pg, 3dg-205pts), Gloucester (1994-98, 57, 13t, 69c, 142pg, 7dg-650pts). Prolific points-scorer and darling of the Shed, Mark will come under pressure at fly-half after the signing of Mannix. Though he has broken many goal-kicking records since his arrival at Gloucester, he has occasionally failed to launch the potent Gloucester back division and will be looking to add consistency to his attacking play. Educated at Bawnmore Middle and Lawrence Sheriff School in Rugby and Loughborough University, he starred for England 18 Group before the first of two serious knee injuries. Recovered in time to make an outstanding contribution on England's U21 tour of Australia (1993) but after joining Gloucester he again injured knee ligaments, against West Hartlepool. Represented Coventry City Reserves as a schoolboy.

OJOMOH, Stephen Oziegbe (Backrow)
Born Benin City, Nigeria, 25.05.70. 6'3", 16st 7lb. **Rep hons:** England (12, Ire94), A (17, NOtago92, 3t-12pts), Barbarians (94). **ADPR:** Bath (1990-97, 61, 4t-20pts), Gloucester (1997-98, 13, 2t-10pts). A popular signing from old rivals Bath last season, Steve took a few games to regain fitness and form but was at full throttle by the end of the season, earning a recall to Clive Woodward's England squad.

Schoolboy decathlete of note who attended West Buckland School and the West of England University. Steve joined Bath from Rosslyn Park and toured New Zealand and Canada with England A before winning his first cap against Ireland. Outstanding for England in South Africa (1994) and a member of England's RWC95 squad.

PEARCE, Edward (Flanker)
Born Bristol, 02.09.75. 6'5", 17st 10lb. **ADPR:** Bath (1994-96, 2), Gloucester (1996-98, 12). Has yet to make a real impact in Premiership rugby but is young enough to fulfil his potential. Proud owner of size 16 boots, Ed was educated at Clifton College and has developed into an exceptional age-group international. Performed well in Bath's cross-code game against Wigan at Twickenham before moving to Kingsholm in August 1996.

SAINT-ANDRE, Philippe Georges (Wing)
Born Romans, France, 19.04.67. 5'11", 14st 5lb. **Rep hons:** France (69, Rom90, 32t-152pts), Barbarians (90-91). **ADPR:** Gloucester (1997-98, 13, 6t-30pts). Plagued by quadricep muscle injury for much of the season but looked sharp towards the end of Gloucester's campaign. Philippe, who joined Gloucester in May 1997, has been one of the world's great try-scoring wings and also captained France for 29 successive games. Originally joining Montferrand from his home club Romans in 1988, he was first capped against Romania in 1990, an inauspicious day as France slipped to a 12-6 defeat. Scored that sensational try at Twickenham in 1991 when France counter-attacked from behind their own line. In 1994 became the first wing to captain France since Christian Darrouy (1967) and went on to become France's most successful captain in history. Owns an Irish pub in Montferrand.

SANDERS, Ian (Scrum-half)
Born Penzance, 22.01.71. 5'9", 13st 11lb. **ADPR:** Bath (1990-97, 34, 4t-20pts), Gloucester (1997-98, 2). Proud Cornishman who moved to Gloucester from Bath in 1997. Educated at St Ives School and Penwith College, he made his Bath debut in 1990 as a replacement against London Scottish.

SIMS, David (Lock)
Born Gloucester, 22.11.69. 6'7", 17st 10lb. **Rep hons:** England (3, NZ98), A (23, Sp92, 1t-5pts), Barbarians (95-96). **ADPR:** Gloucester (1990-98, 119, 9t-43pts). Popular local hero nominated as this season's captain by coach Richard Hill. Made a delayed start last season after recovering from an Achilles tendon operation and also struggled with a shoulder problem, but was in prime form by the end of the season and was deservedly called into the England summer tour party. Played magnificently in adversity against New Zealand, and South Africa. The grandson of former Cheltenham and England forward Thomas Price, Dave was educated at Churchdown School, played his early rugby for Longlevens and enjoyed a spell with the Sunny-bank club in Brisbane before representing England U21 and touring New Zealand with England B (1992).

TOMBS, Richard Craig (Centre)
Born Te Kuiti, New Zealand, 04.01.68. 6', 14st 6lb. **Rep hons:** Australia (5, Sc92). **ADPR:** Gloucester (1997-98, 22, 4t-20pts). Former Australia centre whose experience and mature play contributed much to Gloucester's best performances. Toured England with Ricky Stuart's Australian Schools squad in 1986 and was a member of Australia's World Cup winning squad in 1991.

VICKERY, Philip John (Prop)
Born Barnstaple, 14.03.76. 6'3", 19st 9lb. **Rep hons:** England (5, Wal98), A (1, NZ97). **ADPR:** Gloucester (1996-98, 21, 1t-5pts). Powerful front row tyro who made an immediate impression on his senior England debut, helping Clive Woodward's side to

a record 60-26 win over Wales. He was subsequently cited for punching an opponent and initially banned for a month, though this was quashed on appeal. Made a big impact on England's ill-starred tour of southern hemisphere. Learned his rugby playing for Bude and Redruth before joining Gloucester. Capped at Schools and Colts level.

WINDO, Anthony John (Prop)
Born Gloucester, 30.04.69. 6´, 17st 6lb. **ADPR:** Gloucester (1989-98, 75, 9t-45pts). Called into England's summer tour party, just reward for another stalwart season of hard graft in the front row. Another of Gloucester's array of powerful props, Tony joined the club from Longlevens and was nominated the Shed's player of the season in 1996-97.

REVIEW

Gloucester's imported stars brought a sense of excitement and drama at Kingsholm – especially Terry Fanolua and Richard Tombs – but Gloucester still have work to do if they are to consistently challenge the Premiership's elite sides. They still look instinctively to their pack when in trouble, underrating the ability of their new-look back line to deliver the goods. They must also learn to win away from home – they managed it just twice last season. Generally, though, a satisfying season with the supporters in marvellous voice and their game against Newcastle possibly the most compelling in the Premiership last season.

GLOUCESTER in Premiership One 1997-98

Aug 23	H	Bristol	Won	35	13	P.Saint-Andre(2T) T.Windo(T) R.Fidler(T) M.Mapletoft(3C, 3P)
30	A	Leicester	Lost	16	33	M.Mapletoft(T, C, D, 2P)
Oct 19	H	London Irish	Won	29	7	T.Fanolua(T) Penalty(T) R.Tombs(T) P.Glanville(T) M.Mapletoft(3C, P)
26	A	Saracens	Lost	24	42	R.Tombs(2T) T.Fanolua(T) M.Mapletoft(T, C) N.Osman(C)
Nov 2	H	Harlequins	Lost	16	17	T.Fanolua(T) M.Mapletoft(C, 3P)
Dec 14	A	Newcastle	Lost	27	37	C.Catling(T) R.Jewell(T) Penalty(T) M.Mapletoft(3C, 2P)
27	H	Richmond	Won	26	20	T.Fanolua(T) B.Johnson(T) A.Lumsden(T) M.Mapletoft(C, 3P)
30	A	Sale	Drew	24	24	Penalty(T) P.Vickery(T) M.Mapletoft(C, 4P)
Jan 11	A	Wasps	Lost	20	26	N.Carter(T) T.Fanolua(T) C.Fortey(T) M.Mapletoft(C, P)
18	A	Bristol	Won	14	13	R.Fidler(T) M.Mapletoft(3P)
Feb 1	H	Leicester	Won	32	25	S.Benton(T) M.Mapletoft(T, 2C, 6P)
11	A	Bath	Lost	3	47	M.Mapletoft(P)
14	H	Northampton	Won	20	15	T.Fanolua(T) A.Lumsden(T) M.Mapletoft(2C, 2P)
Mar 11	H	Wasps	Won	22	15	R.Fidler(T) B.Johnson(T) R.Tombs(T) M.Mapletoft(2C, P)

15	H	Saracens	Won	38 15	B.Johnson(T) S.Benton(T) T.Windo(T) R.Fidler(T) M.Mapletoft(3C, 4P)
24	A	London Irish	Lost	19 23	S.Devereux(T) M.Mapletoft(C, D, 3P)
29	A	Harlequins	Lost	16 36	Penalty(T) M.Mapletoft(C, 3P)
Apr 11	H	Newcastle	Lost	27 29	S.Ojomoh(T) P.Saint-Andre(T) M.Mapletoft(C, 5P)
18	H	Bath	Won	27 17	R.Fidler(T) P.Saint-Andre(T) M.Mapletoft(C, 5P)
25	A	Richmond	Lost	22 33	M.Mapletoft(T, 2C, P) S.Ojomoh(T) P.Saint-Andre(T)
May 2	H	Sale	Won	31 19	T.Fanolua(T) B.Johnson(T) N.McCarthy(T) P.Saint-Andre(T) M.Mapletoft(4C, P)
17	A	Northampton	Won	24 22	B.Johnson(T) M.Mapletoft(T, C, 4P)

Summary of Premiership scorers:

275 – M.Mapletoft (5T, 35C, 2D, 58P); 35 – T.Fanolua (7T); 30 – P.Saint-Andre (6T); 25 – B.Johnson (5T), R.Fidler (5T); 20 – Penalty (4T), R.Tombs (4T); 10 – T.Windo (2T), S.Ojomoh (2T), A.Lumsden (2T), S.Benton (2T); 5 – P.Vickery (T), N.McCarthy (T), R.Jewell (T), P.Glanville (T), C.Fortey (T), S.Devereux (T), N.Carter (T), C.Catling (T); 2 – N.Osman (C).

Summary of Premiership appearances:

22 – R.Tombs, M.Mapletoft, T.Fanolua, N.Carter (+1); 20 – T.Windo, R.Fidler, C.Catling; 19 – S.Benton; 18 – P.Glanville, S.Devereux (+1); 17 – M.Cornwell (+5); 16 – P.Vickery; 15 – D.Sims (+3); 13 – P.Saint-Andre, S.Ojomoh (+6), A.Lumsden (+2), B.Johnson, C.Fortey (+2); 10 – N.McCarthy (+4); 9 – A.Deacon (+2); 8 – P.Greening (+3); 6 – L.Beck (+3); 5 – R.Jewell (+3); 4 – R.Saint-Andre, A.Powles (+3), E.Pearce (+1), 3 – C.Emmerson (+2); 2 – I.Sanders (+2), N.Osman (+2), M.Lloyd; 1 – A.Hazell (+1).

HARLEQUINS

Formation of club: 1866
Ground: Stoop Memorial Ground, Craneford Way, Twickenham TW2 7SX
Capacity: 9,750 (All seated)
Colours: Light blue, magenta, chocolate, french grey, black and light green
Honours: Cup Winners (2) – 1988, 1991
Best League finish: 3rd in Division One 1987-88, 1990-91, 1995-96 and 1996-97
Last season: ADP1 – 10th. Heineken European Cup – Q/F (lost 10-51 to Toulouse).
    Tetley's Bitter Cup – 4th round (lost 26-31 to Wasps)
Owner: NEC Electronics
Director of Rugby: John Gallagher
Coaches: Bernie McCahill (backs), Adrian Skeggs (forwards)
Captain: TBC

ALLISON, Gareth Vincent (Flanker)
Born New Malden, 31.01.70. 6'5", 16st 2lb. **Rep hons:** England A (2, SA96). **ADPR:** Rosslyn Park (1991-93, 5, 2t-10pts), Harlequins (1995-98, 25, 4t-20pts). Struggled badly with injury last season after making a successful switch from full-back to flanker the previous winter. Educated at St Paul's and an England Colts cap at full-back, Gareth continued his studies at Reading University and Oxford University where he graduated with an MSc in Management Studies and won a Blue at flanker (1994). Has also played for Toulouse and Rosslyn Park.

BROOKE, Zinzan Valentine (Backrow)
Born Waiuku, New Zealand, 04.02.65. 6'3", 16st 7lb. **Rep hons:** New Zealand (Arg87, 58, 17t, 3dg-89pts). Hugely skilled and versatile former All Black who starts his playing career at Harlequins this season, having helped out with the coaching at the end of last season. Started as a sevens expert with New Zealand and developed into one of their most accomplished backrow forwards in history. Also proved a popular and effective captain of Auckland. Famed for his outrageous touch kicks and dropped goals – he landed one from 40 metres against England in the 1995 World Cup and kicked two others, against South Africa and Wales, in international rugby. Brother Robin continues to carry the family honour in an All Black shirt.

COLLIER, Tim (Lock)
Born Farnborough, 27.10.77. 6'6", 19st 4lb. **ADPR:** Harlequins (1997-98, 7). Formerly a pupil at Ravenswood School, Tim played for Westcombe Park before moving to NEC Harlequins. Played in South Africa for Durban Quins in 1997.

DAVISON, William (No 8)
Born Kitwe, Zambia, 08.04.69. 6'6", 16st 8lb. **Rep hons:** England A (2, Arg96). **ADPR:** Richmond (1990-91, 1), Rosslyn Park (1991-94, 23, 2t-10pts), Harlequins (1994-98, 52, 4t-20pts). Much travelled and ultra-reliable utility forward who often stepped in as a deputy captain during Keith Wood's absences last season and retained his reputation of being Harlequins' most reliable forward. Educated at Hinchlewood School, Esher Sixth Form College and Sheffield Polytechnic, he numbers Cobham, Sheffield, Hawkes Bay and Rosslyn Park among his previous clubs. Played for Hawkes Bay in 1993 when they defeated the British Lions.

HALPIN, Garrett Francis (Prop)
Born Dublin, 14.02.66. 6', 17st 6lb. **Rep hons:** Ireland (11, Eng90, 1t-5pts), A (2, Arg90), Barbarians (94). **ADPR:** London Irish (1991-98, 101, 10t-50pts). Inspirational former London Irish captain who has moved three miles up the M3 during the summer to join Harlequins. An 'amateur' by inclination, Gary has nonetheless put his teaching career on hold this season to concentrate fully on a professional rugby career. Educated at Rockwell College, Tipperary, Gary won schools caps in 1983 and 1984 before attending University of Manhattan on an athletics scholarship. He represented Ireland in the hammer at the 1987 World Championships in Rome and has a personal best of 73.84m. First capped against England in 1990, Gary won six caps in the next five years before becoming first choice at RWC95, which he will remember chiefly for a tapped penalty try against New Zealand . . . and the celebrations. Renewed his acquaintance with various New Zealand friends when he captained the Ireland Development XV in 1997.

HARRIES, Huw (Scrum-half)
Born Cardiff, 21.02.73. 5'11", 13st 7lb. **Rep hons:** Wales A (2, Ire97). **ADPR:** Harlequins (1996-98, 31, 9t-45pts). Razor-sharp around the fringes, Huw found it a little tougher in the Premiership last season when the opposition defences were waiting for him. A star product of the Wales age-group system, Huw has captained every Welsh side he has represented. Educated at Ysgol Glantaf, New College Cardiff and Cardiff University. A qualified pharmacist.

JENKINS, Rory Harry John (Flanker)
Born Leicester, 29.06.70. 6'2", 15st 12lb. **Rep hons:** England A (16, It94, 1t-5pts).
ADPR: London Irish (1993-94, 15, 1t-5pts), Harlequins (1994-98, 67, 3t-15pts).
Powerful destructive flanker. The son of former Leicester and Cambridge University
lock John Jenkins, Rory was also educated at Oundle and Cambridge University
where he won Blues in rugby, cricket and athletics. Formerly with Brixham, he joined
London Irish and played against the 1993 All Blacks for London before joining
Harlequins. Toured Argentina with England in 1997 but failed to make the break-
through at full England level. Qualified solicitor.

KEYTER, Jason (Centre/wing)
Born Pt Elizabeth, S Africa, 20.12.73. 5'11", 14st 2lb. **Rep hons:** England A (2,
Vict95). **ADPR:** Harlequins (1993-95, 12, 5t-25pts), Bristol (1995-96, 9), Harlequins
(1996-98, 27, 6t-30pts). Talented utility back and one of Harlequins' more consistent
performers behind the scrum last season. Jason arrived in England in 1986 and
played his junior rugby with Weston-Super-Mare. Joined Harlequins as a Colt and
made rapid progress before quitting the club and joining Bristol midway through
1994-95 season. Toured Australia and Fiji with England A in 1995 and rejoined
Quins from Bristol last season.

LACROIX, Thierry (Fly-half)
Born Nogaro, France, 02.03.67. 5'11", 13st 12lb. **Rep hons:** France (43, Aus89, 6t, 32c,
89pg, 2dg-367pts). **ADPR:** Harlequins (1996-98, 27, 5t, 55c, 65pg, 5dg-345pts).
Bedevilled by a long-term hamstring problem for much of the season, Lacroix
remained a significant force at fly-half whenever fully fit. His experience and
playmaking ability was badly missed in many key games. Lacroix, a lifelong member
of Dax before joining Harlequins, made his international debut as a replacement
against Australia in 1989 and subsequently scored 367 points in his 38 international
appearances. Appeared at fly-half in France's unsuccessful 1991 World Cup campaign but thereafter switched to centre. Enjoyed his finest moment in the 1995 World
Cup when he emerged as the tournament's top scorer with 116 points in six games.
He stayed on in South Africa that summer and his goal-kicking helped Natal to
victory in the Currie Cup.

LEACH, Adam (No 8)
Born Corowa, Australia, 24.11.71. 6'2", 15st 6lb. **ADPR:** Harlequins (1997-98, 15,
2t-10pts). Former New South Wales backrow forward who signed for Harlequins
after advertising his services on the Internet.

LEONARD, Jason (Prop)
Born Barking, 14.08.68. 5'10", 17st 2lb. **Rep hons:** England (63, Arg90, 1t-5pts), A (2,
Fiji89), Barbarians (96). **ADPR:** Saracens (1988-90, 19, 1t-4pts), Harlequins (1990-
98, 93, 2t-9pts). A disappointing season for England's most-capped prop started with
a contractual dispute with the club and scarcely got better, Jason struggling to find
the form and fitness that had made him one of the world's most reliable props. Easy
to forget that he probably should not be playing at all after undergoing complicated
surgery to his neck which required a bone graft from his hip. Educated at Warren
Comprehensive School, Chadwell Heath, Jason joined Barking RFC before moving
to Saracens and on to Harlequins.

LILEY, Robert James (Fly-half)
Born Wakefield, 03.04.70. 6'1", 12st 8lb. **Rep hons:** England A (2, Qld96, 2c,
1pg-7pts), Barbarians (96-97). **ADPR:** Wakefield (1991-94, 23, 3t, 23c, 51pg, 2dg-
219pts), Sale (1994-96, 25, 3t, 28c, 44pg, 2dg-209pts), Leicester (1996-97, 13, 3t, 7c,
5pg-44pts), Harlequins (1997-98, 13, 2t, 22c, 7pg-75pts). Failed to make a huge
impact after his arrival from Leicester. Rob also numbers Sandal, Wakefield, Sale and
Cahors in France amongst his previous clubs. He is the younger brother of John and

shares many of his footballing skills. Served a patient apprenticeship under Paul Turner at Sale but emerged in 1995-96 to amass 167 League points before signing for Leicester. Yorkshire debut against Cumbria in 1992. Enjoys classical guitar.

LLEWELLYN, Gareth Owen (Lock)
Born Cardiff, 27.02.69. 6'6", 17st 10lb. **Rep hons:** Wales (62, NZ89, 5t-24pts), A (6, Can89, 1t-5pts), Barbarians (89-90). **ADPR:** Harlequins (1996-98, 37, 3t-15pts). Another big name who endured a disappointing season, Gareth joined Harlequins from Neath after captaining the Welsh All Blacks to the Heineken League champi-onship in 1995-96 and a SWALEC Cup final appearance against Pontypridd. The most capped Welsh lock in history, he has also captained his country against Zimbabwe and Namibia on tour and against France (twice), Italy and South Africa. Gareth was educated at Bryntiron Comprehensive and won Youth and U19 honours from Llanharan before moving to the Gnoll. Switched briefly, without conspicuous success, to blindside flanker during RWC95.

LUGER, Dan (Wing)
Born Chiswick, 11.01.75. 6'1", 14st. **Rep hons:** England A (4, Arg96, 2t-10pts). **ADPR:** Richmond (1994-96, 20, 5t-25pts), Orrell (1995-96, 5, 1t-5pts), Harlequins (1996-98, 20, 10t-50pts). Back to his try-scoring best after finally recovering from surgery to a serious knee injury. Dan joined Quins from Orrell, and was formerly with Richmond. Played for London U21 against NZ U21 in 1994 and appeared for England Students and U21 in 1995-96. A member of England's squad in the World Students Cup in South Africa in 1996, Luger showed glimpses of his exciting potential on his return before injury struck.

MENSAH, Peter (Centre)
Born Ghana, 10.11.66. 6', 13st 8lb. **Rep hons:** England A (8, SA95, 3t-15pts). **ADPR:** Harlequins (1994-98, 49, 16t-80pts). Wholehearted team performer, occasionally let down by poor hands. Peter came to the senior game late when he joined from Old Millhillians in 1994. Has slotted in well at the Stoop and has also earned England A honours. Scored three tries for an England Select XV against a Springbok Veteran XV in a fund-raising game for Max Brito in Ghana in May 96.

NEBBETT, Ricky (Prop)
Born Kingston, 16.08.77. 5'11", 17st. **ADPR:** Harlequins (1997-98, 9, 1t-5pts). Powerful former England Schools prop who gained valuable first-team experience later in the season as Harlequins struggled with injury. Educated at John Fisher School in Purley.

NGAUAMO, Johnny F. (Centre)
Born Tonga, 20.07.69. 6'1", 14st. **Rep hons:** Tonga. **ADPR:** Harlequins (1997-98, 15, 3t-15pts). Experienced Tongan international who has also played provincial rugby for Auckland.

OFFICER, David Gordon (Utility back)
Born Aberdeen, 9.5.73. 6'2", 14st. **Rep hons:** Scotland A (3, Fr98, 2t-10pts). Moves to Harlequins from the Currie club having played in Europe last season with Caledonia – proving his versatility by appearing at centre, wing and scrum-half. Had previously played club rugby for Montrose, Edinburgh University and Heriot's before joining Currie two years ago. Broke into the Scotland A squad at the end of last season and toured Fiji and Australia with the senior Scotland team.

O'LEARY, Daren S. (Wing)
Born Harold Wood, Essex, 27.06.73. 6'0", 13st 10lb. **Rep hons:** England A (1, It96). **ADPR:** Saracens (1992-93, 10, 3t-15pts), Harlequins (1993-98, 80, 50t, 1dg-253pts). Try-poacher par excellence, Daren scored 15 League tries in 1996-97 to lead the chart

with Adedayo Adebayo, having topped the chart the previous season with 14. Last season was less productive, though he comfortably topped Quins' list with 9. Educated at Campion School and West London Institute, Daren developed his try-scoring habits at Saracens before moving to Harlequins in 1993, making his debut that September against Lansdowne. Was called into the England training squad for the 1993 Five Nations and was deservedly recalled for England's visit to Argentina in 1997.

OZDEMIR, Altan Mustafa (Prop)
Born Cyprus, 03.09.74. 5'9", 16st. **ADPR:** Bristol (1994-95, 7), Harlequins (1996-98, 8). A strong young prop, Altan moved from Cyprus at the age of six, was educated at Hurstpierpoint College and joined Harlequins after a short spell with Bristol.

SHEASBY, Christopher Mark Andrew (No 8)
Born Windsor, 30.11.66. 6'3", 16st. **Rep hons:** England (7, 1t96, 1t-5pts), A (8, 1t94, 5t-25pts), Barbarians (89-90). **ADPR:** Harlequins (1987-96, 63, 8t-39pts), Wasps (1996-98, 27, 8t-40pts), Harlequins (1997-98, 6, 1t-5pts). Returned to the club in February after a spell at Wasps where he finally won England recognition. Has shed his reputation of being only a sevens specialist to become a model of consistency for Wasps. Educated at Radley, London University and Hughes Hall, Cambridge, where he gained two Blues (90, 91), Chris is a maths teacher at Pangbourne College. Still enjoys sevens and represented England at the Hong Kong tournament in 1996 and 1997.

STAPLES, James Edward (Full-back)
Born Bermondsey, 20.10.65. 6'2", 13st 10lb. **Rep hons:** Ireland (26, Wal91, 5t, 2c-25pts), A (4, Sc89, 1t-5pts), Barbarians (92-93). **ADPR:** London Irish (1987-94, 56, 14t, 1dg-59pts), Harlequins (1994-98, 40, 16t, 5c, 2pg, 2dg-102pts). Chose to pursue his lucrative career in the City, so his first-team opportunities last season were inevitably limited. Educated at St Mary's, Sidcup, and played for Sidcup before joining London Irish. Played for the Irish Wolfhounds in the 1989 Hong Kong Sevens and won three U25 caps against Italy, USA and Spain before making a try-scoring international debut against Wales in 1991. Starred for Ireland in RWC91 and did well to survive a crude, late and high tackle from Scotland's Finlay Calder in their group games. Prolapsed disc and serious knee ligament injury problems blighted his career. A useful footballer who once partnered Arsenal's Ian Wright up front for Greenwich Borough.

STEWART, D. Scott (Full-back)
Born Vancouver, Canada, 16.01.69. 6'2", 13st 13lb. **Rep hons:** Canada (41, US89, 4t-19pts). **ADPR:** Harlequins (1997-98, 14, 1t-5pts). Strong-tackling and vastly experienced Canadian, starting his second season in the Premiership.

WALSHE, Nicholas Patrick James (Scrum-half)
Born Chiswick, 01.11.73. 5'11", 13st 4lb. **Rep hons:** England A (2, Arg96). **ADPR:** Rosslyn Park (1993-95, 25, 2t-10pts), Harlequins (1995-98, 27, 7t, 2c-39pts). Formerly at Rosslyn Park, Nick impressed at full-back for London U21 v NZ U21 in 1994 but then switched to scrum-half and continued to press Huw Harries hard for the starting spot last season. Educated at Worth Abbey.

WHITE-COOPER, Steve (No 8)
Born Cape Town, South Africa, 15.07.74. 6'4", 16st. **ADPR:** Harlequins (1997-98, 4). Versatile backrow performer who did not disgrace himself when called upon late last season.

WILLIAMS, Jamie (Wing/Full-back)
Born Marton, New Zealand, 16.03.76. 6'1", 13st 9lb. **ADPR:** Harlequins (1996-98, 16, 5t-25pts). Versatile young New Zealander who has rarely let Quins down since making his debut against London Irish in September 1995. Has real pace when

released on the outside, something he demonstrated at Wasps in the Tetley's Bitter
Cup when he scored a spectacular hat-trick. Educated at St Patrick's College,
Wellington, and Surrey University.

WOOD, Keith Gerard Mallinson (Hooker)
Born Limerick, 27.01.72. 6′, 15st 10lb. **Rep hons:** Ireland (17, Aus94, 2t-10pts), A (2,
Sc93). **ADPR:** Harlequins (1996-98, 30, 8t-40pts). Endured a frustrating season as
captain with injury again causing problems, not to mention sheer fatigue after his
exertions on behalf of the British Lions the previous summer. Did, however, recover
sufficiently to play in both of Ireland's Tests in South Africa, though not as captain.
Had missed much of the 1996-97 season with shoulder problems, after missing all of
the previous season with Garryowen having re-injured his right shoulder in the
opening minutes of Ireland's group game against Japan in RWC95. The son of
former Ireland and British Lions hooker Gordon Wood, Keith was educated at St
Munchin's College, Limerick, and was an exceptional age-group international. Made
his full debut on the Australian tour (1994).

YATES, Alan John (Prop)
Born Sale, 05.01.63. 6′, 18st. **ADPR:** Broughton Park (1990-92, 2t-8pts), Sale
(1995-97, 16), Wakefield (1997-98, 3), Harlequins (1997-98, 11). Signed from Wakefield as a stop-gap when Quins were hit by an injury crisis in the front row.
Enormously strong bodybuilder, and soccer player with Oldham.

REVIEW

Flattered briefly to deceive early on last season, but their season disintegrated
following a humiliating European Cup defeat away to Toulouse. They dropped away
alarmingly in the League, Will Carling departed, coach Andy Keach was shifted
sideways before being dispensed with altogether and All Black legend Zinzan Brooke
arrived, only for his side to plummet to new depths. Harlequins were a shambles for
much of the second half of the season and must improve dramatically if they are to
compete. The presence, on the field, of Brooke should help but generally the standard
and motivation of their recruits has been Harlequins' biggest problem. A key season
in the club's history awaits.

HARLEQUINS in Premiership One 1997-98

Aug 23	A	Northampton	Won	26	23	D.O'Leary(T) W.Carling(T) T.Lacroix(2C, 4P)
30	H	Bath	Lost	20	27	J.Ngauamo(T) J.Williams(T) T.Lacroix(2C, 2P)
Oct 18	A	Richmond	Lost	16	37	S.Stewart(T) R.Liley(C, 3P)
25	H	Sale	Won	52	41	D.O'Leary(2T, D) T.Tollett(T) S.Bromley(T) K.Wood(T) R.Jenkins(T) A.Leach(T) R.Liley(7C)
Nov 2	A	Gloucester	Won	17	16	J.Williams(T) Gar.Llewellyn(T) T.Lacroix(2C, P)
Dec 13	H	Wasps	Won	53	17	D.O'Leary(2T) T.Tollett(T) T.Lacroix(T, 3C, 2D, 3P) Penalty(T) J.Williams(T) P.Challinor(C)
20	A	Leicester	Lost	3	27	T.Lacroix(P)

27	H	London Irish	Won	26	24	B.Davison(T) R.Nebbett(T) T.Lacroix(2C, 4P)
31	H	Bristol	Lost	38	40	J.Keyter(2T) R.Liley(T, 3C) J.Ngauamo(T) D.Luger(T) P.Challinor(T) T.Lacroix(C)
Jan 11	A	Saracens	Lost	16	25	D.Luger(T) T.Lacroix(C, 3P)
18	H	Northampton	Lost	5	30	T.Tollett(T)
Feb 15	A	Newcastle	Lost	15	43	D.O'Leary(T) D.Luger(T) R.Liley(C, P)
28	A	Bath	Lost	13	39	D.Luger(T) R.Liley(C, 2P)
Mar 7	H	Richmond	Won	41	12	D.O'Leary(2T) B.Davison(T) T.Lacroix(T, 5C, 2P) P.Mensah(T)
14	A	Sale	Lost	13	23	D.Luger(T) T.Lacroix(C, 2P)
29	H	Gloucester	Won	36	16	Gar.Llewellyn(T) N.Walshe(T) C.Sheasby(T) D.O'Leary(T) P.Mensah(T) R.Liley(4C, P)
Apr 12	A	Wasps	Lost	26	29	J.Ngauamo(T) D.Luger(T) N.Walshe(T) R.Liley(T, 3C)
18	H	Leicester	Lost	14	23	J.Keyter(T) A.Leach(T) R.Liley(2C)
25	A	London Irish	Lost	14	62	J.Keyter(T) Penalty(T) T.Lacroix(C) N.Walshe(C)
29	H	Saracens	Lost	26	28	J.Williams(T) T.Lacroix(T, 2C, 4P)
May 3	A	Bristol	Won	26	19	D.Luger(T) K.Wood(T) T.Lacroix(2C, 4P)
17	H	Newcastle	Lost	20	44	D.Luger(T) H.Harries(T) T.Lacroix(2C, 2P)

Summary of Premiership scorers:

169 – T.Lacroix (3T, 26C, 2D, 32P); 75 – R.Liley (2T, 22C, 7P); 48 – D.O'Leary (9T, D); 40 – D.Luger (8T); 20 – J.Williams (4T), J.Keyter (4T); 17 – P.Challinor (3T, C); 15 – T.Tollett (3T), J.Ngauamo (3T); 12 – N.Walshe (2T, C); 10 – K.Wood (2T), P.Mensah (2T), Gar.Llewellyn (2T), Penalty (2T), A.Leach (2T), B.Davison (2T); 5 – S.Stewart (T), R.Nebbett (T), R.Jenkins (T), H.Harries (T), W.Carling (T), S.Bromley (T).

Summary of Premiership appearances:

21 – R.Jenkins (+3), B.Davison; 20 – Gar.Llewellyn (+2), J.Keyter (+13); 19 – L.Cabannes (+4); 18 – D.O'Leary; 17 – J.Leonard; 16 – H.Harries (+7); 15 – K.Wood (+2), N.Walshe (+2), J.Ngauamo (+1), A.Leach (+2); 14 – S.Stewart (+1), D.Luger, T.Lacroix (+1); 13 – R.Liley (+2), T.Billups (+5); 11 – T.Tollett (+4), P.Mensah; 10 – M.Cuttitta (+3); 9 – J.Williams (+1), R.Nebbett (+3); 7 – C.Wright (+4), T.Collier (+4), P.Challinor (+4); 6 – L.Gross; 5 – W.Carling (+1); 4 – S.White-Cooper (+1), R.Strudwick, A.Ozdemir (+2), S.Bromley (+2), L.Belligoi, G.Allison (+2); 3 – S.Power (+1); 2 – J.Staples, D.Rouse, P.Delaney (+1); 1 – I.Pickup, A.Mullins.

LEICESTER

Formation of club: 1880
Ground: Welford Road Stadium, Aylestone Road, Leicester LE2 7TR
Capacity: 16,250 (Seated 12,500)
Colours: Scarlet, green and white
Honours: Cup Winners (5) – 1979, 1980, 1981, 1993, 1996. League Champions (2) –
1987-88, 1994-95
Last season: ADP1 – 4th. Heineken European Cup – Q/F (lost 18-35 to Pau). Tetley's
Bitter Cup – 5th round (lost 13-14 to Saracens)
Owner: Members
Team Manager: Dean Richards. Assistants: John Wells, Joel Stransky
Captain: Martin Johnson

ALDWINCKLE, Jason Malcolm (Hooker)
Born Leicester, 08.10.69. 5'9", 15st 7lb. **ADPR:** Rugby (1991-93, 6), Leicester
(1993-98, 5). Loyal club man who was finally, after eight years, awarded his tie for 20
first-team appearances after the game at Wasps last season.

BACK, Neil Antony (Flanker)
Born Coventry, 16.01.69. 5'10", 14st 9lb. **Rep hons:** England (12, Sc94, 3t-15pts), A
(26, Aus90, 10t-45pts), Barbarians (90-91). **ADPR:** Nottingham (1988-90, 7, 2t-8pts),
Leicester (1990-98, 100, 24t-119pts). England's player of the season internationally
although a groin strain, unfortunately, prevented him from touring the southern
hemisphere. Educated at Woodlands School, Coventry, Neil played for Earlsdon and
Barkers Butts before moving to Nottingham and then to Welford Road. Toured New
Zealand and Canada with England A, made his full international debut against
Scotland (1994). Treated with mistrust by various England regimes until Clive
Woodward made him the side's pivotal player. Outstanding Lions tour to South
Africa in 1997.

BALDING, Adam (Backrow)
Born Coventry, 07.12.79. 6'4", 16st 8lb. Outstanding backrow prospect from Caludon
Castle School who has been ever-present in the England Schools 18 Group side over
the last two seasons, playing a prominent role in their successful tour of Australia in
1997. Accompanied England Colts to Argentina in August 1998.

COCKERILL, Richard (Hooker)
Born Rugby, 16.12.70. 5'10", 17st. **Rep hons:** England (13, Arg97, 2t-10pts), A (6,
It95), Barbarians (94). **ADPR:** Coventry (1991-92, 12), Leicester (1992-98, 93,
5t-25pts). Came of age internationally last season, initially against New Zealand and
then in the Five Nations. Richard won his first cap as a replacement for great rival
Phil Greening in England's first Test against Argentina in May 1997. Voluble
character, who has become a favourite at Leicester, his aggressive play served
England well on their tour of the southern hemisphere last summer. Formerly an
antiques restorer, he is now a full-time professional. Educated at Harris Church of
England School, Richard played for Newbold-on-Avon and Coventry before joining
Leicester.

CORRY, Martin Edward (Backrow)
Born Birmingham, 12.10.73. 6'5", 17st 8lb. **Rep hons:** England (2, Arg97), A (10,
Vic95). **ADPR:** Newcastle (1993-95, 25, 7t-35pts), Bristol (1995-97, 32, 8t-40pts),
Leicester (1997-98, 17). After doing well for England in Argentina in May 1997,
Martin slipped out of the national reckoning last season and generally endured a
disappointing season. Educated at Tunbridge Wells GS and Newcastle Polytechnic,

Martin played lock for the England Schools Grand Slam side in 1992. Toured Australia and Fiji with England A in 1995. Numbers Newcastle and Bristol among his former clubs.

EDWARDS, Roland (Scrum-half)
Born Derby, 11.11.77. 5'8", 10st 10lb. **ADPR:** Leicester (1996-98, 3). Useful backup scrum-half to Austin Healey and Jamie Hamilton. Educated at Ashby Grammar School.

FRESHWATER, Perry Thomas (Prop)
Born Wellington, New Zealand, 27.07.73. 6', 17st 5lb. **Rep hons:** Barbarians (96-97). **ADPR:** Leicester (1995-98, 17). Tough New Zealand-reared prop who provides front row back-up to the ABC club. Has played for New Zealand U21s.

GARFORTH, Darren James (Prop)
Born Coventry, 09.04.66. 5'10", 18st 7lb. **Rep hons:** England (11, Wal97), A (17, Sp93, 3t-15pts), Barbarians (94). **ADPR:** Nuneaton (1988-89, 1t-4pts), Leicester (1991-98, 119, 4t-19pts). Disappointed to be dropped from England's summer tour. Rugged tight-head prop with a surprising turn of speed, Darren made his senior England debut as a replacement against Wales in March 1997, commanded a place in the starting line-up in 1997 and was rarely out of the reckoning last season. Educated at Binley Park School, Coventry, he played for Nuneaton before moving to Leicester in 1991-92.

GREENWOOD, William John Heaton (Centre)
Born Blackburn, 20.10.72. 6'4", 15st. **Rep hons:** England (8, Aus97, 1t-5pts), A (13, SAus95, 6t-30pts), Barbarians (95-96). **ADPR:** Waterloo (1991-94, 4, 1t-5pts), Harlequins (1994-96, 25, 6t, 1c, 5pg-47pts), Leicester (1996-98, 31, 14t-70pts). Finally emulated father Dick and played for England last season, but missed the summer tour to have a much-needed shoulder operation, the legacy of his bad knock against the Free State playing for the Lions in 1997. Signed from Harlequins in June 1996, Will comes from the same Sedbergh/Durham University stable as former Quins colleague Will Carling. Formerly with Preston Grasshoppers and Waterloo, he toured Australia with England U21 (1993). Scored a hat-trick for England A against Western Samoa in December 1995.

GUSTARD, Paul Simon Keith (Flanker)
Born Newcastle-upon-Tyne, 02.02.76. 6'4", 17st 3lb. **ADPR:** Leicester (1997-98, 16, 4t-20pts). Dynamic young flanker who is rapidly demanding inclusion in Leicester's first choice line-up. Captained the England U21 team in Australia in 1997.

HAMILTON, James Garth (Scrum-half)
Born Guildford, 01.07.70. 5'9", 12st 5lb. **ADPR:** Leicester (1990-96, 15, 1t-5pts), London Scottish (1996-97, 7, 1t-5pts), Leicester (1997-98, 12, 2t-10pts). Fast and aggressive around the base of the scrum, made a welcome return from London Scottish last season.

HEALEY, Austin Sean (Scrum-half)
Born Wallasey, 26.10.73. 5'10", 13st 5lb. **Rep hons:** England (14, Ire97, 2t-10pts), A (3, NSW96, 1t-5pts), Barbarians (95-96). **ADPR:** Waterloo (1992-94, 20, 3t, 1dg-18pts), Orrell (1994-96, 33, 4t, 2c, 1pg-27pts), Leicester (1996-98, 36, 5t-25pts). England think he's a wing but Austin wants to revert to scrum-half for Leicester this season. Talented but voluble character who fell out with former Leicester coach Bob Dwyer last season. Transferred from Orrell after switching from wing to scrum-half in 1995-96. Educated at St Anselm's College, he first joined Birkenhead Park and came to national prominence when helping Waterloo to a third-round Pilkington Cup victory over Bath. A try-scorer in December 1994 when England U21 beat New

Zealand U21, Austin made his A team debut against New South Wales at Leicester in January 1995. Would have been called Jensen had he been born a girl!

HORAK, Michael John (Full-back)
Born Johannesburg, 03.06.77. 6′2″, 14st 3lb. **ADPR:** Leicester (1997-98, 19, 8t, 2c, 2pg-50pts). Long striding former Free State U21 and Perth Reds full-back with a nose for tries. Played for England U21s last season.

HOWARD, Patrick William (Utility back)
Born Brisbane, Australia, 14.11.73. 5′10″, 14st 2lb. **Rep hons:** Australia (20, NZ93, 2t-10pts). Barbarians 94. Talented all-rounder behind the scrum who has not yet given up on continuing his international career. Started with Queensland but has enjoyed success in recent seasons with ACT Brumbies.

JOHNSON, Martin Osborne (Lock)
Born Solihull, 09.03.70. 6′6″, 18st. **Rep hons:** England (37, Fr93, 1t-5pts), A (8, Fr92, 1t-5pts), Barbarians (91-92). **ADPR:** Leicester (1988-98, 107, 3t-15pts). Enjoyed a summer off from England duties to undergo a second groin operation. Martin has been an immense force for England since making his debut against France in 1993 after a last-minute call-up for Wade Dooley. Was touring Canada with an England XV in May 93 when he was again called on to replace Dooley, this time for the Lions in New Zealand, immediately winning Test selection. Captained the British Lions on their successful 1997 tour to South Africa. Educated at Welland Park and Robert Smythe Upper School, Market Harborough, Martin had already represented England Schools when he travelled to New Zealand to play for King Country, and subsequently toured Australia with New Zealand Colts (U21).

JOHNSON, William Warwick (Flanker)
Born Solihull, 18.03.74. 6′4″, 17st 4lb. **ADPR:** Leicester (1995-98, 20, 1t-5pts). Hard-grafting flanker, younger brother of club captain Martin Johnson.

JOINER, Craig Alexander (Wing/centre)
Born Glasgow, 21.04.74. 5′10″, 14st. **Rep hons:** Scotland (21, Arg94, 3t-15pts), A (3, SA94). **ADPR:** Leicester (1996-98, 24, 9t-45pts). Elusive Scottish wing who joined Leicester from Melrose and has finally overcome a troublesome groin injury. Craig was educated at Dunfermline HS and Merchiston Castle School, where he was a national schools sprint champion and won 10 schools rugby caps. Making his international debut while on tour in Argentina (94), Craig was ever-present throughout Scotland's RWC95 campaign. Toured Australia and Fiji in summer 1998.

LLOYD, Leon David (Wing)
Born Coventry, 22.09.77. 6′4″, 14st. **Rep hons:** Barbarians (97). **ADPR:** Leicester (1996-98, 25, 4t-20pts). Strong-running England Colts wing who is still finding his way in senior rugby. Represented England in the Six Nations U21 Festival in Cape Town in July 1998.

LOUGHEED, David (Wing/centre)
Born Toronto, 04.11.68. 6′2″, 14st 4lb. **Rep hons:** Canada (22, Arg90, 4t-20pts). Barbarians 1995. Powerful Canadian best remembered for his two tries against England at Twickenham in 1994. Long-time member of the Canadian Sevens team, often playing prop. Joins Leicester from the Balmy Beach club in Toronto.

MALONE, Niall Gareth (Utility back)
Born Leeds, 30.04.71. 5′11″, 14st. **Rep hons:** Ireland (3, Sc93, 3pg-9pts), A (4, Sc92, 1t, 1c, 2pg-13pts), Barbarians (97-98). **ADPR:** London Irish (1992-93, 1), Leicester (1993-98, 31, 2t, 1pg, 1dg-16pts). Educated at Methodist College, Belfast, and

Loughborough University, Niall also won a Blue for Oxford (1992) and earned his first full cap two months later, against Scotland. Scored a try in the 1995-96 Pilkington Cup final.

MILLER, Eric Roger Patrick (Backrow)
Born Dublin, 23.09.75. 6'3", 15st 12lb. **Rep hons:** Ireland (8, It97, 1t-5pts), A (2, Sc96, 1t-5pts). **ADPR:** Leicester (1995-98, 28, 1t-5pts). Another to suffer a hangover from the Lions trip, Eric was also hampered by a long-term ankle problem last year and was forced to miss Ireland's tour of South Africa. He remains an important player for Ireland as they build towards RWC99. Educated at Wesley College, Eric has emerged as a more than useful line-out operator and a useful left-footed touch-kicker, as befits a former Dublin Schools soccer representative. PE student at Loughborough University.

MOODY, Lewis Walton (Flanker)
Born Berkshire, 12.06.78. 6'4", 15st 11lb. **ADPR:** Leicester (1996-98, 16, 1t-5pts). Strong, driving openside flanker who toured Australia with Clive Woodward's England U21 squad in 1997, and made a big enough impression with Leicester last season to receive a call-up for the senior squad's vist to the southern hemisphere in the summer. Educated at Oakham School.

MURPHY, Geordan Edward Andrew (Full-back)
Born Dublin, 19.04.78. 6', 12st 7lb. **ADPR:** Leicester (1997-98, 3). Promising Irish-born full-back who has opted for England. Played for Naas in Ireland before joining the Tigers last season.

POOLE, Matthew David (Lock)
Born Keyham, Leicester, 06.02.69. 6'6", 19st 6lb. **Rep hons:** Barbarians (93-94). **ADPR:** Leicester (1988-98, 97, 5t-25pts). Unsung but invaluable member of Leicester's pack who was troubled by injury last season. Matt has toured Argentina (1990) and South Africa (1994) with the senior England squads without being capped. Educated at Roundhill and originally a member of Syston College, he made his Tigers debut in 1989 against Oxford University.

POTTER, Stuart (Centre)
Born Lichfield, 11.11.67. 5'11", 14st 7lb. **Rep hons:** England (1, Aus98), A (18, It93, 5t-25pts), Barbarians (93-94). **ADPR:** Nottingham (1989-92, 30, 5t-20pts), Leicester (1992-98, 87, 16t-80pts). Stalwart performer for Leicester, Stuart's consistency was rewarded when he was called into England's tour party for the southern hemisphere. A powerful centre, Stuart also toured Canada with England A (1993) and South Africa with England (1994). Educated at Friary Grange School, he first came to prominence with Nottingham and helped the Midlands win the Divisional Championship (1991) before joining Leicester.

ROWNTREE, Graham Christopher (Prop)
Born Stockton-on-Tees, 18.04.71. 6', 17st 4lb. **Rep hons:** England (19, Sc95), A (5, BritCol93), Barbarians (93-94). **ADPR:** Leicester (1990-98, 105, 2t-10pts). Dropped out of the England reckoning last season before being recalled for the summer tour. Educated at Hastings HS and John Cleveland College in Hinckley, Graham emerged from the Nuneaton club and was an outstanding age-group international. He toured Canada with an England XV in 1993, playing in both 'Tests'.

STIMPSON, Timothy Richard George (Full-back)
Born Liverpool, 10.09.73. 6'3", 15st 7lb. **Rep hons:** England (11, It96, 1t, 2c, 2pg-15pts), A (7, Vic95, 2t, 15c, 14pg-82pts), Barbarians (96-97). **ADPR:** Wakefield (1992-93, 1), West Hartlepool (1994-96, 23, 7t, 21c, 42pg-203pts), Newcastle (1996-98, 25, 14t, 29c, 4pg-140pts). Joins Leicester after a winter of discontent with

Newcastle. Powerful, long-striding full-back who performed wonders in adversity with West Hartlepool in 1995-96 before moving to Newcastle. Educated at Silcoates School, Wakefield, Tim earned England Schools caps at 16 and 18 Group and then moved to Durham University, where he obtained a BA in Anthropology. Toured Australia with the England U21 team in 1993, became an A team regular in 1995-96 and moved to Newcastle in May 1996.

STRANSKY, Joel Theodore (Fly-half)
Born Pietermaritzburg, South Africa, 16.07.67. 5'10", 13st 7lb. **Rep hons:** South Africa (23, Aus93, 6t, 30c, 47pg, 3dg-240pts), Barbarians (96-97). **ADPR:** Leicester (1996-98, 30, 7t, 47c, 72pg, 3dg-354pts). Will combine playing and coaching duties this season. Will forever be remembered as the man who delivered the dream for the rainbow nation in 1995, when his extra-time dropped goal clinched victory against the All Blacks in the World Cup. Had made his international debut two years earlier against Australia in Sydney when the Springboks won 19-12. Subsequently lost out to Henry Honniball in the South Africa squad but remains a player of true international quality. Has also played for Natal and Western Province.

VAN HEERDEN, Frederick 'Fritz' Johannes (Lock)
Born Roodepoort, South Africa, 29.06.70. 6'6", 16st 7lb. **Rep hons:** South Africa (13, Eng94, 1t-5pts). **ADPR:** Leicester (1997-98, 15, 1t-5pts). Athletic Springbok forward who gave up a place in the national squad to play for Leicester. Formerly with Western Province.

WEBB, Elliot (Prop)
Born Bromley, 28.03.78. 6'2", 17st 1lb. **Rep hons:** England U21. A student at Loughborough University, Elliott was educated at Eltham College and has also represented England Colts.

WEST, Dorian Edward (Hooker)
Born Wrexham, 05.10.67. 5'11", 16st. **Rep hons:** England (2, Fr98), A (2, Otago97). **ADPR:** Nottingham (1990-95, 41, 6t-30pts), Leicester (1995-98, 20, 1t-5pts). Understudy to Richard Cockerill, Dorian was educated at Ibstock and Ashby GS and is a former captain of Nottingham. Made his England debut as a replacement against France last season.

REVIEW

Not a memorable season for Leicester, with a comprehensive defeat at Pau in the European Cup quarter-finals, a distant fourth place in the Premiership and defeat at Saracens in the Tetley's Bitter Cup. The services of coach Bob Dwyer were mysteriously dispensed with after Christmas and, alas, the signing of Waisale Serevi did not prove a success – mainly because Tigers were reluctant to play him in his best position of fly-half. The triumvirate of Dean Richards, John Wells and Joel Stransky will be on trial this season. On the positive side, young flankers Paul Gustard and Lewis Moody made rapid progress.

LEICESTER in Premiership One 1997-98

Aug 30	H	Gloucester	Won	33	16	M.Horak(T) W.Greenwood(T) N.Back(T) J.Stransky(3C, 4P)
Oct 18	A	Northampton	Lost	6	25	J.Stransky(2P)
25	H	Bath	Won	33	22	W.Greenwood(T) J.Stransky(T, 3C, 4P) A.Healey(T)

Dec 13	H	Sale	Won	55	15	M.Horak(2T) P.Gustard(T) M.Johnson(T) L.Moody(T) Penalty(T) D.West(T) J.Stransky(4C, 4P)
16	A	Richmond	Lost	15	32	S.Potter(T) W.Greenwood(T) M.Horak(C, P)
20	H	Harlequins	Won	27	3	W.Greenwood(T) N.Back(T) Penalty(T) M.Horak(C, P) W.Serevi(2C, P)
26	A	Saracens	Won	22	21	F.Van Heerden(T) J.Stransky(C, D, 4P)
30	H	Newcastle	Lost	19	25	Penalty(T) J.Stransky(C, 4P)
Jan 17	H	Wasps	Won	45	21	A.Healey(T) M.Horak(T) Penalty(T) W.Serevi(T) J.Stransky(T, 4C, 4P)
Feb 1	A	Gloucester	Lost	25	32	M.Horak(2T) C.Joiner(T) W.Serevi(2C) J.Stransky(2P)
14	H	London Irish	Won	34	19	W.Greenwood(2T) L.Lloyd(T) J.Stransky(2C, 5P)
28	A	Bristol	Won	27	24	N.Back(T) L.Lloyd(T) S.Potter(T) J.Stransky(3C, 2P)
Mar 7	H	Northampton	Drew	15	15	N.Back(T) C.Joiner(T) J.Stransky(C, P)
14	A	Bath	Lost	5	16	C.Joiner(T)
28	H	Richmond	Won	42	19	W.Greenwood(3T) N.Back(T) S.Potter(T) G.Rowntree(T) J.Stransky(3C, D, P)
Apr 11	A	Sale	Lost	21	35	R.Cockerill(T) E.Miller(T) J.Stransky(C, 3P)
18	A	Harlequins	Won	23	14	L.Lloyd(T) J.Stransky(T, 2C, D, 2P)
25	H	Saracens	Drew	10	10	J.Hamilton(T) J.Stransky(C, P)
29	A	Wasps	Lost	13	17	C.Joiner(2T) J.Stransky(P)
May 4	A	Newcastle	Lost	10	27	N.Back(T) J.Stransky(C, P)
10	H	Bristol	Won	34	25	J.Stransky(2T, 3C, P) C.Joiner(T) A.Healey(T) P.Gustard(T)
17	A	London Irish	Won	55	16	M.Horak(2T) P.Gustard(2T) N.Back(2T) T.Barlow(T) J.Hamilton(T) J.Stransky(6C, P)

Summary of Premiership scorers:

253 – J.Stransky (5T, 39C, 3D, 47P); 50 – M.Horak (8T, 2C, 2P);
45 – W.Greenwood (9T); 40 – N.Back (8T); 30 – C.Joiner (6T); 20 – Penalty(4T),
P.Gustard (4T); 16 – W.Serevi (T, 4C, P); 15 – S.Potter (3T), L.Lloyd (3T),
A.Healey (3T); 10 – J.Hamilton (2T); 5 – D.West (T), F.Van Heerden (T),
G.Rowntree (T), L.Moody (T), E.Miller (T), M.Johnson (T), R.Cockerill (T),
T.Barlow (T).

Summary of Premiership appearances:

22 – D.Garforth (+1); 21 – J.Stransky, G.Rowntree, M.Johnson; 19 – M.Horak;
18 – A.Healey (+2), N.Back; 17 – W.Greenwood, R.Cockerill (+2), M.Corry (+4);
16 – S.Potter, L.Lloyd (+2), P.Gustard (+7); 15 – F.Van Heerden; 14 – E.Miller
(+1), C.Joiner; 13 – L.Moody (+5), P.Freshwater (+11); 12 – D.West (+6),
J.Overend (+3), J.Hamilton (+4); 11 – W.Johnson (+3); 8 – W.Serevi (+1);
6 – M.Poole (+2); 4 – A.Leeds (3); 3 – T.Murphy (+3), G.Murphy, N.Malone (+3),
T.Barlow; 2 – R.Edwards (+1), J.Aldwinckle (+1); 1 – D.Roke (+1), D.Richards,
M.Read, P.Delaney, D.Addison (+1).

LONDON IRISH

Formation of club: 1898
Ground: The Avenue, Sunbury-on-Thames, Middlesex, TW16 5RQ
Capacity: 6,800
Colours: Emerald green and white
Honours: None
Best League finish: 7th in Division One 1992-93
Best Cup run: Losing finalist in 1979-80
Last season: ADP1 – 11th. Tetley's Bitter Cup – Q/F (lost 7-41 to Wasps)
Owner: Consortium of Members
Director of Rugby: Dick Best
Captain: Conor O'Shea

BACHOP, Stephen John (Fly-half)
Born Lyttleton, New Zealand, 02.04.66. 5'10", 14st 2lb. **Rep hons:** Western Samoa (4, Wal91, 1t, 1pg-7pts), New Zealand (5, Fra94). Barbarians 1995-96. Experienced former dual international who represented Western Samoa in the 1991 World Cup before switching allegiance to New Zealand. Educated at Hagley HS in Christchurch and played his Provincial rugby for Otago. Younger brother Graeme, now playing in Japan, is a former All Black scrum-half. The two brothers combined at half-back in New Zealand's three-match series against South Africa in 1994.

BERRIDGE, Simon (Wing)
Born England, 29.07.65. 6'1", 14st 2lb. **Rep hons:** South Africa A. English-born speedster who joins from Western Province. Played for Western Province against the 1997 British Lions.

BISHOP, Justin Patrick (Wing)
Born Crawley, 08.11.74. 6', 13st. **Rep hons:** Ireland (2, SA98, 1t-5pts), A (1, Can97).
ADPR: London Irish (1994-98, 72, 15t-75pts). A hectic end of season for this talented wing, with Justin scoring in both play-off games against Rotherham before being called into the Ireland tour party of South Africa following an injury to James Topping. Made his Test debut against South Africa at Bloemfontein. An elusive runner who arrived at London Irish from East Grinstead RFC, Justin helped Ireland U21 to victory over England at Northampton in 1995-96, before declaring for England and playing centre for England U21 against Italy. Considered the nationality issue once again the following season, finally decided he was Irish and accompanied the Development XV on their demanding tour of New Zealand where he teamed up with former Sunbury favourite Rob Henderson, who just happened to be his flatmate as well. Educated at Sackville College and the West of England University in Bristol.

BROWN, James (Fly-half)
Born Solihull, 08.12.77. 5'8", 10st 10lb. **ADPR:** Coventry (1996-98, 16, 14c, 23pg, 1dg-100pts). Former Millfield Schoolboy who has played representative rugby for England at Schools and U21 level. Toured Australia with England U21 in 1997.

BURROWS, Nick Paul (Centre/wing)
Born Chester, 19.05.73. 6'1", 13st 12lb. **ADPR:** London Irish (1996-98, 23, 2t-10pts). Resourceful utility back who learned much of his rugby in South Africa, where he played for Eastern Province.

CAMPBELL, Kieran (Scrum-half)
Born London, 06.07.79. **ADPR:** London Irish (1997-98, 1). Exciting young talent who helped Ireland to victory in the Youth World Cup in Toulouse in April 1998.

CHARLES, David Alexander (Wing/full-back)
Born London, 13.11.75. 6'2", 14st 6lb. **ADPR:** London Irish (1996-98, 6). Rangy former England Colts full-back who deputised ably whenever Conor O'Shea was injured. Loads of pace, and will be looking for more first-team exposure this season.

CORCORAN, Michael (Wing)
Born London, 29.11.69. 6'3", 14st 6lb. **ADPR:** London Irish (1989-96, 70, 22t, 64c, 165pg, 1dg-730pts), Harlequins (1996-97, 6, 5t, 3c, 2pg-37pts), London Irish (1997-98, 2, 1c, 4pg-14pts). Scored 301 League points for London Irish in their promotion season 1995-96, including eight tries, but failed to make an impact when he transferred to Harlequins. Returned to Sudbury last season. Educated at John Fisher School, Purley, Michael toured Australia with England Schools in 1988 and was a professional footballer at Chelsea before concentrating on rugby.

DAWSON, Kieron (Flanker)
Born Bangor, 29.01.75. 6'1", 15st 6lb. **Rep hons:** Ireland (3, NZ97), A (5, Wal97). **ADPR:** London Irish (1996-98, 33, 2t-10pts). Ran himself into the ground last season on behalf of Ireland and the Exiles and deservedly took a summer off from touring duties to recuperate. A product of the strong Ulster Schools system, Kieron played for Ireland Schools, U21 and the national sevens team at Hong Kong before making his senior debut against the All Blacks in November. Moved to London Irish from the Bangor club. Educated at Bangor GS and Queen's University, Belfast.

FEA'UNATI, Isaac M. (Backrow)
Born New Zealand, 23.07.73. 6'1", 16st 11lb. **Rep hons:** Western Samoa. **ADPR:** London Irish (1997-98, 13, 5t-25pts). Arguably the Exiles' player of the season in 1997-98 after a series of powerful displays after Christmas. Cruelly, he injured knee ligaments in their final play-off game against Rotherham and faces a delayed start to this season. Learned his rugby in Auckland and with the Canterbury Crusaders before moving to England. Another player to benefit from his love of sevens, being a regular with Western Samoa in Hong Kong. Also played for Melrose in Scotland.

HARDWICK, Robin John Kieran (Prop)
Born Kenilworth, 29.03.69. 6', 19st 10lb. **Rep hons:** England (1, It96), A (14, Ire95), Barbarians (96-97). **ADPR:** Coventry (1989-98, 88, 8t-39pts). Strong-scrummaging prop who joins from Coventry, where he was a former club captain. At the height of RFU-Epruc power struggle, he was the only England squad member to defy training boycott. Gained first full England cap against Italy, at Twickenham in November 96 as 72nd-minute replacement for Jason Leonard, and toured Argentina with the full England team in 1997. He had already toured Australia and Fiji with England A in summer 1995, and played for winning England A teams against France in Paris in

January 96 and Italy two months later. Suffered a two-and-a-half year absence from the game with career-threatening knee ligament trouble shortly after joining Coventry from Barkers Butts.

HARVEY, Nicholas Andrew (Back five forward)
Born New South Wales, Australia, 21.10.74. 6'6", 17st 13lb. **ADPR:** London Irish (1997-98, 13, 1t-5pts). Raw-boned Australian who made an immediate impact, both as a forward and leader, when cleared to play after Christmas. Played for New South Wales and ACT and has also represented the Australian Barbarians.

HENNESSY, Raymond Gerard (Wing)
Born Limerick, 18.02.70. 5'11", 14st 11lb. **Rep hons:** Barbarians (93-94). **ADPR:** London Irish (1991-98, 53, 12t, 1dg-61pts). Stalwart team man who played his early representative rugby for Ireland U21 at full-back. Educated at Oatland in Ireland and St Mary's College, Teddington.

HOWE, Mike (Hooker)
Born New Zealand, 11.06.73. 6', 15st. Combative New Zealand-reared hooker who has played Provincial rugby for Bay of Plenty.

JONES, Matthew Brian (Fly-half)
Born Tonbridge, 03.01.76. 5'10", 12st. **ADPR:** Leicester (1996-97, 2), Moseley (1997-98, 17, 3t, 26c, 32pg, 5dg-178pts). Former Millfield schoolboy, capped by England Schools and U21.

KELLAM, Robert John (Hooker)
Born Newbury, 04.02.71. 5'10", 15st 2lb. **Rep hons:** England A (1, Arg96). **ADPR:** London Irish (1993-98, 81, 1t-5pts). A combative hooker, Rob is a graduate of Portsmouth University and was formerly with Wasps Colts and Newbury. His consistent form was rewarded in December 1996 when he made his England A debut against Argentina.

KIRKE, Richard Paull (Hooker)
Born Fairlie, New Zealand, 16.11.71. 6', 17st. **ADPR:** Bedford (1997-98, 12, 1t-5pts). Experienced New Zealand hooker who joined Bedford June 1997 before moving to the Exiles this summer. Former Waikato U21 captain who has played provincial rugby for Auckland and Canterbury. A BSc graduate from Waikato (89-91) and former corrosion consultant. His father is a farmer, mother runs real estate company. Leisure interests include all sports. A member of the Hamilton Marist club.

McLAUGHLIN, Ian Philip (Prop)
Born Dublin, 04.01.77. 6'1", 17st 6lb. **ADPR:** London Irish (1996-98, 10, 1t-5pts). Fast-developing young prop who is beginning to push for a regular starting spot.

MEADOWS, Alistair James (Lock)
Born Kendal, 20.04.71. 6'5", 17st. **ADPR:** Newcastle (1991-94, 19, 2t-9pts), London Irish (1995-98, 12). Educated at Sedbergh, Newcastle University and Cambridge University, where he won Blues in 1993 and 94. Alistair is a former member of the Newcastle club.

MOONEY, Liam Thomas (Prop)
Born Dublin, 18.05.73. 6', 17st 10lb. **ADPR:** London Irish (1992-98, 38). Educated St Boniface College, Plymouth, and Cardiff University. Liam joined London Irish from Plymouth in 1991. Earned Blues at Cambridge in 1993 and 94 and holds the unusual distinction of having represented three countries – Irish Exiles, England Students and Welsh Universities.

O'KELLY, Malcolm Eamonn (Lock)
Born Chelmsford, 19.07.74. 6'7", 16st 2lb. **Rep hons:** Ireland (9, NZ97), A (4, Sc96). **ADPR:** London Irish (1996-98, 31, 1t-5pts). Ireland's discovery of the season, Malcolm produced a string of superlative performances for Ireland both before Christmas and in the Five Nations. Tall, rangy and athletic, an illustrious career beckons if he can stay clear of injury. Joined the Exiles from the St Mary's club in Dublin. Educated at Templeogue and Trinity College, Dublin. Toured South Africa with Ireland in the summer and the subject of much transfer speculation, with big bids reportedly coming from Bath and Brive.

O'SHEA, Conor Michael Patrick (Full-back)
Born Limerick, 21.10.70. 6'2", 15st. **Rep hons:** Ireland (20, Rom93, 1c, 3pg, 1dg-14pts), A (7, Wal95, 4t, 3pg-29pts). **ADPR:** London Irish (1995-98, 58, 26t, 4c, 4pg, 1dg-153pts). Fine club captain who returned to his best form last season, regaining his place in the Ireland side before he was sidelined with a fractured cheekbone. Adventurous, pacey full-back who joined the Exiles from Lansdowne in 1995. Conor was educated at Terenure College and University College, Dublin, and represented Ireland in the World Students Cup in 1992. Made his international debut against Romania in 1993 and played in ten consecutive internationals before losing out to his friend and rival, Jim Staples, against France in March 1995. Staples' injury against New Zealand in Ireland's opening game of RWC95 saw O'Shea called in against Japan, Wales and France. In and out of the national team before making the place his own last season.

PETERS, David Laurence (Back five forward)
Born London, 06.10.73. 6'6", 16st 9lb. **ADPR:** London Irish (1995-98, 13, 1t-5pts). Useful utility forward. Educated at London Oratory and Kingston Polytechnic.

PUTT, Kevin Barry (Srum-half)
Born Cambridge, New Zealand, 28.07.65. 5'8", 12st 4lb. **Rep hons:** South Africa squad, South Africa Sevens team. Dynamic performer at scrum-half who has proved an inspiration for Natal over the last five years. New Zealand born and bred, Kevin emigrated to South Africa and toured Britain with South Africa in 1994 and Argentina and France with the 1996 Springboks.

REDMOND, Anthony Francis (Hooker)
Born Bromley, 14.01.71. 5'10", 15st 10lb. **ADPR:** Orrell (1994-95, 10), London Irish (1995-98, 26, 1t-5pts). Reliable front row backup who joined the club from Orrell. Has played for England Students and Welsh Universities.

RICHARDS, Peter Charles (Scrum-half)
Born Portsmouth, 10.03.78. 5'9", 13st 3lb. **Rep hons:** England A (2, Sc98). **ADPR:** London Irish (1996-98, 17, 3t-15pts). Jonny Wilkinson's half-back partner at Bishop Wandsworth School just two years ago, Peter was also selected for the tour of Australia, New Zealand and South Africa. A powerful runner and fierce competitor, Peter has been capped by England at every level from U16 to England A.

RODGERS, Pieter Heinrich (Prop)
Born Harrismith, South Africa, 23.06.62. 6'0", 16st 9lb. **Rep hons:** South Africa (5, WorldXV89). Experienced South Africa and Guateng prop. Educated at Pretoria University.

SPICER, Kevin Michael John (Backrow)
Born Dublin, 28.07.73. 6'4", 16st 9lb. **ADPR:** London Irish (1996-98, 25, 1t-5pts). A valuable addition to the Exiles squad, Kevin won a second Blue at Oxford last season before concentrating on Premiership duties. Educated at Clongowes Wood College and University College, Dublin, where he read Engineering. Moved to Oxford to study for an MSc in Industrial Relations.

TODD, Robert (Wing)
Born Auckland, New Zealand, 19.04.71. 5'11", 15st 3lb. **ADPR:** London Scottish (1997-98, 7, 2t-10pts). Blockbusting New Zealand wing who had forced his way into the side by the end of last season. An exciting prospect.

VENTER, Brendan (Centre)
Born Johannesburg, South Africa, 29.12.69. 6'1", 13st 7lb. **Rep hons:** South Africa (14, Eng94, 1t-5pts). **ADPR:** London Irish (1997-98, 11). A crucial late-season signing, the stylish former Springbok centre brought a high degree of professionalism and expertise to the Exiles – not to mention confidence. Losing is not something he endured on a regular basis with either Free State or South Africa. A qualified doctor, Brendan was a member of the 1995 World Cup-winning squad.

WOODS, Niall Kevin Patrick John (Wing)
Born Dublin, 21.06.71. 6', 12st 13lb. **Rep hons:** Ireland (7, Aus94, 1t-5pts), A (13,Sc92, 4t, 3c, 3pg-35pts), Barbarians (93-94). **ADPR:** London Irish (1996-98, 43, 17t, 37c, 57pg-330pts). Made great strides as a goal-kicker throughout the season, his steadiness ensuring there were no slip-ups in the play-offs against Rotherham. Elusive wing who looks a world-beater on his day but is prone to lapses in both concentration and form. Educated at Blackrock College, he moved to the Blackrock club and was soon a regular with Ireland U21. Toured southern Africa with Ireland (1993), scoring three tries in their 53-15 win over South Africa Provinces. First capped on tour in Australia (1994).

YEABSLEY, Richard Stuart (No 8)
Born St Albans, 02.11.73. **ADPR:** London Irish (1996-98, 12, 2t-10pts). Cricket and rugby Blue at Oxford. Educated at Haberdashers Askes and Keble College, Oxford.

REVIEW

Avoided relegation for the second consecutive season by performing well in the play-offs. Made an appalling start, winning just one of their first 12 games. A serious knee injury to Jeremy Davidson was a major blow but the team showed a curious inconsistency, having performed well in their competitive European Conference group. Director of rugby Willie Anderson, a popular figure, was eventually held to account and Dick Best took over as caretaker coach with encouraging results, though the need to contest the play-offs could not be avoided. Having left their recruiting too late last season, Irish moved quickly this summer to sign Stephen Bachop and Kevin Putt but were bitterly disappointed to lose Jeremy Davidson to big spending Castres.

LONDON IRISH in Premiership One 1997-98

Aug 23	A	Richmond	Lost	12	32	N.Woods(4P)
30	H	Sale	Lost	20	26	C.O'Shea(T) C.Bird(T) N.Woods(2C, 2P) D.Humphreys(D)
Oct 19	A	Gloucester	Lost	7	29	N.Woods(T, C)
26	H	Wasps	Won	22	17	N.Burrows(T) N.Woods(C, 3P) D.Humphreys(D) C.O'Shea(D)
Nov 1	H	Newcastle	Lost	19	35	N.Hogan(T) M.Corcoran(C, 4P)
Dec 13	H	Northampton	Lost	10	51	M.McCall(T) N.Woods(C, P)
27	A	Harlequins	Lost	24	26	C.O'Shea(2T) J.Bishop(T) N.Woods(3C, P)

	30	H	Saracens	Lost	10 25	C.O'Shea(T) N.Woods(C, P)
Jan 11		A	Newcastle	Lost	13 46	J.Bishop(T) N.Woods(C, P) D.Humphreys(D)
	17	H	Richmond	Lost	14 45	N.Woods(T, 3P)
Feb 1		A	Sale	Lost	16 41	J.Fitzpatrick(T) N.Woods(C, 3P)
	14	A	Leicester	Lost	19 34	K.Dawson(T) N.Woods(C, 4P)
	20	H	Bristol	Won	38 23	J.Bishop(T) I.Fea'unati(T) C.O'Shea(T) N.Woods(T, 3C, 4P)
Mar 15		A	Wasps	Won	38 19	C.O'Shea(T) D.Humphreys(T) I.McLaughlin(T) I.Fea'unati(T) N.Woods(3C, 4P)
	24	H	Gloucester	Won	23 19	N.Woods(2T, C, 2P) P.Richards(T)
	28	H	Bath	Lost	35 49	I.Fea'unati(2T) Penalty(T) P.Richards(T) N.Woods(3C, 3P)
Apr 19		A	Bristol	Won	17 5	S.Burns(T) I.Fea'unati(T) N.Woods(2C, P)
	22	A	Northampton	Lost	18 33	C.O'Shea(T) N.Harvey(T) N.Woods(C, 2P)
	25	H	Harlequins	Won	62 14	J.Bishop(3T) N.Woods(2T, 8C, 2P) N.Hogan(T) M.O'Kelly(T) C.O'Shea(T)
	28	A	Bath	Lost	3 20	N.Woods(P)
May 3		A	Saracens	Lost	21 29	N.Hogan(T) N.Woods(TC, 2P) D.Humphreys(D)
	17	H	Leicester	Lost	16 55	S.Amor(T, 2P) M.Jarvis(T)

Play-offs

	20	A	Rotherham	Won	16 13	J.Bishop(T) N.Woods(C, 3P)
	24	H	Rotherham	Won	26 14	J.Bishop(T) N.Woods(7P)

Summary of Premiership scorers:

237 – N.Woods (8T, 34C, 43P); 43 – C.O'Shea (8T, D); 30 – J.Bishop (6T);
25 – I.Fea'unati (5T); 17 – D.Humphreys (T, 4D); 15 – N.Hogan (3T); 14 –
M.Corcoran (C, 4P); 11 – S.Amor (T, 2P); 10 – P.Richards (2T); 5 – M.O'Kelly (T),
M.McCall, I.McLaughlin (T), M.Jarvis (T), N.Harvey (T) J.Fitzpatrick (T),
K.Dawson (T), N.Burrows (T), S.Burns (T), C.Bird (T), Penalty (T).

Summary of Premiership appearances:

22 – J.Bishop; 20 – N.Woods; 19 – M.O'Kelly (+1), D.Humphreys; 18 – C.O'Shea,
M.McCall, G.Halpin (+1); 17 – R.Kellam (+3), C.Bird (+9); 16 – K.Spicer (+2),
N.Hogan (+3), K.Dawson (+1); 15 – J.Fitzpatrick (+3), S.Burns (+6);
14 – T.Redmond (+6), G.Fulcher (+2); 13 – L.Mooney (+3); 12 – N.Burrows (+1);
11 – P.Richards (+3), K.O'Connell, N.Harvey, I.Fea'unati; 9 – B.Venter;
7 – M.Morahan (+3); 6 – I.McLaughlin (+1); 5 – A.Kershaw (+5), D.Charles (+2);
3 – R.Yeabsley (+2), J.Davidson; 2 – D.Peters (+1), R.Hennessy (+2), M.Corcoran
(+1); 1 – A.Meadows (+1), M.Jarvis, A.Flavin (+1).

LONDON SCOTTISH

Formation of club: 1878
Ground: Stoop Memorial Ground, Craneford Way, Twickenham TW2 7SX
Capacity: 9,750 (All seated)
Colours: Dark blue, white and red
Honours: Division Three Champions – 1989-90. Division Two Champions – 1991-92
Best League finish: 10th in Division One 1992-93
Best Cup run: Losing finalist 1973-74
Last season: ADP2 – 3rd. Tetley's Bitter Cup – 4th round (lost 23-24 to Bath)
Owner: Tony Tiarks
Director of Rugby: John Steele
Coach: Alan Zonda
Captain: TBC

BONNEY, Jan (Centre)
Born Chingford, 27.01.71. **ADPR:** Moseley (1991-97, 62, 4t, 1dg-23pts), London
Scottish (1997-98, 9). Former England Colts centre who joined from Moseley.

BURNELL, Andrew Paul (Prop)
Born Edinburgh, 29.09.65. 6'1″, 17st 2lb. **Rep hons:** Scotland (42, Eng89, 1t-5pts), A
(3, Sp91), Barbarians (89-90). **ADPR:** Leicester (1987-88, 1), London Scottish
(1988-98, 121, 3t-15pts). Former club captain, Paul enjoyed an 'Indian summer' of a
season, even winning a recall to Scottish colours against England. His experience will
be important for the Exiles as they attempt to compete in the Premiership. Paul was
Scotland's Grand Slam tight-head 1990 and played all six games for Scotland in the
1991 World Cup. Played 23 consecutive Five Nations internationals until missing the
1995 Championship. One of the eight Scots who played for the British Lions on the
1993 tour to New Zealand. Selected for seven of the 13 matches, including first Test.
Studied Law and Land Management at Leicester Polytechnic and played for the
Tigers for four seasons. Former sales director in the leisure industry.

CAMERON, Jamie (Fly-half)
Born Stratford, New Zealand, 23.03.70. 5'11″, 13st 4lb. **ADPR:** Havant (1995-96,
1t-5pts), London Scottish (1997-98, 18, 5t, 7c, 11pg, 2dg-78pts). Class performer at
fly-half where his first instinct is always to attack. Jamie was a star product of the
New Zealand age-group system, playing for the national U17, Schools and U21
teams before missing out on selection for their 1991 World Cup squad. Played Super
12 rugby with Wellington before joining Scottish at the start of last season.

COOK, Stephen (Scrum-half)
Born St Helens, 04.08.73. 5'9″, 13st 2lb. **ADPR:** Liverpool St Helens (1991-92, 4),
West Hartlepool (1993-96, 23, 4t-20pts), Orrell (1996-97, 19, 3t-15pts), London
Scottish (1997-98, 11, 1t-5pts). More than useful scrum-half who joined from Orrell
at the beginning of last season. Played for Liverpool St Helens as a 17-year-old
before studying at Newcastle University, when he joined West Hartlepool club.
Former England Students representative who also enjoyed a spell at Orrell.

DAVIES, Rhodri (Utility back)
Born Carmarthen, Wales, 04.08.74. 5'10″, 13st 8lb. **ADPR:** London Scottish (1997-
98, 12). Talented former Wales U21 representative who moved from Harlequins in an
attempt to secure regular senior rugby. Showed up well in the play-off games against
Bristol in May.

DAVIES, Tom (Flanker)
Born Sutton-in-Ashfield, 29.05.76. 6'2″, 16st. **ADPR:** London Scottish (1997-98, 6).
Rugged young flanker who joined the club from Worcester.

EASTERBY, Guy (Scrum-half)
Born Tadcaster, 21.03.71. 6'1", 14st. **Rep hons:** Ireland A (1, Can97). **ADPR:** Harrogate (1990-96, 77, 17t, 7c, 8pg, 2dg-127pts), Rotherham (1996-98, 44, 18t-90pts). Summer signing from Rotherham. Former England U21 scrum-half who has now opted for Ireland.

ERIKSSON, Bo Ronald Sheehan (Centre)
Born Athlone, Ireland, 22.04.72. 6'1", 15st 6lb. **Rep hons:** Scotland (3, NZ96, 1t-5pts), A (8, Fr95, 2t-10pts). **ADPR:** London Scottish (1992-98, 74, 18t, 1dg-93pts). The Exiles' captain proved a tower of strength last season though it ended disappointingly with him having to miss Scotland's summer tour to undergo surgery on a complicated finger break. Ronnie made debut for Scotland against New Zealand in the first Test of the 1996 summer tour. Sampled international atmosphere for first time on 1995 Zimbabwe tour when he played in both non-cap Tests. Made his debut for London Scottish against Gloucester in 1992 and played briefly at Harlequins before returning to the Richmond-based club. Played seven times for Scottish Exiles in their Grand Slam district championships 94, 95, 96. Represented Scottish Select against South Africa at Aberdeen November 94. Toured South Africa with full Scotland squad on non-cap tour summer 1997. Educated at Merchiston Castle.

FENN, Simon (Flanker)
Born Manly, Australia, 24.04.71. 15st 10lb. **ADPR:** London Scottish (1997-98, 9). Powerful Australian flanker whose name will forever be linked with the ear-biting incident against Bath, when he was forced off with a ripped ear that required over 20 stitches. Bath prop Kevin Yates was later suspended for six months though he still vigorously protests his innocence. All of which detracted from a solid second half of the season from Fenn, including eye-catching performances in the play-offs.

HOLMES, Simon David (Flanker)
Born Workington, 12.12.66. 5'10", 16st. **Rep hons:** Scotland (3, It98), A (4, SA96), Barbarians (89-90). **ADPR:** London Scottish (1994-98, 51, 7t-35pts). Simon started last season with a bang and finally forced his way into the Scotland side before his international season was ended by a broken hand. Returned just in time to help the Exiles in the play-offs and tour Australia with Scotland. Educated at Cockermouth GS and Cambridge University, Simon toured South Africa in summer 1997 with Scotland Development squad but the matches were designated non-cap occasions. Still works full-time in the communications business.

HUNTER, Robert Stuart (Back five forward)
Born Scotland, 23.05.72. 6'4", 17st 2lb. **ADPR:** London Scottish (1995-98, 44, 5t-25pts). Army regular before turning professional with London Scottish. Bob is a line-out specialist jumper, who started at Saffron Walden and has played for the Army and Combined Services.

JACKSON, Adam (Lock)
Born Blackpool, 28.01.73. 6'6", 17st. **ADPR:** Orrell (1992-95, 5), London Scottish (1996-98, 19, 2t-10pts). With dual nationality, Adam played for England Colts in 1992 but came to prominence representing Wales in the 1996 World Students Cup. Strapping Lancastrian lock who learned his rugby playing for Orrell and appeared in three Colts County Cup finals for Lancashire at Twickenham. Member of the Harlequins squad at the start of 1996-97, but wanted first-team action so moved to London Scottish.

JOHNSTONE, Paul (Prop)
Born Bulawayo, Zimbabwe, 16.10.70. 5'11", 16st 12lb. **Rep hons:** Zimbabwe (35). **ADPR:** Clifton (1996-97, 1t-5pts), London Scottish (1996-98, 31, 3t-15pts). Ultra-consistent Zimbabwe international who missed just two games in the regular League season. Fast and mobile, Paul joined the Exiles from Clifton in September 1996.

JONES, Eddie (Lock)
Born Horahora, New Zealand, 22.03.68. 6'4", 17st 10lb. **ADPR:** London Scottish (1996-98, 27). Regular in the North Auckland side between 1992 and 1996 and played for Taranaki in 1995 and 1996. A member of the Horahora club back in New Zealand, Eddie joined Scottish in November 1996.

KELLY, James Robert (Prop)
Born Aldershot, 16.02.76. 6'3", 18st. **ADPR:** London Scottish (1995-98, 15). Aggressive and athletic young prop who has represented Scotland U21 and Scottish Exiles.

LEE, Derrick James (Full-back)
Born Ayr, 01.10.73. 5'9", 13st 5lb. **Rep hons:** Scotland (7, Ire98, 4c, 7pg-29pts), A (5, SA96, 3t-15pts). **ADPR:** London Scottish (1996-98, 19, 6t, 18c, 29pg, 2dg-159pts). Exciting counter-attacking full-back who went through the full gamut of emotions last season. Made his debut as a last-minute replacement against Ireland and was denied a £10,000 bonus because his contract insisted he only became a full international if he played more than 10 minutes as a replacement or started a Test. Starred for exactly an hour in the Exiles' play-off game against Bristol before he punched David Corkery and was sent off. Despite that, was allowed to tour Australia with Scotland, appearing in both Tests. Formerly with Watsonians, Derrick first came to national prominence when he did well for Scotland A in South Africa in 1997.

McATAMNEY, Mark Robert (Flanker)
Born Dunedin, New Zealand, 19.02.68. 6'8", 18st. **ADPR:** Moseley (1997-98, 7, 1t-5pts). Former Canterbury lock who joined Blackheath at the end of last season from Moseley.

McAUSLAND, Ian Cameron (Utility back)
Born, Sydney, Australia, 15.01.76. 5'9", 13st. **ADPR:** London Scottish (1997-98, 18, 4c, 8pg, 1dg-35pts). Australian-reared utility back with impeccable Scottish qualifications, via his Glasgow-born father. Represented Australia U19 and U21 while playing for Eastern Suburbs and did well with Scottish last season, forcing his way into the successful Scotland A squad.

McLELLAN, James William (Hooker)
Born Bournemouth, 12.05.69. **ADPR:** London Scottish (1993-98, 26, 1t-5pts). James has fought hard for first-team recognition since joining the club from junior rugby on the south coast. Passionate trainer and one of the club's fittest men. Quiet, skilled in one-line jokes.

MILLARD, David Bruce (Scrum-half)
Born 19.09.64. 6'1", 13st 9lb. **Rep hons:** Scotland A (1, Fr93), Barbarians (93-94). **ADPR:** London Scottish (1988-98, 107, 29t, 1dg-138pts). Evergreen scrum-half who seems to be playing as well as ever. Sevens expert who runs an orthopaedic clinic.

MILLIGAN, Kenneth (Wing/centre)
Born Edinburgh, 19.07.72. 5'10", 12st 7lb. **Rep hons:** Scotland A (4, Fr93). **ADPR:** London Scottish (1996-98, 14, 5t-25pts). Utility back with plenty of pace, Ken has played for Scotland at every representative level except senior international. Formerly with the Stewart's Melville club.

MORLEY, Colin (Wing/scrum-half)
Born Slough, 17.12.73. 5'10", 12st 7lb. **ADPR:** London Scottish (1996-98, 9). Joined London Scottish August 1996 as a centre but has also appeared at scrum-half. Loyal squad member who was selected for the England U21 squad and has represented Scottish Exiles.

RAYNER, Edward John (Centre)
Born Ottawa, Canada, 07.06.71. **Rep hons:** Barbarians (94). **ADPR:** Bath (1993-95, 4, 1c, 4pg, 1dg-17pts), Rosslyn Park (1995-96, 1t-5pts), London Scottish (1996-98, 26, 2t-10pts). Talented centre whose RAF duties have not always enabled him to fulfil his potential at senior level. Educated at Dauntseys and an Oxford Blue in 1993.

SHARMAN, Conan (Wing)
Born Harare, Zimbabwe, 12.09.73. 6'1", 14st. **ADPR:** London Scottish (1997-98, 20, 14t-70pts). Exciting arrival from South Africa who scored 14 tries last season, including an outstanding hat-trick against champions Bedford, and looked dangerous whenever in possession.

SKRYPEC, Mark (Lock)
Born Nottingham, 27.01.74. 6'7", 17st. **ADPR:** Nottingham (1993-94, 3), Blackheath (1996-97, 10), London Scottish (1997-98, 2). Experienced lock whose first-team opportunities have been limited since joining from Blackheath.

TARBUCK, Christopher Richard (Backrow)
Born Harlow, Essex, 20.08.68. 6'4", 15st 7lb. **ADPR:** Saracens (1989-93, 44, 3t-12pts), Leicester (1993-96, 18, 4t-20pts), London Scottish (1996-98, 43, 11t-55pts). Underrated backrow grafter who appeared in 21 League games last season and was the model of consistency. Learned his rugby at Harlow and Southend and also enjoyed a long spell at the old Borough Road College before joining Saracens. Also spent three seasons at Leicester without getting regular first-team rugby. Represented England in the 1992 World Students Cup in Italy. Educated at Mark Hall School in Harlow.

THOMPSON, Gavin John (Centre)
Born Croydon, 20.08.69. 6', 13st 5lb. **Rep hons:** England A (10, Aus90, 2t-8pts). **ADPR:** Harlequins (1989-95, 59, 11t-49pts), London Scottish (1995-98, 14, 3t-15pts). Former England Schools and Colts cap who was educated at Trinity School, Croydon, Gavin looked headed for full England honours at one stage and formed a much-respected centre pairing for Harlequins with Will Carling. Injury interrupted at a crucial stage, however, but he has shown signs of returning to full fitness and form with Scottish.

WATSON, Michael Derek (No 8)
Born Sunderland, 02.08.69. 6'6", 18st. **ADPR:** West Hartlepool (1992-95, 27, 8t-40pts), Harlequins (1994-97, 26, 6t-30pts), London Scottish (1997-98, 22, 5t-25pts). Abrasive but highly effective ex-Army backrow star who joined Quins from West Hartlepool, having also represented Alton RFC. Hampered by injury in 1996-97 season but back to his rumbustious best last winter.

REVIEW

Never a dull moment at London Scottish last season. The much-discussed Simon Fenn affair threatened to overshadow everything and enough has probably been said on that matter – except that it seems obscene that the Exiles were left with a large legal bill simply to achieve justice for their aggrieved player. Happily there was also a lot of rugby to admire, and months of honest endeavour came to fruition when the Exiles beat Bristol in both play-off games to book a place in the Premiership. A potent back division could surprise a few sides and Scottish embarked on a late recruitment, signing Hull Sharks Rugby League star Brad Hepi, Manly hooker Damien Cummins, and Western Province No 8 Guy Manson-Bishop.

LONDON SCOTTISH in Premiership Two 1997-98

Aug 30	H	Fylde	Won	35	9	R.Eriksson(3T) D.Lee(T, C) C.Sharman(T) J.Cameron(C, 2P)
Sep 7	H	Blackheath	Won	34	6	G.Smith(T) R.Eriksson(T) J.Cameron(T, C, P) D.Lee(C, D, 3P)
13	A	Waterloo	Won	36	17	C.Sharman(2T) S.Cook(T) R.Hunter(T) D.Lee(2C, D, 3P)
20	A	Bedford	Lost	33	45	C.Sharman(3T) Penalty(T) D.Lee(2C, 3P)
27	H	Orrell	Won	20	19	C.Sharman(T) I.McAusland(5P)
Oct 4	A	Rotherham	Lost	3	24	I.McAusland(P)
11	H	Wakefield	Won	30	13	C.Sharman(2T) J.Cameron(T) P.Johnstone(T) G.Smith(T) D.Lee(C, P)
18	A	Exeter	Won	22	16	D.Lee(T, 4P) G.Thompson(T)
25	H	Bedford	Lost	15	22	A.Jackson(T) M.Watson(T) I.McAusland(C) J.Cameron(D)
Nov 8	A	Orrell	Won	27	13	D.Lee(T, 2C) D.Millard(T) K.Milligan(T) M.Watson(T) I.McAusland(D)
Dec 13	H	Rotherham	Won	35	29	J.Cameron(T, D) S.Holmes(T) K.Milligan(T) C.Tarbuck(T) D.Lee(3C, 2P)
20	A	Wakefield	Lost	10	15	P.Johnstone(T) D.Lee(P) I.McAusland(C)
Jan 17	A	Blackheath	Lost	25	34	Penalty(T) C.Sharman(T) C.Tarbuck(T) I.McAusland(2C, 2P)
24	H	Exeter	Won	22	10	J.Cameron(T, 2C, P) K.Milligan(T) T.Jankovich-Besan(T)
31	A	Moseley	Won	29	18	D.Millard(T) E.Rayner(T) J.Cameron(C, 3P) D.Lee(C, 2P)
Feb 14	H	Coventry	Drew	18	18	R.Eriksson(T) D.Lee(T, P) C.Tarbuck(T)
Mar 8	H	West Hartlepool	Won	31	17	J.Cameron(T, 2C, 4P) R.Todd(T) G.French(T)
14	A	Coventry	Lost	10	37	C.Sharman(T) M.Watson(T)
28	H	Moseley	Won	24	18	R.Eriksson(T) C.Sharman(T) R.Todd(T) M.Watson(T) D.Lee(2C)
Apr 11	A	Fylde	Won	22	7	C.Sharman(2T) D.Lee(4P)
18	H	Waterloo	Won	26	6	D.Millard(2T) D.Lee(T, C, 3P)
25	A	West Hartlepool	Lost	10	11	M.Watson(T) D.Lee(C, P)

Summary of Premiership scorers:

149 – D.Lee (5T, 17C, 2D, 28P); 78 – J.Cameron (5T, 7C, 2D, 11P);
70 – C.Sharman (14T); 35 – I.McAusland (4C, D, 8P); 30 – R.Eriksson (6T);
25 – M.Watson (5T); 20 – D.Millard (4T); 15 – C.Tarbuck (3T) K.Milligan (3T);
10 – Penalty (2T), R.Todd (2T), G.Smith (2T), P.Johnstone (2T); 5 – G.Thompson
(T), E.Rayner (T), A.Jackson (T), T.Jankovich-Besan (T), R.Hunter (T), S.Holmes
(T), G.French (T), S.Cook (T).

Summary of Premiership appearances:

22 – M.Watson (+1); 21 – C.Tarbuck (+3); 20 – C.Sharman, P.Johnstone,
R.Hunter; 19 – P.Burnell; 18 – I.McAusland (+6), J.Cameron; 16 – D.Lee (+2),
E.Jones (+1); 15 – R.Eriksson, J.Allan; 13 – D.Millard (+7); 12 – E.Rayner (+2),
S.Holmes, R.Davies (+4); 11 – S.Cook (+1); 10 – T.Jankovich-Besan (+8);
9 – J.Kelly (+5), G.French (+2), S.Fenn, J.Bonney (+1); 8 – A.Jackson (+1);
7 – C.Wright (+4), R.Todd (+1), G.Thompson (+2), K.Milligan; 6 – G.Smith,
T.Davis; 3 – C.Smith, S.Owen (+3), C.Morley; 2 – M.Skrypec (+2), M.MacDonald
(+1); 1 – J.McLellan (+1).

MANCHESTER SALE

Formation of club: 1861
Ground: Heywood Road, Sale, Cheshire M33 3WB
Capacity: 7,500 (Seated 750)
Colours: Royal blue and white
Honours: Division Two Champions – 1993-94
Best League finish: 4th in Division One 1994-95
Best Cup run: Losing finalist in 1996-97
Last season: ADP1 – 6th. Tetley's Bitter Cup – S/F (lost 9-15 to Wasps)
Owner: Tourney Events Group
Coach: John Mitchell
Rugby Manager: Adrian Hadley
Captain: Jim Mallinder

ANGLESEA, Peter (Flanker)
Born Blackrod, Bolton, 30.10.71. 6'3", 16st 2lb. **ADPR:** Orrell (1995-97, 27, 5t-25pts),
Bedford (1997-98, 4), Sale (1997-98, 6, 1t-5pts). Former England A squad flanker
who returns to the north-west after a spell at Bedford.

BALDWIN, David Neil (Lock)
Born Ilkley, 03.09.65. 6'6", 19st 4lb. **Rep hons:** England A (5, Rus89), Barbarians (94).
ADPR: Wakefield (1987-89, 14, 2t-8pts), Sale (1988-98, 132, 13t-63pts). Much-
respected and vastly experienced front-of-the-line jumper. This former Bramley and
Wakefield lock made his Yorkshire county debut against Northumberland in 1985.
Toured New Zealand with England B in 1992. Ever-present in the Premiership last
season and four games short of making 150 League appearances.

BAXENDELL, Joshua John Neill (Centre)
Born Manchester, 03.12.72. 6', 14st 4lb. **Rep hons:** England (2, NZ98), A (2, SA96).
ADPR: Sheffield (1992-94, 14, 2t-10pts), Sale (1993-98, 82, 16t-80pts). Educated at
King's, Macclesfield, Jos played first with Wilmslow and then moved to Heywood

Road from Sheffield where he studied at the local University. Dextrous with the ball in hand as befits a keen basketball player. A qualified surveyor, he toured Argentina with England in 1997 and after recovering from a groin operation finished strongly last season to clinch a place on the southern hemisphere tour where he was one of the few back to further his career.

BEIM, Thomas David (Wing)
Born Frimley, 11.12.75. 5'11", 13st 9lb. **Rep hons:** England (2, NZ98, 1t-5pts), Barbarians (97). **ADPR:** Gloucester (1995-96, 2, 1t-5pts), Sale (1996-98, 38, 27t-135pts). Long-striding wing with a try-scoring instinct, Tom opted for England in 1997 when he toured Australia with Clive Woodward's U21 squad. Maintained his excellent strike rate last season and deservedly earned selection for the senior tour of Australia, New Zealand and South Africa. Ever-present in the Premiership last season. Former Cheltenham College schoolboy who has played hockey for Wales U18 and professional polo.

BELL, Duncan Stuart Crampton (Prop)
Born King's Lynn, 01.10.74. 6'2", 18st. **ADPR:** Sale (1997-98, 16, 2t-10pts). Former England Schools and Bath Colts lock who has switched to the front row with marked success, winning a place on England's summer tour of the southern hemisphere. Numbers Harlequins, London Irish and Ebbw Vale among his former clubs.

DEVEREUX, John Anthony (Centre/wing)
Born Pontycymmer, 30.03.66. 6'1", 17st. **Rep hons:** Wales (21, Eng86, 5t-20pts), Barbarians (85-86). **ADPR:** Sale (1996-98, 6). Another serious ankle injury has hampered John's attempt to make a meaningful return to rugby union but when fully fit he remains a formidable competitor. Educated at Ynysawdre Comprehensive and South Glamorgan Institute, John was plucked from the Students side to make his international debut against England in 1986, having played just 17 minutes of senior rugby with Bridgend, against Newport. A powerful centre, John won his last Welsh cap against Ireland (1989) and toured Australia with the Lions before signing for Widnes RL.

DIAMOND, Steve (Hooker)
Born Manchester, 03.02.68. 5'10", 14st 11lb. **Rep hons:** Barbarians (97-98). **ADPR:** Sale (1990-98, 104, 4t-20pts). Durable hooker who toured Argentina with England in 1997. Spent five years with the Metrovick club before joining Sale. Joker in the pack but an upbeat and inspiring character. Former captain of the North Division. Fully qualified RFU coach.

DRIVER, Murray John (Prop)
Born Hamilton, New Zealand, 05.04.72. 5'11", 17st 4lb. **ADPR:** Sale (1996-98, 18, 2t-10pts). A British passport holder, Driver played representative age-group cricket and rugby league in New Zealand. The powerful prop also has a certificate in Sports Studies and a diploma in personal training. Father was an All Black triallist.

ELLIS, Kevin (Scrum-half)
Born Bridgend, 29.05.65. 5'9", 13st. **ADPR:** Sale (1997-98, 16, 6t-30pts). Former Bridgend scrum-half who joined Sale after a RL career with Widnes, from where he won GB honours against France in Perpignan in 1991.

ERSKINE, David James (Flanker/lock)
Born London, 14.10.69. 6'4", 16st. **Rep hons:** Ireland (3, NZ97), A (3, Sc98). **ADPR:** Sale (1990-98, 87, 13t-65pts). Versatile forward who developed apace under the tutelage of John Mitchell and made his Ireland international debut against New Zealand in November 1997. Works as an insurance inspector for club sponsors Independent Insurance. Formerly with CIYMS in Ulster and Boroughmuir.

FOWLER, John (Lock)
Born Bexley, Kent, 6.02.68. 6'8", 17st 8lb. **Rep hons:** England A (6, SAus95). **ADPR:** Richmond (1t-4pts), Sale (5t-25pts). Athletic line-out operator who is on the comeback trail after a year out with damaged anterior cruciate knee ligaments. Formerly with Richmond, Rosslyn Park and Newcastle Gosforth, John has also benefited from two spells in New Zealand, playing for King Country and Hawkes Bay, representing the latter against the 1993 British Lions. Toured Australia and Fiji with England A 1995 and made a significant contribution in the line-out during England's 27-19 win over Australia at Brisbane.

HADLEY, Adrian Michael (Centre/wing)
Born Cardiff, 01.03.63. 6'2", 15st 8lb. **Rep hons:** Wales (27, Rom83, 9t-36pts), Barbarians (84-85). **ADPR:** Sale (1996-98, 15, 2t, 6c, 3pg-31pts). Veteran Welshman who spent much of last season sidelined with injury. Adrian was educated at Lady Mary HS, Cardiff, where he played full-back or centre and scored 26 tries in his debut season with Cardiff. Played in non-capped internationals against Spain and Japan before making his full debut in Wales' defeat in Romania (1983). Last appeared for Wales against France in 1988 before signing for Salford RL. Moved to Widnes RL in August 1992.

HOWARTH, Shane Paul (Fly-half/full-back)
Born Auckland, New Zealand, 08.07.68. 5'9", 14st. **Rep hons:** New Zealand (4, SA94, 1t, 2c, 15pg-54pts). **ADPR:** Sale (1997-98, 21, 4t, 39c, 41pg, 1dg-224pts). Versatile former All Black full-back who deputised for Simon Mannix at fly-half in the second half of the season. Fine goal-kicker who scored 54 points in his four New Zealand Tests before being dropped!

MACHACEK, Jan (No 8)
Born Prague, Czech Republic, 15.02.72. 6'5", 17st. **Rep hons:** Czech Republic (20, 4t-20pts). Barbarians and Barbarians Sevens squad. Athletic Czech No 8 who learned his rugby with the Slavia club in Prague and then moved to New Zealand to play for the Pirates club in Dunedin. Graduated with a BSc in computer science from Prague University and is currently completing a Masters degree in Manchester. Joins from the Newport club. Generally identified by his colourful bandanas.

MALLINDER, David James (Full-back)
Born Halifax, 16.03.66. 6'3", 16st. **Rep hons:** England (2, Arg97), A (3, Qld96, 3t-15pts). **ADPR:** Sale (1989-98, 132, 36t, 2dg-174pts). Stalwart club captain who was ever-present in the Premiership last season and rallied the side after Christmas when the season threatened to deteriorate. Long-striding full-back who narrowly missed out on selection for the 1997 British Lions. Educated at Porter GS, Halifax, and Carnegie College. Formerly with Old Crossleyans and Roundhay. Plays squash and has swum for Yorkshire.

MATHER, Barrie-Jon (Centre)
Born 15.01.73. Athletic former England Schoolboy lock who remarkably switched to centre when he joined Wigan RL. Will transfer to Sale from Castleford when his RL contract expires in the autumn. His christian name derives from his father's admiration for Wales fly-half Barry John.

MILLS, Simon (Flanker)
Born 28.10.76. 6', 14st 7lb. **Rep hons:** England U21. Educated at Holmwood House and Douai and currently at Salford University. Formerly at Blackheath.

MOORE, Matthew Thomas (Wing)
Born 02.04.76. 5'11", 13st. **ADPR:** Sale (1996-98, 13, 6t-30pts). Enjoyed a startling end of the season when deputising for England wing, and flatmate, David Rees – so

much so that he earned selection for England's demanding summer tour. Played his early representative rugby for Sussex and currently a student at Manchester Metropolitan University.

MURPHY, Christopher Ian (Lock)
Born Hull, 02.02.76. 6'8", 17st 10lb. **Rep hons:** England A (2, Ire96). **ADPR:** West Hartlepool (1994-97, 37), Sale (1997-98, 12, 1t-5pts). Giant young former England Schools lock who attended Hymer's School in Hull.

O'CUINNEAGAIN, Dion (No 8)
Born Cape Town, South Africa, 24.05.72. 6'4", 16st. **Rep hons:** Ireland (2, SA98), A (1, Eng98). **ADPR:** Sale (1997-98, 16, 3t-15pts). Former South Africa Sevens captain who made a big impact last season and attracted the attention of the Ireland selectors who took him on their summer tour of South Africa where he made his Test debut.

O'GRADY, Dylan (Flanker)
Born Manchester, 19.01.71. 6'3", 16st 7lb. **Rep hons:** Ireland (1, It97), A (1,Sc98). **ADPR:** Sale (1992-98, 57, 10t-50pts). Known to his friends as 'Dangerous' and formerly a nightclub bouncer, O'Grady was hampered last season by a groin injury but did make his full Ireland debut against Italy. Local lad who joined Sale from the Metrovick Club.

RAIWALUI, Simon Vereneki (Lock)
Born Auckland, New Zealand, 08.09.74. 6'6", 17st. **Rep hons:** Fiji. **ADPR:** Sale (1997-98, 19, 2t-10pts). Mobile Fijian lock who has played provincial rugby for Queensland, and helped Fiji demolish Scotland in Suva in May.

REES, David Llewellyn (Wing)
Born London, 15.10.74. 5'9", 13st 10lb. **Rep hons:** England (6, Aus97, 3t-15pts), A (1, Otago97). **ADPR:** Sale (1995-98, 37, 11t-55pts). Exciting, scuttling runner and fearless tackler who broke into the senior England ranks under Clive Woodward before he became yet another Sale player to succumb to a groin injury. A graphic design and advertising student at Manchester Metropolitan University, he represented England in the World Students Cup in 1996. Educated at Gosforth HS and RGS, Newcastle. A sporting all-rounder, David has played soccer for Newcastle Boys, was a Northumberland Schools sprint champion and county tennis player and a nationally ranked table tennis junior. Represented Northumberland in the 1995 CIS County final against Warwickshire.

SANDERSON, Alex (Flanker)
Devastatingly quick openside flanker who starred for England Schools during their triumphant tour of Australia in 1997 and then captained the Schools side throughout last season. Like older brother Pat, educated at Kirkham HS and headed straight for top honours.

SANDERSON, Patrick Harold (Flanker)
Born Chester, 06.09.77. 6'4", 16st 7lb. **Rep hons:** England (3, NZ98), A (3, NZ97). **ADPR:** Sale (1996-98, 20, 6t-30pts). Enjoyed a marvellous end of the season to force his way into England's summer tour party, though illness cruelly deprived him of a debut against Australia. Undaunted he was one of England's best forwards in their two Tests against New Zealand and also did well against South Africa. Educated at Kirkham GS, Pat is blessed with pace and the handling skills of a basketball player and represented England Schools before joining Sale. Made a good impression playing for England A against New Zealand in November 1997.

SMITH, Andrew George (Prop)
Born Nantwich, 28.03.69. 6'1", 17st 6lb. **ADPR:** Sale (1990-98, 79, 1t-5pts). Educated at Rossall School and member of Chester RFC before joining Sale. Toured South Africa with North (1994). Good ball handler and sound scrummager.

SMITH, Paul Leslie (Prop)
Born Nantwich, 28.03.69. 6'1", 17st 6lb. **ADPR:** Sale (1989-98, 50). Twin brother of Andrew and equally uncompromising in the front row. Also educated at Rossall, Paul was another to fight against injury last season, being impeded with a sore back.

SMITH, Richard Malcolm (Scrum-half)
Born Wales, 06.06.73. 5'10", 12st 12lb. **ADPR:** Bristol (1996-97, 3, 1t-5pts), Sale (1997-98, 8, 2t-10pts). Useful backup scrum-half who learned his rugby with Newbridge in Wales.

TETLOW, Matt Philip (Centre)
Born Birmingham, 11.12.73. 6'2", 15st 10lb. **ADPR:** Newcastle (1993-97, 29, 6t-30pts), Sale (1997-98, 4). Powerful centre who joined from Newcastle.

WINSTANLEY, Philip (Prop)
Born Orrell, 16.09.68. 5'11", 16st 10lb. **ADPR:** Orrell (1988-96, 39, 3t, 1pg-17pts), Sale (1996-98, 28, 5t-25pts). Goal-kicking prop who graduated into senior rugby via Orrell Colts, having spent his early years playing in the backrow or even the wing. Remains extremely mobile and established himself as a first choice last season.

YATES, Christian Jude (Wing/centre)
Born Otahuhu, New Zealand, 13.05.71. 6'1", 16st. **ADPR:** Sale (1994-98, 47, 14t, 2dg-76pts). Powerful Anglo/Kiwi wing, represented England in the 1995 Hong Kong Sevens. Originally travelled to England with the intention of playing rugby league but got diverted and played briefly for Old Aldwinians before joining Sale. A member of the Universities club in Auckland while in New Zealand.

REVIEW

Sale, now officially known as Manchester Sale, finished last season strongly and reached the semi-final of the Tetley's Bitter Cup but struggled to recover from indifferent form before Christmas. An outbreak of groin and hernia injuries did not help but the situation did underline Sale's slender squad resources. A very public falling-out with talented New Zealand fly-half Simon Mannix also rocked the club, but the spirit that has served them so well in recent decades again came to the fore and Sale finished full of optimism. Wings David Rees, Tom Beim and Matt Moore all went on England's tour along with Jos Baxendell, Pat Sanderson and Duncan Bell.

SALE in Premiership One 1997-98

Aug 24	H	Saracens	Lost	10	19	D.Erskine(T) S.Howarth(C, D)
30	A	London Irish	Won	26	20	C.Yates(T) K.Ellis(T) S.Howarth(2C, 4P)
Oct 18	H	Newcastle	Lost	26	33	M.Moore(T) R.Smith(T) S.Howarth(2C, 4P)

25	A	Harlequins	Lost	41	52	M.Moore(T) C.Yates(T) T.Beim(T) P.Sanderson(T) K.Ellis(T) S.Howarth(5C, 2P)
Nov 2	A	Wasps	Won	38	22	D.Rees(2T) S.Mannix(T, D) P.Sanderson(T) S.Howarth(3C, 3P)
9	H	Bristol	Won	76	0	T.Beim(4T) D.Rees(3T) P.Winstanley(2T) K.Ellis(T) J.Mallinder(T) P.Sanderson(T) S.Howarth(8C)
Dec 13	A	Leicester	Lost	15	55	S.Howarth(T, C, P) S.Raiwalui(T)
27	H	Bath	Lost	11	13	T.Beim(T) S.Howarth(2P)
30	H	Gloucester	Drew	24	24	J.Baxendell(T) K.Ellis(T) S.Howarth(C, 4P)
Jan 10	A	Northampton	Lost	14	33	T.Beim(2T) S.Mannix(2C)
Feb 1	H	London Irish	Won	41	16	P.Sanderson(2T) D.Bell(T) K.Ellis(T) C.Yates(T) S.Mannix(2C, 4P)
15	A	Richmond	Won	28	20	J.Baxendell(T) J.Mallinder(T) D.O'Cuinneagain(T) S.Mannix(2C, 2P) S.Howarth(P)
24	A	Saracens	Lost	20	42	T.Beim(2T) S.Mannix(2C, 2P)
Mar 10	A	Newcastle	Lost	18	23	T.Beim(T) D.Erskine(T) S.Howarth(C, 2P)
14	H	Harlequins	Won	23	13	D.Bell(T) D.O'Cuinneagain(T) P.Winstanley(T) S.Howarth(C, 2P)
Apr 11	H	Leicester	Won	35	21	M.Moore(2T) J.Baxendell(T) T.Beim(T) K.Ellis(T) S.Howarth(2C, 2P)
15	A	Bristol	Won	25	15	J.Baxendell(T) S.Raiwalui(T) P.Anglesea(T) S.Howarth(2C, 2P)
18	H	Wasps	Drew	28	28	M.Moore(T) S.Howarth(C, 7P)
25	A	Bath	Won	29	19	J.Baxendell(T) M.Moore(T) P.Sanderson(T) R.Smith(T) S.Howarth(3C, P)
May 2	A	Gloucester	Lost	19	31	T.Beim(T) D.Erskine(T) S.Howarth(T, 2C)
10	H	Northampton	Won	30	19	J.Mallinder(T) S.Howarth(T, 3C, 3P) C.Murphy(T)
17	H	Richmond	Lost	28	40	T.Beim(T) S.Howarth(T, C, P) P.Winstanley(T) D.O'Cuinneagain(T) C.Yates(D)

Summary of Premiership scorers:

224 – S.Howarth (4T, 39C, D, 41P); 70 – T.Beim (14T); 48 – S.Mannix (T, 8C, D, 8P); 30 – P.Sanderson (6T), M.Moore (6T), K.Ellis (6T); 25 – D.Rees (5T), J.Baxendell (5T); 20 – P.Winstanley (4T); 18 – C.Yates (3T, D); 15 – D.O'Cuinneagain (3T), J.Mallinder (3T), D.Erskine (3T); 10 – R.Smith (2T), S.Raiwalui (2T), D.Bell (2T); 5 – C.Murphy (T).

Summary of Premiership appearances:

22 – J.Mallinder (+1), T.Beim, D.Baldwin; 21 – S.Howarth (+2); 20 – S.Diamond (+1); 19 – S.Raiwalui; 18 – P.Sanderson (+2); 17 – J.Baxendell; 16 – D.O'Cuinneagain (+4), K.Ellis (+1), D.Bell (+2); 15 – D.Erskine (+1); 14 – P.Winstanley; 13 – C.Yates (+3), D.O'Grady (+2); 12 – C.Murphy (+8), M.Moore (+1); 11 – D.Rees; 10 – S.Mannix, M.Driver (+4), G.Dawe (+7); 9 – D.Williamson (+4); 8 – R.Smith (+2); 7 – C.Vyvyan (+1); 6 – A.Hadley, S.Davidson (+2); 4 – M.Tetlow (+3), P.Smith; 2 – A.Smith; 1 – A.Morris, M.Kirke, D.Kenny (+1), J.Devereux (+1).

NEWCASTLE

Formation of club: 1995 (Gosforth formed in 1877)
Ground: Kingston Park, Brunton Road, Kenton Bank Foot, Newcastle NE13 8AF
Capacity: 6,900 (Seated 600)
Colours: Black and white
Honours: Cup Winners (2) – 1976, 1977 (when Gosforth RFC). Premiership Champions – 1997-98. Division Two Champions – 1992-93
Last season: ADP1 – Champions. Heineken European Cup – S/F (lost 9-12 to Agen). Tetley's Bitter Cup – Q/F (lost 7-17 to Northampton).
Owner: Sir John Hall
Director of Rugby: Rob Andrew
Coach: Steve Bates
Captain: Dean Ryan

ANDREW, Christopher Robert (Fly-half)
Born Richmond, Yorks. 18.02.63. 5'9", 12st 8lb. **Rep hons:** England (71, Rom85, 2t, 33c, 86pg, 21dg-396pts), Barbarians (85-86). **ADPR:** Wasps (1987-96, 77, 16t, 82c, 161pg, 11dg-748pts), Newcastle (1995-98, 47, 12t, 146c, 62pg, 2dg-544pts). After masterminding Newcastle's League success last season, and playing as well as ever, Rob stated his intention of continuing for at least one more season. Rob's signing as director of rugby in October 1995 heralded the beginning of modern professionalism. Educated at Barnard Castle School, Durham, and Cambridge University, where he won rugby and cricket Blues – Rob has also played for Nottingham, Gordon in Sydney and Toulouse. First capped against Romania 1985 when he scored 24 points in a 54-3 win, Rob won 69 of his 71 caps at fly-half, a world record. He also holds the world record for dropped goals in internationals with 22, including two for the British Lions. Other individual highlights include a 30-point haul against Canada (December 94), with a 12 out of 12 kicking record, and 27 points against South Africa in Pretoria (94). A member of England's three World Cup squads, Rob shared in three Grand Slam triumphs and was a Lion in 1989 and 1993.

ARCHER, Garath Stuart (Lock)
Born South Shields, 15.12.74. 6'6", 18st 7lb. **Rep hons:** England (12, Sc96), A (12, Ire95). **ADPR:** Newcastle (1993-95, 19, 2t-10pts), Bristol (1994-96, 16, 1t-5pts), Newcastle (1996-98, 38, 10t-50pts). Emerged as a major force throughout England's testing autumn internationals and the Five Nations tournament. Aggressive lock who rejoined Newcastle from Bristol at the end of the 1995-96 season. Garath, the son of former Gosforth wing Stuart Archer, was educated at Biddick School and Durham School and was a member of the England Schools 18 Group Grand Slam team in 1992. Toured Australia and Fiji with England A in 1995 and made his senior debut against Scotland at Murrayfield the following year.

ARMSTRONG, Gary (Scrum-half)
Born Edinburgh, 30.09.66. 5'8", 13st 8lb. **Rep hons:** Scotland (40, Aus88, 4t-16pts), A (3, It92), Barbarians (89-90). **ADPR:** Newcastle (1995-98, 46, 38t-190pts). As combative as ever, Gary took over as Scotland captain from Rob Wainwright for the Five Nations, but rested up during the summer in an attempt to ensure his battered body gets through to the 1999 World Cup. Gary was educated at Jedburgh GS and Dunfermline HS and won Scotland recognition out of the Jedburgh club, where he succeeded Roy Laidlaw at scrum-half. Made his international debut against Australia in 1988. Played a massive part in Scotland's 1990 Grand Slam triumph and produced possibly the best rugby of his career the following year during RWC91. A British Lion in 1989.

ARNOLD, Richard Karl (Backrow)
Born Taranaki, New Zealand, 16.08.65. 6'4", 15st 12lb. **ADPR:** Newcastle (1991-98, 95, 15t-69pts). Abrasive Kiwi forward who has played for Newcastle since before the professional era, after arriving from New Zealand where he was a member of the Eltham club. A stalwart in the backrow last season, making big hits and scoring important tries.

BEATTIE, Ross (No 8)
Born 15.11.77. 6'5", 17st 7lb. **Rep hons:** England U21. Immensely promising No 8 who shone successively for England Schools, Colts and U21. Educated at Hymer's College, Hull.

CHILDS, Graham Christopher (Centre/wing)
Born Fareham, 03.04.68. 6', 13st 10lb. **Rep hons:** England A (6, Fr90, 1t-4pts). **ADPR:** Wasps (1990-95, 60, 11t-50pts), Newcastle (1995-98, 28, 8t-40pts). Ultra-reliable centre who was voted Wasps player of the year in 94-95 before a job move brought him back to the north-east. Toured Argentina with England in 1990. Educated at Worthing HS and Newcastle Polytechnic.

FRANKLAND, Neil (Hooker/flanker)
Born Leeds, 16.02.63. 5'11", 16st. **ADPR:** Gosforth (1987-90, 26, 1t-4pts), Newcastle (1990-98, 76, 6t, 1dg-30pts). Educated at Ilkley GS and Aston University and a former Ilkley player, Neil is equally at home hooking or at wing forward. A chemist by profession.

GRAHAM, George (Prop)
Born Stirling, 19.01.66. 5'7", 17st. **Rep hons:** Scotland (5, Aus97), A (3, Ire89). **ADPR:** Newcastle (1996-98, 31, 7t-35pts). Joined Newcastle in 1996 after signing from Carlisle RL. Toured Zimbabwe with Scotland back in 1988 and was finally capped, as a replacement, against Australia in November 1997. Also a Scotland RL representative.

HORTON, Richard Lee (Hooker)
Born Middlesbrough, 22.06.76. 5'10", 15st. **ADPR:** Newcastle (1997-98, 2). Locally developed talent who has won a place in the England U21 squad.

HURTER, Marius Hofmeyr (Prop)
Born Potchefstroom, South Africa, 08.10.70. 6'2", 17st 13lb. **Rep hons:** South Africa (13, Rom95). Powerful Springbok lock who was a member of their 1995 World Cup-winning squad. Has played Currie Cup rugby for the Northern Bulls and Western Province.

LEGG, Stuart James (Wing)
Born Solihull, 27.09.75. 6'1", 14st. **ADPR:** Newcastle (1997-98, 21, 6t, 1c-32pts). Former England Colt who was a stalwart of the championship-winning side at

full-back. The circumstances of his selection above Tim Stimpson were not of his making – he simply grabbed his opportunity with both hands. Formerly with the Birmingham & Solihull club.

MASSEY, Peter Martin (Full-back)
Born Pontefract, 03.04.75. 5′11″, 13st 7lb. **ADPR:** Wakefield (1996-97, 22, 7t-35pts), Moseley (1997-98, 12, 3t-15pts). Joins from Moseley. Peter was a member of the North U21 Championship-winning team in 1995-96 and toured Italy in 1996 with the North Development squad before leaving neighbouring Morley to join Wakefield, progressing to Moseley after one season at Wakefield. A former England U21 squad member who works as a teacher.

NAYLOR, James Richard (Wing)
Born Halifax, 06.02.74. 5′11″, 15st 1lb. **Rep hons:** England A (6, SAus95, 3t-15pts). **ADPR:** Orrell (1993-97, 60, 17t-85pts), Newcastle (1997-98, 18, 8t-40pts). Speedy wing who proved a major success after transferring from Orrell, so much that Newcastle were able to release British Lion John Bentley to Rotherham on loan. Scored four tries in four matches for England Colts in 1993 before graduating to the England U21 squad and then making an England A debut against Fiji in 1995. Educated at Crossley Heath School and Wigan Tech and played his early rugby for Crossley Heath RFC.

NESDALE, Ross Patrick (Hooker)
Born Auckland, New Zealand, 30.07.68. 5′10″, 16st 2lb. **Rep hons:** Ireland (7, Wal97), A (1, Fr97). **ADPR:** Newcastle (1996-98, 41, 13t-65pts). No-nonsense New Zealand-reared hooker at the very heart of Newcastle's championship efforts, delaying a much-needed knee operation until the job was safely completed at Harlequins. Has also done well for Ireland whenever called upon. The Irish connection is real enough – Tom Nesdale, a cousin of his father's, played for Ireland in 1961. Educated at St Patrick's College, Silverstream, and Waikato Polytechnic, Ross then played for Auckland University and spent four years as Sean Fitzpatrick's understudy with the Provincial side.

O'NEILL, Stephan (Flanker)
Born Blaydon, 10.10.72. 6′1″, 16st 7lb. **ADPR:** London Irish (1987-90, 2), Newcastle (1996-98, 18, 4t, 1pg-23pts). Powerfully built flanker, developed locally.

POPPLEWELL, Nicholas John (Prop)
Born Dublin, 06.04.64. 5′10″, 17st 4lb. **Rep hons:** Ireland (48, NZ89, 3t-13pts), A (1, Eng91, 1t-5pts), Barbarians (89-90). **ADPR:** Wasps (1994-96, 13), Newcastle (1995-98, 39, 15t-75pts). Immensely powerful prop who has announced his retirement from international rugby but played a full part in Newcastle's championship effort. First capped against New Zealand in 1989 and toured New Zealand with the 1993 British Lions, becoming the only non-English player in the Test pack. Missed Ireland's tour to Australia in 1994 to undergo surgery to a serious cruciate ligament injury to his knee. Educated at Newton Secondary School in Wexford, 'Poppy' was a schools hockey international and played for Greystones before venturing across the Irish Sea, first to join Wasps and then Newcastle.

RYAN, Dean (No 8/lock)
Born Tuxford, 22.06.66. 6′6″, 17st. **Rep hons:** England (4, Arg90, 1t-4pts), A (9, Aus88, 3t-13pts), Barbarians (88-89). **ADPR:** Saracens (1987-89, 11), Wasps (1989-96, 69, 13t-61pts), Newcastle (1995-98, 45, 15t-75pts). Charismatic captain, immensely forceful No 8 and a good man to have when the going gets tough. Dean's season started with controversy – being banned for a month, later reduced to two weeks, after retaliating against Nathan Thomas at Bath – but ended on a high note with an England recall against Scotland and a well-deserved championship. First

capped on tour in Argentina in 1990, Dean left Saracens to join Wasps and then transferred to Newcastle soon after Rob Andrew's departure from Wasps in October 95.

SHAW, Martin (Wing)
Born Bishop Auckland, 02.09.75. 5′11″, 14st. **Rep hons:** England A (1, Sc98). **ADPR:** Newcastle (1996-98, 17, 3t-15pts). Educated at Durham School and Northumbria University, Martin represented England Colts and U21 before making his England A debut, as a replacement, against Scotland in March 1998. Formerly with Durham City and West Hartlepool.

TUIGAMALA, Va'aiga Lealuga (Wing/centre)
Born Faleasiu, Western Samoa, 04.09.69. 5′10″, 17st 4lb. **Rep hons:** New Zealand (19, US91, 5t-21pts), Western Samoa (1, Ire96). **ADPR:** Wasps (1996-97, 8, 3t-15pts), Newcastle (1996-98, 27, 15t, 1c-77pts). Inga's effectiveness as a player was often reduced by injury last season but he remains a wonderful 'professional' presence, reminding everybody how they should conduct themselves on and off the pitch. Returned to Union after a successful spell in RL with Wigan. Although born in Western Samoa, Va'aiga was brought up in Auckland and first came to the attention of the All Black selectors when he scored five tries against Mid Canterbury in 1989. Made his full international debut against USA in the 1991 World Cup. Last capped for New Zealand when defeated by England in 1993. Now fully committed to the Western Samoan cause.

UNDERWOOD, Tony (Wing)
Born Ipoh,Malaysia, 17.02.69. 5′9″, 13st 7lb. **Rep hons:** England (25, Can92, 13t-65pts), A (18, Fr89, 16t-68pts), Barbarians (89-90). **ADPR:** Leicester (1988-95, 42, 24t-111pts), Newcastle (1995-98, 31, 18t-90pts). After another season marred with injury Tony took the summer off to try and fully rehabilitate a troublesome knee. Still looked sharp in flashes for Newcastle but longs to string a series of games together. Tony was educated at Barnard Castle School and Cambridge University (Blues in 1990 and 91), and played for England in the World Students Cup (1988) before touring Argentina with England (1990), when another knee injury again restricted his effectiveness. After an outstanding season for England B in 1992, he won his first senior cap against Canada at Wembley later that year. Shared in England's Grand Slam (95) and played in four games during RWC95.

VAN ZANDVLIET, Paul (Prop)
Born Newcastle, 14.10.66. 6′, 17st 10lb. **ADPR:** Newcastle (1993-98, 81, 9t-45pts). Respected and experienced scrummager who joined Newcastle after spells with Whitley Bay and Rockcliff. Best remembered last season for his cynical trip on Mark Mapletoft at Gloucester that should have resulted in a sending off, and those ugly press pictures after the game against Leicester which seem to show him biting Neil Back – no further action was taken.

WALTON, Peter (Flanker)
Born Alnwick, 03.06.69. 6′3″, 18st. **Rep hons:** Scotland (13, Eng94, 3t-15pts), A (9, It93, 1t-5pts), Barbarians (95-96). **ADPR:** Newcastle (1991-92, 11, 10t-40pts), Northampton (1992-95, 31, 2t-10pts), Newcastle (1995-98, 31, 6t-30pts). Showed tremendous late-season form, just when Newcastle needed his power and strength most. Anglo/Scot who played club rugby for Alnwick, Gosforth and Northampton before rejoining the newly constituted Newcastle Gosforth club. Educated at Merchiston Castle School and the Royal Agriculture College, Cirencester.

WEIR, George Wilson (Lock)
Born Edinburgh, 04.07.70. 6′6″, 17st 7lb. **Rep hons:** Scotland (50, Arg90, 4t-19pts), A (7, Ire89, 2t-10pts), Barbarians (92-93). **ADPR:** London Scottish (1989-91, 5,

1t-4pts), Newcastle (1995-98, 45, 5t-25pts). Another to take the summer off in an attempt to ensure his fitness for this season and the World Cup that follows. Versatile, experienced and much-travelled Scottish forward who moved to Newcastle from Melrose where he was a member of five championship-winning teams. Doddie was educated at Stewart's Melville College and toured New Zealand with Scottish Schools in 1988, when he played in seven of the eight games. Has subsequently toured New Zealand with the full Scottish squad, North America, Australia and the South Pacific. Father played for Gala, as does brother Tom. Keen horse rider (one-day eventing) and enjoys clay pigeon shooting.

WILKINSON, Jonathan (Fly-half)
Born Surrey, 25.06.79. 5'10", 12st 9lb. **Rep hons:** England (3, Ire98). **ADPR:** Newcastle (1997-98, 11). Became England's youngest capped international for 71 years when he came on as a replacement against Ireland in March, aged 18 years 301 days. Jonny has been content to bide his time at Newcastle where Rob Andrew has been playing as well as ever. Clive Woodward, however, had no hesitation in asking him to start at outside half against Australia in the opening game of their summer tour, having played centre for England Schools against Australia just 12 months earlier. Wilkinson had also accumulated 38 points from fly-half for England 18 Group the previous winter when they claimed the junior Grand Slam. Educated at Lord Wandsworth School in Hampshire.

WOOD, Michael Denis (Wing)
Born Stockton-on-Tees, 15.07.76. 5'11", 12st 2lb. **ADPR:** West Hartlepool (1995-97, 23, 6t-30pts), Bath (1997-98, 1), West Hartlepool (1997-98, 11, 3t-15pts). Moved to Newcastle in the summer after spells with Bath and West Hartlepool. Educated at Sedbergh, Will Carling's old school, Michael also attended Newcastle University. Has been capped by England Schools and U21.

REVIEW

Sir John Hall gave Rob Andrew five years to form a championship-winning side when he signed the England fly-half from Wasps – ultimately Andrew delivered the goods with over two years to spare. Newcastle were worthy champions – consistent, remorseless and cool under pressure. They lost just three Premiership games all season, a remarkable achievement. Andrew was admirably supported by coach Steve Bates and inspiring captain Dean Ryan – a trio of former Wasps who did not miss a trick. On the field Pat Lam, Doddie Weir, Gary Armstrong, Alan Tait and Ross Nesdale were also immense figures, while Jim Naylor and Stuart Legg came through well.

NEWCASTLE in Premiership One 1997-98

Aug 23	A	Bath	Won	20	13	V.Tuigamala(T) S.Legg(T) T.Stimpson(2C, 2P)
Oct 8	H	Northampton	Won	37	12	J.Naylor(2T) G.Armstrong(T) P.Lam(T) N.Popplewell(T) T.Stimpson(3C, 2P)
	18	A	Sale	Won	33	26	G.Archer(T) P.Lam(T) S.O'Neill(T) D.Ryan(T) R.Andrew(2C, 3P)
	26	H	Richmond	Won	18	12	R.Andrew(6P)
Nov 1	A	London Irish	Won	35	19	N.Popplewell(2T) R.Nesdale(T) P.Lam(T) R.Andrew(3C, 3P)

Date	H/A	Opponent	Result			Scorers
Dec 14	H	Gloucester	Won	37	27	G.Armstrong(2T) S.Legg(T) T.Underwood(T) P.Van Zandvliet(T) R.Metcalfe(T) D.Ryan(T) R.Andrew(C)
27	A	Bristol	Won	50	8	G.Armstrong(3T) G.Childs(T) P.Lam(T) J.Naylor(T) A.Tait(T) V.Tuigamala(T) R.Andrew(2C, 2P)
30	A	Leicester	Won	25	19	P.Lam(2T) N.Popplewell(T) R.Andrew(2C, D, P)
Jan 11	H	London Irish	Won	46	13	J.Naylor(3T) G.Archer(2T) V.Tuigamala(T) G.Armstrong(T) R.Nesdale(T) S.Legg(C) R.Andrew(2C)
31	A	Northampton	Won	21	17	J.Naylor(T) V.Tuigamala(T) R.Andrew(C, 3P)
Feb 15	H	Harlequins	Won	43	15	T.Underwood(2T) J.Naylor(T) A.Tait(T) D.Ryan(T) M.Shaw(T) R.Andrew(5C, P)
Mar 10	H	Sale	Won	23	18	T.Underwood(T) G.Childs(T) R.Andrew(T, C, 2P)
14	A	Richmond	Lost	17	30	Penalty(T) T.Underwood(T) R.Andrew(2C, P)
25	H	Saracens	Won	30	25	S.Legg(T) N.Popplewell(T) P.Walton(T) R.Andrew(3C, 3P)
Apr 7	H	Wasps	Won	20	13	S.Legg(2T) R.Andrew(T, C, P)
11	A	Gloucester	Won	29	27	R.Andrew(2T, 3C, P) Penalty(T) P.Walton(T)
19	A	Saracens	Lost	10	12	P.Lam(T) R.Andrew(C, P)
22	A	Wasps	Lost	17	18	G.Armstrong(2T) R.Andrew(2C, P)
26	H	Bristol	Won	43	18	G.Childs(2T) R.Andrew(T, 4C) G.Armstrong(T) S.Legg(T) Penalty(T) M.Shaw(T)
May 4	H	Leicester	Won	27	10	G.Armstrong(T) P.Lam(T) P.Walton(T) R.Andrew(3C, 2P)
11	H	Bath	Won	20	15	T.Underwood(T) R.Arnold(T) R.Andrew(2C, 2P)
17	A	Harlequins	Won	44	20	G.Armstrong(2T) R.Andrew(T, 4C, 2P) N.Popplewell(T) P.Lam(T) R.Arnold(T)

Summary of Premiership scorers:

226 – R.Andrew (6T, 44C, D, 35P); 65 – G.Armstrong (13T); 40 – J.Naylor (8T), P.Lam (8T); 32 – S.Legg (6T, C); 30 – T.Underwood (6T), N.Popplewell (6T); 22 – T.Stimpson (5C, 4P); 20 – V.Tuigamala (4T), G.Childs (4T); 15 – P.Walton (3T), D.Ryan (3T), G.Archer (3T), Penalty (3T); 10 – A.Tait (2T), M.Shaw (2T), R.Nesdale (2T), R.Arnold (2T); 5 – P.Van Zandvliet (T), S.O'Neill (T), R.Metcalfe (T).

Summary of Premiership appearances:

22 – P.Van Zandvliet, P.Lam (+1), G.Armstrong (+1), R.Andrew; 21 – D.Weir (+1), D.Ryan, R.Nesdale, S.Legg (+1); 20 – G.Archer; 19 – A.Tait (+1), N.Popplewell (+1), R.Arnold (+1); 18 – J.Naylor; 16 – V.Tuigamala (+2); 15 – P.Walton (+10); 12 – G.Graham (+8); 11 – J.Wilkinson (+3), T.Underwood; 10 – G.Childs, J.Bentley; 8 – M.Shaw (+2); 6 – R.Metcalfe (+2); 4 – T.Stimpson (+2); 2 – S.O'Neill (+1), R.Horton (+1); 1 – C.Simpson-Daniel, N.Frankland (+1).

NORTHAMPTON

Formation of club: 1880
Ground: Franklin's Gardens, Weedon Road, Northampton NN5 5BG
Capacity: 9,500 (Seated 2,500)
Colours: Black, gold and green
Honours: Division Two Champions – 1989-90, 1995-96
Best League finish: 3rd in Division One 1991-92
Best Cup run: Losing finalist in 1990-91
Last season: ADP1 – 8th. Tetley's Bitter Cup – S/F (lost 10-25 to Saracens)
Owner: Keith Barwell
Coach: Ian McGeechan
Captain: Tim Rodber

ALLEN, Matt Charles (Centre)
Born Farnborough, 28.02.74. 6'2", 15st 2lb. **Rep hons:** England A (6, Otago97, 1t-5pts), Barbarians (96-97). **ADPR:** Northampton (1994-98, 66, 31t-155pts). Solid performer in Northampton's midfield who knows exactly how to score tries, witness his League record of 31 in 66 appearances. Educated at St Dunstan's and Loughborough University, Matt toured Argentina with England in 1997 and returned there at the end of last season with the Barbarians.

BEAL, Nick David (Full-back/wing)
Born York, 02.12.70. 6'2", 13st 8lb. **Rep hons:** England (5, Arg96), A (10, Ire93, 2t-10pts), Barbarians (94). **ADPR:** Northampton (1992-98, 76, 11c, 12pg, 1dg-151pts). Missed much of last season after undergoing knee surgery but returned to action just in time to earn selection on England's tour of the southern hemisphere, where he did service at centre. A sevens expert who represented England in the RWC Sevens in 1993 and Hong Kong (1996), Nick won his first senior cap against Argentina in December 1996. His versatility also helped him win a place on the Lions tour to South Africa in 1997. Nick was educated at RGS, High Wycombe, and 'discovered' playing for High Wycombe.

BRAMHALL, James Patrick (Scrum-half)
Born Northampton, 20.05.78. 5'11", 12st 6lb. **ADPR:** Northampton (1996-98, 7). Useful scrum-half reserve who finished the season on the England U21 bench.

CASSELL, Justyn Paul Sheldon (Backrow)
Born Reading, 25.05.67. 6'3", 15st 8lb. **Rep hons:** England A (4, Fr92, 1t-4pts), Barbarians (91-92). **ADPR:** Saracens (1989-93, 33, 3t-13pts), Harlequins (1993-95, 12, 2t-10pts), Northampton (1994-98, 22, 3t-15pts). Experienced former Saracens and Harlequins flanker who played for the triumphant England side at the RWC Sevens in 1993.

CHANDLER, Jason William (Lock)
Born Wellington, New Zealand, 23.09.70. 6'6", 17st. **ADPR:** Northampton (1996-98, 25, 2t-10pts). Typically abrasive and mobile former Auckland Provincial lock, who has contributed well in the loose but occasionally struggled in the jungle of British-style line-outs.

COHEN, Ben Christopher (Wing)
Born Northampton, 14.09.78. 6'3", 15st. **ADPR:** Northampton (1996-98, 13, 1t-5pts). A real speed merchant, Ben has done well for England Colts and U21 in successive seasons. Educated at King's Thorpe Upper School, he represented East Midlands Colts in their three championship-winning years, 1995-97. Nephew of England 1966 World Cup soccer star George Cohen.

DANTIACQ, David (Centre)
Born Clichy, France, 10.01.70. 5'10", 13st. **Rep hons:** France (1, Rom97), French Barbarians. Quicksilver French centre who has signed from Pau. Learned his rugby originally with Grenoble.

DAWSON, Matthew James Sutherland (Scrum-half)
Born Birkenhead, 31.10.72. 5'11", 12st 10lb. **Rep hons:** England (14, WS95, 4t, 1c, 1pg-25pts), A (11, Fr93, 7t-35pts), Barbarians (94). **ADPR:** Northampton (1991-98, 90, 23t, 6c, 16pg, 1dg-177pts). Started the representative season by being left out of Clive Woodward's first England squad but nine months later captained the England tour party to the southern hemisphere, where he did a superb job in the most difficult circumstances. The previous season he recovered from knee surgery to make the 1997 Lions tour party, playing in all three Tests and scoring two tries. Played junior rugby for the Marlow club and represented England U21 at centre, before reverting to scrum-half and successfully challenging Kyran Bracken for the senior berth in the 1995-6 Five Nations campaign. Useful wicketkeeper and played soccer for Chelsea Boys.

FOALE, Simon Edward (Lock)
Born Northampton, 29.08.67. 6'4", 16st 9lb. **Rep hons:** Barbarians (97-98). **ADPR:** Northampton (1991-98, 41, 2t-10pts). A product of the local Bugbrook RFC, Simon is a versatile back five forward who has yet to command a regular place in Saints' starting line-up. Joined the club in 1990.

GRAYSON, Paul James (Fly-half)
Born Chorley, 30.05.71. 6', 12st 7lb. **Rep hons:** England (15, WS95, 1t, 23c, 47pg, 5dg-207pts), A (9, BCPres93, 16c, 26pg, 3dg-119pts). **ADPR:** Waterloo (1992-93, 10, 1t, 8c, 29pg, 6dg-126pts), Northampton (1993-98, 79, 11t, 134c, 172pg, 13dg-878pts). Paul bounced back from the disappointment of being 'invalided' off the British Lions tour in 1997 to produce the best form of his career, though the imminent arrival of his first child prevented him from travelling to the southern hemisphere with England. A convert from soccer, Paul enjoyed an excellent debut season for England in 1995-96, scoring 58-plus in the Five Nations. Educated at Parklands High in Chorley and Dr Tuson College, Preston, Paul arrived at Northampton via Preston Grasshoppers and Waterloo, for whom he starred in their famous Pilkington Cup victory over Bath in 1992. Useful club cricketer.

HEPHER, Alastair Mark (Fly-half)
Born Yardley Gobian, 03.10.74. 5'11", 13st. **Rep hons:** Barbarians (97). **ADPR:** Northampton (1994-98, 10, 2t, 10c, 20pg, 2dg-96pts). Promising young fly-half whose opportunities have inevitably been few and far between with Paul Grayson and, until this season, Gregor Townsend at Franklin's Gardens. Captained East Midlands in their CIS U21 County Championship final at Twickenham in 1996.

HUNTER, Ian (Full-back/wing)
Born Harrow, 15.02.69. 6'2", 14st 10lb. **Rep hons:** England (7, Can92, 3t-15pts), A (17, Aus90, 10t, 1c-44pts), Barbarians (90-91). **ADPR:** Nottingham (1988-89, 2), Northampton (1989-98, 83, 16t, 3pg, 1dg-84pts). Richly talented but injury-prone back who has the ability to excel in the top flight. Educated at Lake School, Windermere, Ian scored two tries on his international debut against Canada at Wembley, and another on his Five Nations debut against France before injuring an eye against Wales. Selected for the 1993 British Lions tour of New Zealand, he reappeared for England against Wales in 1994 and was also a member of the 1995 RWC squad.

HYNES, Martin Peter (Prop)
Born Wigan, 23.08.68. 5'9", 16st. **Rep hons:** England A (10, NOtago92). **ADPR:** Orrell (1988-94, 64, 1t-4pts), Northampton (1994-98, 44). A tough scrummager, Martin was educated at Wigan Tech and moved to Northampton from Orrell. Played in the inaugural U21 international when England beat Romania 54-13 in Bucharest. Was a bench reserve for England throughout the 1992 Five Nations.

JOHNSON, Christopher Andrew Philip (Hooker)
Born Oldham, 23.05.73. 5'11", 15st 7lb. **ADPR:** Leicester (1993-96, 7, 1t-5pts), Northampton (1996-98, 19, 2t-10pts). Experienced former England Students captain who challenges Clarke hard at hooker.

LAM, Patrick Richard (Backrow)
Born Auckland, New Zealand, 29.09.68. 6'2", 16st. **Rep hons:** Western Samoa. **ADPR:** Newcastle (1996-98, 33, 22t-110pts). Sensationally signed from Newcastle for £100,000 in July after contract negotiations broke down at Kingston Park. A revelation last season with his explosive running and tackling, Pat was deservedly voted Premiership player of the season. Experienced Western Samoa captain who helped his country to both the 1991 and 1995 World Cup quarter-finals. Played against Wales, Argentina and Scotland in 1991 and was ever-present four years later. Learned his rugby with Auckland and represented New Zealand Colts and the national seven at Hong Kong, but his first allegiance has always been Manu Samoa. Will miss the opening weeks of the season to concentrate on Western Samoa's World Cup qualifying tournament in Australia.

MACKINNON, Don Charles (Flanker)
Born Sydney, Australia, 27.03.71. 6'3", 15st 7lb. **ADPR:** Northampton (1996-98, 19, 1t-5pts). Athletic Australian who provides useful backrow cover.

MERLIN, David Jonathan (Flanker/lock)
Born Leeds, 22.05.72. 6'4", 16st 5lb. **ADPR:** Northampton (1992-98, 23, 5t-25pts). Former Worcester utility forward who continues to impress with his mobility and improving ball skills. Tim Rodber's injury problems gave him plenty of chances to shine last season.

METCALFE, Richard (Lock)
Born Leeds, 21.11.73. 7'1", 19st. **Rep hons:** England A (2, Vict95, 1t-5pts), Scotland A (3, Fr98). **ADPR:** Newcastle (1993-98, 42, 3t-15pts). Moved from Newcastle in July 1998. The only senior player in Britain currently topping 7ft, Richard is a talented all-round forward who switched allegiance last season and was immediately rewarded with a Scotland cap and a place on their summer tour of Fiji and Australia. Educated at Rodillian School, Wakefield.

MOIR, Craig Calder (Wing)
Born Aberdeen, 25.09.73. 5'10", 14st 10lb. **ADPR:** Northampton (1993-98, 38, 12t-60pts). Welsh speedster from Milford Haven who played for Llanelli in 1991-92

before attending Nene College and joining Saints. Has represented the Welsh Seven in Taipei and Uruguay and spent much of the 1996 summer playing and coaching at Sciotto Valley in Columbus, Ohio.

NORTHEY, Andrew John (Centre)
Born 17.02.72. **ADPR:** Waterloo (1991-95, 14, 2t-9pts), Northampton (1997-98, 16). Convert from rugby league who joined from St Helens.

PAGEL, Garry Louis (Prop)
Born King Williams Town, South Africa, 17.09.66. 6'4", 17st. **Rep hons:** South Africa (5, Aus95). **ADPR:** Northampton (1997-98, 16, 2t-10pts). Pagel's arrival in midseason from Western Province resulted in an immediate improvement in Northampton's scrummaging, and his international experience proved very beneficial in a young pack when injuries took their toll. Also appeared for Eastern Province before breaking into the Springbok side in 1995. Had previously achieved notoriety in 1993, when involved in an incident with Jeff Tordo that resulted in the France captain requiring over 50 stitches in a cut face.

PHILLIPS, Jon-Lee (Lock)
Born Peterborough, 16.08.72. 6'6", 17st. **ADPR:** Northampton (1991-98, 88, 5t-25pts). Raw-boned utility forward who came of age on the England U21 tour of Australia in 1993 when he forced his way into the Test side. The long-term injury to Martin Bayfield has seen a lot of responsibility heaped on the shoulders of Phillips. Many still believe his best position would be blindside wing forward.

POUNTNEY, Anthony Charles (Flanker)
Born Southampton, 13.11.73. 6'2", 15st. **Rep hons:** Scotland A (2, Ire98). **ADPR:** Northampton (1994-98, 63, 13t-65pts). A tireless scavenging flanker in the old-fashioned style, Budge's consistent form resulted in a call-up for the Scotland squad last season – he qualifies because a grandparent was born in the Channel Islands – though he was mysteriously overlooked when it came to the summer tour of Fiji and Australia. A former member of Winchester (1989-91) and attended King's School, Winchester, before studying for a BA in European Studies at Bedford University and joining Northampton. Member of England's squad in the 1996 World Students Cup.

RODBER, Timothy Andrew Keith (Backrow)
Born Richmond, Yorkshire, 02.07.69. 6'6", 16st 7lb. **Rep hons:** England (32, Sc92, 3t-15pts), A (6, Fr90, 2t-8pts), Barbarians (92-93). **ADPR:** Northampton (1989-98, 100, 17t-82pts). After contributing hugely to the British Lions series victory over South Africa, Tim endured a miserable injury-ravaged season, with first a persistent hamstring problem and then a knee cartilage problem keeping him on the sidelines for long stretches. Educated at Churchers, Hampshire, and Oxford Polytechnic, he played for Petersfield and Oxford Old Boys before joining Northampton. Developed rapidly under the tutelage of All Black Wayne Shelford, made his England debut against Scotland in 1992 and was a member of England 1993 RWC Sevens-winning team. Performed wonderfully well in South Africa during England's 1994 tour, but career suffered a blip when dismissed for punching against Eastern Province at Port Elizabeth. Played throughout England's RWC95 campaign.

SEELY, Grant Lionel (Backrow)
Born Aylesbury, 07.01.74. 6'4", 16st 2lb. **ADPR:** Northampton (1994-98, 53, 22t-110pts). Like Pountney, has learned from playing alongside Rodber in the backrow. Grant has developed out of all recognition since joining Northampton from Aylesbury in 1991. Former England U21 captain.

SLEIGHTHOLME, Jonathan Mark (Wing)
Born Malton, 05.08.72. 5'10", 13st 5lb. **Rep hons:** England (12, Fr96, 4t-20pts), A (9, Ire95, 3t-15pts), Barbarians (92-93). **ADPR:** Wakefield (1991-94, 38, 27t-127pts), Bath (1994-98, 39, 22t-110pts), Northampton (1997-98, 14, 1t-5pts). Looking to relaunch his representative career after moving from Bath last season. Educated at Whitgift School, Grimsby, and Chester College, John played for Grimsby and Hull Ionians before moving to Wakefield, where he scored 42 tries in 60 appearances. Gradually became established at Bath, made England A debut against Ireland in January 1995 and full debut at Parc des Princes in February 96.

STEWART, Matthew James (Prop)
Born Dartford, 18.05.73. 5'11", 17st. **Rep hons:** Scotland (12, It96). **ADPR:** Blackheath (1993-96, 41, 2t-10pts), Northampton (1996-98, 26). With a grandfather from Dunfermline, Lance Corporal Mattie Stewart is a PT instructor with the Princess of Wales regiment and came to rugby late, only taking the game up when he entered the Army, aged 16. Immediately showed promise, joined the Blackheath club and broke into the Scotland Development XV in 1995 before making his senior debut against Italy in 1996. Keen boxer.

TATUPU, Shem J. (Backrow)
Born Western Samoa, 18.02.68. 6'3", 16st. **Rep hons:** Western Samoa, Barbarians (97-98). **ADPR:** Northampton (1996-98, 15, 1t-5pts). Again plagued by injury, but a powerful performer when fully fit. Western Samoan flanker who starred in the 1995 World Cup but took a while to settle after returning to rugby union after an unsuccessful spell with Wigan RL.

THORNEYCROFT, Harvey Spencer (Wing)
Born Northampton, 22.02.69. 6', 15st 11lb. **Rep hons:** England A (11, NOtago92, 8t-37pts), Barbarians (91-92). **ADPR:** Northampton (1987-89, 10, 1t-4pts), Nottingham (1989-90, 4, 3t-12pts), Northampton (1990-98, 118, 30t-144pts). Remains a popular, hard-running wing who burst on the representative scene in 1988 when he scored a hat-trick in England Colts' 32-12 win over Wales Youth. Toured New Zealand with England B in 1992. Was the mastermind behind the England XV Discovery tour of West Africa in 1996, which helped raise funds for the Max Brito fund by playing games against a Springbok XV in Accra and Ivory Coast in Abidjan.

VOLLAND, Matthew James (Prop)
Born Peterborough, 30.06.74. 6', 16st 7lb. **Rep hons:** England A (2, SA96). **ADPR:** Northampton (1993-98, 52). Powerful prop learning his trade. Formerly with the Peterborough club. Worked as a scaffolder before turning professional.

REVIEW

Despite some useful mid-season form – culminating in a Tetley's Cup quarter-final win over Newcastle – Northampton have failed to shrug off the tag of under-achievers. Saints finished disappointingly in the Premiership, losing four of their last five games. In mitigation they were badly hit by injuries, especially to captain Tim Rodber – a huge influence when playing. The return to form of Paul Grayson heartened everybody at Franklin's Gardens, as did Matt Dawson's selection as England captain for their summer tour. Recruited well in the summer, striking to sign Pat Lam and Richard Metcalfe from champions Newcastle and David Dantiacq from Pau. Leaving the club were Jonathan Bell and Allan Clarke, who have returned to Ulster, and Gregor Townsend who moves to Brive.

NORTHAMPTON in Premiership One 1997-98

Aug 23	H	Harlequins	Lost	23	26	M.Dawson(T, C) J.Phillips(T) S.Tatupu(T) G.Townsend(2P)
Oct 8	A	Newcastle	Lost	12	37	A.Hepher(3P) G.Townsend(D)
18	H	Leicester	Won	25	6	P.Grayson(T) T.Rodber(T) M.Dawson(4P) G.Townsend(P)
26	A	Bristol	Lost	15	22	M.Dawson(5P)
Nov 8	H	Saracens	Lost	13	19	C.Moir(T) M.Dawson(C, 2P)
Dec 13	A	London Irish	Won	51	10	M.Allen(T) M.Dawson(T) P.Grayson(T, 6C, 3P) G.Pagel(T) B.Pountney(T) G.Townsend(T)
21	A	Richmond	Won	24	21	P.Grayson(D, 7P)
27	H	Wasps	Won	18	10	P.Grayson(6P)
30	A	Bath	Lost	3	26	P.Grayson(P)
Jan 10	H	Sale	Won	33	14	M.Allen(2T) G.Townsend(T) P.Grayson(3C, 4P)
18	A	Harlequins	Won	30	5	M.Allen(2T) J.Sleightholme(T) G.Townsend(T) P.Grayson(2C, 2P)
31	H	Newcastle	Lost	17	21	C.Johnson(T) P.Grayson(4P)
Feb 14	A	Gloucester	Lost	15	20	G.Seely(T) H.Thorneycroft(T) P.Grayson(C, P)
Mar 7	A	Leicester	Drew	15	15	P.Grayson(D, 4P)
14	H	Bristol	Won	35	12	H.Thorneycroft(3T) M.Allen(T) J.Chandler(T) C.Johnson(T) P.Grayson(C, P)
Apr 18	H	Richmond	Lost	39	47	M.Dawson(T) Penalty(T) J.Phillips(T) B.Pountney(T) H.Thorneycroft(T) P.Grayson(4C, 2P)
22	H	London Irish	Won	33	18	J.Bell(T) G.Pagel(T) B.Pountney(T) P.Grayson(3C, 4P)
26	A	Wasps	Lost	15	31	M.Allen(T) G.Seely(T) P.Grayson(C, P)
May 2	H	Bath	Won	16	15	J.Bell(T) M.Dawson(C, 3P)
10	A	Sale	Lost	19	30	M.Dawson(2T, 2C) S.Foale(T)
14	A	Saracens	Lost	20	43	N.Beal(T) P.Grayson(T, C, P) S.Tatupu(T)
17	H	Gloucester	Lost	22	24	P.Grayson(T, C, D, 4P)

Summary of Premiership scorers:

210 – P.Grayson (4T, 23C, 3D, 45P); 77 – M.Dawson (5T, 5C, 14P); 30 – M.Allen (6T); 27 – G.Townsend (3T, D, 3P); 25 – H.Thorneycroft (5T); 15 – B.Pountney (3T); 10 – G.Seely (2T), J.Phillips (2T), S.Tatupu (2T), G.Pagel (2T), C.Johnson (2T), J.Bell (2T); 9 – A.Hepher (3P); 5 – T.Rodber (T), C.Moir (T), S.Foale (T), J.Chandler (T), N.Beal (T), Penalty (T).

Summary of Premiership appearances:

22 – J.Phillips; 20 – G.Townsend (+1), B.Pountney; 18 – P.Grayson; 17 – G.Seely (+4), M.Dawson, M.Allen (+3); 16 – M.Stewart, G.Pagel (+1), A.Northey (+3), A.Clarke (+1); 15 – H.Thorneycroft (+3), J.Chandler; 13 – D.Mackinnon (+2), C.Johnson (+6); 12 – T.Rodber, I.Hunter (+2); 11 – M.Volland (+4), J.Bell (+1); 9 – B.Cohen (+1); 8 – M.Hynes (+2); 7 – C.Moir (+1); 6 – S.Tatupu, J.Bramhall (+2), N.Beal; 5 – S.Foale (+2), M.Bayfield; 4 – S.Barnes (+2); 2 – J.Wright (+2), D.Merlin (+2), J.Cassell (+1), C.Allen (+2); 1 – D.Malone, R.MacNaughton, R.Jackson, A.Hepher.

RICHMOND

Formation of club: 1861
Address: Madejski Stadium, Junction 11 – M4, Reading RG2 0FL
Capacity: 25,000 (All seated)
Colours: Old gold, red and black
Honours: Division Two Champions – 1996-97. Division Three Champions – 1991-92.
Best League finish: 5th in Premiership One 1997-98
Best Cup run: Quarter finalist 1973-74, 1974-75, 1978-79, 1989-90 and 1997-98
Last season: ADP1 – 5th. Tetley's Bitter Cup – Q/F (lost 30-36 to Saracens)
Owner: Ashley Levett (copper commodities trader)
Coach: John Kingston
Captain: Ben Clarke

BATEMAN, Allan Glen (Centre)
Born Maesteg, 06.03.65. 5′9″, 14st. **Rep hons:** Wales (15, Sc90, 6t-30pts), A (1, Fr89), Barbarians (96-97). **ADPR:** Richmond (1996-98, 37, 18t-90pts). Ended the season disappointingly by having to miss out on Wales' tour of South Africa to have a nose operation. Remains, however, the fulcrum of Richmond's impressive midfield. Model pro who signed from Cronulla, where he was playing rugby league in Australia. Started his career at Maesteg in 1985 where he played 137 games and was voted player of the year in 1988. Moved to Neath in 1988 and helped them to one Welsh Club Championship and two Welsh Cup successes. Capped four times before he turned professional with Warrington where he played 142 games, sharing in a Regal Cup success and a Club Championship. Played for Cronulla for two seasons before returning to rugby union and gaining selection for the 1997 British Lions.

BEST, Lee (Full-back/wing)
Born 16.10.78. 6′3″, 14st 11lb. **Rep hons:** England 18 Group, 16 Group. Hampered by injury last season, Lee joined Richmond direct from school having made a big impression during England 18 Group's triumphant tour to Australia in 1997.

BROWN, Spencer (Wing)
Born Eton, 11.07.73. 5′10″, 13st. **Rep hons:** England (2, Aus98), A (2, NZ97, 1t-5pts). **ADPR:** Richmond (1994-98, 27, 16t-80pts). Hard-tackling and aggressive wing who made his name last season with two astonishing tackles against Todd Miller and Tana Umaga for the ERP XV against the All Blacks. Spent 13 weeks on the touchline soon after with a badly broken cheekbone but returned in fine fettle to win a place on England's summer tour where he played in two Tests. Educated at Weavers School, Wellingborough. Former Royal Marines musician who trained, on the French horn, at the Marines School of Music in Deal, where he played for Deal RFC. Works in the Marines recruiting office at Kensington.

CABANNES, Laurent (Flanker)
Born Reims, France, 06.02.64. 6'3", 14st 6lb. **Rep hons:** France (49, NZ90, 2t-8pts), Barbarians (90-91). **ADPR:** Harlequins (1996-98, 41, 3t-15pts). Former France flanker who moves from Harlequins. Originally played his rugby for Pau and Bordeaux University, joined Racing in 1986 and helped them to the 1987 French Championship final. Laurent then overcame a serious car accident and returned to help Racing to the 1990 Championship before making his international debut against New Zealand that November. Was an automatic choice until the autumn of 1995 when he was disciplined for arriving back late from South Africa, where he played for Western Province.

CHAPMAN, Dominic (Wing)
Born Kingston, 07.03.76. 5'9", 12st. **Rep hons:** England (1, Aus98), A (3, Fr98, 1t-5pts). **ADPR:** Harlequins (1996-97, 2, 4t-20pts), Richmond (1997-98, 17, 17t-85pts). Prolific try-scorer with exceptional pace and predatory instincts near the line. Logged 31 tries last season, including 23 in Premiership and Cup games. A product initially of the Esher club, he spent a year at Harlequins before finally flourishing at attack-minded Richmond. Was courted by Ireland before opting for England. Undertakes special sprint training with Margot Wells, wife and coach of former Olympic 100m champion Allan.

CLARKE, Benjamin Bevan (Backrow)
Born Bishop's Stortford, 15.04.68. 6'5", 17st 7lb. **Rep hons:** England (37, SA92, 3t-15pts), A (15, Sp91, 2t-8pts), Barbarians (90-91). **ADPR:** Saracens (1989-91, 22, 8t-32pts), Bath (1991-96, 61, 14t-68pts), Richmond (1996-98, 43, 14t-70pts). Captained Richmond to success in Courage League Two in 1996-97 and again skippered the side with authority last season, so much so that he earned a recall to the England squad for their summer tour when he was the squad's outstanding forward. Educated at Bishop's Stortford College and the Royal Agricultural College, Cirencester, Ben was another to benefit from the coaching of Tony Russ at Saracens and was already poised for England honours when he joined Bath in the summer of 1992. After a satisfactory debut against South Africa in 1992 he was outstanding at blindside wing forward for the Lions in New Zealand in 1993. In and out of the side ever since but a class backrow forward who commands respect.

CODLING, Alex (Lock)
Born Lewisham, 25.09.73. 6'6", 18st 3lb. **ADPR:** Blackheath (1994-96, 25, 1t-5pts), Richmond (1996-98, 21, 1t-5pts). Powerful young backup lock. Former England Schools and Colts representative.

CROMPTON, Darren Edward (Prop)
Born Exeter, 12.09.72. 6'1", 17st. **Rep hons:** England A (2, SA95, 1t-5pts). **ADPR:** Bath (1993-96, 6), Richmond (1996-98, 40, 1t-5pts). Rewarded for his excellent form after Christmas with a place on England's summer tour. Educated at Exeter College, Darren captained England 18 Group in 1991 and is a former England Schools and U21 captain. Represented England in the 1992 World Students Cup and toured Australia and Fiji with England A in 1995. Moved to Richmond in May 1996 from Bath, where first-team rugby often proved elusive.

CUSACK, Brian (Lock)
Born Waterford, Ireland, 11.07.72. 6'7", 16st. **Rep hons:** Ireland A (8, Fr97). **ADPR:** Bath (1996-98, 12, 1t-5pts). Struggled to make an impression at Bath last season. Educated at Clongowes Wood College and the Accountancy and Business College in Dublin. Played for Irish Youths for two years and made his Ireland U21 debut in 1993 before touring Zimbabwe, Namibia and South Africa with the Ireland Development XV.

CUTHBERT, Andrew Simon Jonathan (Hooker)
Born East Grinstead, 11.02.68. 5'10", 15st 7lb. **ADPR:** Richmond (1990-98, 58, 13t-65pts). Backup hooker to Barry Williams. Former England U21 and Students cap.

DAVIES, Adrian (Fly-half)
Born Bridgend, 09.02.69. 5'9", 12st. **Rep hons:** Wales (9, Barb90, 2c, 3pg, 3dg-22pts), A (8, Fr89, 2t, 8c, 15pg-71pts). **ADPR:** Richmond (1996-98, 30, 11t, 33c, 23pg, 2dg-196pts). Finished last season impressively despite struggling with a knee injury. Adrian signed for Richmond from Cardiff in May 1996 having amassed 846 points for Cardiff in the last four seasons of Heineken League rugby. After learning his rugby at Pencoed and Neath, he won four rugby Blues at Cambridge where he also represented the University at soccer. Sporadic international career since making his debut as a replacement against the Barbarians in 1990 but has been a member of Wales' RWC91 and 95 squads and toured Australia (91), Zimbabwe and Namibia (92), Canada and the South Pacific (94). Former member of the Mid Glamorgan Youth Orchestra and choir.

DAVIES, John David (Prop)
Born Carmarthen, 01.02.69. 6', 16st 7lb. **Rep hons:** Wales (34, Ire91, 1t-5pts), A (4, Hol90, 1t-5pts). **ADPR:** Richmond (1997-98, 21, 1t-5pts). Former Wales and Neath prop who has adapted well since moving to London and turning professional. Still a formidable scrummager, whose experience is invaluable.

DEANE, Mel (Centre)
Born London, 16.01.75. 5'10", 14st. **ADPR:** Richmond (1996-98, 4, 1t-5pts). Stocky reserve centre with exceptional pace off the mark.

GILLIES, Craig (Lock)
Born Manchester, 06.05.76. 6'9", 15st 7lb. **Rep hons:** England A (4, Fr98, 1t-5pts). **ADPR:** Richmond (1997-98, 21, 1t-5pts). Immensely promising line-out operator who has opted for England after resisting the overtures of the Scottish management. Originally came to prominence with Bath but has not looked back since joining Richmond. Narrowly missed out on selection for England's summer tour.

HUTTON, Robert John (Flanker)
Born London, 11.09.72. 6', 16st. **Rep hons:** England A (1, Ire98). **ADPR:** Richmond (1995-98, 10, 1t-5pts). Younger brother of former Richmond captain Michael and another product of St Benedict's, Ealing. Played rugby league at Nottingham University and has experimented playing hooker, but returned to his schoolboy international position of openside flanker in recent seasons.

McFARLAND, Dan (Prop)
Born Oxfordshire, 10.04.72. 6', 17st 5lb. **ADPR:** Morley (1994-96, 34, 1t-5pts), Richmond (1996-98, 24). Powerful loose head prop who has developed well since joining Richmond from Morley.

MOORE, Andrew Phillip (Scrum-half)
Born Cardiff, 06.09.68. 5'10", 12st 10lb. **Rep hons:** Wales (4, Jap95, 2t-10pts), A (9, SA96, 2t-10pts), Barbarians (96-97). **ADPR:** Richmond (1996-98, 36, 8t, 1pg, 1dg-46pts). Played well enough to hold off the challenge of Pichot for much of last season before breaking a hand and missing the final six weeks. Former Bridgend and Cardiff scrum-half who joined Richmond in tandem with his old Cardiff half-back colleague Adrian Davies. Educated at Llanishen, Andy scored the winning try for Oxford University in the 1990 Varsity Match, and was nominated as the man of the match after Cardiff's SWALEC Cup final victory over Llanelli (1994). Andrew scored a try on his international debut against Japan in Bloemfontein during RWC95. Played against South Africa in September 95 and against Fiji and Italy but has subsequently missed out since the emergence of Robert Howley.

PALMER, Corin (Flanker)
Born Farnborough, 11.08.67. 6'5", 17st 4lb. **ADPR:** Richmond (1994-98, 21, 2t-10pts). Experienced back five forward who has played for the Navy and Combined Services.

PICHOT, Agustin (Scrum-half)
Born Buenos Aires, Argentina, 22.08.74. 5'9", 12st. **Rep hons:** Argentina (13, Aus95, 3t-15pts), Barbarians (95-96). **ADPR:** Richmond (1997-98, 8). Made a startling impression at the end of last season when finally given an extended run in Richmond's starting line-up. Emerged from the formidable Argentinian Colts squad to initially make his name as an outstanding sevens player but won his first senior cap against Australia in 1995. Formerly with the San Isidro club in Buenos Aires.

PINI, Matthew James (Full-back)
Born Canberra, Australia, 21.03.69. 6', 14st 12lb. **Rep hons:** Australia (8, Ire94, 2t-10pts). **ADPR:** Richmond (1997-98, 22, 3t, 3c, 6pg, 1dg-42pts). Former Queensland and Australia full-back who showed that the Australians discarded his services too quickly. A fine attacking player and safe touch-kicker, Matt made an immediate impression in the Premiership.

QUINNELL, Jonathan Craig (Lock)
Born Swansea, 09.07.75. 6'6", 18st. **Rep hons:** Wales (6, Fiji95), Barbarians (96-97). **ADPR:** Richmond (1996-98, 39, 15t-75pts). Rumbustious young giant who can look world-class when the mood takes him, witness an astonishing match-winning performance against Newcastle in March. Arrived at Richmond from Llanelli with an impressive family pedigree that includes brother Scott, father Derek and uncle Barry John. Educated at Llandovery College, where he won schoolboy honours, Craig rocketed through the age-group levels and made his senior debut against Fiji in November 1995 at the age of 20.

QUINNELL, Leon Scott (No 8)
Born Swansea, 20.08.72. 6'4", 16st 8lb. **Rep hons:** Wales (18, Can93, 5t-25pts), A (1, Jap93, 1t-5pts), Barbarians (93-94). **ADPR:** Richmond (1996-98, 38, 31t-155pts). Scott endured a stop-start season, struggling with a groin injury after returning from the British Lions tour of South Africa. The son of Derek and nephew of Barry John, Scott played for Wales at all age-group levels, touring New Zealand in 1990 with the Schools and Canada in 1991 with the Youth before turning to senior rugby with Llanelli. Made his international debut against Canada (November 93) and played a starring role in the Welsh team that won the 1994 Five Nations, including the try of the tournament against France at Cardiff Arms Park. Returned to Welsh colours for the 1997 Five Nations. Scott also represented his country in the 1995 Rugby League World Cup.

VA'A, Earl Valentino (Fly-half)
Born Western Samoa, 01.05.72. 5'6", 13st. **Rep hons:** Western Samoa. **ADPR:** Richmond (1996-98, 22, 2t, 4c, 7pg-39pts). Stocky and immensely powerful fly-half who joined Richmond from Hutt Valley Dolphins RL. Raised in New Zealand, Earl played for Wellington Schools in 1989 before joining Wainuiomata RL and helping them to NZ championships in 1990 and 1992. Subsequently a member of the New Zealand RL sevens team, he also represented Western Samoa in the inaugural RL World Cup. Toured Britain and Ireland with the Manu Samoa squad in autumn of 1996.

VANDER, Adam (Flanker)
Born Turners Hill, Sussex, 27.01.74. 6'2", 15st 7lb. **ADPR:** Rosslyn Park (1994-96, 18, 5t-25pts), Richmond (1996-98, 22, 4t-20pts). Rapidly developing openside flanker whose good form, in concert with that of Robbie Hutton, persuaded Richmond they

could afford to release experienced Argentinian Rolando Martin. Educated at Millfield, Adam has previously played for Haywards Heath, Rosslyn Park and Bath before joining Richmond.

WALNE, Nicholas John (Wing)
Born Scunthorpe, 18.09.75. 6'3", 15st. **Rep hons:** Barbarians (98). Former Wales School, Youth and U21 cap who won three Cambridge Blues while at St Catharines College. Educated at Caerleon CS.

WHITFORD, Tom (Centre)
Born Birmingham, 15.09.71. 6', 14st 7lb. **Rep hons:** Barbarians (96-97). **ADPR:** Leeds (1994-95, 6, 1t-5pts), Richmond (1996-98, 6, 3t-15pts). Reliable centre who will provide valuable backup following the retirement of Michael Hutton and Steve Cottrell. A Cambridge Blue who has represented England Students and also played for Leeds and Northern Suburbs in Australia.

WILLIAMS, Barry Hugh (Hooker)
Born Carmarthen, 06.01.74. 5'11", 16st 6lb. **Rep hons:** Wales (8, Fr96, 2t-10pts), A (9, Ire94). **ADPR:** Richmond (1997-98, 21, 1t-5pts). Impressive Wales hooker who came back from the 1997 British Lions tour of South Africa a more mature player. Spent three years in the Wales Youth side, winning a record 13 caps, before making his full debut against France in September 1996, scoring a try within two minutes. With Garin Jenkins and Jonathan Humphreys still playing well, Barry has failed to make the Wales Test place his own but remains one for the future.

WRIGHT, Jason Anthony (Centre/wing)
Born 05.07.69. 6'2", 14st 9lb. **ADPR:** Richmond (1997-98, 15, 8t-40pts). New Zealand-born but England-qualified utility back who made a big impression when not injured last season, notably in his preferred position of centre. Originally from the Pirates club in Dunedin, Jason has played for Otago and New Zealand Universities.

REVIEW

Spluttered badly in mid-season but finished superbly, playing an exciting brand of rugby that should draw the crowds when they move to the Reading football stadium this season. Earlier in the season injuries had been a problem as the team lost confidence and flattered to deceive on too many occasions. Their away win in the Cup at Bath showed their true mettle and their grandstand finish started when they comprehensively defeated Newcastle despite having Scott Quinnell sent off after only 20 minutes. Ben Clarke again led the side well, and although Richmond's experienced internationals contributed fully it was the emerging talents of Craig Gillies, Dominic Chapman, Spencer Brown and Adam Vander that caught the eye. New South Wales centre Matt Dixon was a late summer signing.

RICHMOND in Premiership One 1997-98

Aug 23	H	London Irish	Won	32	12	A.Vander(2T) J.Wright(2T) S.Quinnell(T) A.Davies(2C, P)
Oct 8	A	Saracens	Lost	9	15	A.Davies(2P) M.Pini(D)
18	H	Harlequins	Won	37	16	A.Bateman(T) D.Chapman(T) R.Martin(T) C.Quinnell(T) E.Va'a(4C, 3P)
26	A	Newcastle	Lost	12	18	E.Va'a(4P)

Nov 1	A	Bath	Lost	31	47	J.Fallon(T) A.Bateman(T) S.Cottrell(T) J.Davies(T) S.Quinnell(T) S.Mason(3C)
Dec 13	A	Bristol	Won	13	12	J.Wright(2T) M.Pini(P)
16	H	Leicester	Won	32	15	S.Cottrell(T) C.Gillies(T) B.Clarke(T) D.Chapman(T) S.Quinnell(T) M.Pini(2C, P)
21	H	Northampton	Lost	21	24	D.Chapman(T) S.Quinnell(T) J.Wright(T) M.Pini(2P)
27	A	Gloucester	Lost	20	26	A.Bateman(T) J.Fallon(T) B.Williams(T) S.Mason(C, P)
30	A	Wasps	Lost	18	22	D.Chapman(2T) M.Pini(C, 2P)
Jan 17	A	London Irish	Won	45	14	D.Chapman(2T) A.Bateman(T) A.Moore(T) S.Quinnell(T) E.Va'a(T) A.Davies(3C, 3P)
31	H	Saracens	Lost	10	15	J.Fallon(T) A.Davies(C, P)
Feb 15	H	Sale	Lost	20	28	J.Fallon(T) A.Davies(5P)
Mar 7	A	Harlequins	Lost	12	41	A.Davies(T, C) R.Hutton(T)
14	H	Newcastle	Won	30	17	D.Chapman(T) A.Moore(T) C.Quinnell(T) J.Wright(T) A.Davies(2C, 2P)
28	A	Leicester	Lost	19	42	A.Bateman(2T) B.Brown(T) A.Davies(2C)
Apr 10	H	Bristol	Won	43	3	D.Chapman(3T) C.Quinnell(2T) A.Bateman(T) B.Brown(T) A.Davies(4C)
13	H	Bath	Won	32	14	B.Clarke(T) Penalty(T) S.Quinnell(T) E.Va'a(T) A.Davies(3C, 2P)
18	A	Northampton	Won	47	39	D.Chapman(2T) A.Bateman(T) B.Clarke(T) M.Pini(T) J.Wright(T) A.Davies(4C, 3P)
25	H	Gloucester	Won	33	22	D.Chapman(2T) Penalty(T) S.Quinnell(T) J.Wright(T) A.Davies(4C)
May 2	H	Wasps	Won	51	29	B.Brown(2T) A.Davies(2T, 4C, P) M.Pini(2T) B.Clarke(T) S.Quinnell(T)
17	A	Sale	Won	40	28	D.Chapman(2T) S.Quinnell(2T) J.Fallon(T) A.Davies(3C, 3P)

Summary of Premiership scorers:

150 – A.Davies (3T, 33C, 23P); 85 – S.Mason (T, 16C, 16P), D.Chapman (17T); 50 – S.Quinnell (10T); 42 – M.Pini (3T, 3C, D, 6P); 40 – J.Wright (8T), A.Bateman (8T); 39 – E.Va'a (2T, 4C, 7P); 25 – J.Fallon (5T); 20 – C.Quinnell (4T), B.Brown (4T); 15 – B.Clarke (3T); 10 – A.Vander (2T), A.Moore (2T), S.Cottrell (2T), Penalty (2T); 5 – B.Williams (T), R.Martin (T), R.Hutton (T), C.Gillies (T), J.Davies (T).

Summary of Premiership appearances:

22 – M.Pini, B.Clarke; 21 – B.Williams (+2), C.Gillies, J.Davies (+4);
20 – C.Quinnell (+1), D.Crompton (+7), A.Bateman; 18 – S.Quinnell;
17 – D.Chapman; 16 – E.Va'a (+6), D.McFarland (+3); 15 – J.Wright (+2);
14 – A.Moore (+1), A.Davies; 13 – R.Martin (+2); 12 – A.Codling (+10), B.Brown;
11 – A.Vander (+4); 10 – S.Mason (+2); 9 – R.Hutton (+3), J.Fallon; 8 – A.Pichot,
S.Cottrell; 5 – C.Palmer (+4), M.Hutton, B.Harvey (+4), A.Cuthbert (+2);
3 – M.Deane (+2); 2 – P.Carr (+1); 1 – T.Whitford (+1), R.West, J.Foster, S.Barlow.

SARACENS

Formation of club: 1876
Ground: Vicarage Road, Watford, Herts WD1 8ER
Capacity: 22,000 (all seated)
Colours: Black, red star and crescent
Honours: Cup Winners – 1998. Division Two Champions – 1988-89 and 1994-95
Best League finish: 2nd in Premiership One 1997-98
Last season: ADP1 – Runners-up. Tetley's Bitter Cup – Winners
Owner: Nigel Wray (Leisure/property entrepreneur)
Player/Coach: Francois Pienaar
Captain: Tony Diprose

BENNETT, Alex (Flanker)
Born Lewisham, 18.01.75. 6'3", 17st 6lb. **Rep hons:** England A (1, Ire98). **ADPR:**
Otley (1994-95, 4), Orrell (1995-97, 21, 4t-20pts), Saracens (1997-98, 10). Underrated
former Orrell flanker who gave a good account of himself whenever called upon last
season. Educated at Carnegie College and Manchester Metropolitan University, Alex
played for Otley before joining Orrell. A member of the England squad at the 1996
World Students Cup.

BOTTERMAN, Greg Richard (Hooker)
Born Welwyn Garden City, 03.03.68. 5'11", 15st 6lb. **ADPR:** Saracens (1989-98, 94,
5t-25pts). Former Datchworth and Bacavians hooker who was a bench reserve for
England in their Grand Slam game against Scotland in 1995. Made his club debut
back in 1988. Educated at Alleyne's, Stevenage, Greg is a director of a glassware
manufacturing company.

BRACKEN, Kyran Paul Patrick (Scrum-half)
Born Dublin, 22.11.71. 5'11", 13st 3lb. **Rep hons:** England (19, NZ93, 2t-10pts), A (6,
BritCol93, 3t-15pts), Barbarians (94). **ADPR:** Bristol (1991-96, 47, 7t-35pts), Saracens (1996-98, 33, 3t-15pts). Bothered by injury for much of the season but in
devastating form in many of Saracens' key matches. Kyran was forced to miss
England's summer tour in order to rest his shoulder. Burst onto the international
scene with a courageous performance against New Zealand in 1993 when he
overcame a painful ankle injury, courtesy of Jamie Joseph's reckless stamp. A regular
for England throughout the 1995 Five Nations, he lost his place to Dewi Morris in
RWC95 and then lost out to Matt Dawson in 1995-96 season after playing against
South Africa in November. Educated at Stonyhurst, Lancashire, and originally
capped by England 16 Group at fly-half.

CHUTER, George (Hooker)
Born Greenwich, 09.07.76. 5'10", 15st 4lb. **Rep hons:** England A (4, Fr98, 1t-5pts).
ADPR: Saracens (1997-98, 21, 1t-5pts). Tough young Londoner who enjoyed a marvellous debut season with Saracens, establishing himself as first-choice hooker and winning a summer tour place with England. Educated at Trinity School, Croydon, George missed out on schoolboy honours but was capped by England Colts. Joined Saracens from his junior club, Old Mid-Whitgiftians.

CONSTABLE, Ryan (Centre/wing)
Born Durban, South Africa, 20.10.71. 6', 13st. **Rep hons:** Australia (1, Ire94). **ADPR:** Saracens (1997-98, 22, 4t-20pts). Former Australia Sevens captain with a devastating burst of pace who made an immediate impact with Saracens during his first season. Australia must be very strong indeed to ignore his blossoming talent. South African-born, moved to Australia with his family when he was 12. Studying for a Bachelor of Business degree in Marketing.

DANIEL, Brendon Wiremu (Wing)
Born New Zealand, 19.07.77. 6'1", 14st 4lb. **ADPR:** Saracens (1997-98, 15, 4t-20pts). Powerful young wing with an excellent pedigree, having been a member of New Zealand's U19 and Academy sides and a member of the All Blacks' renowned sevens squad. Caught Saracens' eye when starring for the Barbarians in the 1997 Middlesex Sevens and did well in his first season of senior rugby. English-qualified after his marriage to an English girl.

DIPROSE, Anthony James (Backrow)
Born Orsett, 22.09.72. 6'5", 17st 8lb. **Rep hons:** England (10, Arg97, 1t-5pts), A (20, Ire94, 5t-25pts). **ADPR:** Saracens (1992-98, 100, 17t-85pts). Took over from the injured Matt Dawson as England captain against Australia in June, a game he will never forget, for the wrong reasons. Remarkably, Saracens' captain did not miss a single minute of Premiership rugby last season. Educated at Campion School, Hornchurch, he graduated from Loughborough University with a BSc in PE and Recreation Management and made his England A debut against Ireland in 1994, being voted the RFU young player of the year that season. Toured Australia with England U21 in 1993 and captained England A to an unbeaten season in 1995-96.

FREE, Bradley John (Scrum-half)
Born Australia 10.06.71. 5'10", 12st 4lb. **Rep hons:** Ireland A (1, Can97). **ADPR:** Saracens (1997-98, 5). Irish-qualified Australian whose season was disrupted by a serious leg injury. Former Australia U21 and Queensland representative who spent a year in Ireland in 1993, playing for Longford.

GRAU, Roberto Diego (Prop)
Born Argentina, 16.07.70. 5'11", 17st. **Rep hons:** Argentina (17, Jap93, 2t-10pts). **ADPR:** Saracens (1997-98, 16). One of the game's most respected scrummagers, who has played for Brive in France and Gauteng Lions in South Africa as well as home club Liceo. Toured England with Argentina in 1996, helping the squad win five of their seven games and playing in the Test team beaten 20-18 by England. His late brother was captain of the Argentina Youth team 1992 and an Argentinian reserve later that year. Roberto missed out on the 1995 World Cup, when Argentina's front row was universally recognised as the best in the tournament, but looks a certainty for RWC99.

GREWCOCK, Daniel Jonathan (Lock)
Born Coventry, 07.11.72. 6'6", 17st 7lb. **Rep hons:** England (7, Arg97, 1t-5pts), A (1, SA96), Barbarians (96-97). **ADPR:** Coventry (1994-97, 33, 3t-15pts), Saracens (1997-98, 21). Immense line-out presence and an athletic performer in the loose last season. Danny was arguably the most improved player in the Premiership, building on an

already promising career forged at Coventry, from where he won his first England cap during their tour of Argentina in 1997. During the summer he was sent off in England's first Test against New Zealand for allegedly stamping on an opponent as a scrummage broke up. Educated at Woodlands School and Crewe & Alsager College, Danny was at Barkers Butts for five years before moving to Coventry.

HILL, Richard Anthony (Flanker)
Born Dormansland, 23.05.73. 6'2", 15st 8lb. **Rep hons:** England (11, Sc97, 3t-15pts), A (8, It95, 3t-15pts), Barbarians (94). **ADPR:** Saracens (1993-98, 66, 13t-65pts). Returns to action after an operation on a long-standing back injury. Clever, constructive and hard-tackling openside flanker who played a conspicuous part in the 1997 British Lions success in South Africa. Richard was educated at Stratford Castle Primary and Bishop Wordsworth School. An outstanding Schools international, he completed his education at Brunel University which now incorporates that well-known rugby nursery West London Institute. Represented England A against Western Samoa in December 1995 and New South Wales in January 1996, before finally receiving the call at senior level in 1997.

JOHNS, Patrick Stephen (Lock)
Born Portadown, 19.02.68. 6'6", 16st 10lb. **Rep hons:** Ireland (43, Arg90, 2t-10pts), A (3, Sc89, 1t-5pts), Barbarians (93-94). **ADPR:** Saracens (1997-98, 37, 2t-10pts). Ended a superb season by being appointed as Ireland's captain in Keith Wood's absence, though the Quins hooker was, eventually, able to tour South Africa. Stalwart lock for club and country who can also double up at No 8 when required. Johns was educated at the Royal School, Dungannon, from where he won schoolboy honours. He played University rugby for Dublin and Newcastle and has appeared regularly for Ulster since 1988. First capped against Argentina in 1990, he next appeared for his country two years later on tour in New Zealand. Regular thereafter, including three appearances in RWC95, but lost his place after a heavy defeat in Paris in 1996. Returned in 1997 and has been a model of consistency ever since.

JOHNSON, Gavin Keith (Full-back/wing)
Born Louis Trichardt, South Africa, 17.10.66. 6'2", 12st 8lb. **Rep hons:** South Africa (7, Arg93, 5t, 14c, 11pg-86pts). **ADPR:** Saracens (1997-98, 14, 2t, 4c, 8pg, 1dg-45pts). Laid-back South African who rediscovered his best form late in the season, so much so he has delayed his decision to retire. Scored a record 22 points on his South Africa debut in 1993 when the Springboks beat Argentina 52-23. Learned his rugby with Pretoria Harlequins and the Pirates club in Johannesburg. A member of South Africa's World Cup-winning squad in 1995.

LEE, Andrew John (Fly-half)
Born Wanstead, 10.11.68. 5'9", 13st 7lb. **ADPR:** Saracens (1989-98, 66, 8t, 27c, 49pg, 16dg-288pts). Talented club stalwart who let nobody down when Michael Lynagh was incapacitated with his cancer scare late in the season. Educated at Chigwell School, Andy is a supreme all-rounder, having represented his country at three sports. Played cricket with Nasser Hussain and Graham Thorpe for England U19 and still plays in the Essex League for Woodford. Also played for England Schools soccer and West Ham Youth despite 'not really liking football'. A former captain of West London Institute.

OLSEN, Marcus James (Scrum-half)
Born Salisbury, 23.06.72. 5'7", 11st 11lb. **ADPR:** Bath (1993-95, 4), Saracens (1996-98, 9, 4t-20pts). Deputised superbly for Kyran Bracken when called upon. A practising aromatherapist, Marcus learned his rugby with the Salisbury club and has represented England Colts and U21. Played for Llandovery and Welsh Universities while studying at Cardiff Institute of Higher Education.

PENAUD, Alain (Fly-half)
Born Juillac, France, 19.7.69. 5'11", 14st. **Rep hons:** France (30, Wal92, 8t, 5pg-52pts). Mercurial French playmaker who has represented France at fly-half and full-back during a stop-go international career in which he never quite fulfilled his potential. His finest moment was probably during the 1996-97 season when he captained and inspired Brive to a spectacular success in the Heineken European Cup, their uninhibited 28-9 demolition of favourites Leicester in the final being one of the most impressive club performances in recent history. Saracens' hope, and gamble, is that Penaud will rediscover that form.

PIENAAR, Jacobus Francois (Flanker)
Born Vereeniging, South Africa, 02.01.67. 6'3", 17st. **Rep hons:** South Africa (29, Fr93, 3t-15pts). **ADPR:** Saracens (1996-98, 30, 10t-50pts). Outstandingly successful in his first full season as player-coach but Pienaar will not rest until Saracens win the Premiership. Captained Transvaal to successive Currie Cup wins in 1993 and 1994, and also led them to victory in the 1993 Super Ten and an excellent 24-21 win over England the following year. Captained South Africa on his debut in 1993 against France in Durban, becoming only the third Springbok to be honoured in such a way – the others being Basil Kenyon and Des van Jaarsveld – and famously led the rainbow nation to the 1995 World Cup at Ellis Park. Unceremoniously dumped later the following year by Andre Markgraaff.

RAVENSCROFT, Stephen Charles Wood (Centre)
Born Bradford, 02.11.70. 5'11", 14st 2lb. **Rep hons:** England (2, Aus98), A (2, Fr98). **ADPR:** Saracens (1990-98, 92, 9t-45pts). Loyal and underrated Saracens stalwart who blossomed under the influence of Philippe Sella and Michael Lynagh – so much so that he was called into the England tour party and named in their side to play Australia in their opening Test. Educated at Bradford GS, Steve previously played for Otley and Bradford and Bingley before joining Saracens. Played Provincial U21 rugby for North Harbour during a prolonged stay in New Zealand and represented England in 1992 World Students Cup.

REIDY, Brendan Philip (Prop)
Born Apia, Western Samoa, 13.09.70. 6'1", 17st. **Rep hons:** Western Samoa (9), Barbarians (95-96). **ADPR:** Saracens (1996-98, 16, 1t-5pts). Western Samoan international prop who has been flirting with a switch to hooker. Appeared in the 1995 World Cup for Samoa. Brendan has played much of his rugby in New Zealand for the Marist St Pats club and Wellington Lions.

ROCQUES, Anthony William Seymour (Flanker)
Born Bromley, 07.09.78. 6'2", 14st. **ADPR:** Saracens (1997-98, 4). Came of age during Saracens' championship run-in when he had to deputise for Francois Pienaar, notably in the drawn game at Leicester. Educated at Sevenoaks School and a former captain of England Schools, for whom he starred during their 1997 tour of Australia.

SINGER, Matthew James (Full-back)
Born Bristol, 07.11.72. 6'6", 13st 5lb. **ADPR:** Saracens (1995-98, 27, 5t, 2c, 1pg-32pts). Talented utility back who won Blues at Cambridge in 1995 and 1996, scoring two tries on his second appearance at the Twickenham showpiece occasion. Educated at Wycliffe College, Stonehouse, and Bristol University, Matt has also played for Neath and Racing Club Narbonne. Called briefly into the Wales squad last season before opting for England.

SORRELL, Kevin James (Centre)
Born Harold Wood, 06.03.77. 6', 12st 8lb. **ADPR:** Saracens (1996-98, 5, 1t-5pts). Another product of Campion School, Kevin played his early club rugby for Upminster. Formerly a member of school barber-shop singing group.

THOMPSON, David Paul Charles (Full-back)
Born 08.02.78. 5'11", 12st 8lb. **ADPR:** Saracens (1997-98, 7, 1t-5pts). Promising former Millfield Schoolboy and England Colts captain.

WALLACE, Paul Stephen (Prop)
Born Cork, 30.12.71. 6'1", 16st. **Rep hons:** Ireland (20, Jap95, 2t-10pts), A (4, Eng95, 1t-5pts). **ADPR:** Saracens (1996-98, 42, 6t-30pts). Many people's player of the year, Paul was an immense figure for Saracens and Ireland last season, despite his strenuous efforts on behalf of the British Lions in South Africa the previous summer. Educated at Crescent College, Limerick, Paul was an exceptional Schools international in 1989 and 1990 and has made smooth progress towards a place in the full Ireland side. Made his senior debut against Japan in RWC95 and has grown in stature ever since. Brother of Ireland wing Richard and promising Ireland A flanker David Wallace.

WALLACE, Richard Mark (Wing)
Born Cork, 16.01.68. 5'11", 14st. **Rep hons:** Ireland (29, Nam91, 5t-23pts), A (9, Sc90, 4t-20pts), Barbarians (91-92). **ADPR:** Saracens (1996-98, 33, 17t-85pts). Hard-running wing with well-developed try-scoring instincts. Educated at St Francis Capuchine College, Cork, and Cork Regional Technical College, Richard made his senior debut as a replacement against Namibia. Ever-present for Ireland in the 1992-93 season, Richard was called into the 1993 British Lions tour of New Zealand as a replacement. Also performed well in 1993-94 international season until he broke his leg and missed the 1994 tour to Australia. Returned against Wales in March 1995 and played in all 1995 World Cup games until losing his place for the quarter-final against France. Keen yachtsman who represented Ireland in the European Junior Laser championships.

REVIEW

An amazing season at Saracens where Francois Pienaar's side won the Tetley's Bitter Cup, took Newcastle to the wire in the Championship and took their home gates from 6,000 to 20,000. Michael Lynagh and Philippe Sella, who both retired after the final game, against Northampton, both contributed hugely but Saracens boasted strength in depth. Roberto Grau, Ryan Constable, Danny Grewcock, Tony Diprose and Paul Wallace were also massively influential, along with player-coach Francois Pienaar. Alain Penaud has been signed to replace Lynagh – further big signings are almost inevitable – and an exciting future is in prospect at Vicarage Road.

SARACENS in Premiership One 1997-98

Aug 24	A	Sale	Won	19	10	T.Diprose(T) M.Lynagh(C, 4P)
Oct 8	H	Richmond	Won	15	9	M.Lynagh(5P)
19	A	Wasps	Won	19	15	R.Constable(T) M.Lynagh(C, 4P)
26	H	Gloucester	Won	42	24	P.Sella(T) M.Lynagh(T, 4C, 3P) G.Botterman(T) P.Wallace(T) G.Chuter(T)
Nov 2	H	Bristol	Won	31	9	M.Lynagh(2T, 3C) F.Pienaar(T) M.Singer(T) D.Thompson(T)
8	A	Northampton	Won	19	13	R.Constable(T) M.Lynagh(T, 3P)

Dec 14	H	Bath	Won	50	23	G.Johnson(2T) R.Wallace(2T) B.Daniel(T) S.Ravenscroft(T) M.Lynagh(4C, 4P)
	26	H	Leicester	Lost	21	22	R.Constable(T) R.Wallace(T) M.Lynagh(C, D, 2P)
	30	A	London Irish	Won	25	10	R.Constable(T) B.Daniel(T) M.Lynagh(T, 2C, 2P)
Jan 11	H	Harlequins	Won	25	16	Penalty(T) M.Lynagh(C, 6P)
	31	A	Richmond	Won	15	10	T.Diprose(2T) M.Lynagh(C, P)
Feb 14	A	Bristol	Won	37	20	R.Wallace(3T) K.Bracken(T) P.Sella(T) M.Lynagh(3C, 2P)
	24	H	Sale	Won	42	20	A.Olver(T) Penalty(T) F.Pienaar(T) B.Sturnham(T) S.Ravenscroft(T) M.Lynagh(4C, 2P) G.Johnson(D)
Mar 8	H	Wasps	Won	33	27	M.Olsen(T) Penalty(T) M.Singer(T) M.Lynagh(3C, 4P)
	15	A	Gloucester	Lost	15	38	F.Pienaar(2T) M.Lynagh(C, P)
	25	A	Newcastle	Lost	25	30	T.Diprose(T) M.Lynagh(C, 6P)
Apr 10	A	Bath	Won	29	13	F.Pienaar(T) R.Wallace(T) M.Lynagh(2C, 5P)
	19	H	Newcastle	Won	12	10	M.Lynagh(D, 3P)
	25	A	Leicester	Drew	10	10	A.Lee(T) G.Johnson(C, P)
	29	A	Harlequins	Won	28	26	S.Ravenscroft(T) T.Copsey(T) B.Reidy(T) G.Johnson(2C, 3P)
May 3	H	London Irish	Won	29	21	B.Daniel(2T) B.Sturnham(T) G.Johnson(C, 4P)
	14	H	Northampton	Won	43	20	M.Olsen(2T) T.Diprose(T) F.Pienaar(T) S.Ravenscroft(T) R.Wallace(T) M.Lynagh(5C, P)

Summary of Premiership scorers:

279 – M.Lynagh (5T, 37C, 2D, 58P); 45 – G.Johnson (2T, 4C, D, 8P);
40 – R.Wallace (8T); 30 – F.Pienaar (6T); 25 – T.Diprose (5T); 20 – S.Ravenscroft
(4T), B.Daniel (4T), R.Constable (4T); 15 – M.Olsen (3T), Penalty (3T);
10 – B.Sturnham (2T), M.Singer (2T), P.Sella (2T); 5 – P.Wallace (T), D.Thompson
(T), B.Reidy (T), A.Olver (T), A.Lee (T), T.Copsey (T), G.Chuter (T), K.Chesney
(T), K.Bracken (T), G.Botterman (T).

Summary of Premiership appearances:

22 – P.Wallace (+1), T.Diprose, R.Constable (+2); 21 – S.Ravenscroft, D.Grewcock,
G.Chuter (+6); 19 – F.Pienaar, M.Lynagh; 18 – P.Johns (+2); 17 – M.Singer (+4);
16 – R.Grau (+1); 15 – B.Daniel (+1); 14 – P.Sella, G.Johnson (+2), K.Bracken
(+1); 13 – R.Wallace (+1), B.Reidy (+2); 12 – B.Sturnham (+4); 11 – A.Olver (+10);
10 – A.Bennett (+2); 9 – A.Lee (+6), T.Copsey (+2), G.Botterman (+3);
7 – D.Thompson (+4), M.Olsen (+3); 6 – R.Hill; 5 – B.Free, K.Chesney (+1);
4 – T.Rocques (+1); 2 – M.Powell (+2); 1 – K.Sorrell.

WASPS

Formation of club: 1867
Ground: Loftus Road Stadium, South Africa Road, Shepherd's Bush, London W12 7PA.
Capacity: 19,000 (all seated)
Colours: Black with gold wasp
Honours: League Champions (2) – 1989-90, 1996-97
Best Cup run: Losing finalist 1985-86, 1986-87, 1994-95 and 1997-98
Last season: ADP1 – 9th. Heineken European Cup – Q/F (lost 18-25 to Brive).
Tetley's Bitter Cup – Losing finalist
Owner: Chris Wright (Chrysalis Records)
Coach: Nigel Melville
Captain: Lawrence Dallaglio

BEARDSHAW, Joe (Lock)
Born 30.10.76. 6'5", 17st. **ADPR:** Wasps (1997-98, 1). A student at Loughborough University, having previously studied at Gresham's School, Holt. Represented England 16 and 18 Group before touring Australia with England U21 in 1997.

CRONIN, Damian Francis (Lock)
Born Wegberg, West Germany, 17.04.63. 6'6", 17st 8lb. **Rep hons:** Scotland (45, Ire88, 5t-23pts), A (7, Sp90, 3t-15pts), Barbarians (87-88). **ADPR:** Bath (1987-91, 21, 3t-12pts), London Scottish (1991-94, 29, 4t-19pts), Wasps (1996-98, 28, 1t-5pts). Formerly with Bath and London Scottish, Damian has overcome serious knee and spine injuries to pursue his rugby career. Was an outstanding member of Scotland's Grand Slam-winning side in 1990, and although his appearances were restricted in RWC91 he contributed fully to their World Cup campaign in 1995. Moved to Wasps from Bourges, France, in July 1996.

DALLAGLIO, Lawrence Bruno Nero (Flanker)
Born Shepherd's Bush, 10.08.72. 6'4", 15st 7lb. **Rep hons:** England (20, SA95, 5t-25pts), A (4, Fr94), Barbarians (95-96). **ADPR:** Wasps (1993-98, 82, 13t-65pts). Took a much-needed break to rest a chronic shoulder problem over the summer. Lawrence captained England in all their eight internationals last winter as well as leading Wasps throughout a difficult domestic campaign. Educated at Ampleforth College, where he starred in their sevens team that won the Open and Festival tournaments at Rosslyn Park (1989), Lawrence missed out on England Schools honours but has been capped at every other age-group level, and represented England when they won the RWC Sevens at Murrayfield (1993). Toured South Africa with England in 1994, missed out on the 1995 World Cup but returned to the Republic in 1997 with the Lions.

DENNEY, Mark Christian Alexander (Centre)
Born Epping Forest, 25.07.75. 5'11", 15st 11lb. **ADPR:** Bedford (1992-93, 2), Bristol (1993-97, 40, 4t-20pts), Wasps (1998, 6). Former Bedford Modern schoolboy who joined the club from Bristol after obtaining a Blue at Cambridge. Mark spent two seasons in the England Schools' 18 Group team, captaining the side in his final year.

FRIDAY, Michael (Scrum-half)
Born 25.04.72. 5'9", 12st 1lb. **ADPR:** Blackheath (1993-97, 64, 19t-95pts), Wasps (1997-98, 12, 5t-25pts). Live-wire scrum-half and sevens specialist who deputised well in Gomarsall's absence.

GOMARSALL, Andrew Charles Thomas (Scrum-half)
Born Durham, 24.07.74. 5'10", 13st 8lb. **Rep hons:** England (6, It96, 4t-20pts), A (10, SAus95, 6t-30pts), Barbarians (94-95). **ADPR:** Wasps (1994-98, 49, 12t-60pts). Last

season was ruined by the need for a back operation but Andy is back to full fitness and anxious to challenge for England honours again. A product of Bedford School, he captained England Schools to their first Grand Slam in 11 years in 1992 but had to wait patiently for regular first-team rugby at Wasps while Steve Bates was in residence.

GREEN, William Robert (Prop)
Born Littlehampton, 25.10.73. 5'11", 17st 4lb. **Rep hons:** England (2, Aus97), A (2, Wal98). **ADPR:** Wasps (1995-98, 41, 4t-20pts). Powerful scrummager, capped by England Schools and U21 before touring Argentina with the full squad in 1997. Capped by Clive Woodward against Australia in November 1997, he then struggled with injury but returned in time to book a place on England's summer visit to the southern hemisphere. Educated at Eastbourne College.

GREENSTOCK, Nicholas James Jeremy (Centre/wing)
Born Dubai,United Arab Emirates, 03.11.73. 6'3", 15st. **Rep hons:** England (4, Arg97, 2t-10pts), A (11, Ire95, 1t-5pts), Barbarians (94). **ADPR:** Wasps (1993-98, 58, 17t-85pts). Last season was badly disrupted by a recurring shoulder problem but Nick should have benefited from a summer's rest. Educated at Sherborne, where he won England Schools honours, Nick made a massive impact during the 1994-95 season when he was voted the RFU young player of the season after figuring prominently for England A, U21 and Emerging England, the Barbarians and the England Seven at Hong Kong. Scored a try on his international debut against Argentina in Buenos Aires. Graduated from Royal Holloway College with a BA (Hons) in Geography and now works as a PR consultant for Christow in London.

HENDERSON, Robert Alexander James (Centre)
Born Dover, 27.10.72. 6'1", 15st 4lb. **Rep hons:** Ireland (7, WS96), A (2, Wal96, 1t-5pts), Barbarians (96-97). **ADPR:** London Irish (1993-97, 56, 22t-110pts), Wasps (1996-98, 22, 4t-20pts). Former London Irish centre who was troubled by a groin injury for much of last season, Rob rediscovered fitness and form in the latter stages and toured South Africa with Ireland. Benefited greatly from the coaching of Clive Woodward while at London Irish. Originally a footballer, Rob was asked to 'make up' the numbers when Kingston found themselves short and hasn't looked back since. Educated at Tiffin and St Mary's, Teddington, he qualifies for Ireland via his mother who comes from Wexford, though Scotland will be distressed to hear his father hails from north of the border.

HOPLEY, Damian Paul (Centre/wing)
Born Lambeth, London, 12.04.70. 6'2", 15st 2lb. **Rep hons:** England (3, WS95), A (23, Aus90, 3t-14pts), Barbarians (94-95). **ADPR:** Wasps (1990-98, 46, 20t-96pts). Has now missed two seasons with a complicated knee ligament injury that has required countless operations. Blockbusting centre/wing and famously good-natured tourist, having visited Australia, Fiji and South Africa with England and New Zealand with England B. After studying theology at St Andrew's University, he won a Blue at Cambridge and was an outstanding member of the England Seven which unexpectedly took the inaugural RWC crown at Murrayfield in 1993. Finally won a full England cap as a replacement against Western Samoa in RWC95. Brilliant pianist, look out also for his rendition of 'Flower of Scotland' using a bar stool as a bagpipe.

IONS, Jonathan Alexis (Flanker)
Born Wakefield, 12.12.76. 6'2", 15st. **ADPR:** West Hartlepool (1995-97, 23, 4t-20pts), Wasps (1997-98, 4, 1t-10pts). Former England Schools captain who provides valuable backrow backup. Educated at Bradford GS and Durham University.

JAMES, Aaron Gordon (Centre)
Born Otautau, New Zealand, 20.09.67. 6′, 13st. **ADPR:** Wasps (1994-98, 23, 1t-5pts).
Former Southland utility back who played against England B (92) and the British
Lions (93).

KING, Alexander David (Fly-half)
Born Brighton, 17.01.75. 6′, 13st 4lb. **Rep hons:** England (1, Arg97, 1t-5pts), A (8,
WS95, 1t, 12c, 13pg, 2dg-74pts), Barbarians (95-96). **ADPR:** Rosslyn Park (1993-96,
7, 2t, 9c, 14pg-70pts), Wasps (1996-98, 32, 5t, 2c, 1pg, 5dg-47pts). Yet another Wasps
back who suffered injury last season, spending over three months on the sidelines
after knee surgery. Returned to mastermind Wasps' Pilkington Cup run and win a
place on England's tour. Originally came to prominence playing for the South West in
the CIS Divisional championship, while a student at Bristol University. Educated at
Brighton College and previously with Rosslyn Park.

LEOTA, Trevor H. (Hooker)
Born Western Samoa, 08.02.75. 5′10″, 17st 4lb. **Rep hons:** Western Samoa. **ADPR:**
Wasps (1997-98, 18, 2t-10pts). Popular hard-tackling Western Samoan hooker.

LEWSEY, Josh (Utility back)
Born Bromley, 30.11.76. 5′10″, 12st 7lb. **Rep hons:** England (3, NZ98). **ADPR:** Bristol
(1996-98, 27, 7t, 1c, 3pg-46pts). Joins Wasps from Bristol after a well publicised
disagreement at the end of last season when he opted to revise for university
examinations rather than appear in their play-off games against London Scottish.
Surprise choice for England's southern hemisphere tour but did as well as any back,
impressing with his strength and tackling. Educated at Watford GS and Bristol
University.

LOGAN, Kenneth McKerrow (Wing)
Born Stirling, 03.04.72. 6′1″, 14st 8lb. **Rep hons:** Scotland (33, Aus92, 7t-35pts), A (8,
Sp92, 4t-20pts), Barbarians (94-95). **ADPR:** Wasps (1996-98, 23, 15t, 1c-77pts).
Missed Scotland's summer tour of Australia and Fiji to undergo an ankle operation.
Kenny endured a tough season after blazing such an auspicious trail in Wasps'
championship-winning season. Logan was the first player out of Stirling County to
be capped when he played full-back in the second Test against Australia in 1992. He
then played in 20 consecutive games, on the wing, before he was dropped for the 1996
Five Nations internationals against Ireland and France. Ever-present in the 1995
World Cup in South Africa. A former pupil of Wallace HS in Stirling.

MITCHELL, Simon John (Hooker)
Born Saltburn, 23.11.65. 5′10″, 16st. **Rep hons:** England A (1, SA96), Barbarians (94).
ADPR: West Hartlepool (1987-95, 82, 6t-28pts), Harlequins (1994-96, 14, 1t-5pts),
Wasps (1996-98, 36, 4t-20pts). Moved from West Hartlepool to Harlequins early in
1995 to successfully challenge Brian Moore at hooker before transferring to Wasps.
Educated at Sacred Heart Comprehensive, Redcar.

MOLLOY, Darren (Prop)
Born Middlesex, 31.08.72. 6′2″, 17st. **Rep hons:** England A (1, Fr98). **ADPR:** Wasps
(1991-98, 67, 1t-5pts). Powerful young prop. Started at Old Gaytonians and also
played for London Irish before joining Wasps. Toured Australia with England U21 in
1993.

REED, Andrew Ian (Lock)
Born St Austell, 04.05.69. 6′7″, 17st 10lb. **Rep hons:** Scotland (15, Ire93), A (1, Ire92).
ADPR: Camborne (1988-89, 11, 2t-8pts), Plymouth Albion (1989-90, 10), Bath
(1990-95, 24), Wasps (1996-98, 32, 2t-10pts). Educated at Bodmin Comp, Bristol
Polytechnic and Cheshire College of Agriculture, Andy arrived at the Recreation

Ground via Bodmin, Camborne, Plymouth Albion and England Colts but soon used his Scottish ancestry to win international honours for Scotland. Toured New Zealand with 1993 British Lions, playing in the first Test. A member of Cornwall's County Championship-winning side in 1991 and a former Cornwall Schools goalkeeper.

REES, Gareth Lloyd (Full-back)
Born Duncan, Canada, 30.06.67. 6', 14st 8lb. **Rep hons:** Canada (43, US86, 7t, 28c, 78pg, 7dg-343pts), , Barbarians (92-93). **ADPR:** Wasps (1996-98, 41, 4t, 79c, 120pg, 3dg-547pts). Goal-kicking Canadian who remains as prolific, and consistent, as ever. Fitness and form permitting, there is every chance that he will captain Canada in the 1999 World Cup and become the only player in history to play in all four World Cups. Prior to arriving at Wasps, Gareth had experienced club rugby with Merignac in France and enjoyed spells with Oxford University and Newport. Educated at Harrow, Gareth represented Wasps in the 1986 Pilkington Cup final as a schoolboy and later that year made his Canadian debut at fly-half against USA. Has been fundamental to their cause ever since playing in all ten World Cup matches in RWC 1987, 1991 and 1995.

ROISER, Shane Maurice (Wing)
Born London, 07.06.73. 5'9", 13st. **ADPR:** Rosslyn Park (1992-94, 26, 10t-50pts), Wasps (1994-98, 60, 18t-90pts). One of the quickest wings around, Shane learned his rugby at Trinity Whitgift and played for Rosslyn Park before joining Wasps.

SAMPSON, Paul Christian (Full-back/wing)
Born Wakefield, 12.07.77. 5'10", 11st 10lb. **Rep hons:** England (1, SA98), A (2, Arg96), Barbarians (97-98). **ADPR:** Otley (1995-96, 2), Wasps (1996-98, 21, 7t-35pts). Failed to gain a regular First XV spot but Paul remains one of the brightest prospects in English rugby and earned a late England call-up for the final Test of their southern hemisphere tour against South Africa. Probably the quickest player in the British game, Paul posted a startling 10.48 seconds to win the 1996 English Schools 100m Championship in Sheffield and intends to combine both athletics and rugby. Came to prominence with Woodhouse Grove School in 1994-95, playing in all six internationals for England 18 Group, including a famous 30-3 win over Australia at Kingsholm.

SCRASE, Laurence William (Wing/centre)
Born Dubai,United Arab Emirates, 19.09.72. 6', 12st 7lb. **ADPR:** Wasps (1992-98, 34, 7t-35pts). Joined Wasps as a Colt in 1990 and achieved a regular starting place on the wing last season. Pole vaulter and 200m specialist in the summer.

SCRIVENER, Peter (Backrow)
Born 27.10.73. 6'5", 16st. **Rep hons:** Barbarians (97). **ADPR:** Wasps (1993-98, 43, 8t-40pts). Held back by a shoulder injury, Peter remains a forward for the future with all the physical attributes to reach the top. Educated at Coopers & Co, Coburn, and currently a student at Brunel University, Peter starred in the England Schools Grand Slam of 1992 and appeared for the England Seven in Hong Kong in 1995.

SHAW, Simon Dalton (Lock)
Born Nairobi, Kenya, 01.09.73. 6'9", 19st. **Rep hons:** England (8, It96), A (5, Ire95), Barbarians (94-95). **ADPR:** Bristol (1992-97, 58, 3t-15pts), Wasps (1997-98, 19, 1t-5pts). Hampered by a back injury last season, Simon was approaching full fitness in April and May when the injury flared up again and prevented him touring with England. Became the biggest-ever Schools international when he made his debut against Ireland at Thomond Park in 1991. Simon was 6'8" and 18st 4lb that day, and for such a big man is a superb athlete. Brought up initially in Spain, he attended Godalming Sixth Form College and was playing a Colts final trial when the selectors realised he was still a schoolboy. Won a Colts cap the next season and rapidly moved

through the age groups, before being called up as a replacement for England's tour to South Africa (1994) and producing two eye-catching performances.

UFTON, Jonathan Derek Giles (Full-back)
Born Dulwich, 31.01.74. 6'1", 12st 7lb. **ADPR:** Wasps (1994-98, 51, 8t, 11c, 4pg, 2dg-80pts). Held back by a serious knee ligament injury last season. Joined Wasps from Old Whitgiftians, having previously been a member of the England Schools 18 Group squad that achieved the Grand Slam in 1992. Surrey schoolboy cricketer and fencer, father Derek was a distinguished former Charlton Athletic and England soccer player and Kent wicketkeeper.

VOLLEY, Paul (Flanker)
Born 02.11.71. 6'1", 15st 6lb. **ADPR:** Wasps (1996-98, 4). Aggressive, big-tackling flanker who had just broken into the first team, against Brive in the European Cup quarter-final, when struck down by a knee injury. Returned later in the season to score a try for Wasps in the Tetley's Bitter Cup final.

WEEDON, Mark (Lock)
Born Tauranga, New Zealand, 31.07.68. 6'6", 18st 8lb. **ADPR:** Wasps (1997-98, 15, 2t-10pts). Consistent New Zealand-reared lock, good in the loose.

WHITE, Michael Kevin (Flanker)
Born Poole, 30.03.66. 6'1", 14st 8lb. **Rep hons:** Barbarians (96-97). **ADPR:** Wasps (1987-98, 116, 13t-62pts). Whole-hearted flanker who has given everything for the club in his 116 appearances that span the entire history of League rugby in England. Used as a battering ram in offence, he is one of the bravest tacklers in the game. High representative honours somehow seem to have passed him by, but he has the total respect and admiration of all opponents. Attended Purbeck School and played for Swanage before joining Wasps in 1985.

WINTERBOTTOM, James (Second row)
Born Norwich 26.1.78. 6'6", 17st 2lb. **Rep hons:** England U21. Educated at Diss HS and currently studying at St Mary's College, Twickenham. Also represented England Schools and Colts before making his U21 debut against France in February 1998.

WORSLEY, Joe Paul Richard (Backrow)
Born London, 14.06.77. 6'5", 17st. **Rep hons:** Barbarians (97-98). **ADPR:** Wasps (1995-98, 14). Educated at Hitchin Boys HS, played his early rugby at Welwyn RFC and an outstanding member of England 18 Group side that won Grand Slam in 1994-95. Capped by England Colts and U21 last winter. Talented saxophone player.

REVIEW

There is only one thing more difficult than getting to the top – and that's staying there. Wasps, champions in 1996-97, endured the toughest of seasons when defending their title and at one stage looked candidates for relegation. A horrific casualty list, especially among the backs, was a major problem and once the slide started it was difficult to stop. Recovered sufficiently in the spring to banish talk of relegation and mount an encouraging Cup run, though they will have few happy memories of a heavy defeat against Saracens in the final. With disappointing gates at Loftus Road, Wasps need a big season to reconfirm their position as an elite club.

WASPS in Premiership One 1997-98

Aug 30	A	Bristol	Won	38	21	N.Greenstock(T) K.Logan(T) M.Weedon(T) G.Rees(T, 3C, 3P) J.Ufton(P)
Oct 19	H	Saracens	Lost	15	19	G.Rees(5P)
26	A	London Irish	Lost	17	22	M.Wood(T) L.Scrase(T) G.Rees(C, P) K.Logan(C)
Nov 2	H	Sale	Lost	22	38	M.Wood(T) G.Rees(C, 5P)
Dec 13	A	Harlequins	Lost	17	53	J.Ions(T) Penalty(T) G.Rees(2C, P)
27	A	Northampton	Lost	10	18	M.Friday(T) G.Rees(C, P)
30	H	Richmond	Won	22	18	P.Sampson(T) G.Rees(C, 5P)
Jan 11	H	Gloucester	Won	26	20	M.Friday(T) Penalty(T) G.Rees(2C, 4P)
17	A	Leicester	Lost	21	45	K.Logan(2T) G.Rees(C, 3P)
Feb 1	H	Bristol	Won	32	18	Penalty(T) P.Scrivener(T) G.Rees(2C, D, 5P)
14	A	Bath	Lost	27	43	K.Logan(T) P.Scrivener(T) C.Sheasby(T) G.Rees(3C, 2P)
Mar 8	A	Saracens	Lost	27	33	N.Greenstock(T) Penalty(T) P.Sampson(T) G.Rees(3C, 2P)
11	A	Gloucester	Lost	15	22	M.Friday(T) P.Scrivener(T) G.Rees(C, P)
15	H	London Irish	Lost	19	38	S.Shaw(T) W.Green(T) G.Rees(3P)
Apr 7	A	Newcastle	Lost	13	20	A.King(T) G.Rees(C, 2P)
12	H	Harlequins	Won	29	26	W.Green(T) Penalty(T) G.Rees(2C, 5P)
18	A	Sale	Drew	28	28	T.Leota(2T) M.Friday(T) G.Rees(2C, D, 2P)
22	H	Newcastle	Won	18	17	L.Scrase(T) M.Friday(T) G.Rees(C, 2P)
26	H	Northampton	Won	31	15	L.Dallaglio(T) W.Green(T) P.Sampson(T) M.Weedon(T) G.Rees(4C, P)
29	H	Leicester	Won	17	13	S.Mitchell(T) G.Rees(D, 3P)
May 2	A	Richmond	Lost	29	51	A.Black(T) A.Gomarsall(T) S.Roiser(T) P.Scrivener(T) G.Rees(3C, P)
17	H	Bath	Lost	17	31	J.Ufton(T, C) J.Ions(T) P.Sampson(T)

Summary of Premiership scorers:

253 – G.Rees (T, 34C, 3D, 57P); 25 – M.Friday (5T), Penalty (5T); 22 – K.Logan (4T, C); 20 – P.Scrivener (4T), P.Sampson (4T); 15 – W.Green (3T); 10 – M.Wood (2T), M.Weedon (2T), J.Ufton (T, C, P), C.Sheasby (2T), L.Scrase (2T), T.Leota (2T), J.Ions (2T), N.Greenstock (2T); 5 – S.Shaw (T), S.Roiser (T), S.Mitchell (T), A.King (T), A.Gomarsall (T), L.Dallaglio (T), A.Black (T).

Summary of Premiership appearances:

21 – G.Rees (+1), D.Molloy (+1); 20 – L.Scrase (+1); 19 – S.Shaw (+5), W.Green;
18 – M.White, S.Roiser, T.Leota (+11); 17 – S.Mitchell (+2), L.Dallaglio;
16 – A.Reed (+8); 15 – M.Weedon (+1), C.Sheasby (+5), N.Greenstock;
14 – P.Scrivener (+1), K.Logan (+1); 13 – P.Sampson (+2), A.King; 12 – J.Worsley
(+5), M.Friday (+4); 11 – R.Henderson (+1), A.Gomarsall (+2); 10 – D.Cronin
(+2); 9 – A.Black (+7); 7 – M.Wood (+2); 4 – J.Ufton (+1), A.James (+1), J.Ions
(+1), I.Dunston (+1); 3 – P.Volley (+1); 2 – D.Walton (+1), D.Macer (+2),
G.Gregory, D.Alexopoulos (+2); 1 – D.Hopley (+1), J.Beardshaw.

WEST HARTLEPOOL

Formation of club: 1881
Ground: Victoria Park, Clarence Road, Hartlepool TS24 8BZ
Capacity: 7,500 (Seated 4,000)
Colours: Blue, red and white
Honours: Division Three Champions – 1990-91
Best League finish: 9th in Division One 1994-95
Best Cup run: Quarter finalist 1982-83, 1992-93, 1995-96 and 1997-98
Last season: ADP2 – Runners-up. Tetley's Bitter Cup – Q/F (lost 21-36 to Sale)
Owners: Members
Director of Rugby: Mike Brewer
Captain: Tu Nu'uali'itia

BEAL, Paul Andrew (Prop)
Born Redcar, 10.02.68. 5'11", 16st 4lb. **ADPR:** West Hartlepool (1994-98, 29). Joined
West Hartlepool July 1994. Made his first-team debut at Orrell in the Pilkington Cup,
December 1994. Three weeks later rewarded with a League debut. A product of
Redcar juniors.

BELGIAN, Philip (Full-back/centre)
Born Gateshead, 31.10.75. 6'1", 14st 1lb. **ADPR:** Newcastle (1995-97, 6, 1t, 4c,
5pg-28pts), West Hartlepool (1997-98, 10, 2t, 5c, 13pg-59pts). Former RGS Newcastle schoolboy who kicked a huge dropped goal against Mount St Mary's in the 1994
Daily Mail U18 Cup final at Twickenham. Joined Newcastle from Bath and was
formerly with Gateshead Fell.

BENSON, Jonathan (Wing)
Born Co. Durham, 11.01.76. 5'10", 11st 10lb. **ADPR:** West Hartlepool (1995-98, 14,
3t, 3c, 6pg-39pts). Former Durham player whose career was badly interrupted by a
knee injury. Worked hard to regain his place in the first-team squad. Scored a try
against his former club on his debut appearance for Wests. Made his Allied Dunbar
League debut against Sale, October 1995.

BISHOP, Hugo (utility back)
Born Brighton, 17.06.76. 6', 13st 6lb. **ADPR:** West Hartlepool (1997-98, 9, 2t-10pts).
Joined West Hartlepool August 1997, while a student at Durham University. Per-
formed with promise when called upon.

BREWER, Michael Robert (Backrow)
Born Pukekohe, New Zealand, 06.11.64. 6'5", 16st 3lb. **Rep hons:** New Zealand (32,
Fr86, 1t-4pts), Barbarians (95-96). **ADPR:** West Hartlepool (1997-98, 7). Influential

player-coach with massive experience of the game worldwide who took Wests back into the Premiership at the first time of asking after joining from Blackrock. Member of the All Black team beaten by South Africa in the 1995 World Cup final in Johannesburg. Also played in New Zealand's 45-29 win against England in the semi-finals. A former marketing manager, Michael made his international debut against France in 1986 but injury has often disrupted his international career. Missed 1987 World Cup through injury and was controversially omitted from 1991 World Cup squad, which he was due to captain, after failing NZRU fitness test. Returned in 1992 as member of All Black team that beat Ireland 59-6 in Wellington Test. Skippered Otago in 1986, aged 21, leading team to national championship in 1991. Relinquished Otago captaincy 1992. Hobbies include golf and fishing.

CASSIDY, Shaun (Flanker)
Born Middlesbrough, 13.10.69. **ADPR:** Wasps (1988-90, 2), West Hartlepool (1990-92, 7), Newcastle (1993-96, 31, 1t-5pts), Bedford (1996-97, 2), West Hartlepool (1997-98, 19, 1t-5pts). Former England Students cap. Experienced, abrasive flanker.

CONNOLLY, James Francis (Centre)
Born Wellington, New Zealand, 06.02.73. 5'11", 14st. **ADPR:** West Hartlepool (1996-98, 39, 6t-30pts). Consistent young New Zealand centre who missed just one League game last season. Educated at St Bede's College and Lincoln University in New Zealand and a Canterbury A representative before moving to Wests. Enjoys squash and golf.

CULLINANE, Brett John (Hooker/prop)
Born Otahuhu, New Zealand, 14.05.73. **ADPR:** West Hartlepool (1997-98, 9). Reliable reserve hooker who joined from the Pukekohe club in New Zealand.

ELWINE, Anthony (Centre)
Born Hartlepool, 23.11.70. 6'2", 15st 7lb. **ADPR:** West Hartlepool (1988-98, 39, 3t-15pts). Strong, bustling centre who rejoined the club from Middlesbrough in 1997. Originally a product of the club's mini section.

FARNER, Philippe Albert (Lock)
Born Dar-es-Salaam,Tanzania, 09.01.70. 6'7", 16st 9lb. **Rep hons:** France A (1, Eng96). **ADPR:** West Hartlepool (1997-98, 19, 2t-10pts). Joined Wests from Racing Club in Paris and was a key member of their powerful pack.

FARRELL, Emmet Anthony (Full-back/fly-half)
Born Dublin, 06.03.77. 5'10", 13st 7lb. **ADPR:** West Hartlepool (1997-98, 22, 10t, 1dg-53pts). Multi-talented young Irish back who has already shown his try-scoring ability, claiming 10 in the League last season when he was ever-present. Has played Gaelic football for Dublin Minors and attended soccer trials at Leeds United. A member of Ireland Schools squad who were unbeaten in Australia in 1996, he has also represented Ireland U21.

FLETCHER, Willie (Hooker/prop)
5'11", 16st. Versatile front row performer who arrives from New Zealand where he played provincial rugby for Nelson Bays. Appeared for the South Island Development team against Scotland in 1996. Was player/coach at Sandal last season.

FULLER, William Paul (Lock)
Born 19.10.76. 6'5", 17st. **Rep hons:** England U21. Joins from Leicester where he failed to make a significant impact, due largely to a bad ankle break last season. An outstanding member of England Schools and Colts sides before graduating to England U21, Bill is a talented all-rounder having represented the GB U20 athletics

squad in the shot put. A capable musician, he is a grade 7 pianist and has achieved grade 4 on the clarinet. Has recently graduated from Loughborough University.

GIACHERI, Mark Renato Giulio (Flanker)
Born Sydney, Australia, 01.02.69. 6'8", 17st 11lb. **Rep hons:** Italy (24, Rom92), Barbarians (95-96). **ADPR:** West Hartlepool (1997-98, 10, 2t-10pts). Rangy Australian-born lock who returned to the land of his fathers to become a distinguished Italian international. Formerly with Randwick in Australia and Treviso in Italy. Absent from the Italy squad last season, he will be hoping to return to the international fold in time for RWC99.

HERBERT, Timothy James (Hooker)
Born London, 28.09.67. 6', 15st 4lb. **ADPR:** West Hartlepool (1994-98, 34, 2t-10pts). Experienced former Northern hooker who enjoyed a spell with Manly in Australia before joining Wests. Educated at Hurstpierpoint College and Newcastle Polytechnic.

JOHN, Stephen (Wing/centre)
Born Cardiff, 11.10.73. 5'10", 13st. **ADPR:** West Hartlepool (1996-98, 42, 19t, 1pg-98pts). Versatile utility back who joined the club in August 1996 when Mark Ring, then director of rugby, signed him from Cardiff. Scored a remarkable 13 tries when they were relegated in 1996-97 and added six more last season. Represented Wales Schools and studied at Loughborough University.

MARSTON, Jonathon (Lock)
Born Otley, 15.12.77. 6'4", 17st. **ADPR:** West Hartlepool (1996-98, 2). Educated at Bradford GS where he played in their Daily Mail U18 Cup-winning side. Represented England Schools at lock.

MITCHELL, David Charles (Lock/No 8)
Born Peterborough, 19.10.71. 6'4", 15st 7lb. **ADPR:** West Hartlepool (1987-98, 80, 9t-41pts). Club stalwart, able to play anywhere in the back five, who again contributed well last season.

MORGAN, Ivan Edward (Backrow)
Born New Zealand, 30.01.76. **ADPR:** West Hartlepool (1996-98, 39, 9t-45pts). Forceful New Zealand flanker who claimed seven League tries last season. Joined West in August 1996 from Canterbury.

NIKORA, Emerson (Centre)
Born Feilding, New Zealand, 01.06.71. **ADPR:** West Hartlepool (1997-98, 4). Played club rugby in Perth, Western Australia, before moving to Brierton Lane.

NU'UALI'ITIA, Toetu (Scrum-half)
Born Auckland, New Zealand, 22.06.66. 5'7", 13st 6lb. **Rep hons:** Western Samoa. **ADPR:** West Hartlepool (1997-98, 21, 5t-25pts). A veritable pocket battleship at scrum-half, Toetu was one of West's most influential players last season. Member of the Western Samoan team beaten 42-14 by South Africa in the RWC95 quarter-finals, having also played in all their group games.

PEACOCK, Andrew (Hooker)
Born Newport, 03.12.68. 5'11", 15st 12lb. **ADPR:** West Hartlepool (1996-98, 36, 1t-5pts). Another Mark Ring signing who has done well over the past two seasons. Formerly with Newport and Pontypool, Andrew won Wales schoolboy honours from Gwent College and also went on to play for Wales Youth.

PONTON, James William (Flanker)
Born 31.07.74. **ADPR:** West Hartlepool (1997-98, 19, 3t-15pts). Hard-tackling flanker who made an outstanding contribution to West's promotion effort last season.

REDPATH, Nicholas James (Centre)
Born Ashington, 19.08.76. **ADPR:** West Hartlepool (1997-98, 1, 1t-5pts). Young centre who enjoyed spells at Leicester and Morpeth before joining West.

SCHRADER, Russell John (Lock)
Born Featherston, New Zealand, 02.05.74. **ADPR:** West Hartlepool (1997-98, 12). Towering lock who joined from the Petone club in New Zealand.

SEYMOUR, Patrick John (Prop)
Born Northallerton, 18.07.78. **ADPR:** West Hartlepool (1997-98, 3). Front row backup who has previously played for Harrogate and Middlesbrough.

SPARKS, Steven Joseph (Prop)
Born 07.07.74. **ADPR:** West Hartlepool (1995-98, 24, 3t-15pts). Former England Schoolboy prop who was the model of consistency last season, appearing in all 22 League games for West.

VILE, Steven Jeremy (Fly-half)
Born Waratah, Australia, 16.07.70. 5'11", 13st 1lb. **ADPR:** West Hartlepool (1997-98, 18, 8t, 33c, 43pg, 2dg-241pts). Prolific Australian who made a huge impact in his first season with West. Arrived via France, where he played for Castres.

REVIEW

After years of alternating between the top two divisions West will be determined to cement a place in Premiership One. Securing the necessary finance will obviously be a key element and West spent much of the summer looking at various proposals. Began last season with two disheartening defeats against Waterloo and Rotherham, but with the experienced Mike Brewer at the helm they refused to panic and recovered momentum well. Finished the season strongly with victories over London Scottish and Bedford, who join them in the Premiership.

WEST HARTLEPOOL in Premiership Two 1997-98

Aug 30	H	Waterloo	Lost	19	21	S.John(T) S.Vile(C, 4P)
Sep 13	A	Moseley	Won	21	16	I.Morgan(T) T.Nu'uali'itia(T) S.Vile(C, D, 2P)
20	A	Rotherham	Lost	21	33	L.Botham(T) E.Farrell(T) S.Vile(C, D, P) S.John(P)
27	H	Wakefield	Won	31	20	J.Connolly(2T) T.Nu'uali'itia(T) S.Vile(2C, 3P) P.Belgian(P)
Oct 4	A	Exeter	Won	20	19	E.Farrell(T) S.Vile(5P)
11	H	Blackheath	Won	32	21	S.Jones(2T) I.Morgan(2T) P.Farner(T) S.Vile(2C, P)
18	A	Bedford	Lost	9	22	S.Vile(3P)
25	H	Rotherham	Won	22	21	S.John(T) S.Vile(T, 3P) P.Belgian(P)
Nov 8	A	Wakefield	Won	28	12	P.Belgian(T) S.John(T) J.Ponton(T) J.Benson(2C, 3P)

Dec 13	H	Exeter	Won	34	14	S.Vile(2T, 3C, P) J.Benson(T)
						E.Farrell(T) S.John(T)
20	A	Blackheath	Lost	22	25	M.Wood(T) S.Vile(C, 5P)
Jan 17	A	Orrell	Won	35	30	E.Farrell(T, D) I.Morgan(T)
						S.Vile(2C, 6P)
31	A	Coventry	Lost	16	21	S.John(T) S.Vile(C, 3P)
Feb 14	H	Fylde	Won	66	12	E.Farrell(2T) S.Sparks(2T)
						S.Vile(7T, 8C) S.John(T) Penalty(T)
						J.Ponton(T) N.Redpath(T)
22	H	Orrell	Won	20	11	M.Wood(T) J.Benson(T)
						S.Vile(T, C, P)
Mar 8	A	London Scottish	Lost	17	31	J.Connolly(T) J.Benson(T)
						T.Nu'uali'itia(T) P.Belgian(C)
14	A	Fylde	Won	34	8	E.Farrell(T) P.Belgian(T)
						M.Giacheri(T) J.Ponton(T)
						T.Nu'uali'itia(T) S.Vile(3C, P)
28	H	Coventry	Won	42	31	P.Farner(T) M.Giacheri(T)
						D.Hyde(T) I.Morgan(T)
						S.Vile(T, 4C, 3P)
Apr 11	A	Waterloo	Won	51	6	E.Farrell(2T) H.Bishop(T)
						I.Morgan(T) T.Nu'uali'itia(T)
						S.Sparks(T) S.Vile(T, 3C, P)
						M.Wood(T) P.Belgian(C)
18	H	Moseley	Drew	18	18	P.Belgian(6P)
25	H	London Scottish	Won	11	10	I.Morgan(T) P.Belgian(P)
						J.Benson(P)
May 2	H	Bedford	Won	48	29	D.Mitchell(2T) H.Bishop(T)
						S.Cassidy(T) J.Connolly(T)
						E.Farrell(T) P.Belgian(3C, 4P)

Summary of Premiership scorers:

241 – S.Vile (8T, 33C, 2D, 43P); 59 – P.Belgian (2T, 5C, 13P); 53 – E.Farrell (10T, D); 35 – I.Morgan (7T); 33 – S.John (6T, P); 31 – J.Benson (3T, 2C, 4P); 25 – T.Nu'uali'itia (5T); 20 – J.Connolly (4T); 15 – M.Wood (3T), S.Sparks (3T), J.Ponton (3T); 10 – D.Mitchell (2T), S.Jones (2T), M.Giacheri (2T), P.Farner (2T), H.Bishop (2T); 5 – Penalty (T), N.Redpath (T), D.Hyde (T), S.Cassidy (T), L.Botham (T).

Summary of Premiership appearances:

22 – S.Sparks (+2), E.Farrell; 21 – T.Nu'uali'itia (+1), J.Connolly; 20 – S.John; 19 – J.Ponton (+1), I.Morgan, P.Farner, S.Cassidy (+2); 18 – S.Vile (+1), A.Peacock (+3); 15 – P.Beal (+1); 12 – R.Schrader (+1), J.Benson (+5); 11 – M.Wood, T.Elwine (+3); 10 – D.Mitchell (+2), M.Giacheri, P.Belgian (+2); 9 – S.Whitehead (+7), B.Cullinane (+6), H.Bishop; 7 – M.Brewer (+3); 6 – T.Herbert (+2), P.Harvey (+4); 5 – J.Painter (+3), D.Hyde (+4); 4 – E.Nikora (+3), V.Hartland (+1); 3 – G.Truelove, P.Seymour (+1), S.Jones (+1); 2 – L.Botham; 1 – C.Webb, N.Redpath, J.Marston, N.Hood, T.Handley (+1), M.Hathaway.

ALLIED DUNBAR PREMIERSHIP

Premiership Two

BLACKHEATH

Formation of club: 1858
Ground: Rectory Field, Charlton Road, Blackheath SE3 8SR
Capacity: 5,072 (Seated 572)
Colours: Red and black
Honours: None
Best League finish: 7th in Division Two, 1995-96
Best Cup run: Last 16 1982-83, 1983-84, 1984-85, 1985-86 and 1996-97
Last season: ADP2 – 9th. Tetley's Bitter Cup – 4th round (lost 31-59 to Saracens)
Owner: Members
Coach: TBC
Captain: TBC

BOOTH, Toby (Flanker)
Born Folkestone, 06.02.70. 5′11″, 15st 6lb. **ADPR:** Blackheath (1990-98, 71, 5t-25pts). Loyal former club captain who joined Blackheath back in 1991. Career badly interrupted for two years by mystery knee injury that eventually cleared. Graduate of St Mary's College, Twickenham.

BOYLE, Laurence Stuart (Centre)
Born Warwick, 29.01.70. 5′10″, 13st 7lb. **Rep hons:** Ireland A (2, Sc95). **ADPR:** Moseley (1989-91, 18, 3t, 1dg-15pts), Leicester (1991-94, 19, 3t-14pts), Harlequins (1994-95, 1), Blackheath (1997-98, 4, 1t-5pts). Former England Colts and U21 representative. Educated at Binswood College and Keble College, Oxford, where he gained a Blue in 1993.

BRAITHWAITE, Christopher (Fly-half)
Born Amersham, 26.12.71. 5′11″, 12st 10lb. **ADPR:** Wasps (1993-96, 10, 6t, 8c, 8pg, 2dg-76pts), Blackheath (1996-98, 28, 3t, 40c, 38pg, 4dg-221pts). Seemed the heir apparent to Rob Andrew at Wasps but slipped down the pecking order after the signing of Gareth Rees and Alex King. Moved to the Rectory Field where his goal-kicking has proved invaluable. Works as a financial executive.

CALDER, Ian Robert (Fly-half)
Born Helensville, New Zealand, 12.01.66. **ADPR:** Blackheath (1997-98, 3, 2c, 4pg-16pts). Formerly with Neath and College Rovers in South Africa.

CLARKE, John Fa'aususa (Scrum-half)
Born Lower Hutt, New Zealand, 30.05.75. 6′, 14st 6lb. **Rep hons:** Western Samoa. **ADPR:** Blackheath (1997-98, 14, 13t-65pts). Dynamic Western Samoan international scrum-half who was averaging nearly a try a game when injury struck midway through last season – Blackheath's form fell away appreciably thereafter. Played much of his rugby for Western Suburbs, New Zealand.

COOKE, Paul James (Wing)
Born Hastings, New Zealand, 09.01.67. **ADPR:** Blackheath (1997-98, 5, 1t-5pts). New Zealand-reared wing who arrived at Blackheath via Newport.

COYNE, Owen (Centre)
Born Harrow, 24.08.70. 5'10", 14st 6lb. **ADPR:** Blackheath (1992-98, 67, 3t-15pts). Former club captain who has played for England U21 and represented Transvaal U21 during a stay in South Africa. Joined from Upper Clapton in 1991 and worked as an engineering company salesman before turning professional last season.

FITZGERALD, David John (Centre)
Born Farnborough, 12.06.74. 5'10", 14st. **ADPR:** Blackheath (1996-98, 37, 7t-35pts). Another former England U21 squad member who was possibly Blackheath's most consistent back last season. Formerly with Rosslyn Park, David enjoyed spells with Narberth and Whitland in West Wales while a student at Swansea University.

GOLLINGS, Andrew Neil (Utility back)
Born Solihull, 08.08.71. 6'2", 14st 7lb. **ADPR:** Blackheath (1997-98, 2). Formerly with the Walsall club, Andrew enjoyed a brief spell playing with North Harbour in New Zealand.

GRAHAM, David Dominic **Paul** (Prop)
Born Stratford, New Zealand, 28.04.67. **ADPR:** Blackheath (1997-98, 20, 2t-10pts). One of Blackheath's Auckland contingent, David proved a reliable prop, missing just two League games last season.

GRIFFITHS, Matthew James (Wing)
Born London, 30.03.72. 5'8", 13st 4lb. **ADPR:** Blackheath (1991-95, 40, 9t-44pts), Wasps (1995-96, 1), Blackheath (1996-98, 26, 7t-35pts). Former England U21 wing who has also appeared in various England Sevens squads. Began his career with Blackheath, left to join Wasps in 1995 but returned the following year. Trained as a journalist.

HOARE, Mitch (Utility back)
Born Coventry, 28.12.73. 5'10", 13st 5lb. **ADPR:** Blackheath (1995-98, 19, 3t-15pts). Began his career at Wasps and moved briefly to Coventry before joining Blackheath. Works as an advertising executive.

HOWE, Robert Kevin (Hooker)
Born Beckenham, 12.04.63. 5'8", 14st. **ADPR:** London Scottish (1987-89, 8, 2t-8pts), Blackheath (1990-98, 30). Bobby started his career with London Scottish before joining Blackheath in 1990. Left for Askeans in 1994 but returned the following year. Works as a pipe-fitter.

JOHNSON, Steven John (Back five forward)
Born Swansea, 10.10.73. 6'6", 15st 7lb. **ADPR:** Blackheath (1996-98, 5). Former Wales U21 squad member who is attempting to regain full fitness after surgery to rebuild his knee.

JONES, David Royce (Lock)
Born Christchurch, New Zealand, 15.06.65. **ADPR:** Blackheath (1997-98, 13). Kiwi lock who enjoyed a spell with Chambery in France before arriving in England and joining Blackheath.

McCORDUCK, Robert Richard (Back five forward)
Born Galway, Ireland, 09.01.72. 6'4", 16st. **ADPR:** Blackheath (1996-98, 32, 1t-5pts). Doughty Irish backrow forward who was ever-present in the League for Blackheath last season. Capped for Welsh Universities while a student in Wales, where he also played club rugby for Abertillery.

MASON, Simon John Peter (Full-back)
Born Birkenhead, 22.10.73. 6'1", 14st 4lb. **Rep hons:** Ireland (3, Wal96, 3c, 12pg-42pts), A (1, SC96, 1t, 1c-7pts). **ADPR:** Liverpool St Helens (1993-94, 3t, 16c, 30pg, 1dg-140pts), Newcastle (1994-95, 18, 1t, 22c, 46pg, 2dg-193pts), Orrell (1995-96, 16, 4t, 16c, 38pg-166pts), Richmond (1996-98, 24, 10t, 87c, 36pg-332pts), Blackheath (1997-98, 7, 1t, 12c, 15pg-74pts). Loaned out to Blackheath for a spell last season but remained a top-rate goal-kicker and a valuable member of Richmond's first-team squad. Arrived at Blackheath towards the end of last season on loan from Richmond. Had originally travelled to Richmond via Liverpool St Helens, Newcastle Gosforth and Orrell, after being educated at St Anselm's, Liverpool. Simon narrowly missed out on England Schools and England U21 honours and, with three Irish grandparents in Dublin, happily answered the call.

MAYHEW, David William (Lock)
Born Matamata, New Zealand, 13.01.67. 6'6", 17st 6lb. **ADPR:** Blackheath (1997-98, 19). Another of Blackheath's imports from New Zealand, David originally played for North Harbour. He was one of the *New Zealand Rugby Almanack*'s Promising Players of the Year in 1990.

PAWSON, Christopher (Utility back)
Born Bromley, 21.09.76. 5'11", 13st 5lb. **ADPR:** Blackheath (1997-98, 10, 5t-25pts). Promising utility back capped by England Schools, Colts and U21. Gradually regaining full fitness and form after a serious groin injury. Educated at Skinners School, Tunbridge Wells, and Exeter University.

PENALUNA, Jason (Fly-half)
Born Winnepeg, Canada, 11.10.73. 5'10", 12st 7lb. **Rep hons:** Canada. **ADPR:** Blackheath (1997-98, 9, 1t, 4pg, 1dg-20pts). Canadian international back who has yet to find his feet in British conditions. Member of the James Bay club in Vancouver.

PERCIVAL, Mark John (Scrum-half)
Born Epsom, 20.04.76. **ADPR:** Blackheath (1997-98, 8, 2t-10pts). Former England Colts scrum-half who graduated from the Sutton & Epsom club.

POPE, Stephen (Prop)
Born Harlow, 24.11.73. 5'11", 17st 2lb. **ADPR:** Blackheath (1995-98, 35). Rapidly developing prop who played for England U16 and London U21. Enjoyed a brief spell at Wasps.

POWELL, Keith Thomas (Wing)
Born Sidcup, 01.06.73. **ADPR:** Blackheath (1997-98, 8). Kent wing who has also played for Sidcup and Old Colfeians.

REID, Hikatarewa Rockcliffe (Hooker)
Born Rotorua, 08.04.58. **Rep hons:** New Zealand (9, Aus80, 2t-8pts). **ADPR:** Blackheath (1997-98, 1). The former New Zealand hooker has retained his playing registration, though at 40 he will be hoping he is not required too often.

RIDGWAY, Colin John (Hooker)
Born Strood, 22.04.72. 5'11", 16st. **ADPR:** Blackheath (1993-98, 79, 12t-60pts). Former England U21 representative who has established himself as Blackheath's first-choice hooker after recovering from serious knee and groin injuries. A financial controller with an engineering company.

RUSSELL, Mark Peter (Back five forward)
Born Nairobi, Kenya, 16.12.65. 6'4", 17st 6lb. **Rep hons:** England A (4,NOtago92, 1t-4pts). **ADPR:** Blackheath (1987-88, 1) Harlequins (1990-95, 37, 2t-9pts), Harlequins

(1995-96, 7, 1t-5pts), Blackheath (1996-98, 34, 2t-10pts). Experienced former England A and Western Province forward who has moved between Blackheath and Harlequins. Voted Blackheath player of the year in 1996-97 and was again a tower of strength last season.

SCHUSTER, Nesetorio Johnny (Centre)
Born Apia, Western Samoa, 17.01.64. **Rep hons:** New Zealand (10, Aus88, 1t-4pts). **ADPR:** Blackheath (1997-98, 4, 1t, 4c, 9pg-40pts). Wonderfully gifted Western Samoan who opted for New Zealand and was a member of their 1987 World Cup squad. Joined Halifax RL for a long spell but returned to rugby union last season with the declared aim of representing Western Samoa in the 1999 World Cup. Badly damaged a shoulder after just four games for Blackheath but is determined to make amends this season.

SHARPLES, Richard William (Scrum-half)
Born Tunbridge Wells, 24.05.77. 5'9", 12st. **ADPR:** Harlequins (1996-97, 1), Blackheath (1997-98, 6). Lively scrum-half who played with Pawson at Skinners School and emerged via the Tunbridge Wells club.

SHORTLAND, Stephen Michael (Lock)
Born Sheffield, 12.01.68. 6'7", 18st 6lb. **ADPR:** Headingley (1987-90, 28), Northampton (1990-91, 4, 1t-4pts), Harlequins (1991-92, 5, 1t-4pts), Wasps (1992-95, 12, 3t-15pts), Blackheath (1996-98, 24, 1t-5pts). Experienced and much-travelled campaigner who has played for England Students and U21. Missed the 1995-96 season with a knee injury. Works as a college lecturer.

SMITH, Richard Paul (Utility back)
Born London, 14.06.67. 6', 14st. **ADPR:** Blackheath (1987-92, 22, 2t-8pts), London Irish (1992-93, 1), Blackheath (1993-98, 65, 3t-15pts). Reliable back enjoying a second spell with the club. Works as a Lloyd's insurance executive.

TASSELL, Matthew John (Centre)
Born Greenwich, 23.12.77. 5'8", 14st. **ADPR:** Blackheath (1996-98, 5). Promising centre who joined Blackheath from Harlequins and is looking to break through into the starting line-up.

TAYLOR, Josh (Prop)
BORN London, 06.01.70. 6'2", 18st. **ADPR:** Blackheath (1992-98, 47, 2t-10pts). Strong prop who established himself as a first choice by the end of last season.

WILKINS, Christopher John (Backrow)
Born Farnborough, 03.07.71. 6'3", 16st 2lb. **Rep hons:** England A (1, It95). **ADPR:** Wasps (1993-96, 17, 1t-5pts), Blackheath (1996-98, 41, 6t-30pts). Talented wing forward who was talked of as a future England prospect during his time at Wasps, where unfortunately a nasty neck injury brought him to a shuddering halt. Has rebuilt his career well at Blackheath. Educated at Brentwood School.

REVIEW

A tough season for Blackheath but one of the world's oldest clubs is still in there fighting to survive in the professional era. The much vaunted line-up with Auckland unfortunately ended in tears, the shell company going into receivership, but the club itself remains in business. Biggest disappointment of the season was probably John Schuster's serious shoulder injury – with the former All Black at the helm Blackheath would have been much more competitive, though they never entertained serious hopes of promotion. Hopefully Schuster can direct operations this season.

BLACKHEATH in Premiership Two 1997-98

Aug 30	A	Orrell	Lost	17	26	O.Coyne(T) C.Wilkins(T) C.Braithwaite(2C, P)
Sep 7	A	London Scottish	Lost	6	34	C.Braithwaite(D, P)
13	H	Wakefield	Won	29	27	J.Clarke(2T) D.Fitzgerald(T) P.Graham(T) C.Braithwaite(3C, P)
20	H	Fylde	Won	50	16	J.Clarke(4T) C.Wilkins(2T) C.Ridgway(T) J.Schuster(T, 2C) C.Braithwaite(3C)
27	A	Waterloo	Lost	16	51	C.Ridgway(T) J.Schuster(C, 3P)
Oct 4	H	Coventry	Won	28	27	J.Clarke(T) J.Schuster(C, 6P) J.Penaluna(D)
11	A	West Hartlepool	Lost	21	32	J.Clarke(T) D.Fitzgerald(T) P.Graham(T) J.Penaluna(2P)
18	H	Moseley	Lost	11	19	J.Clarke(T) J.Penaluna(2P)
25	A	Fylde	Won	31	6	J.Clarke(T) R.McCorduck(T) Penalty(T) I.Calder(2C, 4P)
Nov 8	H	Waterloo	Lost	14	15	C.Ridgway(T) M.Russell(T) C.Braithwaite(2C)
Dec 13	A	Coventry	Lost	22	24	C.Ridgway(T) C.Braithwaite(C, 5P)
20	H	West Hartlepool	Won	25	22	C.Pawson(T) J.Clarke(T) C.Braithwaite(2C, 2P)
Jan 17	H	London Scottish	Won	34	25	J.Christian(T) J.Clarke(T) J.Gallagher(T) C.Pawson(T) C.Ridgway(T) C.Braithwaite(3C, 3P)
31	A	Exeter	Lost	18	20	J.Clarke(T) M.Griffiths(T) J.Penaluna(T) C.Braithwaite(P)
Feb 14	H	Rotherham	Lost	18	31	M.Percival(T) C.Wilkins(T) C.Braithwaite(C, 2P)
28	A	Moseley	Lost	16	29	M.Percival(T) S.Mason(C, 3P)
Mar 7	H	Bedford	Lost	13	37	P.Cook(T) S.Mason(C, 2P)
14	A	Rotherham	Lost	10	40	C.Pawson(T) S.Mason(C, P)
28	H	Exeter	Won	26	15	L.Boyle(T) D.Fitzgerald(T) S.Mason(2C, 4P)
Apr 11	H	Orrell	Lost	14	32	T.Booth(T) S.Mason(3P)
18	A	Wakefield	Won	24	21	M.Griffiths(T) S.Mason(T, 3C, P) C.Pawson(T)
25	A	Bedford	Lost	31	72	W.Stanley(2T) C.Braithwaite(T) C.Pawson(T) S.Mason(4C, P)

Summary of Premiership scorers:

84 – C.Braithwaite (T, 17C, D, 14P); 74 – S.Mason (T, 12C, 15P); 65 – J.Clarke (13T); 40 – J.Schuster (T, 4C, 9P); 30 – C.Ridgway (6T); 25 – C.Pawson (5T); 20 – C.Wilkins (4T), J.Penaluna (T, D, 4P); 16 – I.Calder (2C, 4P); 15 – D.Fitzgerald (3T); 10 – W.Stanley (2T), M.Percival (2T), P.Graham (2T), M.Griffiths (2T); 5 – Penalty (T), M.Russell (T), R.McCorduck (T), J.Gallagher (T), O.Coyne (T), P.Cook (T), J.Christian (T), T.Booth (T), L.Boyle (T).

Summary of Premiership appearances:

22 – R.McCorduck; 21 – C.Wilkins, C.Ridgway; 20 – D.Graham, D.Fitzgerald (+1); 19 – D.Mayhew (+1); 18 – S.Pope (+3); 17 – J.Gallagher; 16 – M.Russell; 15 – M.Griffiths; 14 – J.Taylor (+5), J.Clarke, C.Braithwaite (+1); 13 – D.Jones; 12 – W.Stanley (+3); 11 – R.Smith (+1), T.Booth (+1); 10 – C.Pawson; 9 – J.Penaluna; 8 – K.Powell (+3), M.Percival (+1); 7 – S.Shortland (+2), S.Mason; 6 – R.Sharples (+5); 5 – O.Coyne (+1), P.Cook (+1); 4 – J.Schuster, S.Johnson (+1), L.Boyle; 3 – J.Christian (+2), I.Calder (+2); 2 – S.Read (+2), B.Howe (+1), A.Gollings (+1); 1 – M.Tassle (+1), H.Reid (+1), M.Karaitiana, M.Hoare (+1).

BRISTOL

Formation of club: 1888
Ground: The Memorial Ground, Filton Avenue, Horfield, Bristol BS7 0AQ
Capacity: 10,780 (Seated 1,780)
Colours: Navy blue and white
Honours: Cup Winners (1) – 1983.
Best League finish: 4th in Division One 1993-94
Last season: ADP1 – 12th. Tetley's Bitter Cup – 4th round (lost 12-14 to Worcester)
Owner: Club in receivership
Coaches: Darryl Jones, Dave Egerton
Captain: Paul Burke

ADAMS, Phil (Lock)
Born Bristol, 02.03.63. 6'6", 17st. **ADPR:** Bristol (1987-98, 67). Reliable grafter in the second row. Formerly with Bristol combination side BAC.

ARMSTRONG, Mark (Fly-half)
Born Rush Green, Essex, 10.09.74. 5'8", 13st 8lb. **ADPR:** Bristol (1997-98, 4, 2pg-6pts). Promising fly-half who deputised when Paul Burke was injured last season.

BABER, Gareth (Scrum-half)
Born 23.05.72. 5'10", 12st 2lb. **ADPR:** Bristol (1997-98, 12, 2t-10pts). Versatile former Aberavon scrum-half who also played fly-half, with some distinction, during Bristol's injury crisis.

BENNETT, Anthony Mark (Flanker)
Born Neath, 26.01.68. 6'2", 15st 3lb. **Rep hons:** Wales (3, NZ95, 1t-5pts), A (1, Ire95). Underrated Welsh flanker who made an outstanding international debut against New Zealand at Ellis Park in the 1995 World Cup, then was curiously discarded by Wales soon after. Arrives at the Memorial Ground after spells at Cardiff and Neath.

BREEZE, Ben (Wing)
Born Exeter, 08.04.74. 5'10", 13st. **ADPR:** Bristol (1995-98, 38, 5t-25pts). Promising wing who returned to action late season after surgery to a serious knee injury. Educated at Queen Elizabeth School, Crediton, and Loughborough University, Ben graduated through Bristol Colts and U21 sides. Represented England in the World Students Cup in South Africa in 1996.

BROWNRIGG, Jim (Back five forward)
Born Chichester, 04.06.77. 6'6", 15st. **ADPR:** Bristol (1996-98, 20, 1t-5pts). A regular source of encouragement during a miserable season for Bristol, Jim's athleticism and line-out skills sustained Bristol during many Premiership games. Educated at Wellington School and University of the West of England, Bristol, where he is studying for a degree in Business Studies. Selected for the England U21 team to play in the Six Nations tournament in Cape Town in July 1998.

BURKE, Paul Anthony (Fly-half)
Born London, 01.05.73. 5'8", 12st. **Rep hons:** Ireland (10, Eng95, 11c, 26pg, 1dg-103pts), A (6, Wal94, 1t, 8c, 16pg-69pts). Barbarians (94). **ADPR:** London Irish (1992-94, 21, 3c, 12pg, 7dg-63pts), Bristol (1996-98, 40, 4t, 53c, 81pg, 2dg-375pts). A knee injury sustained playing for Ireland A against Wales A early in March cruelly deprived Bristol of their most consistent performer for the last two months of the season, though he recovered in time for the play-offs. An Anglo-Irishman who was educated at Epsom College and came up through the English age-group system, Paul captained England Colts before opting for Ireland. His father is from Galway and mother from Kildare. Moved from London Irish to Cork Constitution in 1994 and made his senior Ireland debut against England in 1995. Was dropped after his next game, against Scotland, but returned as a replacement against Wales. His 1995 World Cup was confined to a game against Japan. Equalled the world record of eight penalties against Italy in January 1997 before being dropped for the 1997 Five Nations.

CHARRON, Alan John (Back five forward)
Born Ottawa, Canada, 27.07.66. 6'6", 17st 7lb. **Rep hons:** Canada (34, WalesB89, 5t-24pts), Barbarians (94). **ADPR:** Moseley (1996-98, 18, 3t-15pts), Bristol (1997-98, 5). Powerful and versatile back five Canadian forward, who moved from Moseley last season. A veteran of two World Cups.

CHESNEY, Kris (Wing)
Born Ilford, 02.03.74. 6'6", 16st 12lb. **ADPR:** Saracens (1995-98, 20, 5t-25pts), Bristol (1997-98, 5, 2t-10pts). Formerly with Barking and Saracens, Kris is a frightening sight on the wing. Back in December 94 played for London U21 against New Zealand U21 at lock. Trained as a chef.

COLLINS, Andy (Prop)
Born 11.11.74. 6'1", 17st. **ADPR:** Bristol (1996-98, 6). Developing prop who let nobody down when called upon last season.

CORKERY, Sean David (Flanker)
Born Cork, 06.11.72. 6'4", 16st 2lb. **Rep hons:** Ireland (25, Aus94, 3t-15pts), A (2, Sc95). Barbarians (94). **ADPR:** Bristol (1996-98, 33, 6t-30pts). Missed much of the early season with a complicated knee injury and rarely played to his known ability thereafter, though he showed up more prominently for Ireland in the Five Nations. Bristol will rely heavily on Corkery returning to his best form if they are to bounce back up into Premiership One. David is a product of the Christian Brothers College in Cork and was an outstanding Irish Schools blindside flanker in 1991. Emerged through the U21 set-up and made a big impression on his full debut against Australia in 1994. Retained his place against USA but was dropped after the England game in the Five Nations and only reappeared in RWC95, when he was Ireland's best forward. Missed out on selection for the 1997 British Lions after foolishly playing the last two Five Nations games with a broken hand.

DEWDNEY, Dean (Scrum-half)
Born Zimbabwe 5.11.74. 5'10", 11st. Joined Bristol from Clifton where he made seven League appearances in 1994-95. Made his Bristol debut in a friendly against Northampton in November 1995 and his League debut, as a replacement, against Orrell in April 1996.

DUNN, Kevin Anthony (Hooker)
Born Gloucester, 05.06.65. 5'9", 14st 7lb. **Rep hons:** England A (17, Aus88, 4t-17pts). **ADPR:** Gloucester (1987-92, 45, 4t-16pts), Wasps (1992-97, 61, 2t-10pts), Bristol (1997-98, 14). Formerly with Spartans, Lydney, Gloucester, Wasps and Waratahs RFC in Australia, Kevin was educated at Churchdown Comprehensive.

EAGLE, Chad (Lock)
Born New Zealand, 24.08.71. 6'5", 18st. **ADPR:** Bristol (1996-98, 33, 1t-5pts). Strong-scrummaging New Zealand-reared lock who has struggled a little in the line-outs.

EVANS, Jonathan William (Hooker)
Born Swansea, 05.04.72. 5'9", 14st. Dynamic former Wales Schools and Welsh Youth captain who was educated at Neath Tertiary College and Emmanuel GS in Swansea. Gained a Cambridge Blue in 1995 while at Homerton College.

FULLMAN, Kris (Prop)
Born Bristol, 07.12.72. 5'11", 16st. **ADPR:** Bristol (1995-98, 43). Promising young prop who played for England in the 1996 World Students Cup in South Africa. Made his Bristol League debut against Gloucester in October 1995. Former captain of Bristol Colts.

HINKINS, David John (Prop)
Born Exeter, 20.10.66. 6'1", 18st 7lb. **ADPR:** Bristol (1989-97, 103), Bedford (1997-98, 12, 1t-5pts). Returns to Bristol after a season with Bedford. A PE and science teacher at the John Cabot City Tech, Dave is a solid prop who also contributes usefully in the loose. Educated at Plymouth College and St Paul's College, Cheltenham, Dave played for England in the 1988 Students World Cup and enjoyed a short spell with Moseley before joining Bristol.

HULL, Paul Anthony (Full-back)
Born Lambeth, 17.05.68. 5'9", 12st 10lb. **Rep hons:** England (4, SA94), A (19, Fij89, 6t, 6c, 3pg-50pts), Barbarians (94). **ADPR:** Bristol (1987-98, 133, 24t, 5c, 16pg-171pts). Endured a poor season by his own high standards; it's a long time since the Memorial Ground faithful have seen Hull run with the abandon and imagination that marked his early seasons with the club. A genuine talent, Paul is another who must regain his best form if Bristol are to return to the top flight. Outstanding for England in South Africa (1994), when he won two caps, but was unluckily dropped on his return after getting injured against Canada. Captained England A on their tour of Australia and Fiji (1995) and also led Bristol in 1995-96. Educated at Gordon Boys' School in Woking, Paul had soccer trials for Southampton FC before concentrating on rugby.

JONES, Ian Wynn (Full-back)
Born Carmarthen, 12.05.71. 5'10", 13st 3lb. **Rep hons:** Wales A (6, Aus92, 1t-5pts). **ADPR:** Bristol (1997-98, 4). Talented former Llanelli and Cardiff full-back who has struggled badly with injury.

JONES, Philip Steffan (Utility back)
Born Llanelli, 09.02.74. 6'2", 14st. **ADPR:** Bristol (1997-98, 7), Exeter (1997-98, 3). Versatile former Swansea and Wales U21 utility back. Had a brief spell on loan to Exeter last season.

JONES, Robert Nicholas (Scrum-half)
Born Trebanos, 10.11.65. 5'8", 11st 8lb. **Rep hons:** Wales (54, Eng86, 4t-19pts), Barbarians (85-86). **ADPR:** Bristol (1996-98, 38, 4t-20pts). Badly disrupted by a serious back injury in the 1996-97 season, Robert was hindered last winter by a virus and Bristol have yet to see the best from the former Wales captain. Slick distributor who reached the height of his powers in Australia in 1989. Impressed for many seasons in moderate Welsh teams. A talented cricketer who represented Wales at three age-group levels. Enjoyed a testimonial match from Western Province at Stellenbosch in June 1997 when his side played a World XV.

LARKIN, Adam (Centre)
Born Sydney, Australia, 14.02.74. 5'11", 13st 12lb. **ADPR:** Bristol (1997-98, 6, 3t-15pts). Skilful centre who signed from North Harbour but was then held back by injury.

McCONNELL, Barry (Front row)
Born 31.7.75. 5'10", 15st 10lb. A powerful and versatile front row operator who deservedly won selection for Ireland's short tour of New Zealand in 1997, Barry spent last season regaining fitness after a serious knee injury. Made his senior debut for Bristol as a prop against West Hartlepool in May 1996 but increasingly looks an international prospect at hooker. Student at Bristol University where he is studying Civil Engineering.

MAGGS, Kevin Michael (Centre)
Born Bristol, 03.06.74. 5'11", 14st. **Rep hons:** Ireland (7, NZ97, 1t-5pts). **ADPR:** Bristol (1995-98, 53, 6t-30pts). Despite playing in a struggling Bristol side, Kevin established himself as a first-choice centre with Ireland last season, his brave tackling making a big impression. Was originally called into the Ireland Development squad to tour New Zealand and Western Samoa in 1997, following the withdrawal of Northampton's Jonathan Bell. Bristol League debut against Saracens in September 1995.

MARTIN, Simon (Centre)
Born Thornbury, Bristol, 24.01.75. 5'10", 13st 7lb. **ADPR:** Bristol (1995-98, 26, 3t-15pts). Another former Bristol Colts captain, Simon is Bristol-born and bred. His centre partnership with Maggs could be a key element of Bristol's game this season.

MILLETT, Nathan (Wing)
Born Bristol 16.11.77. 6', 14st. A former pupil of Colston's Collegiate, Nathan starred in two Daily Mail U18 Cup final victories at Twickenham, scoring two tries in the 1996 final against QEGS Wakefield. While at Colston's he beat the record of former Bristol star Alan Morley of 72 tries in two seasons.

PEARCE, Stephen (Backrow)
Born 15.09.68. 6'5", 18st. **ADPR:** Bristol (1997-98, 11, 2t-10pts). Reliable backrow backup who has taken his opportunities well.

POOLE, Alex (Prop)
Born, 18.09.73. 5'11", 16st 7lb. **ADPR:** Bristol (1997-98, 10). Former England Schools representative who was pressed into service last season during Bristol's injury crisis.

ROBINSON Tom (Hooker)
Born 8.1.77. 5'11" 15st 9lb. Promising addition to the squad who has represented England U21. Former captain of Cheltenham College, who also skippered Bristol University last season.

ROLLITT, Eben David (Backrow)
Born Bristol, 23.11.72. 6'3", 16st 5lb. **ADPR:** Richmond (1992-95, 2), Bristol (1995-98, 53, 6t-30pts). A qualified architect, Eben was educated at St Paul's School, London, and Cambridge University where he won a Blue (1994). Also played club rugby for Randwick in Sydney and Richmond. Son of former Bristol favourite Dave Rollitt, who won 11 caps for England between 1967 and 1975.

SHORT, Craig (Flanker)
Born Kingswood, 26.06.75. 6'1", 14st 2lb. **ADPR:** Bristol (1996-98, 25, 1t-5pts). Fast-developing openside flanker with plenty of pace and aggression.

TEMPERLEY, Nick (Flanker)
Born 04.11.71. 6'5", 15st. **ADPR:** Bristol (1996-98, 3, 1t-5pts). Formerly with Norwich, Nick joined the club from Sussex University where he took a first-class honours degree in History. Bristol debut against Loughborough University in Nov 1994.

TIUETI, David (Wing)
Born Tonga, 06.06.73. 6', 14st 2lb. **Rep hons:** Tonga. **ADPR:** Bristol (1995-98, 39, 19t-95pts). Spent much of the second half of the season in dispute with the club but remained one of their most dangerous runners, either on the wing or at centre. Made five senior appearances for North Harbour in New Zealand before moving to England. Bristol debut at Bridgend in March 1996, followed by League debut against Bath.

WATKINS, Neil (Second row)
Born 10.11.75. 6'7", 17st 5lb. **Rep hons:** Wales A (2, Rom97, 1t-5pts). Talented former Wales Schools and Youth lock who became available last summer when Neath had to cut their costs in order to survive. Spring-heeled line-out jumper who looked destined for the very top when playing Youth rugby.

WORSLEY, Michael Anthony (Prop)
Born Warrington, 01.12.76. 6'1", 17st. **ADPR:** Orrell (1996-97, 17, 1t-5pts), Bristol (1997-98, 9). England U21 prop and another Bristol player to suffer from injury last season.

YAPP, Darren (Utility back)
Born Wolverhampton, 19.02.75. 6', 15st. **ADPR:** Bristol (1996-98, 16, 3t-15pts). Long-striding wing who has appeared in England U21 squads.

REVIEW

A traumatic season for Bristol, including just two Premiership victories, ended with 15 consecutive defeats and relegation to Premiership Two after losing to London Scottish in both play-off games. Injuries did not help but Bristol looked off the pace, on and off the field, from the beginning of the season. The club's position deteriorated further throughout the summer until late July when the receiver was called in.

BRISTOL in Premiership One 1997-98

Aug 23	A	Gloucester	Lost	13	35	D.Corkery(T) P.Burke(C, 2P)
30	H	Wasps	Lost	21	38	J.Lewsey(T) D.Tiueti(T) Penalty(T) P.Burke(3C)
Oct 18	A	Bath	Lost	15	44	K.Maggs(T) S.Pearce(T) P.Burke(C, P)
26	H	Northampton	Won	22	15	D.Tiueti(T) P.Burke(C2, D, 3P)
Nov 2	A	Saracens	Lost	9	31	P.Burke(3P)
9	A	Sale	Lost	0	76	
Dec 13	H	Richmond	Lost	12	13	P.Burke(4P)
27	H	Newcastle	Lost	8	50	D.Tiueti(T) P.Burke(P)
31	A	Harlequins	Won	40	38	J.Lewsey(T) D.Tiueti(T) P.Burke(T, 4C, 4P) J.Brownrigg(T)
Jan 18	H	Gloucester	Lost	13	14	Penalty(T) P.Burke(C, 2P)
Feb 1	A	Wasps	Lost	18	32	J.Lewsey(T) D.Tiueti(T) P.Burke(C, 2P)
14	H	Saracens	Lost	20	37	A.Larkin(T) J.Lewsey(T) P.Burke(2C, 2P)
20	A	London Irish	Lost	23	38	A.Larkin(T) D.Tiueti(T) P.Burke(2C, 3P)
28	H	Leicester	Lost	24	27	G.Baber(T) A.Larkin(T) S.Pearce(T) P.Burke(3C, P)
Mar 8	H	Bath	Lost	16	22	P.Burke(T, C, 3P)
14	A	Northampton	Lost	12	35	G.Baber(T) D.Yapp(T) J.Lewsey(C)
Apr 10	A	Richmond	Lost	3	43	P.Hull(P)
15	H	Sale	Lost	15	25	D.Tiueti(T) S.Martin(T) P.Hull(C, P)
19	H	London Irish	Lost	5	17	S.Martin(T)
26	A	Newcastle	Lost	18	43	D.Yapp(2T) C.Moore(T) J.Lewsey(P)
May 3	H	Harlequins	Lost	19	26	F.Landreau(T) J.Lewsey(T, 2P) P.Hull(P)
10	A	Leicester	Lost	25	34	K.Chesney(T) E.Rollitt(T) D.Corkery(T) M.Armstrong(2P) P.Burke(2C)

Play-offs

May 17	A	London Scottish	Lost	25	29	P.Hull(T) K.Chesney(T) K.Maggs(T) P.Burke(2C, 2P)
23	H	London Scottish	Lost	15	17	P.Burke(5P)

Summary of Premiership scorers:

153 – P.Burke (2T, 22C, 2D, 31P); 36 – J.Lewsey (5T, C, 3P); 35 – D.Tiueti (7T); 15 – D.Yapp (3T), A.Larkin (3T); 11 – P.Hull (C, 3P); 10 – S.Pearce (2T), S.Martin (2T), D.Corkery (2T), G.Baber (2T); 6 – M.Armstrong (2P); 5 – E.Rollitt (T), C.Moore (T), K.Maggs (T), F.Landreau (T), J.Brownrigg (T).

Summary of Premiership appearances:

21 – K.Fullman (+1); 20 – E.Rollitt (+3); 17 – C.Short (+2), J.Lewsey (+2), P.Hull (+1); 16 – D.Tiueti, K.Maggs, R.Jones, P.Burke (+1), J.Brownrigg (+4); 15 – C.Eagle, T.Devergie (+2), P.Adams (+6); 13 – D.Yapp (+1), S.Martin (+2); 12 – F.Landreau, K.Dunn (+3), D.Corkery (+1); 11 – S.Pearce (+2), G.Baber (+2); 10 – A.Poole (+2), S.Jones (+1); 8 – M.Worsley; 7 – M.Morgan (+3), M.Denney (+2), B.Breeze (+1); 5 – J.Wring (+3), A.Larkin, A.Collins (+4); 4 – I.Jones, M.Armstrong (+3); 2 – J.Wakeford, F.Waters, C.Moore (+1), J.Dickin (+1), R.Collins (+1); 1 – N.Temperley (+1), J.Coad, A.Adams.

COVENTRY

Formation of club: 1874
Ground: Coundon Road, Barker Butts Lane, Coventry CV6 1DU
Capacity: 10,000 (Seated 1,100)
Colours: Navy blue and white
Honours: Cup Winners (2) – 1972-73, 1973-74. Division Three Champions – 1993-94, 1995-96
Best League Finish: 11th in Division One, 1987-88
Last season: ADP2 – 7th. Tetley's Bitter Cup – 4th round (lost 14-50 to Leicester)
Owners: Club in receivership
Director of Rugby: Derek Eves
Coach: Ralph Knibbs
Captain: TBC

ADDLETON, David James (Hooker)
Born Coventry, 30.03.63. 5'9", 14st 2lb. **ADPR:** Coventry (1989-98, 108, 3t-15pts). Club stalwart Dave made his Warwickshire debut in the CIS semi-final against Berkshire at Rugby in 1995-96. A product of the Barkers Butts academy, the club that nurtured Neil Back and Bill Gittings, he has also represented Irish Exiles. Educated at Woodlands, a water engineer by profession.

CROFTS, Lee Bryan (Flanker)
Born Coventry, 07.09.68. 6'4", 17st 7lb. **ADPR:** Coventry (1993-98, 64, 7t-35pts). Police officer who converted from second row to backrow 1995-96 when he was voted Coventry's most improved player. Represented the Midlands against Argentina in 1996. British Police heavyweight boxing champion. Learned his rugby at the Broad-street club.

DAWSON, Anthony Richard (Scrum-half)
Born Crewe, 29.01.75. 5'10", 11st. **ADPR:** Coventry (1996-98, 38, 9t-45pts). Joined Coventry in January 96. 'Tigger', a former teacher, has made a good impression over the last two seasons. Educated at Crewe & Alsager College and a former member of the Whitchurch and Stourbridge clubs.

EVES, Derek John (Flanker)
Born Bristol, 07.01.66. 5'10", 15st 5lb. **Rep hons:** England A (2, SAus95, 2t-10pts), Barbarians (93-94). **ADPR:** Bristol (1987-95, 88, 18t-85pts), Coventry (1995-98, 53, 13t-65pts). Player/coach Derek remains a great enthusiast for the game and a quality performer at openside flanker. Derek made 88 appearances in nine years with Bristol

before moving to Coventry three seasons ago. Was a member of the Barbarians team that won Middlesex Sevens for the last two years and has represented England at Hong Kong Sevens as well as in RWC95.

GALLAGHER, Matthew David (Utility back)
Born Solihull, 21.03.73. 6'1", 13st. **ADPR:** Nottingham (1993-96, 44, 4t, 8c, 26pg-114pts), Coventry (1996-98, 42, 7t, 6c, 2pg, 5dg-68pts). A contemporary at Solihull School of Coventry team-mate Andy Smallwood, Matt is taking an HND in Building at Sheffield Hallam University. Made an early impression playing for Warwickshire Schools, going on to gain Midlands U21 selection and represent the English University side. He and Smallwood were members of Warwickshire's County Championship-winning team against Northumberland in 1994-95.

HEWLETT, Jason (Scrum-half)
Born 30.05.74. 5'8", 12st 10lb. **Rep hons:** Barbarians (97). **ADPR:** Coventry (1997-98, 2, 1t-5pts). Outstanding age-group international for Wales who played in every position behind the scrum for Cardiff.

HORROBIN, Julian Keith (Flanker)
Born Lydney, 17.04.69. 6'3", 15st 4lb. **ADPR:** Bristol (1990-91, 10, 4t-16pts), Coventry (1993-98, 78, 23t-115pts). Rugged West Country flanker who was voted Coventry's player of the year 1995-96 when he scored 20 tries in 28 first-team appearances. Originally from the Berry Hill club in the Forest of Dean. England U21 and Schoolboy cap.

KILFORD, Wayne Ashley (Full-back)
Born Malvern, 25.09.68. 5'11", 13st. **ADPR:** Nottingham (1988-92, 20, 1t, 2c, 5pg-23pts), Leicester (1992-96, 22, 4t, 1pg-23pts), Coventry (1996-98, 34, 9t-45pts). An outstanding all-round sportsman, he has also represented Nottinghamshire County Cricket Club second team as a batsman. Capped by England U21 and Colts, Wayne was at Nottingham and Leicester before joining Coventry. Educated at Joseph Whitaker School, Notts.

LLOYD, Richard Raymond (Flanker)
Born Aylesbury, 02.12.77. 5'11", 14st. **ADPR:** Coventry (1996-98, 5, 1t-5pts). Former England Schools flanker who joined Coventry May 1996. First-team opportunities have inevitably been limited by Derek Eves' continuing good form.

McADAM, Andrew (Wing)
Born Coventry, 29.03.71. 6'1", 14st. **ADPR:** Leicester (1994-96, 6), Coventry (1996-98, 30, 15t-75pts). Former England Colts and Leicester wing, hampered by injury last season. Financial advisor by profession.

MINSHULL, Jason Stuart (Centre/wing)
Born Leamington Spa, 20.12.67. 5'11", 13st 5lb. **ADPR:** Coventry (1987-98, 54, 11t-49pts). Experienced former England Schools and Colts centre who enjoyed a spell with the Tukapi club in New Zealand and represented Taranaki against Australia in 1990. Has also played for Kenilworth and Barkers Butts.

ROBINSON, Richard Philip (Centre)
Born Liverpool, 05.07.67. 6'1", 14st. **Rep hons:** Barbarians (96-97). **ADPR:** Leicester (1993-96, 24, 3t-15pts), Coventry (1996-98, 35, 9t-45pts). An accountant, Richie joined from Leicester in 1996, having played in the 1996 Pilkington Cup final against Bath. Formerly played for Blackpool and Market Bosworth.

SHARP, Alan Victor (Prop)
Born Bristol, 07.10.68. 5'10", 17st 4lb. **Rep hons:** Scotland (6, Eng94), England A (1, Sp89), Scotland A (2, It93), Barbarians (96-97). **ADPR:** Bristol (1987-90, 16), Coventry (1989-90, 1), Bristol (1990-97, 61, 2t-10pts), Clifton (1991-92, 1t-4pts), Coventry (1996-98, 12). Much-travelled prop, formidable scrummager with a short fuse. Has struggled with back problems in recent seasons.

SMALLWOOD, Andrew Mark Charles (Wing)
Born Solihull, 13.08.72. 5'10", 13st 11lb. **ADPR:** Nottingham (1993-96, 47, 11t-55pts), Coventry (1996-98, 38, 22t-110pts). Quick and elusive wing. Educated at Solihull and Nottingham University. A member of Warwickshire's County Championship-winning team that beat Northumberland 1994-95.

STEWART, Keith (Lock)
Born 23.01.72. 6'8", 17st 11lb. **ADPR:** Coventry (1997-98, 3). Experienced lock who joined in the summer, having played on loan from Cardiff at the end of last season. Has represented Scottish Exiles.

REVIEW

Coventry's very future was in doubt this summer as they went into receivership with debts of £3.5m, having already off-loaded many of their best players. Last September they were joint favourites, with Bedford, to win Premiership Two yet Derek Eve's team badly underperformed to finish a miserable seventh. How a team can beat promoted London Scottish 36-10 yet capitulate against the likes of Exeter remains a mystery. Coventry should be a powerhouse in Midlands rugby but as we go to press their very existence is in doubt.

COVENTRY in Premiership Two 1997-98

Aug 30	H	Moseley	Won	20	12	J.Horrobin(T) J.Harris(5P)
Sep 7	H	Exeter	Won	29	8	A.McAdam(T) A.Smallwood(T) T.Dawson(T) J.Brown(C, 4P)
13	A	Fylde	Won	23	15	J.Horrobin(T) J.Harris(6P)
20	A	Wakefield	Won	17	6	M.Curtis(T) D.Eves(T) A.Smallwood(T) J.Brown(C)
27	H	Bedford	Lost	15	22	I.Patten(T) R.Robinson(T) J.Brown(C, P)
Oct 4	A	Blackheath	Lost	27	28	M.Curtis(T) R.Robinson(T) J.Harris(C, 5P)
11	H	Rotherham	Won	18	12	J.Harris(D, 4P) M.Gallagher(D)
18	A	Orrell	Lost	13	38	W.Kilford(2T) J.Brown(P)
25	H	Wakefield	Won	24	17	A.Irwin(T) A.Blackmore(T) T.Dawson(T) J.Harris(3P)
Nov 8	A	Bedford	Lost	3	77	J.Harris(P)
Dec 13	H	Blackheath	Won	24	22	J.Hewlett(T) R.Robinson(T) J.Harris(C, 4P)
20	A	Rotherham	Lost	8	46	W.Kilford(T) J.Harris(P)
Jan 17	A	Exeter	Lost	14	18	W.Kilford(T) J.Brown(3P)

	24	H	Orrell	Lost	21	30	J.Harris(D, 6P)
	31	H	West Hartlepool	Won	21	16	M.Curtis(T) M.Gallagher(T, D) J.Brown(C, D, P)
Feb	14	A	London Scottish	Drew	18	18	D.Duley(2T) J.Brown(C, 2P)
Mar	7	H	Waterloo	Won	41	33	J.Minshull(3T) M.Gallagher(T, D) J.Horrobin(T) A.Smallwood(T) J.Brown(C, P) J.Harris(P)
	14	H	London Scottish	Won	37	10	A.Smallwood(2T) T.Dawson(2T) G.Jones(T) J.Brown(3C, 2P)
	28	A	West Hartlepool	Lost	31	42	J.Horrobin(3T) D.Addleton(T) M.Gallagher(T) J.Brown(C) J.Harris(2C)
Apr	18	H	Fylde	Won	16	7	D.Eves(T) J.Harris(C, 3P)
	22	A	Moseley	Lost	3	31	J.Brown(P)
	25	A	Waterloo	Lost	21	24	A.Irwin(T) R.Lloyd(T) J.Brown(C, 3P)

Summary of Premiership scorers:

133 – J.Harris (5C, 2D, 39P); 82 – J.Brown (11C, D, 19P); 30 – J.Horrobin (6T); 25 – A.Smallwood (5T); 24 – M.Gallagher (3T, 3D); 20 – W.Kilford (4T), T.Dawson (4T); 15 – R.Robinson (3T), J.Minshull (3T), M.Curtis (3T); 10 – A.Irwin (2T), D.Eves (2T), D.Duley (2T); 5 – I.Patten (T), A.McAdam (T), R.Lloyd (T), G.Jones (T), J.Hewlett (T), A.Blackmore (T), D.Addleton (T).

Summary of Premiership appearances:

21 – I.Patten; 20 – D.Eves (+2), D.Addleton; 19 – M.Gallagher (+2); 18 – J.Minshull, L.Crofts (+3); 17 – W.Kilford (+1), T.Dawson (+2); 16 – A.Smallwood; 15 – R.Hardwick (+1), D.Duley (+2); 14 – J.Horrobin, J.Harris (+5), J.Brown (+1); 13 – R.Robinson (+2), M.Curtis; 12 – D.Zaltzman, W.Bullock (+2); 10 – A.McAdam; 8 – V.Hartland (+2), A.Blackmore; 6 – R.Salisbury (+3), R.Morgan (+1), A.Irwin (+2); 5 – A.Sharp, J.Farr; 4 – R.Lloyd (+1), R.Faiers (+1); 3 – K.Stewart, J.Soden (+1), G.Jones; 2 – B.Williams (+1), G.Reayer, J.Hewlett; 1 – P.Lydster (+1), C.M.Fripp (+1), S.Edwards (+1).

EXETER

Formation of club: 1872
Ground: County Ground, Church Road, St Thomas, Exeter EX2 9BQ
Capacity: 6,000 (Seated 900)
Colours: Black and white
Honours: Division Four Champions – 1995-96. Division Three Champions – 1996-97
Best League finish: 1st Division Three, 1996-97
Best Cup Run: Q/F 1992-93, 1994-95
Last season: ADP2 – 11th. Tetley's Bitter Cup – 4th round (lost 10-34 to Newcastle)
Owner: Members
Director of Rugby/Coach: Ian Bremner
Captain: Rob Baxter

ALVIS, James Nicholas (Prop)
Born Clifton, 19.12.70. 5′11″, 18st 10lb. **ADPR:** Exeter (1997-98, 22, 6t-30pts). James could be banished from the front row union after finishing as Exeter's top try-scorer last season with six. His tally was just reward for the ex-Newport, Cardiff and Pontypridd prop who was ever-present in the Premiership. Teaches at Blundell's School.

ARMSTRONG, Robert William (Backrow)
Born Liverpool, 17.08.67. 6′4″, 18st. **ADPR:** Plymouth Albion (1990-92, 17, 2t-8pts), Bristol (1992-96, 40), Exeter (1996-98, 35, 10t-50pts). Strong, influential and highly experienced, Bob has represented Plymouth, Bristol and Exeter in the English League. He is a drill sergeant in the Royal Marines, whose 1997-98 season was disrupted by a 10-week military tour of duty. Former Services super-heavyweight boxing champion who has appeared regularly for the Combined Services XV, notably in their game against the 1993 All Blacks.

BARROW, Craig Anthony (Backrow)
Born Leicester, 26.02.69. 6′6″, 16st 7lb. **ADPR:** Exeter (1990-91, 6), Bristol (1991-97, 61, 3t-14pts), Exeter (1997-98, 22, 2t-10pts). A former Exeter University student and Exeter player, Craig retained links with the club and returned to the south west at the beginning of last season after leaving Bristol. Athletic operator at No 8 who is also something of a sevens specialist. Represented England Students.

BATCHELOR, John Lester (Backrow)
Born Essex, 10.03.71. 6′4″, 17st 7lb. **ADPR:** Exeter (1992-98, 68, 7t-35pts). A strong, blindside wing forward, who joined Exeter in 1992 after spells with Upper Clapton and Loughborough University. Works as a teacher.

BAXTER, Richard John (Flanker)
Born Exeter, 23.06.78. **ADPR:** Exeter (1997-98, 11, 2t-10pts). Promising product of Exeter's Youth team who broke into the senior side last season.

BAXTER, Rob (Lock)
Born Tavistock, 10.03.71. 6′5″, 16st 7lb. **ADPR:** Exeter (1989-98, 107, 6t-29pts). Succeeded Andy Maunder as Exeter's captain last season. Rob is a former England Colt and South West divisional player who has spent his rugby career at the County Ground save a short spell at Gloucester. He is the son of John Baxter, Exeter's chairman. Works as a farmer.

BIRKETT, Andrew Peter (Fly-half)
Born Exeter, 20.11.75. **ADPR:** Leeds (1995-96, 1, 1c, 2pg-8pts), Exeter (1997-98, 6, 1t-5pts). Backup fly-half who has yet to make an impression at this level.

CARTER, Simon James (Wing)
Born Barnstaple, 21.12.68. **ADPR:** Exeter (1997-98, 6, 3t-15pts). Experienced former South Molton wing who made an immediate impression in the First XV, scoring three tries in six games.

CROSS, Derek Lionel (Lock)
Born Watford, 05.08.71. **ADPR:** Exeter (1996-98, 12). Reliable backup lock who joined from Devonport Services.

CUDMORE, Andrew (Wing)
Born Truro, 02.09.73. 5′9″, 12st 4lb. **ADPR:** Exeter (1997-98, 4). Emerging wing who joined from Leicester, where opportunities were limited.

CURRY, Mark David (Lock)
Born Taunton, 22.10.73. 6'7", 17st. **ADPR:** Exeter (1996-98, 31, 4t-20pts). Highly promising young lock who first sprang to attention with Bristol U21s. Became the first Exeter player since 1984 to appear in the County Championship final, when he played for Somerset against Cumbria at Twickenham in April 1997. He was elected Exeter's most improved player in 1996-97. His hobbies include mountaineering. Works as a dispensing chemist.

DOYLE, Sean Michael (Utility back)
Born Exeter, 21.08.74. 6', 14st 10lb. **ADPR:** Exeter (1992-98, 75, 18t-90pts). Powerful runner who hailed originally from the Tiverton club. Works for SW Telecoms.

FABIAN, Jon Geoffrey (Full-back)
Born Plymouth, 18.09.76. 6'3", 14st 7lb. **ADPR:** Exeter (1996-98, 28, 3t, 23c, 50pg-211pts). Immensely promising young full-back who is a student at Exeter University. Has represented England Students and was selected by England U21 for the Six Nations tournament in Cape Town in July 1998. Missed just one game for Exeter last season and finished as the club's top points-scorer with 174.

GIBBINS, Richard John (Prop)
Born 06.08.67. **ADPR:** Exeter (1987-98, 128, 5t-25pts). Ever-loyal clubman who missed just one League game last season.

GREEN, Andrew John (Fly-half)
Born Barnstaple, 23.05.64. 5'5", 10st 7lb. **ADPR:** Exeter (1987-98, 134, 23t, 140c, 214pg, 21dg-1090pts). Andy's availability is not certain this season but he has proved one of the most prolific points-scorers in League history. Established a club record of 300 in their promotion season of 1996-97. Veterinary goods salesman.

HUTCHINSON, Roger Anthony (Flanker)
Born Singapore, 21.11.69. 6', 14st 7lb. **ADPR:** Exeter (1991-98, 79, 11t-55pts). Former England Students representative.

JOHN, Richard Simon (Scrum-half)
Born Exeter, 30.05.74. 5'10", 13st. **ADPR:** Exeter (1995-98, 29, 3t-15pts). Educated at Sealehayne Agricultural College and works as a conservationist. Backup scrum-half who joined from Crediton.

JOHNSON, Simon Patrick (Scrum-half)
Born Swindon, 15.03.73. **ADPR:** Bath (1994-96, 3), Exeter (1997-98, 1). Joined Exeter after a season with the Kurita club in Japan.

McLOUGHLIN, Matthew Brendan Joseph (Fly-half)
Born Harare, Zimbabwe, 06.08.72. **ADPR:** Exeter (1997-98, 6, 1dg-3pts). Played for Mashonaland and Old Georgians in Harare.

MAUNDER, Andrew John Lloyd (Scrum-half)
Born Tiverton, 08.04.66. 6', 14st. **ADPR:** Exeter (1987-98, 146, 42t-198pts). Inspirational former club captain and South West scrum-half whose availability is uncertain for the coming season. In 1995-96 he became the first player in England to make 100 consecutive League appearances. Runs the family butcher's.

PATIDAR, Sachin Meeku Punit (Fly-half)
Born Ndola, Zambia, 08.02.74. **ADPR:** Exeter (1994-98, 6, 4pg, 2dg-18pts). Joined the club from Sutton Coldfield.

POOLEY, Steve (Hooker)
Born Devizes, 19.09.66. **ADPR:** Plymouth Albion (1993-96, 65, 4t-20pts), Exeter (1997-98, 2). Backup hooker with loads of experience.

REED, Wayne (Prop)
Born Tiverton, 27.10.71. 5'10", 17st 4lb. **ADPR:** Exeter (1995-98, 27, 2t-10pts). Joined Exeter from Crediton. Works as a builder.

SLUMAN, Philip John (Prop)
Born Exeter, 15.03.67. 6', 17st. **ADPR:** Exeter (1989-98, 74, 2t-9pts). A one-club man who emerged via Exeter Colts, Philip became a first-team regular in 1996-97. Works as a tarmac layer.

SOUTHERN, William Nicholas (Flanker)
Born Plymouth, 30.08.67. 5'11", 14st. **ADPR:** Exeter (1993-98, 64, 6t-30pts). Classy openside flanker who has played for the South West. Policeman.

TCHAHARDEHI, Farhad (Centre)
Born Teheran, Iran, 06.09.76. **ADPR:** Exeter (1997-98, 5, 1dg-3pts). Much-vaunted centre who arrived from Marmande in France. Failed to impress in his League appearances, though he did score 23 points in a Cheltenham & Gloucester Cup game against Orrell.

THOMAS, Jason Paul (Centre)
Born Aberdare, 02.03.71. 5'9", 11st 7lb. **ADPR:** Exeter (1994-98, 68, 11t, 1dg-58pts). Former Paignton centre who became a first-team regular last season.

TURNER, Andrew Keith (Centre)
Born Saddleworth, 27.11.70. 6'1", 14st. **ADPR:** Exeter (1989-98, 96, 11t-55pts). Another club stalwart. Manufacturer of pharmaceutical products.

WASLEY, Richard Lindsay (Hooker)
Born Adelaide, Australia, 03.11.71. **ADPR:** Exeter (1997-98, 7, 1t-5pts). Joined from the Brighton club in Australia.

WEBBER, Lee Robert (Centre)
Born Plymouth, 25.10.75. **ADPR:** Exeter (1997-98, 7). Strong midfield player who started with Tavistock and then joined Exeter from Northampton.

WILLIAMS, Craig Ian (Flanker)
Born Lower Hutt, New Zealand, 03.09.73. **ADPR:** Exeter (1997-98, 11). New Zealand wing forward who has played for the Arks club in Western Australia and Avalon in New Zealand.

WOODMAN, Mark Charles (Wing)
Born Exeter, 18.09.70. 6', 15st. **ADPR:** Bath (1993-94, 1, 1t-5pts), Exeter (1995-98, 59, 20t-100pts). Former Crediton and Bath wing who moved to the County Ground in August 1995.

WOOLTORTON, Martyn John (Hooker)
Born Leeds, 03.03.67. 5'10", 14st. **ADPR:** Exeter (1994-98, 45, 2t-10pts). Royal Marine who numbers Morley, Plymouth and Huddersfield YMCA among his former clubs.

REVIEW

Started the season brightly with wins over Wakefield and Waterloo, but Exeter flattered to deceive and eventually finished last but one, avoiding relegation only by virtue of the reconstituted League. Exeter failed to recruit adequately after gaining promotion the previous season and, lacking the financial backing of a big sponsor, that could again prove a problem. The appointment of Ian Bremner – who has worked with Cardiff, Sweden and Ireland U21 – as team manager would seem a step in the right direction but a tough season undoubtedly awaits.

EXETER in Premiership Two 1997-98

Aug 30	A	Wakefield	Won	19	15	M.Woodman(T) J.Fabian(C, 4P)
Sep 7	A	Coventry	Lost	8	29	M.Woodman(T) J.Fabian(P)
13	H	Bedford	Lost	17	32	R.John(T) J.Fabian(2P) M.Patidar(2D)
20	H	Waterloo	Won	24	20	J.Fabian(2T, C, 3P) M.McLoughlin(D)
27	A	Moseley	Lost	22	23	R.Wasley(T) J.Fabian(C, 5P)
Oct 4	H	West Hartlepool	Lost	19	20	J.Alvis(T) J.Fabian(C, 4P)
11	A	Fylde	Lost	10	18	Penalty(T) J.Fabian(C, P)
18	H	London Scottish	Lost	16	22	A.Maunder(T) N.Southern(T) M.Patidar(P) F.Tchahardehi(D)
25	A	Waterloo	Lost	13	44	J.Hudson(T) J.Fabian(C, 2P)
Nov 8	H	Moseley	Lost	10	20	J.Thomas(T) J.Fabian(C, P)
Dec 13	A	West Hartlepool	Lost	14	34	B.Armstrong(T) C.Barrow(T) J.Fabian(2C)
20	H	Fylde	Won	24	15	J.Alvis(T) R.Gibbins(T) J.Fabian(C, 4P)
Jan 17	H	Coventry	Won	18	14	J.Alvis(T) R.Baxter(T) J.Fabian(C, 2P)
24	A	London Scottish	Lost	10	22	M.Woodman(T) A.Birkitt(T)
Jan 31	H	Blackheath	Won	20	18	J.Alvis(T) R.Baxter(T) J.Fabian(2C, 2P)
Feb 14	A	Orrell	Lost	3	38	J.Fabian(P)
Mar 7	H	Rotherham	Lost	8	33	C.Barrow(T) J.Fabian(P)
14	H	Orrell	Won	17	14	M.Woodman(T) J.Fabian(4P)
28	A	Blackheath	Lost	15	24	J.Alvis(T) S.Carter(T) J.Fabian(C, P)
Apr 11	H	Wakefield	Lost	17	30	S.Carter(T) R.Gibbins(T) R.John(T) J.Fabian(C)
18	A	Bedford	Lost	3	16	J.Fabian(P)
25	A	Rotherham	Lost	27	50	J.Alvis(T) S.Carter(T) J.Fabian(C, 5P)

Summary of Premiership scorers:

174 – J.Fabian (2T, 16C, 44P); 30 – J.Alvis (6T); 20 – M.Woodman (4T);
15 – S.Carter (3T); 10 – R.John (2T), R.Gibbins (2T), C.Barrow (2T), R.Baxter
(2T); 9 – M.Patidar (2D, P); 5 – Penalty (T), R.Wasley (T), J.Thomas (T),
N.Southern (T), A.Maunder (T), J.Hudson (T), A.Birkitt (T), B.Armstrong (T);
3 – F.Tchahardehi (D), M.McLoughlin (D).

Summary of Premiership appearances:

22 – R.Gibbins, C.Barrow (+1), J.Alvis (+3); 21 – J.Fabian (+2); 20 – M.Woodman,
R.Baxter; 17 – J.Thomas, R.John (+1); 16 – R.Hutchinson (+1); 15 – A.Turner
(+4), N.Southern (+8), S.Doyle (+2); 14 – M.Wooltorton, B.Armstrong;
11 – C.Williams (+7), A.Green (+1), R.Baxter (+1); 8 – W.Newman (+2), M.Curry
(+2), J.Batchelor (+4); 7 – L.Webber (+3), R.Wasley (+1); 6 – W.Reed (+3),
M.McLoughlin, D.Cross, S.Carter, A.Birkitt (+1); 5 – F.Tchahardehi (+1);
4 – P.Sluman (+4), A.Maunder (+1), A.Cudmore (+1); 3 – L.Wilkinson (+1),
M.Patidar, P.Livingstone (+1), S.Jones; 2 – M.Webb (+1), S.Pooley (+1);
1 – R.Ward (+1), H.Thomas, J.Sussex (+1), R.Pugsley, G.May (+1), S.Kelly (+1),
S.Johnson, J.Hudson, J.Collins (+1), J.Adams (+1).

FYLDE

Formation of club: 1919
Ground: The Woodlands Memorial Ground, Blackpool Road, Ansdell, Lytham St
    Annes FY8 4EL
Capacity: 5,440 (Seated 440)
Colours: Claret, gold and white
Honours: None
Best League finish: 9th in Division Two, 1994-95
Best Cup run: Q/F, in 1976-77
Last season: ADP2 – 12th. Tetley's Bitter Cup – 5th round (lost 8-34 to Wasps)
Owners: Members
Rugby Manager: Andy MacFarlane
Coach: Brendan Hanavan
Captain: TBC

AINGE, Damian Thomas (Full-back)
Born Lytham, 19.11.69. **ADPR:** Fylde (1997-98, 1). Joined Fylde from Oldham RL.

ASHURST, Neil Eric (Flanker)
Born St Helens, 12.05.69. 6'2", 16st 7lb. **ADPR:** Orrell (1989-94, 40, 7t-31pts), Sale
(1994-97, 41, 7t-35pts), Wakefield (1997-98, 3), Fylde (1997-98, 5, 1t-5pts). Powerful
blindside wing forward with bags of senior experience with Orrell and Sale. Appeared
in the 1997 Pilkington Cup final for Sale.

BARCLAY, Ian James (Utility back)
Born Lytham St Annes, 29.07.69. 5'11", 14st. **ADPR:** Fylde (1987-98, 119, 17t, 3c,
11pg, 7dg-145pts). Useful all-rounder behind the scrum. Works as an insurance
executive.

BELL, Alistair James (Backrow)
Born Carlisle, 15.04.74. 6'4", 16st 7lb. **ADPR:** Fylde (1994-98, 54, 4t-20pts). A versatile player capable of filling several positions, including wing, although coaches have persuaded him to concentrate on filling the No 8 shirt. Lacks finesse and still has raw edges, but is firmly one for the future. Played consistently well in Fylde's promotion season in 1996-97. Joined from Wigton. Works as a salesman.

BIRD, Ian Phillip (Wing)
Born Burnley, 29.06.78. 5'10", 14st. **ADPR:** Fylde (1997-98, 8). Joined from Vale of Lune. Educated at Lancaster and Morecambe College.

BURNS, Thomas Craig (Prop)
Born Blackburn, 01.08.64. 6', 14st 7lb. **ADPR:** Fylde (1989-98, 101, 4t-19pts). Works on the family farm at Accrington. A powerful athletic prop who recorded his 100th League appearance for Fylde last season. Originally learned his trade with Blackburn RFC.

CONNELL, Stuart Ronald (Centre)
Born Bolton, 17.04.67. 5'11", 14st. **ADPR:** Fylde (1990-98, 55, 2t-8pts). A long-term servant to Fylde for nearly a decade since joining from Cockermouth.

DAVY, John Richard Harry (Hooker)
Born Solihull, 01.03.73. 6', 15st. **ADPR:** Fylde (1996-98, 4). Joined Fylde 1995-96 from Preston Grasshoppers. Works in the restaurant trade.

DUGGAN, John Joseph (Flanker)
Born Leicester, 16.03.74. 6'4", 16st. **ADPR:** Fylde (1995-98, 26, 3t-15pts). Promising flanker who joined from Vipers. Educated at University of Central Lancashire and works as a quantity surveyor.

ECKERSLEY, Nick (Lock)
Born Farnworth, 02.04.61. **ADPR:** Fylde (1987-98, 24). Club stalwart for over a decade whose first-team opportunities have been few and far between.

EVANS, Mark Leslie (Centre)
Born Leeds, 21.02.75. 5'11", 13st. **ADPR:** Fylde (1994-98, 27, 3t-15pts). Centre with plenty of pace who can also play on the wing. Educated at Chester College.

FILIPO, Matthew Tetai (Prop)
Born Otahuhu, New Zealand, 28.10.71. **ADPR:** Fylde (1997-98, 18). Rugged New Zealand-reared prop who was a strong influence in the front row last season. Played for Manawatu/Counties when in New Zealand.

GOUGH, Stephen (Fly-half)
Born Leigh, 22.04.66. 5'10", 13st 7lb. **ADPR:** Fylde (1987-98, 121, 26t, 85c, 142pg, 6dg-739pts), Sheffield (1989-90, 1t-4pts). Prolific fly-half who failed to repeat the points-scoring extravaganza of Fylde's promotion season in 1996-97. Former England Colt and a product of the club's youth policy, Stephen also enjoyed a brief spell at Sheffield and with Leigh RL. Works as an insurance executive.

HANAVAN, Brendan Paul (Wing)
Born Bolton, 27.10.60. **ADPR:** Fylde (1987-88, 9, 10t-40pts), Liverpool St Helens (1988-89, 11, 3t-12pts), Fylde (1989-98, 67, 31t-143pts). Experienced try-scoring wing who prefers to concentrate on his coaching duties these days.

HANSON, Richard John (Prop)
Born Whalley, 11.08.75. **ADPR:** Orrell (1996-97, 1), Fylde (1997-98, 17). Developing prop who joined from Calder Vale.

HOLMES, Paul (Lock)
Born Lancaster, 18.11.75. 6'7", 17st 7lb. **ADPR:** Fylde (1996-98, 36, 1t-5pts). England Students and Scotland U21 lock who joined from Vale of Lune. Educated at Loughborough University, an accountant by profession.

IRELAND, Anthony (Flanker)
Born Lancaster, 05.03.66. 6'2", 16st. **ADPR:** Fylde (1991-93, 13, 4t-16pts), Waterloo (1992-95, 8), Fylde (1996-98, 14). Much-travelled flanker who has also played for Vale of Lune, Waterloo and Orrell. North of England tourist 1991 to Zimbabwe and Namibia.

IRVING, Julien Robert (Centre)
Born Oldham, 13.02.71. 6', 14st 3lb. **ADPR:** Fylde (1996-98, 22, 3t-15pts). Son of Bill Irving, legendary Oldham RL player for many years. Career interrupted two years ago by a broken sternum. Works as an accountant.

KUMBIER, Karl Rainer (Lock)
Born Durban, South Africa, 02.07.71. **Rep hons:** Germany. **ADPR:** Fylde (1997-98, 10). Germany's World Cup lock who learned his rugby in Durban. Has also played for Western Province.

LAVIN, Carl Anthony (Flanker)
Born Blackpool, 14.03.77. 6'2", 15st. **ADPR:** Fylde (1996-98, 6, 1t-5pts). Promising flanker. Student at Oxford University. Educated at King Edward VII, Lytham.

McCARTHY, Brian William (Lock)
Born Brockville, Canada, 15.09.69. **Rep hons:** Canada. **ADPR:** Nottingham (1996-97, 10), Fylde (1997-98, 16, 1t-5pts). Powerful Canadian who enjoyed a spell with Ajax Wanderers before travelling to England.

McCORMICK, Liam Ross (Lock)
Born Coventry, 14.08.72. **ADPR:** Fylde (1997-98, 7). Useful backup lock who has also played for Sutton Coldfield and Guildford.

McINTYRE, Craig Andrew (Hooker)
Born Lytham, 19.04.69. 6', 15st 2lb. **ADPR:** Fylde (1990-98, 52, 1t-5pts). Mobile hooker. Educated at Manchester University, works as a premium bonds administrator. Formerly with Richmond.

MOFFAT, Gavin Richard (Full-back)
Born Lancaster, 09.09.72. 6'3", 15st 7lb. **ADPR:** Fylde (1996-98, 19, 3t-15pts). Talented full-back who has yet to fulfil his full potential. Joined from Vale of Lune, teaches at RGS Lancaster.

O'NEILL, Colm Patrick (Lock)
Born Chesterfield, 17.08.68. 6'7", 17st 9lb. **ADPR:** Fylde (1991-96, 46) Orrell (1995-97, 6), Fylde (1997-98, 6). Imposing lock who returned from Orrell to provide valuable backup in the second row.

O'TOOLE, Christopher Mark (Scrum-half)
Born St Helens, 08.02.66. 5'10", 14st 10lb. **ADPR:** Liverpool St Helens (1987-88, 5, 2t-8pts), Orrell (1988-91, 6, 2t-8pts), Liverpool St Helens (1991-92, 1), Fylde (1993-98, 84, 13t, 1dg-68pts). Much-travelled scrum-half who finally settled at Fylde. Bricklayer who also once considered a career as a boxer.

PEACOCK, Alun Wayne (Fly-half)
Born Billinge, 16.01.74. **ADPR:** Orrell (1993-96, 10, 2c, 2pg-10pts), Morley (1996-97, 14, 3t, 22c, 23pg-128pts), Fylde (1997-98, 16, 1c, 20pg, 1dg-65pts). Underrated former England U21 and Lancashire fly-half.

PRESTON, David Mark (Wing)
Born Lytham, 03.04.67. **Rep hons:** England A (1, It88, 1t-4pts). **ADPR:** Fylde (1987-98, 54, 35t-167pts). A real man of Fylde, who joined the club as a youngster and has maintained strong links ever since, despite an outstanding RL career. Left Fylde to join Wigan before moving to Halifax, but returned to Fylde in 1996. Top try-scorer last season with six.

RUSSELL, Gareth Mark (Flanker)
Born Rochdale, 30.07.72. 6', 15st 5lb. **ADPR:** Fylde (1991-98, 99, 10t-50pts). Hard-tackling flanker who captained Fylde in difficult circumstances last season. One game short of completing 100 League appearances.

SAVERIMUTTO, Robin (Scrum-half)
Born Wallasey, 21.08.73. **ADPR:** Coventry (1995-96, 8), Orrell (1996-97, 6, 1t-5pts), Fylde (1997-98, 7). Youngest of the three Saverimutto brothers. Has represented Ireland U21.

SCOTT, Martin William (Hooker)
Born Falkirk, 05.07.67. 6', 15st 10lb. **Rep hons:** Scotland (1, Aus92), A (4, Ire91). **ADPR:** Orrell (1994-97, 28, 1t-5pts), Fylde (1997-98, 22, 2t-10pts). Former Scotland hooker who was ever-present last season. Started his career with Edinburgh Academicals and Dunfermline. Works as a civil servant in telecommunications.

TANNER, David (Centre)
Born Keighley, 29.09.65. 6'1", 15st 7lb. **ADPR:** Fylde (1996-98, 30, 3t, 3pg-24pts). Another former rugby league player who played the 13-man game with St Helens and Swinton.

TASKER, Grahame Douglas (Flanker)
Born Sao Paolo, Brazil, 04.12.69. **ADPR:** Fylde (1994-98, 10). Joined the club from West of Scotland RFC.

TAYLOR, Jonathan Peter Wallington (Lock)
Born Steamer Point, 05.10.66. 6'5", 17st. **ADPR:** Fylde (1989-98, 114, 7t-30pts). Club stalwart for over a decade, logging over 100 League appearances. Works with British Aerospace.

TOPPING, David Anthony (Scrum-half)
Born Billinge, 14.01.74. 5'7", 11st 7lb. **ADPR:** Orrell (1993-95, 7), Waterloo (1996-97, 2), Fylde (1997-98, 8). Former England U21 and England Universities scrum-half who has struggled to regain his best form. Works as a quantity surveyor.

WALLWORK, Martin (Scrum-half)
Born Blackpool, 30.03.78. 5'11", 12st. **ADPR:** Fylde (1997-98, 9). Promising Lancashire Colts scrum-half. Educated at Arnold School and Loughborough University.

WRIGHT, David John (Prop)
Born Nottingham, 18.10.70. 6'1", 16st. **ADPR:** Fylde (1996-98, 15). Former England Schools representative who joined from Nottingham, having previously been at Leicester and Bedford.

REVIEW

Fylde face a massive task to survive in the newly constituted Premiership Two after a dismal season in 1997-98 in which they won just two League games. Try-scoring was their major problem, managing just 22 throughout the Allied Dunbar campaign. Little money exists for recruiting so Fylde will have to largely rely on their existing squad. A good spirit remains, however, typified by their brave performance in the Tetley's Bitter Cup when they eventually lost 34-8 to Wasps.

FYLDE in Premiership Two 1997-98

Aug 30	A	London Scottish	Lost	9	35	S.Gough(3P)
Sep 13	H	Coventry	Lost	15	23	M.Preston(T) J.Duggan(T) S.Gough(C, P)
20	A	Blackheath	Lost	16	50	M.Evans(T) S.Gough(C, 3P)
27	H	Rotherham	Lost	18	25	I.Barclay(T) S.Gough(T, C, 2P)
Oct 4	A	Orrell	Lost	9	35	A.Peacock(3P)
11	H	Exeter	Won	18	10	A.Peacock(6P)
18	A	Wakefield	Lost	17	35	M.Preston(T) A.Peacock(4P)
25	H	Blackheath	Lost	6	31	S.Gough(2P)
Nov 8	A	Rotherham	Lost	16	32	S.Gough(T, C, 3P)
Dec 13	H	Orrell	Lost	9	21	A.Peacock(3P)
20	A	Exeter	Lost	15	24	G.Moffatt(T) M.Scott(T) S.Gough(C, P)
27	H	Bedford	Lost	7	67	Penalty(T) S.Gough(C)
Jan 17	A	Bedford	Lost	14	50	M.Preston(T) A.Peacock(D, 2P)
31	H	Waterloo	Lost	10	25	M.Preston(2T)
Feb 14	A	West Hartlepool	Lost	12	66	B.McCarthy(T) M.Preston(T) S.Gough(C)
28	H	Wakefield	Lost	10	30	M.Scott(T) A.Peacock(C, P)
Mar 14	H	West Hartlepool	Lost	8	34	G.Moffatt(T) A.Peacock(P)
28	A	Waterloo	Lost	12	22	J.Duggan(T) M.Evans(T) S.Gough(C)
Apr 4	H	Moseley	Won	14	13	S.Gough(T, 3P)
11	H	London Scottish	Lost	7	22	I.Barclay(T) S.Gough(C)
18	A	Coventry	Lost	7	16	N.Ashurst(T) S.Gough(C)
25	A	Moseley	Lost	9	44	S.Gough(3P)

Summary of Premiership scorers:

98 – S.Gough (3T, 10C, 21P); 65 – A.Peacock (C, D, 20P); 30 – M.Preston (6T);
10 – M.Scott (2T), G.Moffatt (2T), M.Evans (2T), J.Duggan (2T), I.Barclay (2T);
5 – Penalty (T), B.McCarthy (T), N.Ashurst (T).

Summary of Premiership appearances:

22 – M.Scott; 18 – G.Russell, M.Preston, S.Gough (+3), M.Filipo (+1);
17 – R.Hanson (+3); 16 – A.Peacock (+1), B.McCarthy; 15 – M.Evans (+1);
14 – P.Holmes (+1), J.Duggan (+1), S.Connell (+1), I.Barclay; 12 – D.Tanner,
J.Irving (+2), A.Bell (+3); 11 – G.Moffatt (+1); 10 – K.Kumbier (+1);
9 – M.Wallwork (+1), G.Tasker (+2), S.Rigby (+2); 8 – D.Topping (+3), A.Ireland,
C.Burns (+5), I.Bird (+2); 7 – J.Taylor (+5), R.Saverimutto (+2), L.McCormack
(+1); 6 – C.O'Toole (+2), P.O'Neill; 5 – N.Ashurst (+2); 4 – J.Webster (+4), P.Stott;
3 – C.Lavin (+3); 2 – R.Stowe (+2), C.McIntyre (+2); 1 – D.Wright, S.Williams
(+1), V.Viller, B.Hanavan (+1), N.Eckersley, J.Davy (+1), D.Ainge (+1).

LEEDS

Formation of club: 1992 by merger of Headingley (founded 1878) and Roundhay
(founded 1924)
Ground: Headingley Stadium, St Michaels Lane, Headingley, Leeds LS6 3BR
Capacity: 27,000 (Seated 9,000)
Colours: Royal blue, white and gold
Honours: None
Best League finish: 2nd in Jewson One, 1997-98
Best Cup run: Last 16 1996-97 1997-98
Last season: Jewson One – 2nd. Tetley's Bitter Cup – 2nd round (lost 11-28 to
Worcester)
Owners: Members
Coach: Phil Davies
Captain: TBC

AINSCOUGH, Gerry Christopher (Fly-half/centre)
Born Wigan, 07.08.64. **Rep hons:** England A (1, Sp89). **ADPR:** Orrell (1987-91, 31,
10t, 9c, 28pg, 2dg-148pts), Leicester (1991-92, 6, 2t-8pts), Orrell (1992-95, 37, 2t, 25c,
43pg-189pts), Leeds (1995-98, 33, 15t, 46c, 49pg-314pts). Canny fly-half and goal-
kicker with valuable experience of the top flight.

APPLESON, Mark Edward (Utility back)
Born Islington, 26.02.68. **Rep hons:** Scotland A (4, Ire91, 2c, 1pg-7pts). **ADPR:**
Headingley (1987-89, 11, 3t, 3c, 18pg-72pts), London Scottish (1990-94, 47, 11t, 15c,
13pg, 1dg-121pts), Sale (1994-96, 17, 3t-15pts), Leeds (1995-98, 33, 20t, 3c, 1dg-
109pts). Former England Schools cap who represented Scotland at sevens and
seemed destined for a full Scotland cap before injury intervened. Schoolmaster by
profession.

CAWTHORN, Michael (Scrum-half)
Born Bridlington, 15.05.72. **ADPR:** Wakefield (1993-95, 6), Leeds (1996-98, 43,
12t-60pts). Promising scrum-half who developed nicely last season.

CLAYTON, Paul Richard (Wing)
Born Billinge, 31.12.74. **ADPR:** Orrell (1996-97, 3) Leeds (1997-98, 10, 5t-25pts). Powerful Lancastrian who showed his try-scoring instincts when called upon last season.

DENHAM, Lee Francis (Flanker)
Born 05.03.74. **ADPR:** Leeds (1995-98, 30, 6t-30pts). Fine young flanker who was dubbed 'Supersub' last season after coming off the replacements' bench no fewer than 11 times.

EASTERBY, Simon Henry (Flanker)
Born Harrogate, 21.07.75. **Rep hons:** Ireland A (1, Can97). **ADPR** Harrogate (1994-97, 26, 8t-40pts), Leeds (1997-98, 17, 2t-10pts). Rangy backrow forward who has attracted the attention of the Ireland selectors.

EDWARDS, Diccon (Centre)
Born London, 13.03.73. **Rep hons:** Wales A (2, Fr95). **ADPR:** Wakefield (1992-94, 23, 2t-10pts), Leicester (1994-95, 15), Leeds (1996-98, 31, 4t-20pts). Represented England Schools, Colts and U21 before opting for Wales in 1995 and winning A caps. Joined Leeds from Leicester and overcame knee problems to enjoy an excellent 1997-98 season, missing only four League games. Also enjoyed a spell with Castleford RL.

FOURIE, Timothy Wayne (No 8)
Born Port Elizabeth, South Africa, 12.03.68. **ADPR:** Leeds (1997-98, 24, 10t-50pts). Athletic South African flanker who played his club rugby for the Centurions club back home.

GREEN, Nicholas John (Flanker)
Born Northampton, 26.01.66. **ADPR:** Headingley (1987-92, 20, 1t-4pts), Leeds (1992-93, 10, 3t-15pts), Wakefield (1993-96, 47, 5t-25pts), Leeds (1996-98, 37, 15t-75pts). Experienced flanker who remains committed despite limited first-team opportunities.

GRIFFITHS, Steven Tom (Lock)
Born Morecambe, 04.08.73. **ADPR:** Orrell (1995-96, 3), London Scottish (1996-97, 8, 1t-5pts), Leeds (1997-98, 14, 2t-10pts). Underrated lock who has impoved noticeably since moving from London Scottish.

HENRY, Simon Richard (Lock)
Born Leeds, 26.03.72. **ADPR:** Otley (1992-96, 34, 4t-20pts), Leeds (1996-98, 18). Athletic former England Schools forward who joined from his hometown club of Otley.

JOHNSON, Paul Thomas Andrew (Centre)
Born Huddersfield, 19.05.62. **ADPR:** Headingley (1987-91, 30, 3t-12pts), Leeds (1992-93, 6, 2t-10pts), Orrell (1993-96, 43, 4t, 1dg-23pts), Leeds (1996-98, 32, 5t-25pts). One of the key figures behind Leeds' improvement, Paul has been a tower of strength since returning to the club from Orrell where he was a former club captain.

KELLY, Ronald William (Prop)
Born Wigan, 11.06.68. **ADPR:** Leeds (1996-98, 7). Solid prop who has played previously for Sale and Keighley

KNEALE, Stewart Caine (Hooker)
Born Leeds, 30.04.74. **ADPR:** West Hartlepool (1994-95, 1). Leeds (1996-98, 19). Former England 16 Group cap who continues to develop.

LANCASTER, William Stuart (Flanker)
Born Penrith, 09.10.69. **ADPR:** Leeds (1992-98, 45, 5t-25pts). Long-time club member who remains a solid performer. Joined from Wakefield in 1992.

LUFFMAN, Mark Edward (Hooker)
Born Nottingham, 17.08.71. **ADPR:** Otley (1995-96, 10, 1t-5pts), Leeds (1996-98, 50, 3t-15pts). Established himself as the first-choice hooker last season. Joined from Otley and also played for Ilkley.

MATHIAS, Richard (Wing)
Born Morriston, 28.05.75. **ADPR:** Orrell (1995-96, 3), Leeds (1996-98, 43, 25t-125pts). Has developed into a prolific try-scorer since joining from Orrell. Son of former Great Britain rugby league star Roy Mathias.

MIDDLETON, Simon (Wing)
Born Kellington, 02.02.66. **ADPR:** Otley (1996-97, 8, 2t-10pts), Leeds (1997-98, 18, 17t-85pts). Powerful direct runner who has flourished since joining from Otley. Averaged nearly a try a game in the Jewsons League last season.

PEREGO, Mark Angelo (Flanker)
Born Winchester, 08.02.64. **Rep hons:** Wales (9, Sc90) A (2, Aus92). **ADPR:** Leeds (1996-98, 27, 4t-20pts). Wonderfully athletic, if occasionally eccentric, Welsh flanker who keeps fit by competing in triathlons. A key player for Leeds, Mark was discarded too quickly by Wales. Formerly with Llanelli.

RADACANU, Christian (Lock)
Born Bucharest, Romania, 02.10.67. **Rep hons:** Romania. **ADPR:** Headingley (1990-91, 5), Sale (1991-92, 7, 1t-4pts), Leeds (1994-98, 68, 28t-140pts). Defected from Romania eight years ago to become an honorary 'Tyke'. Considerable line-out operator who also knows how to score tries.

SAILOR, Wendell (Wing)
Born Brisbane, Australia, 16.07.74. **Rep hons:** Australia RL. Giant Australia wing, rated the best in the world in the 13 man code. An ambitious £100,000 deal will see his services shared for 4 months between Leeds and Leeds Rhinos RL.

SAVERIMUTTO, Christian Lingard (Scrum-half)
Born Wallasey, 08.08.71. 5'8", 13st. **Rep hons:** Ireland (3, Fiji95). **ADPR:** Waterloo (1991-94, 36, 5t, 1dg-26pts), Sale (1994-96, 25, 3t-15pts), Leeds (1997-98, 22, 3t-15pts). Resurrected his career with Leeds last season after a serious anterior cruciate knee ligament injury – incurred playing sevens for Ireland in Lisbon – nearly put him out of action forever. Lovely quick service, and young enough to challenge for international honours again.

SHELLEY, Michael (Prop)
Born Leeds, 02.03.74. **ADPR:** West Hartlepool (1994-96, 18, 4t-20pts), Leeds (1996-98, 50, 9t-45pts). Former England Students prop who has become the cornerstone of Leeds' front row since joining from West Hartlepool. Hopes to start attracting the England selectors again this season.

STEPHENS, Colin John (Fly-half)
Born Morriston, 29.11.69. **Rep hons:** Wales (4, Ire92, 2pg, 1dg-9pts), A (3, Can89, 1t, 2pg, 1dg-14pts), Barbarians (90-91). **ADPR:** Leeds (1995-98, 50, 17t, 19c, 23pg, 13dg-231pts). Mercurial Welsh fly-half who as a youngster with Llanelli looked destined for great honours. Duly won four Wales caps, but the selectors moved him on with indecent haste and serious injury plagued him in subsequent years.

THOMAS, Huw Glyn (Prop)
Born St Asaph, Wales, 29.10.74. **ADPR:** Leeds (1997-98, 16). Joined Leeds from Mold in North Wales.

TUIPULOTU, Sateki (Full-back)
Born Nuku'alofa, Tonga, 03.07.71. **Rep hons:** Tonga. **ADPR:** Leeds (1996-98, 54, 26t, 97c, 66pg-522pts). Exciting, multi-talented Tongan full-back who was voted Jewsons player of the season. Ever-present throughout Leeds' campaign, he garnered a massive 327 points. Will miss the early part of this season as he joins Tonga's squad for the World Cup qualifying tournament in Australia.

WHITCOMBE, Martin Alunn (Prop)
Born Keighley, 14.09.62. **Rep hons:** England A (1, Fr89). **ADPR:** Sale (1987-95, 72, 6t-28pts), Leeds (1995-98, 41, 4t-20pts). Hugely experienced prop who can still scrummage with the best. Educated at Bingley GS.

WYNN, Ian (Centre)
Born St Helens, 11.08.68. 6'2", 14st. **ADPR:** Orrell (1989-96, 57, 16t-80pts), Wakefield (1996-97, 22, 3t-15pts), Leeds (1997-98, 17, 4t-20pts). Clever ball-playing centre who has played for Scottish Exiles.

ZOING, Ralph Aleksio (Fly-half)
Born Herford, West Germany, 27.12.65. **ADPR:** Harrogate (1993-97, 58, 8t, 98c, 118pg, 12dg-626pts), Leeds (1997-98, 4, 1t-5pts). Prolific for Harrogate, provides cover for Colin Stephens at fly-half.

REVIEW

Worcester may have denied Leeds the Jewsons title but the Yorkshire club remain an improving outfit and could well take Premiership Two by storm. Individually they boast exceptional players like Sateki Tuipulotu, Mark Perego, Ian Wynn, Paul Johnson and Colin Stephens and there is every likelihood they will recruit well. Have set themselves the aim of becoming Yorkshire's premier side and with that aim in mind have enlisted the help of local sides – Roundhegians, West Leeds, West Park Bramhope, Old Modernians, Leodiensians, Huddersfield and Huddersfield YMCA – to act as feeder clubs.

LEEDS in Jewson One 1997-98

Aug 30	H	Harrogate	Won	27	24	M.Luffman(T) C.Stephens(T) S.Tuipulotu(T, 3C, 2P)
Sep 13	A	London Welsh	Drew	21	21	C.Stephens(T) C.Radacanu(T) S.Tuipulotu(C, 3P)
20	A	Lydney	Won	8	5	S.Tuipulotu(T, P)

	27	H	Morley	Won	27	17	S.Tuipulotu(T, 3C, P) P.Johnson(T) M.Cawthorn(T) C.Stephens(D)
Oct	11	A	Newbury	Won	21	16	S.Middleton(T) M.Perego(T) S.Tuipulotu(C, 3P)
	18	H	Nottingham	Won	46	18	M.Appleson(T) L.Denham(T) S.Middleton(T) S.Tuipulotu(T, 3C, 5P) M.Whitcombe(T)
	25	A	Otley	Lost	21	30	M.Appleson(T) Penalty(T) S.Tuipulotu(C, 3P)
Nov	8	H	Reading	Won	37	27	C.Stephens(T, D) S.Easterby(T) M.Appleson(T) D.Edwards(T) S.Tuipulotu(4C, 2P)
	15	A	Rosslyn Park	Lost	13	18	N.Green(T) S.Tuipulotu(C, 2P)
	22	H	Rugby	Won	28	15	C.Radacanu(T) T.Fourie(T) S.Tuipulotu(5P) C.Stephens(D)
Dec	13	A	Liverpool St Helens	Won	21	6	S.Tuipulotu(T, 3C) C.Saverimutto(T) T.Fourie(T)
	20	A	Wharfedale	Won	31	9	S.Tuipulotu(2T, C, 3P) R.Mathias(T) P.Clayton(T)
	27	H	Worcester	Lost	14	15	N.Green(T) S.Tuipulotu(3P)
Jan	10	H	Rosslyn Park	Won	26	21	S.Tuipulotu(T, C, 3P) T.Fourie(T) D.Edwards(T)
	17	A	Reading	Won	33	22	I.Wynn(T) C.Radacanu(T) G.Ainscough(T) S.Middleton(T) S.Tuipulotu(2C, 3P)
	24	H	Otley	Won	62	10	T.Fourie(2T) R.Mathias(2T) M.Cawthorn(T) L.Denham(T) S.Middleton(T) C.Radacanu(T) S.Tuipulotu(T, 4C) I.Wynn(T) C.Stephens(2C)
	31	A	Nottingham	Won	33	15	S.Middleton(3T) C.Stephens(T) L.Denham(T) S.Tuipulotu(4C)
Feb	7	H	Newbury	Won	37	14	R.Mathias(2T) S.Middleton(T) C.Radacanu(T) S.Tuipulotu(T, 2C, 2P) C.Stephens(C)
	14	H	Morley	Won	69	14	S.Middleton(5T) C.Stephens(2T, 4C) R.Mathias(T) C.Radacanu(T) S.Easterby(T) T.Fourie(T) S.Tuipulotu(3C)
	21	H	Lydney	Won	46	13	R.Mathias(2T) I.Wynn(T) P.Clayton(T) D.Edwards(T) M.Shelley(T) C.Saverimutto(T) S.Tuipulotu(4C, P)
	28	A	Rugby	Won	28	17	D.Edwards(T) R.Mathias(T) C.Radacanu(T) S.Tuipulotu(2C, 3P)
Mar	7	H	London Welsh	Won	44	5	R.Mathias(2T) C.Radacanu(2T) P.Clayton(T) C.Stephens(T) Penalty(T) S.Tuipulotu(3C, P)

14	H	Liverpool St Helens	Won	46	17	R.Mathias(2T) M.Whitcombe(2T) M.Cawthorn(T) T.Fourie(T) R.Zoing(T) S.Tuipulotu(4C, P)
21	A	Harrogate	Won	66	12	T.Fourie(2T) P.Clayton(2T) S.Griffiths(2T) S.Tuipulotu(T, 8C) I.Wynn(T) C.Saverimutto(T) M.Shelley(T)
Apr 18	A	Worcester	Lost	20	25	T.Fourie(T) S.Middleton(T) S.Tuipulotu(2C, P) C.Stephens(D)
25	H	Wharfedale	Won	33	10	S.Middleton(3T) C.Radacanu(2T) S.Tuipulotu(C, 2P)

Summary of League scorers:

327 – S.Tuipulotu (11T, 61C, 50P); 85 – S.Middleton (17T); 65 – R.Mathias (13T); 61 – C.Stephens (7T, 7C, 4D); 55 – C.Radacanu (11T); 50 – T.Fourie (10T); 25 – P.Clayton (5T); 20 – I.Wynn (4T), D.Edwards (4T); 15 – M.Whitcombe (3T), C.Saverimutto (3T), L.Denham (3T), M.Cawthorn (3T), M.Appleson (3T); 10 – Penalty (2T), M.Shelley (2T), N.Green (2T), S.Griffiths (2T), S.Easterby (2T); 5 – R.Zoing (T), M.Perego (T), M.Luffman (T), P.Johnson (T), G.Ainscough (T).

Summary of League appearances:

26 – S.Tuipulotu; 24 – T.Fourie (+1); 23 – C.Stephens (+3); 22 – C.Saverimutto (+4), M.Luffman (+2), D.Edwards (+1); 21 – C.Radacanu (+1), R.Mathias; 20 – M.Shelley (+1); 18 – S.Middleton, L.Denham (+11), M.Cawthorn (+10); 17 – I.Wynn (+1), S.Easterby (+2); 16 – H.Thomas; 15 – M.Perego (+2); 14 – M.Whitcombe (+5), S.Griffiths (+3); 12 – S.Lancaster (+1), M.Burrow (+1); 10 – S.Kneale (+4), P.Clayton; 9 – N.Green; 8 – G.Ainscough (+4); 7 – P.Johnson, S.Henry; 6 – G.Baldwin (+1), M.Appleson; 4 – R.Zoing (+2), R.Kelly (+1), P.Griffin (+4); 3 – P.Williams, R.Morgan, A.Caldwell (+1); 1 – A.Machell (+1).

LONDON WELSH

Formation of club: 1878
Ground: Old Deer Park, Kew Road, Richmond TW9 2AZ
Capacity: 7,200 (Seated 1,200)
Colours: Scarlet and white
Honours: Division Five South Champions – 1994-95
Best League finish: 9th in Division Two, 1987-88
Best Cup run: Losing finalist, 1984-85
Last season: Jewson One – 3rd. Tetley's Bitter Cup – 4th round (lost 18-34 to Gloucester)
Owners: Members
Coach: TBC
Captain: TBC

ALEXANDER, Colin David (Flanker)
Born Johannesburg, South Africa, 31.08.72. **ADPR:** Rugby (1997-98, 19, 3t-15pts).
Rugged South African flanker who joined from the Wanderers club. Established himself as a first-team regular in Jewson One last season.

CHALLINOR, Andrew Paul (Fly-half)
Born Wolverhampton, 05.12.69. 6', 13st 2lb. **Rep hons:** England A (10, Fr93, 3t, 5c, 12pg, 2dg-67pts). **ADPR:** Harlequins (1990-98, 69, 17t, 31c, 65pg, 10dg-370pts), London Welsh (1997-98, 3, 2t-10pts). Experienced former England Schools fly-half who moved to Old Deer Park at the end of last season. Educated at RGS Guildford. Useful cricketer.

CURRIER, Andrew Stephen (Centre)
Born Widnes, 08.04.66. **ADPR:** London Welsh (1997-98, 21, 13t-65pts). Powerful former Great Britain RL centre who played for Widnes and Featherstone before joining London Welsh.

DAWES, Michael (Centre)
Born Walton-on-Thames, 25.01.68. **ADPR:** London Welsh (1990-98, 68, 22t, 12c, 8pg-154pts). Ultra-reliable utility back who missed just two League games last season. Son of former London Welsh, Wales and British Lions captain John Dawes.

EDWARDS, Darren (Scrum-half)
Born Maesteg, 25.03.75. **ADPR:** Saracens (1996-97, 1), Bedford (1996-97, 5, 3t-15pts), London Welsh (1997-98, 26, 5t-25pts). Bundle of energy at scrum-half who was ever-present last season, after joining from Bedford. Regular member of the Wales Sevens squad who also enjoyed a brief spell at Saracens.

EMMS, Simon John (Prop)
Born Carmarthen, 27.01.75. **ADPR:** London Welsh (1997-98, 22). Fast-developing West Walian who joined from Llandovery.

FRENCH, Gary James (Hooker)
Born St Helens, 02.12.67. 5'11", 15st. **Rep hons:** England A (1, Arg96). **ADPR:** Liverpool St Helens (1987-92, 9), Orrell (1993-94, 18, 2t-10pts), Bath (1995-98, 4), London Scottish (1997-98, 9, 1t-5pts). Educated at Cowley HS where father, TV commentator and dual international Ray, taught rugby union. Gary was a first-team regular at Liverpool St Helens and Orrell before joining Bath in 1994. Played last season on loan from Bath.

GIRAUD, Martin (Wing)
Born Essex, 16.11.77. **ADPR:** London Welsh (1995-98, 39, 16t-80pts). With his blistering pace on the wing, Giraud has a 10.5 sec 100m to his credit. Member of various Wales Sevens squads.

HARBINSON, Alfie (Hooker)
Born Belfast, 01.12.71. **ADPR:** London Welsh (1996-98, 15, 1t-5pts). Combative hooker who moved to London Welsh from Abertillery.

HARRIES, David Gwynne (Flanker)
Born Dagenham, 17.06.66. **ADPR:** London Welsh (1989-98, 74, 6t-27pts). A stalwart figure in the backrow during the dark years, David is still a more than useful flanker.

HAYMAN, Miles (Lock)
Born Welwyn, Hertfordshire, 18.05.71. **ADPR:** London Welsh (1996-98, 15, 1t-5pts). Useful second row forward who moved to London Welsh from Lymm RFC.

HOLMES, Garry (Prop)
Born Hampstead, 07.07.65. 5'11", 16st. **Rep hons:** England A (5, Nam90). **ADPR:** Wasps (1987-95, 62, 2t-9pts), Saracens (1995-97, 13, 1t-5pts), Blackheath (1996-97, 14), London Welsh (1997-98, 26). Rock-solid and vastly experienced former England A prop who was ever-present in the Jewson League last season after joining from Blackheath the previous summer.

JOHANSON, Ashley David (Lock)
Born Sydney, Australia, 14.03.69. **ADPR:** London Welsh (1997-98, 10, 1t-5pts). Former New South Wales lock who joined from the Gordon club in Sydney.

JONES, Adam Windsor (Utility back)
Born Basingstoke, 07.11.74. 5'11", 12st 7lb. **ADPR:** Harlequins (1995-96, 1), Richmond (1996-97, 2), London Welsh (1997-98, 5, 8t-40pts). Exciting talent who has yet to fulfil his potential, though he finished last season in a blaze of glory with eight tries in the last five games.

JONES, Luke Evan (Flanker)
Born Suffolk, 06.11.70. 6'3", 14st 7lb. **ADPR:** Richmond (1993-97, 39, 6t-30pts), London Welsh (1997-98, 26, 3t-15pts). Very fit and durable at openside flanker, Luke was ever-present last season. Educated at RGS Guildford and an Oxford Blue in 1991. Formerly a member of the Beccles club.

LANGLEY, Mark Andrew (Lock)
Born Cardiff, 09.06.67. 6'4", 17st 10lb. **ADPR:** Saracens (1990-97, 68, 3t-15pts), London Welsh (1997-98, 15). Experienced second row who played for Swansea and Bridgend while a student in Wales. Served Saracens well before moving to London Welsh.

LEWSEY, Tom Rhys (Scrum-half)
Born Bromley, 03.05.75. **ADPR:** London Welsh (1996-98, 36, 14t-70pts). Educated at Watford GS. Brother of England utility back Josh Lewsey.

LUBLINER, David (Wing)
Born Roehampton, 05.02.71. **ADPR:** London Welsh (1994-98, 52, 21t-105pts). Strong-running wing with an excellent strike rate, though his opportunities were limited last season.

MARVAL, Nicholas James (Centre)
Born Johannesburg, South Africa, 23.09.72. **ADPR:** Bristol (1995-96, 3), Rosslyn Park (1996-98, 9, 4t-20pts), London Welsh (1997-98, 2, 1t-5pts). South African-reared centre struggling to earn a place in the Exiles' starting line-up.

MILLWARD, Andrew John (Prop)
Born Neath, 01.12.71. **ADPR:** London Welsh (1997-98, 12). Joined London Welsh after spells with Aberavon and Penarth while a student at UWIC.

MOORS, Eldon Stephen (Lock)
Born Auckland, New Zealand, 26.12.71. **Rep hons:** Croatia. **ADPR:** London Welsh (1996-98, 36). Capable New Zealand-reared lock who has represented Croatia in the qualifying rounds of the 1999 World Cup.

MUCKALT, David Neil (Flanker)
Born Lancaster, 17.02.75. **ADPR:** London Welsh (1996-98, 39, 5t-25pts). Hard-driving flanker who played an important role in the Exiles' promotion drive last season.

OLNEY, Charles Brendon (Hooker)
Born Taunton, 11.08.71. 5'11", 16st 8lb. **ADPR:** Saracens (1993-97, 18), London Welsh (1997-98, 8, 1t-5pts). Useful addition to the squad after accepting that first-team rugby was unlikely at Saracens and moving to Old Deer Park.

PEACOCK, Graeme John (Flanker)
Born 15.04.66. **ADPR:** London Welsh (1989-98, 119, 12t, 10c, 6pg-96pts). Stalwart flanker who will complete 10 seasons with the Exiles. Accomplished goal-kicker in his youth.

PHILLIPS, Rowland David (Flanker)
Born St David's, 28.07.65. **Rep hons:** Wales (10, USA87). **ADPR:** London Welsh (1996-98, 27, 7t-35pts). Powerful and experienced flanker who has contributed hugely to the London Welsh revival. Graduated via the Welsh Schools and Youth squads before moving to Neath. Turned professional with Workington RL. Returned to the union code with Treorchy before joining London Welsh.

PILGRIM, Stephen John (Full-back)
Born Sidcup, 26.10.67. **Rep hons:** England A (1, Fij89, 1c, 2pg-8pts), Barbarians (92-93). **ADPR:** Wasps (1987-95, 51, 8t, 16c, 34pg-167pts), Harlequins (1996-97, 3, 1pg-3pts), London Welsh (1997-98, 11, 6c, 1pg-15pts). Famously banned for 12 months by the RFU in 1993 for appearing in a rugby league trial with Leeds, a ludicrous over-reaction. His suspension could not have come at a worse time, having been named in England's long squad for the 1995 World Cup. Returned in the autumn of 1995, moved to Harlequins but has been bedevilled by injury ever since.

RAYMOND, Richard Craig (Fly-half)
Born Llanelli, 30.01.69. **ADPR:** London Welsh (1994-98, 76, 21t, 146c, 145pg, 15dg-877pts). Prolific goal-kicking fly-half and tricky runner who has served London Welsh magnificently over the last five seasons. Scored 264 points last season including eight tries.

REYNOLDS, Alfryn James (Wing)
Born Neath, 06.12.72. **ADPR:** London Welsh (1996-98, 24, 17t-85pts). Elusive former Wales Schools and Youth wing who won a Cambridge Blue in 1994. Formerly with Bridgend and Neath. Educated at Christ's, Brecon.

RIONDET, Jerome Maurice Daniel (Centre)
Born Grenoble, France, 19.04.71. **ADPR:** London Welsh (1996-98, 13, 3t-15pts). Former France A centre who gained an Oxford Blue in 1995. Educated at Lycée La Kanal-Paris.

ROBERTS, Rhys Paul (Centre)
Born Plymouth, 17.10.67. **ADPR:** London Welsh (1997-98, 2). Reliable backup centre who numbers Abertillery and Clifton among his former clubs.

ROSKELL, Scott Thomas (Wing)
Born Gold Coast, Australia, 25.06.69. **ADPR:** London Welsh (1997-98, 20, 17t-85pts). Raw-boned Australian utility back who joined the club from London Broncos RL. Strode in for 17 tries last season.

RUFFELL, David Mark (Lock)
Born Gloucester, 11.11.71. **ADPR:** Rosslyn Park (1996-97, 10, 1t-5pts), London Welsh (1997-98, 7, 1t-5pts). Reliable Gloucester born second row.

STOREY, James Stuart (Wing)
Born Harlow, 26.11.76. **ADPR:** London Welsh (1997-98, 1). Former England 16 Group cap. Former school hurdling champion, as befits the son of BBC athletics commentator Stuart Storey. Joined last season from Harlequins. Educated at Hailey-bury.

THOMAS, Richard (Prop)
Born Camberwell, 23.11.67. **ADPR:** London Welsh (1987-98, 93, 2t-9pts). Wonderfully durable prop, who performed as well as ever last season.

TUCKER, Andrew John (Hooker)
Born Pembroke, 06.12.67. **Rep hons:** Zimbabwe. **ADPR:** Bedford (1987-88, 5, 1t-4pts), London Welsh (1989-98, 94, 25t-121pts). Reliable Zimbabwean hooker who has served the Exiles for nearly a decade. A real sniffer of tries.

VINES, Matthew David (Full-back)
Born South Glamorgan, 11.05.76. **ADPR:** London Welsh (1995-98, 22, 4t-20pts). Young utility back with loads of ability, though first-team opportunities have been limited thus far.

VOGL, Clifton (Lock)
Born Karlsruhe, Germany, 01.04.69. **Rep hons:** US (9, Can96). **ADPR:** London Welsh (1997-98, 12, 1t-5pts). Athletic American lock who learned his trade in Colin Meads country when playing for King Country province in New Zealand. Has also played for Bridgend and Belmont Shore in USA.

WHITTAKER, Christopher Michael (Lock)
Born Victoria, Canada, 12.09.71. **Rep hons:** Canada. **ADPR:** London Welsh (1997-98, 5, 1t-5pts). Solid Canadian second row who joined from the James Bay Club on Vancouver Island.

REVIEW

London Welsh were a club in terminal decline three years ago but a massive effort by a hard core of loyal club members has given them a fighting chance of regaining their status as a top club. A consortium led by former Wales and British Lions flanker John Taylor is attempting to provide the finance, while a useful mix of rugby league imports, seasoned Welsh players and promising London-based youngsters produced an attractive brand of rugby in the Jewsons League. This season will provide the acid test but there is a buzz again at Old Deer Park.

LONDON WELSH in Jewson One 1997-98

Aug 30	A	Wharfedale	Won	41	20	A.Currier(2T) R.Phillips(2T) M.Giraud(T) D.Lubliner(T) C.Raymond(4C, P)
Sep 13	H	Leeds	Drew	21	21	G.Peacock(T) A.Tucker(T) C.Raymond(C, 3P)
20	A	Morley	Won	52	24	P.Shaw(2T) M.Giraud(2T) M.Dawes(T) A.Currier(2T) L.Jones(T) R.Westlake(T) C.Raymond(6C)

	27	H	Nottingham	Won	40	14	R.Phillips(2T) J.Reynolds(T) C.Raymond(T, 2C, 2P) D.Edwards(T) M.Dawes(T)
Oct	11	A	Reading	Won	21	5	J.Reynolds(2T) C.Raymond(T, 2P)
	18	H	Rugby	Won	21	15	A.Harbinson(T) J.Reynolds(T) S.Roskell(T) C.Raymond(3C)
	25	A	Worcester	Won	28	13	A.Currier(2T) M.Giraud(T) C.Raymond(2C, D, 2P)
Nov	8	H	Liverpool St Helens	Won	55	12	S.Roskell(2T) D.Edwards(2T) A.Currier(T) C.Raymond(T, 5C) P.Shaw(T) T.Lewsey(T) M.Giraud(T)
	15	A	Lydney	Won	28	10	J.Reynolds(2T) D.Edwards(T) R.Phillips(T) C.Raymond(C, 2P)
	22	H	Newbury	Lost	17	33	M.Giraud(T) Penalty(T) C.Raymond(C, P) M.Dawes(C)
	29	H	Morley	Won	60	7	M.Dawes(2T) S.Roskell(2T) N.Marval(T) P.Shaw(T) C.Raymond(T, 5C) D.Muckalt(T) G.Peacock(T) M.Giraud(T)
Dec	13	A	Harrogate	Won	32	17	A.Currier(T) A.Johanson(T) M.Dawes(T) L.Jones(T) C.Raymond(3C, 2P)
	20	H	Otley	Won	40	20	M.Dawes(T) M.Hayman(T) J.Reynolds(T) R.Phillips(T) D.Russell(T) C.Raymond(3C, 3P)
	27	H	Rosslyn Park	Won	23	22	M.Giraud(T) J.Reynolds(T) S.Roskell(T) M.Dawes(T) C.Raymond(P)
Jan	10	H	Lydney	Won	24	13	S.Roskell(3T) M.Dawes(T) C.Raymond(2C)
	17	A	Liverpool St Helens	Won	50	12	S.Roskell(2T) J.Reynolds(2T) A.Currier(T) D.Griffiths(T) L.Jones(T) C.Raymond(T, 5C)
	31	A	Rugby	Lost	15	21	J.Reynolds(T) C.Vogl(T) C.Raymond(C, P)
Feb	7	H	Reading	Won	37	6	D.Griffiths(2T) C.Olney(T) C.Raymond(T, 3C, 2P) P.Shaw(T)
	14	A	Nottingham	Won	25	23	J.Reynolds(2T) M.Dawes(T) C.Raymond(2C, 2P)
	28	H	Worcester	Lost	22	31	P.Shaw(T) C.Raymond(C, 5P)
Mar	7	A	Leeds	Lost	5	44	S.Roskell(T)
	14	H	Harrogate	Won	38	23	S.Roskell(2T) P.Challinor(2T) A.Currier(T) A.Jones(T) S.Pilgrim(3C) M.Dawes(C)
	21	H	Wharfedale	Won	71	24	A.Jones(2T) S.Roskell(2T) A.Currier(2T) C.Raymond(2T, 8C) D.Edwards(T) J.Reynolds(T) C.Whittaker(T)
Apr	11	A	Rosslyn Park	Won	24	20	A.Jones(2T) R.Campbell(T) S.Pilgrim(3C, P)

18	A	Newbury	Won	20	13	A.Jones(T) A.Currier(T)
						C.Raymond(2C, D, P)
25	A	Otley	Won	38	15	A.Jones(2T) A.Currier(T)
						M.Dawes(T) R.Phillips(T)
						S.Roskell(T) C.Raymond(4C)

Summary of League scorers:

264 – C.Raymond (8T, 64C, 3D, 29P); 85 – S.Roskell (17T); 75 – J.Reynolds (15T);
65 – A.Currier (13T); 54 – M.Dawes (10T, 2C); 40 – A.Jones (8T), M.Giraud (8T);
35 – R.Phillips (7T); 30 – P.Shaw (6T); 25 – D.Edwards (5T); 15 – S.Pilgrim (6C, P),
L.Jones (3T), D.Griffiths (3T); 10 – G.Peacock (2T); 5 – Penalty (T), C.Whittaker
(T), R.Westlake (T), C.Vogl (T), A.Tucker (T), D.Ruffell (T), C.Olney (T),
D.Muckalt (T), N.Marval (T), D.Lubliner (T), T.Lewsey (T), A.Johanson (T),
M.Hayman (T), A.Harbinson (T), R.Campbell (T).

Summary of League appearances:

26 – R.Phillips, L.Jones, G.Holmes (+10), D.Edwards (+1); 24 – C.Raymond,
M.Dawes (+7); 22 – S.Emms (+7); 21 – P.Shaw (+3), A.Currier (+1); 20 – S.Roskell
(+1); 19 – J.Reynolds (+2), D.Muckalt (+12); 17 – M.Giraud (+1); 16 – R.Thomas
(+7), G.Peacock (+5); 15 – M.Langley (+6); 14 – T.Lewsey (+13), A.Harbinson
(+5); 12 – C.Vogl, A.Millward; 11 – A.Tucker (+3), S.Pilgrim (+3);
10 – A.Johanson (+2); 9 – E.Moors, 8 – C.Olney (+3); 7 – D.Ruffell (+3);
6 – M.Vines (+4), G.Sage (+3), D.Griffiths (+2), R.Campbell (+2); 5 – C.Whittaker
(+1), A.Jones, D.Harries (+1); 3 – D.Lubliner, A.Horobin (+3), M.Hayman,
2 – R.Westlake (+2), R.Roberts (+1), J.Riondet, M.McCormack (+2), N.Marval
(+1); 1 – J.Storey, R.Jones (+1).

MOSELEY

Formation of club: 1873
Ground: The Reddings, Reddings Road, Moseley, Birmingham B13 8LW
Capacity: 5,000 (Seated 1,000)
Colours: Red and black
Honours: Cup Winners (1) – 1981-82 (shared with Gloucester)
Best League finish: 7th in Division One 1987-88
Last season: ADP2 – 6th. Tetley's Bitter Cup – 4th round (lost 11-18 to Sale)
Owners: New consortium
Director of Rugby: John White
Coach: Ian Smith
Captain: TBC

BINNS, Andrew Jeremy (Full-back/fly-half)
Born Yorkshire, 29.06.76. 6'2", 13st. **ADPR:** Moseley (1996-98, 25, 6t, 1dg-33pts).
England Universities fly-half, formerly a member of the all-conquering Bradford GS
side. A graduate of Exeter University.

BUXTON, Peter George (Flanker)
Born Cheltenham, 21.08.78. 6'5", 16st 7lb. **ADPR:** Moseley (1997-98, 9). Former
England Colt who joined Moseley in August 1997 from Cheltenham.

CHUDLEIGH, Mark Anthony (Scrum-half)
Born Launceston, 31.01.74. **ADPR:** Moseley (1993-94, 2), Bristol (1994-95, 8, 1t-5pts), Moseley (1995-97, 23, 2t-10pts). Cornish-born former England U21 scrum-half who returns for a third spell at Moseley.

COLDERLEY, John Kenneth (Centre)
Born Cardiff, 12.12.75. **ADPR:** Moseley (1997-98, 9, 2t-10pts). Powerful Wales U21 centre who joined from Newport.

DRAKE-LEE, William Michael (Flanker)
Born Kettering, 09.08.70. 6', 15st. **ADPR:** Leicester (1991-97, 26, 1t-5pts), Moseley (1997-98, 18, 1t-5pts). Experienced former British Universities flanker. Educated at Irwin Academy and de Montfort University, Bill started his career at Kettering RFC before moving to Leicester. Son of former England prop Nick Drake-Lee. Works as an estate agent.

FORTEY, Lee James (Prop)
Born Gloucester, 25.08.75. **ADPR:** Moseley (1997-98, 6). Twin brother of Gloucester hooker Chris Fortey. Played for Gordon League before joining Gloucester. Moved to the Reddings in August 1997.

GERAGHTY, Damien Peter (Hooker)
Born Wellington, New Zealand, 29.03.68. 5'11", 14st. **ADPR:** Moseley (1996-98, 28, 1t-5pts). Former Wellington hooker who plays for Marist St Pats back home in New Zealand.

GRIFFIN, Mark Timothy (Hooker)
Born Oakham, 06.04.75. **ADPR:** Rugby (1996-97, 1), Moseley (1997-98, 3). Backup hooker who joined from Rugby last season.

HARRIS, Daniel (Centre)
Born High Wycombe, 17.05.77. 5'10", 13st 12lb. **ADPR:** Moseley (1996-98, 34, 7t-35pts). Danny toured Australia with England U21 in summer 1997. He is a powerful, explosive inside centre, who has held a regular first-team place since September 1996.

HEALY, Anthony (Lock)
Born 17.07.69. 6'6", 17st 12lb. **Rep hons:** Canada. Product of the James Bay club on Vancouver Island, Tony has also played for Marmande in France. Made his Canadian debut against Hong Kong in June 1996.

HURLEY, Henry Dennis (Prop)
Born Doncaster, 28.12.65. 5'10", 17st 8lb. **Rep hons:** Ireland (2, Fiji95), A (5, Sc93). **ADPR:** Moseley (1996-98, 30). Ireland prop who has proved a reliable servant throughout all Moseley's difficulties since arriving from the Old Wesley club in 1996.

LE'UU, Afato (Prop)
Born Auckland, New Zealand, 02.01.62. 6'1", 18st 11b. **Rep hons:** Western Samoa. **ADPR:** Moseley (1997-98, 8, 1t-5pts). Powerful Western Samoan who, like many of his countrymen, learned his rugby in New Zealand. Afa played his rugby for the Papakura club in Otahuhu.

LONG, Matthew Robert (Prop)
Born Gloucester, 25.05.73. 6'. **ADPR:** Newcastle (1994-97, 31, 1t-5pts), Moseley (1997-98, 9). West Country prop who did well at Newcastle while at university. Moved to Moseley last season.

MACKINNON, Stuart Donald (Prop)
Born 06.01.69. 6', 17st 7lb. **ADPR:** Moseley (1995-98, 25, 5t-25pts). In and out of the Moseley front row over the last three seasons. Joined Moseley from Stratford-upon-Avon in 1995. Works as a shop-fitter.

MARTIN, Roderick Charles Kirk (Utility back)
Born Southend, 25.11.75. 6', 14st. **ADPR:** Moseley (1996-98, 28, 7t-35pts). Rod emerged from Moseley's Development squad to win a first-team place in the second half of 1996-97 and carried that good form on into last season. Represented England Universities while a student at Birmingham University.

MITCHELL, Neil John (Lock)
Born Newcastle, 22.06.66. 6'6", 17st 5lb. **ADPR:** Moseley (1996-98, 25, 3t-15pts). Policeman with the West Midlands force who joined the club from Stourbridge. Gained a first-team place in February 1997 and by end of that season was voted Moseley's most improved player. He is a line-out specialist, determined and aggressive, who toured South Africa with British Police summer 1997.

MULRAINE, Charles Edward (Scrum-half)
Born Leamington Spa, 24.12.73. 5'8", 12st 10lb. **ADPR:** Moseley (1994-95, 11, 1t-5pts), Gloucester (1996-97, 4, 1t-5pts), Moseley (1997-98, 7, 1t-5pts). Talented all-round sportsman who played rugby and cricket for England Schools and first-class cricket for Warwickshire. Started with Moseley before joining Gloucester where a serious knee injury hindered his progress. Rejoined Moseley but his availability is uncertain for the forthcoming season. Educated at Warwick School.

POLL, Robin William (Flanker)
Born Shrewsbury, 16.02.74. 6'4", 16st. **ADPR:** Moseley (1993-98, 28, 3t-15pts). Missed most of 1995-96 season with a shoulder injury after England U21 honours in 1994-95, but returned as a regular replacement in 1996-97, gaining a first-team place in the last two months and again featuring last season. A graduate of Bristol University.

PROTHEROUGH, Richard David (Hooker)
Born Cheltenham, 09.11.76. 5'9", 14st. **ADPR:** Worcester (1996-97, 2, 1t-5pts). Son of former Moseley hooker Dave Protherough, Richard has represented England Schools, Colts and U21. A graduate of Loughborough University.

ROBERTS, Martin John (Centre)
Born Gloucester, 26.01.68. 6'3", 15st 2lb. **ADPR:** Gloucester (1990-98, 48, 3t, 6c, 13pg-66pts). Powerfully-built centre who arrives at Moseley after spells with Cheltenham and Gloucester.

SMITH, Ian Richard (Flanker)
Born Gloucester, 16.03.65. 6'1", 14st 12lb. **Rep hons:** Scotland (25, Eng92), A (8, Ire90), Barbarians (91-92). **ADPR:** Gloucester (1987-97, 108, 6t-25pts), Moseley (1996-98, 23, 2t-10pts). Former Gloucester captain who joined Moseley in 1996 having been declared surplus to requirements at Kingsholm. An England 18 Group triallist who played for England B against a Spanish Select XV in 1989 but opted for Scotland, captaining Scotland B and a member of the Scotland A team that beat South Africa in November 1994. He also played for Anglo-Scots and Scottish Exiles eight times. Keen to get involved with the coaching this season. Educated at Thomas Rich's School and a civil engineer by profession.

STUART, Robert Andrew (Wing/centre)
Born Devizes, 29.09.72. 6', 13st. **ADPR:** Bath (1993-94, 1), Moseley (1995-98, 6, 2c-4pts). Scotland U21 and Scottish Exiles representative who joined from Bath. Works as a quantity surveyor.

WEBBER, Nathan (Prop)
Born Cardiff, 20.06.74. 6'1", 17st. **Rep hons:** England A (1, SA96). **ADPR:** Moseley (1994-98, 60). Powerful Welsh-born scrummager with good mobility and adhesive handling skills, Nathan also makes a contribution to Moseley's play in the loose. He is a member of John Elliott's RFU Development squad, a Midlands regular, who also played for England A in 1996. Educated at Stratford-on-Avon HS.

REVIEW

Moseley remain the great under-achievers of Premiership Two, but even by their standards the 1996-97 season was traumatic, resulting in the club going into receivership midway through the season and contracts having to be cancelled with 12 players, including Canadian Al Charron. A new consortium has stepped in to buy the club out of receivership and all the players will be put on part-time contracts. John White – a former club captain, coach and chairman – has returned from Birmingham & Solihull to become director of rugby and his first task must be to persuade some of the more experienced players to stay. A tough season in prospect, in fact a season that could determine whether Moseley are ever able to compete in the top flight again.

MOSELEY in Premiership Two 1997-98

Aug 30	A	Coventry	Lost	12	20	S.Hackney(T) D.O'Mahony(T) J.Liley(C)
Sep 13	H	West Hartlepool	Lost	16	21	J.Liley(T, C, 3P)
20	A	Orrell	Lost	19	30	R.Martin(T) D.O'Mahony(T) I.Smith(T) J.Liley(2C)
27	H	Exeter	Won	23	22	A.Binns(T) C.Mulraine(T) D.O'Mahony(T) J.Liley(C, 2P)
Oct 4	A	Wakefield	Won	27	15	D.O'Mahony(2T) D.Geraghty(T) S.Moore(T) J.Liley(2C, P)
11	H	Bedford	Lost	16	35	D.Harris(T) M.Jones(C, 3P)
18	A	Blackheath	Won	19	11	R.Martin(T) M.Jones(C, 4P)
25	H	Orrell	Won	18	9	C.Hall(T) M.Jones(T, 2D) J.Liley(C)
Nov 8	A	Exeter	Won	20	10	C.Hall(T) D.O'Mahony(T) M.Jones(2C, P) J.Liley(P)
Dec 13	H	Wakefield	Won	28	10	B.Drake-Lee(T) M.Jones(T, 2C, 3P) S.MacKinnon(T)
20	A	Bedford	Lost	16	32	M.McAtamney(T) M.Jones(C, D, 2P)
27	H	Rotherham	Lost	23	25	A.Charron(T) R.Denhardt(T) J.Liley(T) M.Jones(C, D, P)
Jan 17	A	Rotherham	Won	16	10	D.Harris(T) M.Jones(C, D, 2P)
31	H	London Scottish	Lost	18	29	J.Calderley(T) D.O'Mahony(T) M.Jones(C, 2P)
Feb 14	A	Waterloo	Lost	31	36	D.O'Mahony(3T) A.Le'uu(T) R.Martin(T) M.Jones(3C)

28	H	Blackheath	Won	29	16	R.Denhardt(T) P.Massey(T) N.Mitchell(T) D.O'Mahony(T) M.Jones(3C, P)
Mar 14	H	Waterloo	Won	23	22	R.Martin(T) D.Harris(T) M.Jones(2C, 3P)
28	A	London Scottish	Lost	18	24	D.O'Mahony(2T) M.Jones(C, 2P)
Apr 4	A	Fylde	Lost	13	14	A.Binns(T, D) M.Jones(C, P)
18	A	West Hartlepool	Drew	18	18	J.Cockle(T) N.Mitchell(T) M.Jones(C, 2P)
22	H	Coventry	Won	31	3	P.Massey(T) A.Binns(T) J.Calderley(T) D.O'Mahony(T) M.Jones(C, 3P)
25	H	Fylde	Won	44	9	D.O'Mahony(3T) M.Jones(T, 4C, 2P) R.Martin(T) P.Massey(T)

Summary of Premiership scorers:

178 – M.Jones (3T, 26C, 5D, 32P); 85 – D.O'Mahony (17T); 47 – J.Liley (2T, 8C, 7P); 25 – R.Martin (5T); 18 – A.Binns (3T, D); 15 – P.Massey (3T), D.Harris (3T); 10 – N.Mitchell (2T), C.Hall (2T), R.Denhardt (2T), J.Calderley (2T); 5 – I.Smith (T), C.Mulraine (T), S.Moore (T), M.McAtamney (T), S.MacKinnon (T), A.Le'uu (T), S.Hackney (T), D.Geraghty (T), B.Drake-Lee (T), J.Cockle (T), A.Charron (T).

Summary of Premiership appearances:

20 – D.O'Mahony; 19 – R.Martin (+1), D.Geraghty, R.Denhardt, J.Cockle (+2); 18 – H.Hurley (+2), B.Drake-Lee (+1); 17 – N.Mitchell (+2), M.Jones; 16 – I.Smith (+2), D.Harris; 15 – A.Binns (+1); 12 – R.Rush, P.Massey (+1); 10 – J.Liley (+2); 9 – S.MacKinnon (+3), M.Long (+3), J.Calderley (+1), P.Buxton (+4); 8 – A.Le'uu (+1); 7 – N.Webber, R.Turner (+2), C.Mulraine (+2), S.Moore (+1), M.McAtamney, C.Hall, L.Criscuolo (+1), J.Clark (+5), A.Charron; 6 – L.Fortey (+4); 5 – S.Hackney; 3 – P.Short (+2), R.Poll (+2), M.Griffin (+2); 2 – A.Mitchell (+2), J.Mellors (+2), D.Kings (+1), N.Golby (+2); 1 – B.Stuart, W.James, A.Hubbleday (+1), G.Gregory (+1).

ORRELL

Formation of club: 1927
Ground: Edgehall Road, Orrell, Wigan, Lancashire WN5 8TL
Capacity: 4,950 (Seated 250)
Colours: Amber and black
Honours: None
Best League finish: 2nd in Division One, 1991-92
Best Cup run: S/F, 1973-74, 1986-87, 1990-91, 1993-94
Last season: ADP2 – 5th. Tetley's Bitter Cup – 3rd round (lost 16-26 to Newbury)
Owners: Members
Coach: Ged Glynn
Captain: TBC

BARTLE, James William (Wing)
Born Leeds, 24.09.76. 5'11", 12st. **ADPR:** Wakefield (1996-98, 4), Orrell (1997-98, 3, 2t-10pts). Speed merchant from Mount St Mary's School who has fought hard to overcome knee injuries.

BIBBY, Alexander Guy (Flanker)
Born Leicester, 20.05.74. 6'4", 15st 7lb. **ADPR:** Nottingham (1996-97, 5), Orrell (1997-98, 8). Versatile all-purpose forward who returned to the club last season. Has also played for Leicester Tigers.

CRONIN, Benjamin Michael (Backrow)
Born Limerick, 13.07.68. 6'5", 17st. **Rep hons:** Ireland (2, Sc95), A (5, Sc92, 1t-5pts). **ADPR:** Orrell (1997-98, 19, 2t-10pts). Ben arrived at Orrell from Garryowen after a career badly interrupted by injury. He was an All-Ireland League winner with Garryowen in 1992 and played in the Munster side that defeated the touring Australians that year. An Ireland cap beckoned, but injury intervened and he did not reappear until 1993, when he was a member of the Irish Development XV that toured southern Africa. He was a mid-tour replacement for the full side the following summer in Australia and was due to win his first cap against the USA in November 1994 when injury again struck. Fully recovered, he returned to action and played for Ireland A against their England counterparts in January 1995 before making his full debut against Scotland in 1995. In 1996-97 he impressed for Ireland A against South Africa, France and England going on to win his second cap, again against Scotland.

CUNDICK, Jason Paul (Prop)
Born Manchester, 18.06.71. 6', 17st. **ADPR:** Orrell (1994-98, 43). A promising prop who has re-established himself after a serious back injury. A teacher who has also played for Winnington Park and Old Salians.

CUSANI, Charles Dominic (Lock)
Born Wigan, 22.10.65. 6'6", 17st. **ADPR:** Orrell (1987-98, 97, 1t-5pts). Rugged ball-handling lock who played rugby league for Wigan Schools before turning to rugby union. Appeared for Lancashire and the North at Colts level before graduating to the senior sides at both county and divisional level and has played in Italy for Roma Olympic. Managed to attract the attention of the RFU disciplinary committee in 1996-97 by receiving five yellow cards. Is now the Orrell club steward, looking after all the members' catering needs.

HARRISON, Charles Leslie (Scrum-half)
Born Chippenham, 06.09.75. 5'10", 13st. **ADPR:** Bath (1995-98, 14, 1t, 2c-9pts), Orrell (1997-98, 11, 3t-15pts). Another protégé of Ged Glynn's at Mount St Mary's School. Arrived at Orrell from Bath where he gained valuable Premiership experience. England U21 cap.

HESLOP, Nigel John (Wing)
Born Hartlepool, 04.12.63. 5'10", 13st. **Rep hons:** England (10, Arg90, 3t-12pts), A (3, Sp89) Barbarians (90-91). **ADPR:** Waterloo (1987-89, 11, 1t-4pts), Orrell (1988-98, 72, 26t-112pts). Nigel returned from rugby league in 1995 and showed up well last season. Made his international debut on tour in Argentina and was ever-present during England's 1991 Grand Slam, scoring a try against Scotland at Twickenham. His last international appearance was against Wales as a replacement the following year. Educated at Rainford HS he played rugby league for St Helens.

HITCHEN, Neil Morton (Hooker)
Born Crewe, 14.07.59. **Rep hons:** England A (3, Sp89). **ADPR:** Orrell (1987-98, 74, 3t-12pts). Veteran hooker who returned to help Orrell through an injury crisis last season.

HUXLEY, Jeffrey Ellis (No 8/lock)
Born Billinge, 28.07.63. 6'3", 16st 7lb. **ADPR:** Orrell (1994-98, 44, 2t-10pts). An evergreen backrow forward, who has been a club stalwart in recent years and hopes to utilise his experience helping out with coaching.

KELLY, Stephen Joseph (Prop)
Born Manchester, 11.05.72. **ADPR:** Orrell (1997-98, 13). Rapidly developing prop who performed well in his first season in Premiership Two.

LEDSON, Paul James (Prop)
Born Billinge, 17.02.72. **ADPR:** Orrell (1996-98, 6). Valuable backup prop who has played for Lancashire.

LYON, David Geoffrey (Centre)
Born Wigan, 03.09.65. 6'1", 14st 8lb. **ADPR:** Orrell (1996-98, 30, 8t-40pts). An experienced former Warrington and St Helens rugby league centre, David is the nephew of Billy and Eric Lyon. Versatile but prefers playing at centre.

MANLEY, Paul Edmund (Backrow)
Born Stockport, 25.01.68. 6', 15st 7lb. **ADPR:** Orrell (1987-96, 85, 7t-29pts), Wakefield (1996-97, 19, 5t-25pts), Orrell (1997-98, 21, 6t-30pts). Underrated flanker who was a member of those vintage Orrell packs of the late 80s and early 90s, Paul arrived back at Edgehall Road after a short spell at Wakefield. He joined the club originally from Burnage and made his divisional debut for the North in 1990. An RFU qualified coach, he has tons of ability but sometimes lacks pace. Enjoyed a spell with the Ngtapa club in New Zealand.

MILLACHIP, Peter Charles (Flanker)
Born Bowdon, 01.09.69. **ADPR:** Orrell (1997-98, 17, 1t-5pts). Seasoned flanker who made a big impact last season after signing from Middlesbrough.

MOFFAT, Alexander Graham (Hooker)
Born Workington, 29.06.68. 5'2", 13st. **ADPR:** Fylde (1990-94, 22, 3t-13pts), Orrell (1995-98, 34). Reliable hooker, particularly accurate throwing in, and one of the smallest players in the League.

OLIVER, Matthew James (Utility back)
Born Northampton, 30.11.76. 6'1", 13st 7lb. **ADPR:** Bedford (1994-98, 37, 13t-65pts), Orrell (1997-98, 13, 4t-20pts). Exciting signing from Bedford. Matt is a class centre, having played for England Colts and travelled to South Africa in July 1998 with the England U21 squad.

RAWLINSON, Robert John (Prop)
Born Littleborough, 23.08.76. 6', 16st. **ADPR:** Orrell (1995-98, 18). A combative prop who benefited from a summer with the Pirates club in Johannesburg in 1996.

REES, Paul Michael (Lock)
Born Dagenham, 10.04.73. 6'6", 17st. **ADPR:** Orrell (1996-98, 40, 1t-5pts). Former Winnington Park second row who has done well in the Orrell boiler house. Police officer.

RICHARDSON, Mark (Flanker)
Born Whitehaven, 06.06.61. **Rep hons:** Barbarians (96-97). **ADPR:** Aspatria (1992-96, 23t-115pts), Orrell (1997-98, 8, 1t-5pts). Reliable Cumbrian flanker who impressed whenever called upon last season. Has also played for Egremont.

RUDGE, Benjamin (Wing)
Born Widnes, 06.09.75. 6′, 15st. **ADPR:** Orrell (1997-98, 2, 2t-10pts). Educated at St Edwards, Liverpool, and an Oxford Blue in 1997.

RYAN, Neil Andrew (Utility back)
Born Wigan, 29.11.73. 5′9″, 13st 4lb. **ADPR:** Waterloo (1993-96, 25, 4t, 5pg, 8dg-59pts), Sale (1995-97, 9, 4t-20pts), Orrell (1997-98, 21, 7t, 3c, 1pg-44pts). Enigmatic talent who represented England 16 Group for two seasons as a prelude to U18 and U21 caps. Moved to Waterloo and played for the North in South Africa (1994) before joining Sale, and toured Italy with the North in May 96. Learned much of his rugby under Orrell's director of coaching Ged Glynn while a student at Mount St Mary's and Cambridge.

SCOTT, Michael Thomas (Wing)
Born Carlisle, 05.11.73. **ADPR:** Aspatria (1993-97, 67, 7t, 86c, 122pg, 6dg-591pts), Orrell (1997-98, 9, 8c, 16pg-64pts). More than useful backup goal-kicker recruited from Cumbrian club Aspatria.

TABERNER, Steven (Full-back)
Born Orrell, 15.09.62. 5′10″, 13st. **ADPR:** Orrell (1987-98, 100, 15t, 1dg-70pts). Steve is a one-club man and a former Orrell captain, who also enjoys triathlons and amateur dramatics. Has tried to retire more than once.

TRIVELLA, Douglas Orlando (Full-back)
Born Harare, Zimbabwe, 03.05.74. **Rep hons:** Zimbabwe. **ADPR:** Orrell (1997-98, 15, 3t, 1pg-18pts). Exciting recruit from the College Rovers club in South Africa whose season was cut short by injury. Played for Zimbabwe versus Wales in May.

TUIGAMALA, Toa'lua Lealuga (Centre)
Born Western Samoa, 10.10.74. 6′2″, 14st 8lb. **ADPR:** Orrell (1995-98, 37, 5t, 1c-27pts). The brother of Vai'aga Tuigamala, Lua travelled to England to live with the former All Black after he signed for Wigan. Made his international debut against the Ireland Development XV in the summer of 97.

TURNER, Stuart Charles (Prop)
Born Southport, 22.04.72. **ADPR:** Waterloo (1992-96, 38), Orrell (1996-98, 44, 2t-10pts). Ultra-reliable front row warrior who has scarcely missed a League game for two seasons.

TYRER, Christian Paul (Wing/centre)
Born Leigh, 19.12.73. **ADPR:** Orrell (1997-98, 1). Former Widnes RL utility back who arrived at Orrell last season after an unsuccessful spell at Bath.

VERBICKAS, Simon John (Wing)
Born Manchester, 22.04.75. 6′1″, 13st 7lb. **ADPR:** Broughton Park (1992-93, 1, 1c-2pts), Sale (1993-97, 26, 20t, 7c, 6pg-132pts), Orrell (1997-98, 18, 12t, 24c, 19pg-165pts). After playing for Broughton Park, Simon enjoyed a sensational debut season for Sale, scoring 16 League tries when the club were promoted from League Two in 93-94, including five in Sale's remarkable 88-9 win over Otley. He damaged his spine and missed the following season but gradually returned to action with the Second XV in 1995-96. Still young and blessed with real pace, he is technically qualified to play for Lithuania, Germany, Ireland and England.

WALSH, Brian Andrew (Centre)
Born Ndola, Rhodesia, 21.10.69. 6′1″, 13st 8lb. **Rep hons:** Ireland A (6, Sc92, 2t-10pts). **ADPR:** Orrell (1997-98, 10, 1t-5pts). Brian arrived at Orrell from Cork Constitution, where he was an All-Ireland League winner as long ago as 1991. Made

his Munster debut the following season, broke into the Ireland A team in 1993 and toured southern Africa with Ireland's Development squad that summer. Further A caps followed against Wales and England the following season before he toured Australia with the senior squad in 1994, playing in three provincial games.

WARR, Mark Kevin (Scrum-half)
Born Birmingham, 24.02.67. 5'9", 12st 12lb. **ADPR:** Sale (1992-97, 43, 15t-75pts), Orrell (1997-98, 13). A long-time member of the Barkers Butts club, Mark enjoyed a five-year spell at Sale before moving to Orrell. Has made three County final appearances for Warwickshire. Studied Psychology and PE at Birmingham University.

WRIGHT, Darren Christopher (Centre)
Born Leigh, 17.01.68. **ADPR:** Sale (1996-97, 4), Orrell (1997-98, 12, 3t-15pts). Another useful recruit from Sale, Darren brought experience to Orrell's midfield.

REVIEW

A useful season of consolidation for Orrell after the traumas of relegation the previous season. A bright start, including impressive wins over Rotherham and Moseley, hinted at genuine hopes of promotion but Orrell never really boasted the strength in depth to sustain a challenge, and slip-ups against the likes of Waterloo and Exeter undermined their cause at valuable junctures. Important for Lancashire rugby that Orrell continue to prosper this season, though the search for a major financial backer is proving as difficult as ever.

ORRELL in Premiership Two 1997-98

Aug 30	H	Blackheath	Won	26	17	B.Rudge(2T) D.Wright(T) S.Verbickas(T, P) D.Trivella(P)
Sep 14	A	Rotherham	Won	29	14	D.Wright(T) B.Cronin(T) S.Verbickas(T, C, 4P)
20	H	Moseley	Won	30	19	N.Ryan(2T) Penalty(T) M.Silcock(T) S.Verbickas(2C, P) M.McCarthy(P)
27	A	London Scottish	Lost	19	20	S.Turner(T) D.Trivella(T) M.Silcock(T) S.Verbickas(2C)
Oct 4	H	Fylde	Won	35	9	N.Heslop(3T) M.Silcock(T) M.McCarthy(3C, 3P)
11	A	Waterloo	Lost	14	25	N.Ryan(T) M.McCarthy(D, 2P)
18	H	Coventry	Won	38	13	P.Manley(2T) N.Ryan(2T, 2C) D.Trivella(T) B.Walsh(T) S.Verbickas(2C)
25	A	Moseley	Lost	9	18	S.Verbickas(2P) N.Ryan(P)
Nov 8	H	London Scottish	Lost	13	27	N.Heslop(T) S.Verbickas(C, 2P)
Dec 13	A	Fylde	Won	21	9	N.Heslop(T) P.Millachip(T) M.Scott(C, 3P)
20	H	Waterloo	Won	23	6	P.Manley(T) M.Richardson(T) M.Scott(2C, 3P)
Jan 17	H	West Hartlepool	Lost	30	35	M.Oliver(T) Penalty(T) N.Ryan(T) M.Scott(3C, 3P)

24	A	Coventry	Won	30	21	S.Verbickas(3T) M.Oliver(T) M.Scott(2C, 2P)
31	A	Bedford	Lost	22	47	P.Manley(T) Penalty(T) S.Verbickas(T, 2C) M.Scott(P)
Feb 14	H	Exeter	Won	38	3	S.Verbickas(2T, 3C) J.Bartle(T) C.Cusani(T) N.Ryan(T, C) P.Manley(T)
22	A	West Hartlepool	Lost	11	20	J.Bartle(T) S.Verbickas(2P)
Mar 7	A	Wakefield	Won	26	20	M.Oliver(T) D.Trivella(T) S.Verbickas(2C, 4P)
14	A	Exeter	Lost	14	17	M.Oliver(T) M.Scott(3P)
28	H	Bedford	Lost	16	29	C.Harrison(T) D.Lyon(T) S.Verbickas(2P)
Apr 11	A	Blackheath	Won	32	14	C.Harrison(2T) J.Huxley(T) D.Lyon(T) S.Verbickas(T, 2C, P)
18	H	Rotherham	Lost	3	9	M.Scott(P)
25	H	Wakefield	Won	54	8	S.Verbickas(3T, 7C) D.Lyon(2T) B.Cronin(T) P.Manley(T) D.Wright(T)

Summary of Premiership scorers:

165 – S.Verbickas (12T, 24C, 19P); 64 – M.Scott (8C, 16P); 44 – N.Ryan (7T, 3C, P); 30 – P.Manley (6T); 27 – M.McCarthy (3C, D, 6P); 25 – N.Heslop (5T); 20 – M.Oliver (4T), D.Lyon (4T); 18 – D.Trivella (3T, P); 15 – Penalty (3T), D.Wright (3T), M.Silcock (3T), C.Harrison (3T); 10 – B.Rudge (2T), B.Cronin (2T), J.Bartle (2T); 5 – B.Walsh (T), S.Turner (T), M.Richardson (T), P.Millachip (T), J.Huxley (T), C.Cusani (T).

Summary of Premiership appearances:

22 – S.Turner; 21 – N.Ryan (+2), P.Rees (+2), P.Manley; 19 – B.Cronin; 18 – S.Verbickas (+2), J.Cundick (+2); 17 – P.Millachip (+3), C.Cusani (+1); 15 – D.Trivella (+2); 14 – R.Rawlinson (+8), A.Moffatt (+2); 13 – M.Warr (+3), M.Oliver (+1), S.Kelly (+9), N.Heslop; 12 – D.Wright; 11 – C.Harrison (+1); 10 – A.Whittle (+2), B.Walsh (+3), D.Lyon (+3); 9 – M.Scott (+3), J.Huxley (+4); 8 – M.Richardson (+7), G.Bibby (+3); 6 – S.Taberner, M.Silcock; 4 – P.Horrocks (+1), N.Hitchen; 3 – L.Tuigamala, M.McCarthy (+1), P.Ledson (+1), G.Hope (+1), J.Bartle; 2 – B.Rudge, P.Newton, M.Lacey (+2), N.Gregory (+1), D.Gifford (+1); 1 – C.Tyrer (+1), N.Liptrot (+1), J.Hayter (+1), D.Fletcher (+1), D.Bailey (+1).

ROTHERHAM

Formation of club: 1923
Ground: Clifton Lane Sports Ground, Badsley Moor Lane, Rotherham S65 2AA
Capacity: 1,770 (Seated 270)
Colours: Maroon, sky blue, navy blue and white

Honours: Champions North East 1 – 1989, North 2 – 1990, North 1 – 1992, Division 5 North – 1994, Division 4 – 1995
Best League finish: 4th in Premiership Two in 1997-98
Best Cup run: 6th round 1996-97
Last season: ADP2 – 4th. Tetley's Bitter Cup – 5th round (lost 14-27 to London Irish)
Owners: Members
Director of Rugby: Steve Cousins
Coaches: Jim Kilfoyle, John Phillips
Captain: TBC

AUSTIN, Gregory Mark (Centre)

Born Cootamundra, Australia, 14.06.65. 5'10", 13st. **ADPR:** Leicester (1996-97, 4, 2t-10pts), Rotherham (1997-98, 20, 13t-65pts). Formerly with North Sydney, Rochdale Hornets, Salford, Huddersfield RL and Leicester, Greg joined Rotherham in July 97 after failing to make the grade at Welford Road. Prolific try-scorer in the RL code with more than 300 touchdowns, including 52 in 1994-95 when he set a Regal Trophy record by scoring nine in one game for Huddersfield against Blackpool. Has the distinction of having been born in the same village as Sir Donald Bradman. Greg's father, Roy, is a regular winner of the World Veterans' Sprint Championship and at 62 still runs 100m in 11.1 seconds.

BENTLEY, John (Wing)

Born Dewsbury, 05.09.66. 6', 15st 7lb. **Rep hons:** England (4, Ire88, 1t-4pts), A (3, Fr88, 2t-8pts). **ADPR:** Sale (1987-89, 8, 2t, 1pg-11pts), Newcastle (1996-98, 21, 25t-125pts), Rotherham (1997-98, 7). England and British Lions wing who played on loan from Newcastle last season. Availability will depend on John's commitments with Halifax Blue Sox RL.

BINNS, Simon James (Fly-half)

Born Shipley, 20.09.74. 5'10", 12st 7lb. **Rep hons:** Barbarians (97-98). **ADPR:** Moseley (1995-96, 5, 1t, 2c, 2pg, 1dg-18pts), Rotherham (1996-98, 40, 13t, 43c, 45pg, 3dg-295pts). Talented former England Schools and U21 fly-half who has flourished since his move from Moseley. Was ever-present last season and scored 244 points. Another former Bradford GS student, Simon attended university at Birmingham.

BRAMLEY, Richard Anthony (Lock/flanker)

Born Doncaster, 19.10.71. 6'5", 17st 5lb. **Rep hons:** Barbarians (97-98). **ADPR:** Wakefield (1990-94, 21, 1t-5pts), Rotherham (1996-98, 12, 1t-5pts). Enormously powerful lock who should be available on a regular basis this season after winning a remarkable five Blues at Cambridge, where he took a degree in Animal Science. Former captain of England Schools, Colts and Students. Educated at QEGS Wakefield, Richard is also a boxing Blue.

BUNTING, Simon Colin (Prop)

Born Rotherham, 17.09.70. 6', 16st. **ADPR:** Rotherham (1990-98, 71, 3t-15pts). Former construction worker who is a star product of the Rotherham Youth system. Fast, mobile prop who was ever-present last season and again looks set to anchor the Rotherham front row.

BUZZA, Alan Jan (Full-back)

Born Beverley, 03.03.66. 5'11", 13st. **Rep hons:** England A (7, Fr90, 1t, 2c-9pts). **ADPR:** Wasps (1990-94, 31, 4t, 5c, 11pg-62pts), Rotherham (1996-98, 31, 4t, 1dg-23pts). Experienced former Wasps full-back, Alan represented England at all levels up to A team and gained Cambridge Blues in 88 and 89. Joined Rotherham at the start of the 1996-97 season, when he started studying for Masters degree at Loughborough University. Educated at Redruth CS.

COOK, Daniel James (Lock)
Born Hull, 10.09.74. 6'8", 17st 7lb. **ADPR:** Otley (1994-96, 12), Rotherham (1996-98, 30). Joined Rotherham from Otley in July 1996 and is beginning to make a big impact.

COY, Sam Nicholas (Prop)
Born Rotherham, 19.01.66. 5'11", 17st. **ADPR:** Rotherham (1987-98, 105, 3t-14pts). A club stalwart and respected scrummager, Sam is an avid collector of rugby shirts. He works on the family farm just outside Rotherham.

DAWSON, Martin (Utility back)
Born Nottingham, 21.09.71. 6', 12st 7lb. **ADPR:** Rotherham (1995-98, 26, 8t-40pts). Former student at Mount St Mary's College and an England Schools cap, Martin also attended Loughborough University. Back to his best last season after injury.

DUDLEY, John Robert (No 8)
Born Sheffield, 16.07.66. 6', 16st. **ADPR:** Rotherham (1987-98, 142, 34t-161pts). Almost a legend locally. John has seen it all at Rotherham, helping them rise through seven divisions in the last 11 years. An uncompromising, durable backrow forward who demands respect.

ELLIOTT, Douglas (Centre)
Born 11.04.64. 5'11", 13st 7lb. **ADPR:** Richmond (1990-96, 60, 13t-64pts), Rotherham (1996-98, 3, 1t-5pts). Experienced former Richmond captain who has been struggling with injury. Works as a production manager with United Biscuits.

HARPER, Jonathan Mark (Centre)
Born London, 09.09.74. 6', 13st 7lb. **ADPR:** Rotherham (1994-98, 58, 17t-85pts). Creative ball-handling centre who joined the club while studying at Sheffield University.

KEARNEY, Ian Nicholas (Flanker)
Born 28.05.69. 6'1", 15st 7lb. **ADPR:** Rotherham (1996-98, 17, 1t-5pts). Useful backrow player and another who joined the club while a student at Sheffield Hallam University.

LAX, Dean (Wing)
Born Rotherham, 10.07.74. 6', 13st 7lb. **ADPR:** Rotherham (1996-98, 28, 6t, 10c, 22pg-116pts). Promising wing, who will remember last season chiefly for squandering a certain try in Rotherham's play-off game against London Irish when he lost the ball in-goal. Joined Rotherham from local club Dinnington.

MILLER, Nicholas William Edward (Wing)
Born Wakefield, 24.01.75. 5'10", 12st 7lb. **ADPR:** Wakefield (1995-96, 7, 1t-5pts), Rotherham (1996-98, 13, 5t-25pts). Former England Colts cap. Yet another former Bradford GS student, who also attended Loughborough University.

MILLS, Matthew Peter (Lock)
Born Selby, 29.12.73. 6'4", 16st. **ADPR:** Rotherham (1994-98, 30, 1t-5pts). Developing lock who joined the club from Sheffield Hallam University.

MOFFATT, John Stuart David (Full-back)
Born Edinburgh, 18.08.77. 6'1", 15st. **ADPR:** Rotherham (1996-98, 19, 4t, 1c, 4pg-34pts). Loughborough University student who showed enough promise last season to win a Scotland U21 cap.

MURPHY, Thomas Desmond (Hooker)
Born Longreach, Australia, 25.04.72. 5'11", 15st 5lb. **ADPR:** Rotherham (1997-98, 3). Australian hooker who won Blues at Cambridge in 1996 and 97. Educated at St Joseph's College, Brisbane. Was loaned to Leicester for a short time last year.

SCHMID, Mike (No 8)
Born Canada, 28.11.69. 6'3", 16st 1lb. **Rep hons:** Canada. **ADPR:** Rotherham (1997-98, 12, 6t-30pts). Inspirational Canadian who was a major force last season until an untimely broken jaw left him sidelined. Certain to be included in Canada's squad for RWC99. The first Rotherham player ever to be capped.

SCULLY, David Andrew (Scrum-half)
Born Doncaster, 07.08.65. 5'9", 12st 6lb. **Rep hons:** England A (4, It92, 1t-4pts), Barbarians (96-97). **ADPR:** Wakefield (1987-98, 161, 51t, 6c, 17pg-293pts). Nobody in England has played more League games than Dave, who has notched up 161 during his 12 seasons with Wakefield. Debut for England B 1992, touring New Zealand with them that year. Captained Northern Division against the All Blacks at Liverpool FC 1993. Member of England's World Cup Sevens-winning team in 1993, receiving 'Best Moment' award for cover tackle. Represented England in the 1995 and 1996 Cathay Pacific-Hong Kong Bank Sevens tournaments and has helped the Barbarians to two Middlesex Sevens titles in recent years. Has continually resisted offers from big clubs, notably Sale, to play elsewhere. Works as a firefighter.

SHEPHERD, Jon (Utility back)
Born Dewsbury, 31.07.74. 5'9", 13st. **ADPR:** Morley (1994-97, 63, 18t-90pts), Rotherham (1997-98, 11, 3t-15pts). Former England Colts centre whose career has often been interrupted by injury.

SPENCE, Neil Andrew (Flanker)
Born Hull, 30.08.76. 5'10", 13st. **ADPR:** Rotherham (1996-98, 25, 1t-5pts). Dynamic former England U21 and Schools flanker who joined from Gloucester and recovered well from a knee injury last season. Began his career with Hull Ionians.

UMAGA, Michael T. (Full-back)
Born Auckland, New Zealand, 19.02.66. 6', 14st 2lb. **Rep hons:** Western Samoa. **ADPR:** Rotherham (1997-98, 11, 2t-10pts). Western Samoa's World Cup full-back in 1995, when he was remembered chiefly for a dangerous head-high tackle on Joost Van Der Westhuizen in the quarter-final against South Africa. Played representative rugby for Wellington in New Zealand.

WADE, Simon Ben (Backrow)
Born Leeds, 11.09.74. 6'1", 15st. **ADPR:** Morley (1992-97, 54, 22t-110pts), Rotherham (1997-98, 24, 7t-35pts). Former England Schools and Colts cap who is developing well in the backrow.

WAREHAM, Richard Antony (Hooker)
Born Rugby, 24.01.68. 5'11", 16st. **ADPR:** Moseley (1993-94, 15), Rotherham (1994-98, 58, 3t-15pts). The RFU Youth Development officer for South Yorkshire. Former England Students representative who has switched from prop.

WEBSTER, Gavin (Lock)
Born Northampton, 11.05.73. 6'5", 16st 7lb. **ADPR:** Northampton (1993-95, 12), Rotherham (1996-98, 40, 3t-15pts). Loughborough University graduate who joined the club from Northampton. Represented Ireland in the 1996 World Students Cup.

WEST, Craig John (Flanker)
Born Rotherham, 08.02.64. 6'2", 16st 7lb. **ADPR:** Rotherham (1988-98, 122, 23t-108pts). Another club stalwart who has contributed massively to Rotherham's rise through the Leagues. Self-employed electrician who joined the club from nearby Dinnington.

WILSON, Scott Cameron (Prop)
Born Rotherham, 14.01.72. 5'11", 16st. **ADPR:** Rotherham (1994-98, 40). Developing well as a prop after stints with Otley and Saracens. Engineer by profession.

WORSLEY, Ian David (Scrum-half)
Born Warrington, 07.11.75. 5'8", 13st 7lb. **ADPR:** Rotherham (1996-98, 5). Young scrum-half prospect who joined from Orrell in 1996.

REVIEW

Just missed out on promotion, which may be a blessing in disguise as Rotherham work hard to catch up off the field with their remarkable rise through the Leagues which has seen them promoted on seven occasions in 11 seasons. They possess a hard-working, durable pack and imaginative backs and could well be the pace-setters in Premiership Two this season. Face a tough fight with emerging Leeds to secure pre-eminence in Yorkshire and tap into local sponsorship but Rotherham have responded to every challenge to date.

ROTHERHAM in Premiership Two 1997-98

Aug 30	A	Bedford	Lost	11	18	G.Austin(T) S.Binns(2P)
Sep 14	H	Orrell	Lost	14	29	J.Sinclair(T) S.Binns(3P)
20	H	West Hartlepool	Won	33	21	J.Shepherd(2T) J.Dudley(T) G.Easterby(T) S.Binns(2C, D, 2P)
27	A	Fylde	Won	25	18	S.Moffatt(T) J.Shepherd(T) N.Spence(T) S.Binns(2C, 2P)
Oct 4	H	London Scottish	Won	24	3	S.Binns(T, C, 4P) C.West(T)
11	A	Coventry	Lost	12	18	S.Binns(4P)
18	H	Waterloo	Lost	16	26	J.Dudley(T) D.Lax(C) S.Binns(2P) A.Buzza(D)
25	A	West Hartlepool	Lost	21	22	B.Wade(T) C.West(T) S.Binns(C, 3P)
Nov 8	H	Fylde	Won	32	16	G.Austin(T) D.Elliott(T) S.Moffatt(T) S.Binns(C, 5P)
Dec 13	A	London Scottish	Lost	29	35	G.Austin(T) S.Binns(T, 3C, P) J.Harper(T) S.Moffatt(T)
20	H	Coventry	Won	46	8	J.Harper(2T) G.Austin(T) G.Easterby(T) J.Dudley(T) M.Schmid(T) S.Binns(5C, 2P)
27	A	Moseley	Won	25	23	S.Binns(T, P) Penalty(T) B.Wade(T) D.Lax(2C, P)
Jan 10	A	Waterloo	Won	32	26	G.Easterby(2T) G.Austin(T) S.Binns(T, 2C, P) D.Lax(T)
17	H	Moseley	Lost	10	16	M.Dawson(2T)
31	H	Wakefield	Won	41	9	G.Austin(3T) S.Binns(2T, 3C) M.Schmid(2T)

Feb 14	A	Blackheath	Won	31	18	M.Schmid(2T) J.Harper(T) S.Binns(2C, 4P)
Mar 7	A	Exeter	Won	33	8	G.Austin(T) S.Bunting(T) M.Dawson(T) M.Schmid(T) M.Umaga(T) S.Binns(4C)
14	H	Blackheath	Won	40	10	G.Austin(2T) M.Dawson(T) J.Harper(T) M.Umaga(T) B.Wade(T) S.Binns(5C)
28	A	Wakefield	Lost	14	15	M.Dawson(T) S.Binns(2C)
Apr 11	H	Bedford	Won	18	17	G.Austin(T) J.Harper(T) S.Binns(C, 2P)
18	A	Orrell	Won	9	3	S.Binns(3P)
25	H	Exeter	Won	50	27	B.Wade(4T) S.Binns(2T, 5C) J.Dudley(T) M.Umaga(T)

Summary of Premiership scorers:

244 – S.Binns (8T, 39C, D, 41P); 60 – G.Austin (12T); 35 – B.Wade (7T);
30 – M.Schmid (6T), J.Harper (6T), M.Dawson (6T); 20 – G.Easterby (4T),
J.Dudley (4T); 15 – M.Umaga (3T), J.Shepherd (3T), S.Moffatt (3T); 14 – D.Lax (T,
3C, P); 10 – C.West (2T); 5 – Penalty (T), N.Spence (T), J.Sinclair (T), D.Elliott (T),
S.Bunting (T); 3 – A.Buzza (D).

Summary of Premiership appearances:

22 – B.Wade (+2), R.Wareham, S.Bunting, S.Binns; 21 – G.Easterby;
20 – G.Webster, C.West, J.Dudley (+4); 19 – S.Wilson (+4); 18 – G.Austin;
17 – D.Cook (+7); 16 – M.Dawson (+1); 15 – D.Lax; 14 – J.Harper; 12 – S.Moffatt
(+1); 11 – A.Buzza (+3); 10 – M.Schmid (+2); 9 – M.Umaga, N.Spence (+4),
J.Shepherd (+3); 7 – J.Sinclair (+1), I.Kearney (+2), R.Bramley (+4), J.Bentley,
J.Ashley (+3); 6 – M.Mills (+3); 5 – M.Pinder (+5); 3 – T.Murphy (+3), D.McIntyre
(+2), S.Coy, C.Barrett (+3); 2 – I.Worsley (+2), A.Knight (+2), R.Ashforth (+2);
1 – N.Miller (+1), P.Hennessey (+1), D.Elliott.

RUGBY LIONS

Formation of club: 1994 (originally formed in 1873)
Ground: Webb Ellis Road, Rugby CV22 7AU
Capacity: 3,396 (Seated 240)
Colours: Orange, black and white
Honours: Champions Area League North 1987-88, Division 2 – 1990-91
Best League finish: 11th in Division One 1991-92
Best Cup run: Last 16, 1990-91, 1992-93, 1997-98
Last season: Jewson One – 4th. Tetley's Bitter Cup – 5th round (lost 11-42 to West
Hartlepool)
Owners: Members
Director of Rugby: Geoff Davies
Captain: Mark Ellis

ASHMEAD, Paul Michael (Flanker)
Born Gloucester, 03.01.66. 6'1", 15st 2lb. **ADPR:** Gloucester (1987-95, 44, 10t-42pts), Rugby (1995-98, 13, 2t-10pts). Durable former Gloucester and South West Divisional flanker who has been struggling with injury.

BAKER, Simon James (Scrum-half)
Born Coventry, 01.02.75. 5'7", 12st 8lb. **ADPR:** Harrogate (1993-94, 4t-20pts), Rugby (1996-98, 29, 4t-20pts). Perennial backup at scrum-half to the evergreen David Bishop but a fine player in his own right. Has represented Warwickshire and works as a teacher after graduating from Liverpool University.

BALE, Paul (Wing)
Born Rugby, 20.12.76. **ADPR:** Rugby (1996-98, 42, 14t-70pts). Product of Rugby Youth's set-up who finally cemented a first-team spot last season when he scored seven tries.

BISHOP, David (Scrum-half)
Born Westminster, 05.01.64. 5'10", 13st 8lb. **ADPR:** Rugby (1987-98, 147, 41t, 1dg-191pts). Wonderful club servant and former club captain who remains as sharp and shrewd as ever around the base of the scrum, helping himself to nine League tries last season. Educated at Skinners School, Tunbridge Wells, and Leicester University. David works as a sales manager for Paramount Press in London. Has represented Warwickshire, the Midlands and Irish Exiles.

BURDETT, Robert Leslie (Hooker)
Born Rugby, 26.07.73. 5'11", 14st 7lb. **ADPR:** Rugby (1993-98, 57, 4t-20pts). Promising hooker who was educated at Lawrence Sheriff School, Rugby, and Loughborough University. Rob became a regular in the Warwickshire county side in 95-96 at the expense of Coventry's Dave Addleton, having made his debut against Notts Lincs & Derby in 94-95. His arrival heralded a run of 11 consecutive victories which only ended when they lost to Gloucestershire in the 1996 final. Rob is a physical education teacher at Nicholas Chamberlaine School in Bedworth.

CUMMINS, Damian (Utility back)
Born Tenby, 08.12.64. 5'11", 14st. **ADPR:** Gloucester (1987-96, 65, 7t, 3dg-38pts), Rugby (1996-98, 25, 1t, 1pg-8pts). Much-travelled teacher who has played for Newport, Exeter University, Borough Road College and Tenby as well as Gloucester before arriving at Rugby. Has also represented the Anglo-Scots and played cricket for Middlesex CCC 2nd XI.

CZERPAK, Josef Stefan (Fly-half)
Born Reading, 25.08.75. **ADPR:** Exeter (1994-95, 2, 3pg-9pts), Newbury (1996, 5, 3t, c, pg-20pts), Rugby (1997-98, 7, 1t, 4c, 2pg-19pts). Promising fly-half who joined from the Newbury club.

DAVIES, Martyn Lloyd (Utility back)
Born Ammanford, 12.10.73. **ADPR:** Rugby (1997-98, 13, 11c, 26pg-100pts). Reliable utility back who provides much-needed goal-kicking backup to Jim Quantrill.

ELLIS, Mark Richard (Flanker)
Born Kirby Muxloe, 23.12.68. 5'11", 14st 12lb. **ADPR:** Rugby (1988-98, 97, 12t-56pts). Loyal club servant who really enjoyed himself last season, scoring seven tries in Rugby's promotion push. Represented Warwickshire in the 1995-96 CIS County final. Mark was educated at Mount Grace High, John Cleveland College and Hinckley College. Was a member of Hinckley RFC before joining Rugby in 1988. Works as a builder.

FIELD, Robert John (Lock)
Born Coventry, 22.06.71. 6'7", 18st. **ADPR:** Coventry (1991-94, 20, 1t-5pts), Leicester (1994-97, 6), Rugby (1997-98, 21, 1t-5pts). Strong lock, put behind him the disappointment of never making a breakthrough with Leicester to anchor Rugby's scrum last season.

GILLOOLY, Adrian Michael (Centre)
Born Rugby, 06.04.70. 6', 14st 11b. **ADPR:** Rugby (1988-98, 83, 8t-40pts). Another loyal Rugby man who missed just one game last season. Adrian was educated at Lawrence Sheriff School and Loughborough University and came up through the youth system at Webb Ellis Road. Enjoyed one season with Dundas Valley in NSW (1993). Has played for Irish Exiles U21. Works as an accountant.

GLOVER, Stuart Lawrence (Centre)
Born Bedford, 03.11.69. 6', 14st. **ADPR:** Bedford (1988-91, 24, 1t-4pts), Rugby (1991-98, 61, 5t-25pts). Quality former England Students centre who arrived from Bedford. Graduate of Exeter University.

HARRISON, Ben Richard (Centre)
Born Coventry, 08.09.78. **ADPR:** Rugby (1997-98, 3, 1t-5pts). Young centre looking to break into the First XV this season.

MEE, Richard (Prop)
Born Leicester, 25.05.67. 6', 18st 7lb. **ADPR:** Rugby (1993-98, 51, 2t-10pts). Warwickshire county prop, formerly with Leicester.

MILNER, Robert James (Hooker)
Born Coventry, 05.06.68. 5'11", 14st 9lb. **ADPR:** Nuneaton (1990-91, 1t-4pts), Rugby (1992-98, 45, 6t-30pts). Reliable squad member who joined Rugby from Nuneaton. Educated at Nicholas Chamberlaine Senior, Bedworth, and Warwickshire College of Agriculture. Works as a farmer.

MORGAN, Jonathan Dean (Fly-half)
Born Ammanford, 23.11.71. **ADPR:** Coventry (1989-90, 3) Rugby (1997-98, 26, 6t, 1dg-33pts). Talented Welsh fly-half who was ever-present throughout Rugby's Jewsons campaign last season. Formerly with Dunvant and Bonymaen.

QUANTRILL, James Robert (Full-back)
Born Poole, 30.05.69. 6'2", 15st. **Rep hons:** Barbarians (95-96). **ADPR:** Rugby (1990-98, 106, 13t, 84c, 109pg-559pts). Quality performer at full-back who has represented English Universities and the Midlands. Formerly with Old Silhillians and Birmingham & Solihull, he was educated at Solihull School and Nottingham University. Bank executive.

REES, David (Prop)
Born Merthyr Tydfil, 11.04.66. **ADPR:** Rugby (1997-98, 26, 2t-10pts). Another successful import from Wales, the former Newbridge and Bridgend prop did not miss a League game last season.

REVAN, Samuel Trevor (Prop)
Born Birmingham, 05.12.63. 6'2", 17st 7lb. **Rep hons:** England A (1,Ire91). **ADPR:** Rugby (1988-98, 134, 8t-36pts). Renowned scrummager and club man, Trevor was educated at Hartfield Crescent Comp. A former member of Birmingham Welsh, he has represented Warwickshire for 12 years. Enjoyed a brief spell playing in France but happy to return to Rugby and play his part in their renaissance. Ever-present last season.

SAUNDERS, Edmund (Wing)
Born Nottingham, 02.11.60. 6', 12st 7lb. **Rep hons:** Barbarians (95-96). **ADPR:** Rugby (1987-98, 141, 73t-333pts). An almost legendary figure on the Rugby wing, Eddie has scored more League tries (73) than any player in England. Blessed with natural pace, his appetite for tries showed no sign of slackening last season when he grabbed 12. Received a special award for his services to rugby from the Rugby Writers Club in 1996 and Rugby organised a testimonial game at the end of the season.

SMITH, Steven David (Lock)
Born Solihull, 20.06.68. **ADPR:** Rugby (1991-98, 121, 6t-30pts).Wonderfully committed and loyal club man; Steve was ever-present last season and a key figure in Rugby's combative pack. Powerful lock who joined Rugby after spells with Old Silhillians, Solihull, Coventry and Tukapa in Taranaki. Educated at Lode Heath Secondary and Solihull College. Works as a company accountant and has represented Irish Exiles.

THOMPSON, Paul (No 8)
Born Warwick, 24.09.74. 6'4", 15st 7lb. **ADPR:** Rugby (1995-98, 31, 4t-20pts). Graduate of Hull University. Warwickshire county representative.

UNDERHILL, Neil Barry (Lock)
Born Lutterworth, 23.06.72. 6'10", 17st. **ADPR:** Rugby (1992-98, 56, 6t-30pts). Forges a formidable second row partnership with Steve Smith. Spent a year in Canterbury, New Zealand and came back an improved player. Missed just one game last season.

VAEGA, To'o (Centre)
Born Moto'otua, Western Samoa, 17.08.65. **Rep hons:** Western Samoa. **ADPR:** Rugby (1997-98, 16, 6t-30pts). A class act at centre, To'o Vaega played a starring role in Western Samoa's World Cup campaigns in 1991 and 1995. Has played much of his rugby for Southland in New Zealand and fully intends challenging for a place in Western Samoa's squad for the 1999 World Cup.

WITHERS, James Alexander (Flanker)
Born Stratford-upon-Avon, 15.03.75. **ADPR:** Moseley (1995-97, 2), Rugby (1997-98, 11, 2t-10pts). Rapidly emerging young flanker who joined the club from Moseley.

REVIEW

Bounced back with great spirit from relegation the previous season to earn promotion to Premiership Two by finishing fourth in Jewsons One. Player-coach Andy Earl was a great influence but was superbly supported by loyal Rugby men such as Eddie Saunders, David Bishop, Mark Ellis and Steve Smith. The signing of Western Samoan To'o Vaega also brought much-needed class to the midfield. Though promotion may be beyond them this season, Rugby have nothing to fear.

RUGBY in Jewson One 1997-98

Aug 30	A	Lydney	Won	20 13	D.Bishop(T) B.Harrison(T) J.Quantrill(2C, 2P)
Sep 13	A	Otley	Won	22 3	E.Saunders(2T) C.Alexander(T) M.Ellis(T) J.Quantrill(C)
20	H	Rosslyn Park	Won	34 22	E.Saunders(2T) A.Earl(2T) J.Quantrill(C, 4P)

27	A	Wharfedale	Won	33	29	D.Bishop(2T) S.Smith(T) J.Quantrill(T, 4C) C.Alexander(T)

27	A	Wharfedale	Won	33	29	D.Bishop(2T) S.Smith(T) J.Quantrill(T, 4C) C.Alexander(T)
Oct 11	H	Harrogate	Won	20	13	M.Ellis(T) Penalty(T) S.Smith(T) J.Quantrill(C, P)
18	A	London Welsh	Lost	15	21	P.Bale(T) J.Quantrill(T, C, P)
25	H	Morley	Won	69	3	D.Bishop(2T) S.Baker(T) A.Earl(T) M.Ellis(T) D.Morgan(T) J.Quantrill(T, 5C) D.Rees(T) S.Smith(T) P.Thompson(T) N.Underhill(T) J.Czerpak(2C)
Nov 8	A	Nottingham	Won	39	24	S.Smith(T) A.Earl(T) R.Milner(T) N.Underhill(T) J.Quantrill(2C, 5P)
15	H	Reading	Won	36	10	J.Quantrill(2T, 2C) D.Bishop(T) M.Ellis(T) A.Gillooly(T) T.Vaega(T) J.Czerpak(C)
22	A	Leeds	Lost	15	28	A.Earl(T) D.Bishop(T) J.Quantrill(C, P)
Dec 6	H	Newbury	Won	38	26	N.Underhill(2T) J.Czerpak(T C, 2P) D.Morgan(T) D.Bishop(T) P.Thompson(T)
20	A	Worcester	Lost	16	30	R.Milner(T) J.Quantrill(C, 3P)
27	H	Liverpool St Helens	Won	33	5	T.Harrison(T) D.Morgan(T) J.Quantrill(C, P) M.Davies(6P)
Jan 17	H	Nottingham	Won	24	13	T.Revan(T) P.Thompson(T) M.Davies(C, 4P)
31	H	London Welsh	Won	21	15	D.Rees(T) C.Alexander(T) M.Davies(C, 3P)
Feb 7	A	Harrogate	Won	21	7	M.Ellis(T) Penalty(T) J.Quantrill(C, 3P)
14	H	Wharfedale	Won	42	21	P.Bale(2T) E.Saunders(T) A.Gillooly(T) D.Morgan(T) J.Withers(T) J.Quantrill(3C, 2P)
21	A	Rosslyn Park	Won	39	8	P.Bale(2T) J.Quantrill(T, 4C, 2P) E.Saunders(T) N.Underhill(T)
28	H	Leeds	Lost	17	28	E.Saunders(T) P.Bale(T) M.Davies(2C, P)
Mar 7	H	Otley	Won	22	7	E.Saunders(T) T.Vaega(T) D.Morgan(T) D.Bishop(T) J.Quantrill(C)
14	A	Newbury	Won	20	18	S.Smith(T) J.Withers(T) T.Vaega(T) J.Quantrill(C) D.Morgan(D)
28	A	Reading	Won	54	20	E.Saunders(2T) T.Vaega(2T) R.Field(T) D.Morgan(T) N.Underhill(T) S.Baker(T) M.Davies(4C, 2P)
Apr 4	H	Lydney	Won	31	5	M.Ellis(T) D.Bailey(T) T.Harrison(T) M.Davies(2C, 4P)
11	A	Liverpool St Helens	Won	28	13	E.Saunders(T) D.Bailey(T) P.Thompson(T) A.Gillooly(T) M.Davies(C, 2P)

| 18 | A | Morley | Won | 18 | 10 | T.Vaega(T) P.Bale(T) M.Davies(C, 2P) |
| 25 | H | Worcester | Lost | 6 | 13 | M.Davies(2P) |

Summary of League scorers:

171 – J.Quantrill (6T, 33C, 25P); 100 – M.Davies (11C, 26P); 60 – E.Saunders (12T); 45 – D.Bishop (9T); 35 – M.Ellis (7T), P.Bale (7T); 33 – D.Morgan (6T, D); 30 – T.Vaega (6T), N.Underhill (6T); 25 – A.Earl (5T); 20 – P.Thompson (4T), S.Smith (4T); 19 – J.Czerpak (T, 4C, 2P); 15 – A.Gillooly (3T), C.Alexander (3T); 10 – Penalty (2T), J.Withers (2T), D.Rees (2T), R.Milner (2T), T.Harrison (2T), S.Baker (2T), D.Bailey (2T); 5 – T.Revan (T), B.Harrison (T), R.Field (T).

Summary of League appearances:

26 – S.Smith (+4), D.Rees, T.Revan, D.Morgan (+1); 25 – N.Underhill (+4), J.Quantrill (+4), A.Gillooly (+1); 24 – P.Bale (+2); 22 – P.Thompson (+9), R.Milner (+1), A.Earl, D.Bishop (+5); 21 – R.Field (+12), M.Ellis; 19 – C.Alexander (+2); 18 – E.Saunders; 16 – T.Vaega (+1); 15 – S.Baker (+10); 13 – M.Davies (+3); 11 – J.Withers (+7), R.Mee (+11); 9 – R.Burdett (+4); 7 – J.Czerpak (+3); 6 – M.Davies (+6), D.Cummins (+3), D.Bailey; 5 – T.Harrison (+1), S.Glover; 4 – C.Gubbins (+3); 3 – B.Harrison; 2 – P.Ashmead (+2); 1 – N.Riley (+1), W.Hare (+1).

WAKEFIELD

Formation of club: 1901
Ground: College Grove, Eastmoor Road, Wakefield WF1 3RR
Capacity: 2,450 (Seated 450)
Colours: Black and gold
Honours: Division Three Champions – 1987-88
Best League finish: 2nd in Division Two, 1994-95
Best Cup run: S/F 1975-76
Last season: ADP2 – 10th. Tetley's Bitter Cup – 4th round (lost 13-23 to West Hartlepool)
Owners: Members
Director of Rugby: Stephen Townend
Coaches: Roger Burman, Clive Harris, Max Greenwood, David Heroy
Captain: Neil Summers

BIRKBY, Alex Mark (Scrum-half)
Born Sheffield, 21.07.77. 5'9", 12st 5lb. **ADPR:** Wakefield (1995-98, 10). Youthful scrum-half who is beginning to pick up valuable experieince under the tutelage of David Scully. Has represented Yorkshire U21 and Colts. Student at Leeds University.

BROOKING, Keith Simon (Front row)
Born Torquay, 07.05.73. 6', 16st. **ADPR:** Exeter (1994-97, 36, 1t-5pts), Wakefield (1997-98, 12). Prop turned hooker who joined Wakefield from Exeter last season, having previously played for Bath and Newton Abbot. Has also represented the Welsh Exiles.

144

BROWN, Alan (Flanker)
Born Stockton-on-Tees, 20.09.67. 6'2", 15st 8lb. **ADPR:** West Hartlepool (1990-97, 80, 16t-73pts), Wakefield (1997-98, 6). Underrated former England U21 and Colts openside flanker who joined from West Hartlepool. Formerly with Stockton.

BURROW, Mark (Lock)
Born Chelmsford, 09.07.69. 6'6", 17st 8lb. **ADPR:** Saracens (1993-97, 42), Leeds (1997-98, 12). Hard-grafting lock, always conspicuous by his flaming red hair. Helped form and run an Occasional XV consisting entirely of redheads to play charity games. Joins from Leeds.

CHOLEWA, Lee Roland (Fly-half)
Born Wakefield, 12.05.78. 5'9", 11st 7lb. **ADPR:** Rotherham (1996-97, 2), Wakefield (1997-98, 4, 1t, 2c, 3pg-18pts). England Colts squad member who learned his rugby at QEGS Wakefield.

CROFT, Simon (Lock)
Born Harrogate, 22.03.65. 6'7", 17st 12lb. **ADPR:** Wakefield (1993-98, 91, 4t-20pts). Experienced former North and Yorkshire lock who threatened to hang his boots up at the end of the season – in fact he nailed them to the changing room. Capped by England Colts and formerly with Harrogate. Works as an estate agent.

ELISARA, Faimafili Caine (No 8)
Born Auckland, New Zealand, 30.11.75. **Rep hons:** Netherlands. **ADPR:** Wakefield (1997-98, 9, 2t-10pts). Learned his rugby playing with Otago but arrived after a spell in the Netherlands.

FLINT, Jonathan David (Centre)
Born Harrogate, 06.06.71. 6'2", 13st 8lb. **ADPR:** Nottingham (1990-91, 1), Otley (1993-96, 6t, 1pg-33pts), Wakefield (1997-98, 10). England Students representative who has yet to fulfil his full potential. Educated at Leeds GS. Works as a recruitment consultant.

GARNETT, Terence Anthony (Hooker)
Born Hull, 10.05.67. 6', 16st 6lb. **ADPR:** Wakefield (1988-98, 133, 17t-77pts). Combative flanker turned hooker who has done Wakefield proud over the years. Played for England Colts and the North before representing Irish Exiles. An England Schools swimming international, he is also a judo black belt. Formerly with Hull Ionians.

GLEN, Michael Francis (Utility back)
Born 06.11.76. 6'2", 13st 8lb. **ADPR:** Wakefield (1995-98, 6). Scotland U21 utility back. Educated at Solihull School and Leeds University.

GREENWOOD, Matthew James (Back five forward)
Born Leeds, 25.09.64. 6'5", 17st. **Rep hons:** England A (13, Sp92, 1t-5pts), Barbarians (93-94). **ADPR:** Nottingham (1988-92, 27, 1t-4pts), Wasps (1992-97, 78, 5t-25pts), Wakefield (1997-98, 22, 1t-5pts). After helping Wasps to the 1996-97 League title Matt returned to Yorkshire as Wakefield's player-coach last season. As reliable and hard-working as ever, Matt was ever-present in the League. Toured New Zealand with England B in 1992 and Canada the following summer with an England XV. Started his career with Roundhay and also numbers Nottingham among his former clubs.

HARDCASTLE, Dean (Prop)
Born Doncaster, 26.01.76. 5'10", 16st 7lb. **ADPR:** Wakefield (1996-98, 12). Former England U21 squad player. Dean will be hoping to secure a regular first XV place this season.

JACKSON, Michael (Utility back)
Born Manchester, 21.01.67. 5'10", 13st 2lb. **ADPR:** Fylde (1988-93, 53, 5t, 19c, 52pg-215pts), Wakefield (1993-98, 72, 9t, 82c, 165pg, 1dg-707pts). One of the most consistent accumulators of points in League history. Former captain of the North Divisional team. Works as a bank official.

LATHAM, Rhodri (Prop)
Born Ghana, 01.08.69. 6'1", 18st 4lb. **ADPR:** Wakefield (1987-98, 100). Developed his game as a youngster in Ghana where his father, a mining engineer, played rugby. Fierce scrummager and a regular first-teamer. Played for Selby before joining Wakefield. A builder by trade and keen fisherman who has landed a 32lb pike, or so he says.

LEE, Craig Philip (Centre)
Born Stockton-on-Tees, 05.05.71. 5'10", 13st 5lb. **ADPR:** West Hartlepool (1991-97, 53, 4t, 1c-21pts), Wakefield (1997-98, 8). Useful former England Colt who has also represented the North. Started out with Stockton RFC.

MAYNARD, Philip Michael (Centre)
Born Wakefield, 08.01.70. 5'11", 14st 7lb. **ADPR:** Wakefield (1989-98, 90, 12t-57pts). Home-grown product who has represented England Colts and Schools. Joined Wakefield in July 1989.

MILLER, Gregory Keith (Fly-half)
Born Port Elizabeth, South Africa, 07.05.73. 5'7", 11st. **ADPR:** Wakefield (1997-98, 14, 3t, 12c, 31pg, 3dg-141pts). Arrived midway through last season and had an immediate effect. Provides a smooth link at fly-half and reliable goal-kicking. Has played Currie Cup rugby for Border and also represented the province against the 1997 British Lions.

PLEVEY, Scott Gary (Hooker)
Born Doncaster, 28.09.76. 5'10", 13st 7lb. **ADPR:** Wakefield (1996-98, 3). Yorkshire U21 hooker who provided backup for Terry Garnett last season.

RUSHWORTH, Christopher Robert (Flanker)
Born 27.02.69. 6'2", 16st 3lb. **ADPR:** Wakefield (1994-98, 23, 5t-25pts). Another of Wakefield's firefighting fraternity, Chris joined the fire brigade in 1993 when he left the army. Has suffered badly from shoulder and arm injuries in recent seasons.

SMITHIES, Edward (Full-back)
Born Halifax, 25.05.79. **ADPR:** Wakefield (1997-98, 4). Graduated from Wakefield Colts last season to impress at full-back.

SOWERBY, Mark (No 8)
Born 05.09.69. 6'4", 16st 5lb. **ADPR:** Wakefield (1989-98, 69, 1t-5pts). Talented backrow man whose rugby career was put on hold when he worked in Turkey for two years, acting as site manager for his chemical company. Former England Students representative.

STEWART, Paul Andrew (Flanker)
Born Halifax, 09.10.62. 6'6", 16st 8lb. **ADPR:** Wakefield (1989-98, 116, 10t-49pts). Wakefield's second longest-serving player, Paul served as captain for the 1997-98 season. Member of the North team that beat Western Samoa 1995-96. Competitive and works hard at his game. Nicknamed 'Stick' for his lean appearance on the rugby pitch and behind the wheel of his truck – he is an HGV driver.

SUMMERS, Neil Gary (Full-back)
Born Leeds, 10.10.68. **ADPR:** Headingley (1987-90, 28, 6t-24pts), Wakefield (1997-98, 15, 3t-15pts). Began his career with Headingley before joining Featherstone Rovers RL and Bradford. Returned to the union code last season with Wakefield.

THOMPSON, Richard John (Utility back)
Born Leeds, 03.12.69. 6', 13st 10lb. **ADPR:** Wakefield (1990-95, 58, 19t-93pts), West Hartlepool (1995-96, 6, 1t-5pts), Wakefield (1996-98, 38, 6t-30pts). Former England Schools full-back whose senior career was held back initially after missing two seasons with a badly broken leg. First joined Wakefield as a Colt in July 1987. Left to join West Hartlepool at the start of the 1995-96 season but rejoined Wakefield after a few months. Works as a bank officer.

WHITE, Paul Joseph (Utility back)
Born 15.12.64. 5'10", 12st 7lb. **ADPR:** Morley (1987-93, 37, 6t, 2dg-30pts), Wakefield (1993-98, 62, 10t-50pts). Versatile back who has represented the Irish Exiles. Educated at Bradford GS and a dentist by profession.

WILSON, Glen Richard (Flanker)
Born Wakefield, 31.07.76. 6'1", 15st 2lb. **ADPR:** Wakefield (1996-98, 28, 3t-15pts). England Students and North U21 flanker who is beginning to establish himself as a first-team regular at Wakefield.

YATES, Kern Clinton (Flanker)
Born Wegberg, Germany, 12.02.74. 5'11", 14st. **ADPR:** Wakefield (1994-96, 13, 1t-5pts), Leeds (1995-97, 16, 5t-25pts), Wakefield (1997-98, 12, 1t-5pts). Dynamic openside flanker who captained England 16 Group. Loads of skill and pace.

REVIEW

Wakefield never recovered from a disastrous start, losing their first seven games, and with problems trying to come to terms with the financial implications of professional rugby, will not look back on the 1997-98 season with any great pleasure. It could not have been any tougher for player-coach Matt Greenwood but the former Wasp never lost heart. With Leeds and Rotherham in Premiership Two this season it could be a case of fighting for survival in future years, with Yorkshire really needing to concentrate the county's resources on one or maybe two senior clubs.

WAKEFIELD in Premiership Two 1997-98

Aug 30	H	Exeter	Lost	15	19	D.Scully(5P)
Sep 7	A	Waterloo	Lost	18	30	R.Thompson(T) C.Rushworth(T) L.Cholewa(C, 2P)
13	A	Blackheath	Lost	27	29	D.Scully(2T) L.Cholewa(T) M.Jackson(3C, 2P)
20	H	Coventry	Lost	6	17	M.Jackson(2P)
27	A	West Hartlepool	Lost	20	31	D.Hendry(T) P.Stewart(T) M.Jackson(2C, 2P)
Oct 4	H	Moseley	Lost	15	27	P.White(T) T.Garnett(T) L.Cholewa(C, P)

11	A	London Scottish	Lost	13	30	S.Croft(T) R.Thompson(T) S.Irving(P)
18	H	Fylde	Won	35	17	T.Garnett(T) G.Miller(T, 3C, 3P) Penalty(T) M.Woodward(T)
25	A	Coventry	Lost	17	24	N.Summers(T) G.Miller(4P)
Nov 8	A	West Hartlepool	Lost	12	28	Penalty(T) P.Stewart(T) G.Miller(C)
Dec 13	A	Moseley	Lost	10	28	D.Scully(T) G.Miller(C, P)
20	H	London Scottish	Won	15	10	G.Miller(5P)
Jan 17	H	Waterloo	Won	23	20	P.Maynard(T) G.Miller(T, C, 2P) P.Stewart(T)
31	A	Rotherham	Lost	9	41	G.Miller(3P)
Feb 14	H	Bedford	Lost	13	24	P.White(T) D.Scully(C, 2P)
28	A	Fylde	Won	30	10	S.Croft(T) C.Elisara(T) N.Summers(T) P.White(T) G.Miller(2C, 2P)
Mar 7	H	Orrell	Won	20	26	D.Scully(T) G.Wilson(T) K.Yates(T) G.Miller(C, P)
14	A	Bedford	Lost	10	36	N.Summers(T) G.Miller(C) D.Scully(P)
28	H	Rotherham	Won	15	14	D.Scully(2P) G.Miller(2D, P)
Apr 11	A	Exeter	Won	30	17	C.Elisara(T) M.Greenwood(T) D.Scully(T) R.Thompson(T) G.Miller(2C, 2P)
18	H	Blackheath	Lost	21	24	G.Miller(D, 6P)
25	A	Orrell	Lost	8	54	G.Miller(T, P)

Summary of Premiership scorers:

141 – G.Miller (3T, 12C, 3D, 31P); 57 – D.Scully (5T, C, 10P); 28 – M.Jackson (5C, 6P); 18 – L.Cholewa (T, 2C, 3P); 15 – P.White (3T), R.Thompson (3T), N.Summers (3T), P.Stewart (3T); 10 – Penalty (2T), T.Garnett (2T), C.Elisara (2T), S.Croft (2T); 5 – K.Yates (T), M.Woodward (T), G.Wilson (T), C.Rushworth (T), P.Maynard (T), D.Hendry (T), M.Greenwood (T); 3 – S.Irving (P).

Summary of Premiership appearances:

22 – R.Latham (+1), M.Greenwood; 21 – P.White (+1), R.Thompson (+1), D.Scully, T.Garnett (+4), S.Croft (+2); 20 – P.Stewart (+2); 19 – P.Lancaster (+4); 15 – N.Summers; 14 – M.Woodward (+3), G.Miller (+2); 13 – G.Wilson (+1); 12 – K.Yates (+4), P.Maynard (+2), K.Brooking (+7); 11 – M.Sowerby (+7); 10 – J.Flint (+1); 9 – D.Hendry (+1), C.Elisara (+3); 8 – C.Lee, D.Hardcastle (+3); 6 – C.Rushworth, I.Brehenny (+1), A.Brown (+2); 5 – S.Irving, A.Birkby (+1); 4 – E.Smithies, M.Jackson, L.Cholewa (+1); 3 – A.Yates, J.Skurr (+3), A.McClarron, N.Ashurst; 2 – R.Szabo (+2); 1 – S.Plevey (+1), M.Glen (+1), J.Bartle (+1), A.Bailey (+1).

WATERLOO

Formation of club: 1882
Ground: The Pavilion, St Anthony's Road, Blundellsands, Liverpool L23 8TW
Capacity: 8,900 (Seated 900)
Colours: Myrtle, scarlet and white
Honours: None
Best League finish: 10th Division One, 1987-88
Best Cup run: Losing finalist, 1975-76
Last season: ADP2 – 8th. Tetley's Bitter Cup – 3rd round (lost 34-36 to London Welsh)
Owners: Members
Director of Rugby/Coach: Tony Russ
Captain: David Blyth

BECKETT, Mark Douglas (Prop)
Born Hartlepool, 16.10.65. 6'2", 19st 7lb. **ADPR:** Waterloo (1991-98, 95, 6t-29pts). Missing just one League game last season, Mark remains as reliable as ever in the front row. A graduate of Sheffield University, he started life as a No 8 but moved to prop when he arrived at Blundellsands. Played for Waterloo in their famous Pilkington Cup win over Bath. Works as a financial advisor and known as Onslow because of an alleged resemblance to the TV character.

BLYTH, David John (Backrow)
Born Liverpool, 14.03.71. 6'3", 17st. **ADPR:** Newcastle (1991-92, 1), Waterloo (1991-92, 6), West Hartlepool (1992-93, 9), Waterloo (1993-98, 71, 12t-60pts). Club captain who led by example last year, not missing a League game. Educated at Rossall School and North Mercia University, David represented England Universities, England U21 and Scottish Exiles. Works as a corporate marketing hospitality manager. Lover of French and Chinese cusine.

BRITTIN, Jason Mark (Front row)
Born Hastings, New Zealand, 24.10.73. 5'11", 14st 2lb. **ADPR:** Waterloo (1996-98, 6). PE teacher who arrived at Waterloo from Hawkes Bay. Keen cricketer.

CLAPINSON, Nicholas Paul (Prop)
Born Lachine, Canada, 26.08.70. **Rep hons:** Canada. **ADPR:** Waterloo (1997-98, 19, 1t-5pts). Formidable Canadian lock who became a fixture in the Waterloo front row last season. Enjoyed a brief spell with Leicester before moving to Blundellsands.

COAST, Marcus (Utility back)
Born Bebington, 14.05.76. 6'1", 14st 7lb. **ADPR:** Waterloo (1996-98, 41, 12t-60pts). Promising wing/centre who was joint top try-scorer for Waterloo last season with seven. Educated at Calday Grange GS and Staffordshire University, he joined Waterloo from New Brighton. Keen fisherman.

DONOVAN, John Terence Michael (Hooker)
Born Liverpool, 06.05.75. **ADPR:** Waterloo (1994-98, 5). Developing young hooker who joined from the Hoylake club.

GRAHAM, Philip John (Wing)
Born Carlisle, 02.12.76. 5'10", 13st. **ADPR:** Liverpool St Helens (1995-97, 8t-40pts), Waterloo (1997-98, 21, 4t-20pts). Talented wing who joined from the Wigton club. Educated at Caldew School, Dalsoton, and Liverpool John Moores University. Talented squash player.

GRIFFITHS, Lyndon Alun (Fly-half)
Born Bridgend, 17.02.74. **ADPR:** Waterloo (1996-98, 32, 2t, 46c, 86pg-360pts).
Prolific points-scorer who amassed a staggering 261 for Waterloo last season. Gained
valuable experience with Swansea and Bridgend in Wales.

HACKETT, Paul (Hooker)
Born Liverpool, 28.02.64. 5'11", 15st. **ADPR:** Waterloo (1987-98, 96, 5t-21pts).
Former England Colt who rejoined the club after a brief spell with Crewe &
Nantwich.

HACKNEY, Stephen Thomas (Wing)
Born Stockton-on-Tees, 13.06.68. 5'11", 13st 10lb. **Rep hons:** England A (13, Aus88,
13t-61pts), Barbarians (87-88). **ADPR:** Nottingham (1988-91, 25, 2t-8pts), Leicester
(1991-97, 77, 25t-121pts), Moseley (1997-98, 5, 1t-5pts), Waterloo (1997-98, 5,
2t-10pts). Experienced former England A wing who still possesses plenty of pace.

HANDLEY, Anthony Francis (Fly-half/full-back)
Born Salford, 12.11.73. 5'11", 13st 5lb. **ADPR:** Waterloo (1992-98, 84, 3t, 9c, 15pg,
2dg-84pts). Spent two years in the England Colts side and was capped by England
U21. Tony has never quite fulfilled his exciting early potential but remains a fine
player. Educated at De La Salle College, Salford and St Ambrose Barlow High
School. Played soccer for Salford Boys and the North in 1989.

HART, Peter Gerard (Full-back)
Born Birkenhead, 27.03.71. **ADPR:** Gloucester (1995-97, 7), Waterloo (1997-98, 12,
3t-15pts). Former Birkenhead Park back who returned to the north west after a
two-year spell with Gloucester.

HILL, Nigel David (Centre)
Born Amersham, 04.12.67. 6', 14st 7lb. **ADPR:** Waterloo (1989-94, 42, 1t-5pts),
Moseley (1994-95, 5), Waterloo (1995-98, 32). Played cricket for British Polytechnics
and in the Minor Counties for Oxfordshire. Joined Waterloo on qualifying for sports
science course at Liverpool Polytechnic. Educated at King Alfred's, Wantage, and
Liverpool Polytechnic. Teaches at Meole Brace School, Shrewsbury. Can also play at
fly-half.

HOLT, Matthew Robert (Hooker)
Born Ipswich, Australia, 30.10.71. **ADPR:** Waterloo (1996-98, 29, 4t-20pts). Tough
Australian who has added greatly to Waterloo's front row strength since joining the
club.

KAY, Benedict James (Flanker)
Born Liverpool, 14.12.75. 6'6", 17st 10lb. **ADPR:** Waterloo (1994-98, 46, 1t-5pts).
Son of Waterloo president and High Court judge John Kay. Fully recovered from
injury received last season. Nicknamed 'M'lud', he played for England Students in
the 1996 Students World Cup in South Africa. Educated at Merchant Taylor's
School, Crosby, and Loughborough University.

KIRBY, Russell Paul (Prop)
Born Solihull, 30.05.71. 6', 16st 7lb. **ADPR:** Rugby (1994-97, 19), Waterloo (1997-98,
2). Backup prop who has also played for Birkenhead Park.

LARUE, Stephane (Flanker)
Born Grenoble, France, 09.08.72. 6'5", 17st. Powerhouse France A flanker who joins
Waterloo from Grenoble.

McGOWAN, Louis Joseph (Lock)
Born Liverpool, 17.10.77. 6'5", 16st 4lb. **ADPR:** Waterloo (1997-98, 1). Promising lock with a big future. Educated at Nugent HS.

MORRIS, Stewart Wayne (Scrum-half)
Born Swansea, 06.12.72. **ADPR:** Waterloo (1996-98, 22, 8t-40pts). Educated at Neath College and played for Bridgend, Pontypool and Aberavon before moving to the north west.

MULLINS, Michael John (Centre)
Born Auckland, New Zealand, 29.10.70. **ADPR:** Waterloo (1996-98, 23, 5t-25pts). Played for North Harbour in New Zealand before travelling to Waterloo.

O'KEEFE, Anthony John (Flanker)
Born Birkenhead, 26.11.73. **ADPR:** Waterloo (1997-98, 2). Middle O'Keefe brother. Previous experience with New Brighton and Birkenhead Park.

O'KEEFE, Martin David (Prop)
Born Birkenhead, 28.04.78. 6'2", 17st. **ADPR:** Waterloo (1997-98, 7). Product of the Youth team. Educated at St Anselm's College and Manchester Metropolitan University. Has represented Merseyside at badminton.

O'KEEFE, Stephen James (Prop)
Born Birkenhead, 30.10.71. 6', 17st. **ADPR:** Waterloo (1997-98, 3). Martin's older brother, educated at Nottingham University. Works as a quality control engineer. Formerly with Liverpool St Helens.

O'REILLY, John Paul (Scrum-half)
Born Belebi Pikwe, Botswana, 07.01.76. 5'10", 13st 8lb. **ADPR:** Sale (1996-97, 7), Waterloo (1997-98, 8). Promising England U21 scrum-half whose first-team opportunities at Sale were limited.

O'SHAUGHNESSY, Mark Aidan (Flanker)
Born Napier, New Zealand, 20.09.74. **ADPR:** Waterloo (1997-98, 12, 4t-20pts). Typically abrasive Kiwi who has played for Waikato.

REGENVANU, Nikil Periv (Flanker)
Born Brisbane, Australia, 06.02.74. **ADPR:** Waterloo (1996-98, 13). Another New Zealand-reared backrow man who played for the Hamilton Marist club.

TEMMEN, Karl (Lock)
Born Salisbury, 23.09.74. 6'9", 18st 10lb. **ADPR:** Waterloo (1996-98, 28, 1t-5pts). Stalwart in the second row last season, missing just two games. Educated at Wellfield HS, Leyland. Works as a mechanical engineer.

THOMAS, Ceri Howell Anthony (Flanker)
Born Swansea, 05.10.73. **ADPR:** Waterloo (1997-98, 18, 3t-15pts). Experienced Welsh flanker who has also played for Dunvant, Ystradgynlais and Aberavon.

THOMPSON, Christopher Michael (Utility back)
Born Widnes, 13.11.71. 6', 12st. **ADPR:** Waterloo (1994-98, 29, 17c, 30pg-124pts). Educated at St Anselm's College, Millfield and Sheffield Polytechnic, played for England in World Students Cup quarter-final match against France 1992. Has represented England U18 at golf. Broke a leg on the North's tour to Zimbabwe 1992. Watches Liverpool FC when time permits. Gifted runner but a string of injuries have seriously disrupted his performances in recent seasons, hence nickname 'Physio'.

WHITE, Paul Andrew (Lock)
Born Brighton, 08.05.70. 6'4", 17st 7lb. **ADPR:** Waterloo (1990-98, 71, 5t-25pts).
England U17 basketball triallist, life-saving expert and keen fell-walker, his career
highlights include Waterloo's 1992-93 Pilkington Cup defeat of Bath. Best line-out
jumper in the club. Sports science graduate, educated at Durrington HS and
Liverpool Polytechnic. Nicknamed 'Duke'. Policeman.

WOLFENDEN, Christopher Thomas (Flanker)
Born Waterloo, 05.02.69. 6'2", 15st 11lb. **ADPR:** Waterloo (1993-98, 24, 5t-25pts).
Educated at St Mary's College, Crosby, works as a tyre retailer. Represented Anti
Assassins against Oxford University (1994) and Cambridge University (1995). An
England Schools' Championships 110m hurdles qualifier with a temperament for the
big-occasion matches . . . hobbies include saloon car racing and boxing.

WOOF, Shaun Anthony (Centre)
Born Liverpool, 06.03.77. 6'2", 14st 7lb. **ADPR:** Waterloo (1996-98, 27, 11t-55pts).
Emerging young talent who was joint top try-scorer last season with seven. Educated
at Calday GS and a former member of the Calday club. Represented England U21 in
the SANZAR tournament in South Africa in July 1998.

WRIGHT, Simon Andrew (Scrum-half)
Born Heswall, 15.02.65. 5'8", 12st 7lb. **ADPR:** Bath (1988-89, 1), Liverpool St Helens
(1990-91, 7), Waterloo (1993-98, 56, 10t, 1dg-53pts). Educated at Birkenhead School
and works as an independent financial advisor. Hampered by injury in recent
seasons. Simon comes from a famous rugby-playing family containing brother Chris,
who has played for Harlequins, Paul, a regular at New Brighton, and Mike, a
Waterloo occasional.

REVIEW

Failed to make a real impact in the League last season despite the encouragement of
early wins over West Hartlepool and Wakefield. Consistency was always their
problem, plus an over-reliance on the boot of Lyndon Griffiths, their talented Welsh
fly-half. Subsequent wins over Orrell, Rotherham and Coventry all hinted at the
potential of the club but there were simply to many slip-ups against lesser clubs.
Need to improve their strength in depth if they are to challenge for honours this
season.

WATERLOO in Premiership Two 1997-98

Aug 30	A	West Hartlepool	Won	21	19	M.Coast(T) M.Beckett(T) D.Blyth(T) L.Griffiths(2P)
Sep 7	H	Wakefield	Won	30	18	M.Coast(T) M.Mullins(T) M.Holt(T) L.Griffiths(3C, 3P)
13	H	London Scottish	Lost	17	36	P.Hart(T) M.Coast(T) L.Griffiths(2C, P)
20	A	Exeter	Lost	20	24	M.Holt(T) W.Morris(T) L.Griffiths(2C, 2P)
27	H	Blackheath	Won	51	16	M.Beckett(2T) M.Coast(T) P.Graham(T) W.Morris(T) S.Woof(T) L.Griffiths(6C, 3P)

Oct	4	A	Bedford	Lost	21	34	M.Coast(T) S.Woof(T) L.Griffiths(C, 3P)
	11	H	Orrell	Won	25	14	W.Morris(2T) P.Graham(T) S.Woof(T) L.Griffiths(C, P)
	18	A	Rotherham	Won	26	16	P.Graham(T) W.Morris(T) L.Griffiths(C, 4P) C.Thompson(C)
	25	H	Exeter	Won	44	13	S.Woof(T) M.Coast(T) P.Graham(T) C.Thomas(T) C.Thompson(C) L.Griffiths(2C, 6P)
Nov	8	A	Blackheath	Won	15	14	L.Griffiths(5P)
Dec	13	H	Bedford	Lost	14	28	W.Morris(T) L.Griffiths(3P)
	20	A	Orrell	Lost	6	23	L.Griffiths(2P)
Jan	10	H	Rotherham	Lost	26	32	P.Hart(T) M.Holt(T) M.Mullins(T) M.O'Shaughnessy(T) L.Griffiths(3C)
	17	A	Wakefield	Lost	20	23	P.Hart(T) L.Griffiths(5P)
	31	A	Fylde	Won	25	10	S.Woof(2T) M.O'Shaughnessy(T) L.Griffiths(2C, 2P)
Feb	14	H	Moseley	Won	36	31	N.Clapinson(T) M.O'Shaughnessy(T) C.Thomas(T) S.Woof(T) L.Griffiths(2C, 4P)
Mar	7	A	Coventry	Lost	33	41	D.Blyth(2T) S.Hackney(T) K.Temmen(T) L.Griffiths(2C, 3P)
	14	A	Moseley	Lost	22	23	L.Griffiths(T, C, 5P)
	28	H	Fylde	Won	22	12	M.O'Shaughnessy(T) C.Thomas(T) L.Griffiths(4P)
Apr	11	H	West Hartlepool	Lost	6	51	L.Griffiths(2P)
	18	A	London Scottish	Lost	6	26	L.Griffiths(2P)
	25	H	Coventry	Won	24	21	M.Coast(T) S.Hackney(T) L.Griffiths(C, 4P)

Summary of Premiership scorers:

261 – L.Griffiths (T, 29C, 66P); 35 – S.Woof (7T), M.Coast (7T); 30 – W.Morris (6T); 20 – M.O'Shaughnessy (4T), P.Graham (4T); 15 – C.Thomas (3T), M.Holt (3T), P.Hart (3T), D.Blyth (3T), M.Beckett (3T); 10 – M.Mullins (2T), S.Hackney (2T); 5 – K.Temmen (T) N.Clapinson (T); 4 – C.Thompson (2C).

Summary of Premiership appearances:

22 – L.Griffiths, D.Blyth; 21 – P.White, P.Graham, M.Beckett (+1); 20 – S.Woof; 19 – K.Temmen, M.Holt (+3), M.Coast (+1), N.Clapinson; 18 – C.Thomas (+6), W.Morris, T.Handley (+3); 17 – B.Kay (+1); 15 – M.Mullins; 12 – M.O'Shaughnessy (+2), P.Hart (+5); 10 – P.Hackett (+4); 9 – N.Allott (+9); 8 – N.Reganvanu, J.O'Reilly (+4); 7 – M.O'Keefe (+5); 6 – N.Hill; 5 – C.Wolfendon (+4), C.Thompson (+2), S.Hackney; 3 – S.O'Keefe (+1); 2 – A.O'Keefe (+1), R.Kirby (+1), B.Johnson (+2), J.Britten (+2); 1 – S.Wright (+1), L.McGowan (+1), T.Donovan (+1).

WORCESTER

Formation of club: 1871
Ground: Sixways, Pershore Lane, Hindlip, Worcester WR3 8SU
Capacity: 3,500 (Seated 850)
Colours: Navy blue and gold
Honours: Champions North Midlands 1 – 1990, Midlands 1 – 1995, Division 4
North – 1997, Jewsons 1 – 1998
Best League finish: 1st in Jewson Division One in 1997-98
Best Cup run: Last 16 1997-98
Last season: Jewson One – Champions. Tetley's Bitter Cup – 5th round (lost 0-10 to
Newcastle)
Owner: Cecil Duckworth
Director of Rugby: Les Cusworth
Coach: Duncan Hall
Captain: TBC

BAILEY, Alistair Joseph (Lock)
Born Essex, 27.06.73. 6'7", 17st 3lb. **ADPR:** Wakefield (1994-98, 31). Young England
Colts and Scottish Exiles lock who failed to cement a first-team place last season.

BALL, Dean John (Hooker)
Born 24.07.71. 5'7", 15st 4lb. **ADPR:** Moseley (1991-97, 62, 2t-10pts), Worcester
(1997-98, 21, 3t-15pts). A former carpenter who joined the club from Moseley. Played
divisional rugby for the Midlands.

BAXTER, Nick (Wing)
Born Birmingham, 13.04.73. **ADPR:** Worcester (1995-98, 50, 50t-250pts). Phenom-
enal try-scorer with a strike rate of exactly one per game. Joined from Kings Norton.
Nick is a keen basketball player and also enjoys poetry. Called into England's
Commonwealth Games Sevens squad.

BRADLEY, Spencer (Flanker)
Born Worcester, 24.05.69. **ADPR:** Worcester (1988-98, 68, 34t-155pts). A homegrown
talent, 'Spanner' was the club's leading try-scorer in 1995-96.

CLARK, Gary (Flanker)
Born 03.05.65. 6'3", 17st. **ADPR:** Saracens (1996-97, 9, 2t-10pts), Worcester (1997-
98, 24, 4t-20pts). Experienced flanker who captained Saracens Second XV for three
years before seizing the opportunity of regular First XV rugby by joining Worcester.

CRANE, Mark (Prop)
Born Bristol, 10.10.71. 6'3", 20st. **ADPR:** Bath (1988-92, 5, 1t-4pts), Clifton (1995-
96, 24, 4t-20pts), Coventry (1996-97, 21, 3t-15pts), Worcester (1997-98, 10, 1t-5pts).
Experienced prop who has also played divisional rugby for the Midlands.

DENHARDT, Richard David Ian (Lock)
Born Birmingham, 13.09.67. 6'5", 18st. **ADPR:** Moseley (1987-98, 59, 3t-15pts).
Former Moseley captain who moved to Worcester at the end of last season. Former
New Zealand Colt who has played provincial rugby for Wellington.

EVANS, Barry John (Wing)
Born Hinckley, 10.10.62. **Rep hons:** England (2, Aus88), B (4, It85, 1t-4pts), Barbarians (82-83). **ADPR:** Leicester (1987-95, 28, 11t-44pts), Coventry (1991-94, 33,

154

9t-45pts), Worcester (1996-98, 24, 8t-40pts). Vastly experienced former England wing who scored 170 tries in 273 games for Leicester and is also a former Coventry club captain.

FENLEY, Bruce (Scrum-half)
Born 07.09.68. 5'8", 12st. **ADPR:** Moseley (1987-93, 38, 3t-14pts), Gloucester (1993-96, 41, 4t-20pts), Worcester (1996-98, 50, 21t-105pts). Qualified as a chartered surveyor, Bruce was Worcester's player of the season in 1996-97 and remains a key element of their rise through the Leagues. Former Midlands representative player.

HARVEY, Ben (Scrum-half)
Born Redruth, 26.06.74. 5'9", 13st. **ADPR:** Bristol (1995-96, 4), Richmond (1996-98, 7, 1t-5pts). Former England Students representative who has joined Worcester from Richmond where First team opportunities were limited. Educated at St. Thomas' Exmouth. Nephew of actress Jan Harvey.

HARWOOD, Greg (Fly-half)
Born Hereford, 28.01.67. 5'7", 11st 8lb. **ADPR:** Coventry (1992-93, 4, 1t, 2c-9pts), Worcester (1995-98, 21, 1t, 6c, 2dg-23pts). Superfit former Army man who works as a sports consultant. Has played for Hereford and the Army as well as Coventry.

HICKEY, Kevin (No 8)
Born Solihull, 02.03.66. 6'1", 14st 7lb. **ADPR:** Moseley (1987-88, 2), Coventry (1988-95, 62, 18t-83pts), Worcester (1997-98, 7, 4t-20pts). Former Moseley and Coventry man who adds experience to the backrow.

HOLFORD, Paul Curtis (Wing)
Born Gloucester, 02.12.69. 5'1", 13st. **Rep hons:** England A (2, Vic95, 1t-5pts). **ADPR:** Gloucester (1992-97, 56, 17t-85pts), Worcester (1997-98, 21, 14t-70pts). Fast, strong and elusive, Paul has the ability to shine again at the top level.

HOUSTON, Gordy (Hooker)
Born Bangor, Northern Ireland, 22.03.67. 6'1", 15st 7lb. **ADPR:** Worcester (1996-98, 27, 3t-15pts). Former Ireland U21 hooker who reverted to his favourite position last season. Arrived at Worcester via Edinburgh Wanderers and Selly Oak.

HUGHES, Duncan (Centre)
Born Derby, 14.07.72. 5'11", 14st. **ADPR:** Worcester (1991-98, 55, 16t, 11c, 7pg-123pts). Former captain at King's School, Worcester, Duncan joined the club straight from school before playing for Llanelli and Newport while at university in Wales.

JENNER, James William (No 8)
Born Reading, 27.11.71. 6'4", 16st 7lb. **ADPR:** Worcester (1997-98, 14, 15t-75pts). Try-scoring No 8 who enjoyed himself immensely last season with 15 to his name. Joined from Exeter. Has been called into the England squad for the Commonwealth Games.

JOHAL, Jag (Flanker)
Born Hitchin, 19.07.74. 5'10", 16st 10lb. **ADPR:** Moseley (1994-97, 22, 2t-10pts), Worcester (1997-98, 4). Powerful flanker with real pace. Joined Worcester from Moseley at the end of last season.

LE BAS, Richard Leslie Joffre (Fly-half)
Born Carterton, New Zealand, 26.07.71. 5'10", 14st. **ADPR:** Moseley (1996-97, 14, 3t, 27c, 36pg-177pts), Worcester (1997-98, 22, 9t, 60c, 16pg, 1dg-216pts). Former New Zealand U19 and U21 fly-half who joined Worcester from Moseley.

LILEY, John Garin (Full-back)
Born Wakefield, 21.08.67. 6′, 13st 10lb. **Rep hons:** England A (4, Nam90, 6c, 7pg-33pts). **ADPR:** Wakefield (1987-88, 5, 2t, 4c, 2pg-22pts), Leicester (1988-97, 102, 25t, 129c, 232pg, 1dg-1070pts), Moseley (1997-98, 10, 2t, 8c, 7pg-47pts), Worcester (1997-98, 1). The second highest points-scorer in the history of League rugby, John joined Worcester at the end of last season from Moseley.

LINNETT, Mark Stuart (Prop)
Born Rugby, 17.02.63. 5′11″, 17st. **Rep hons:** England (1, Fiji89, 1t-4pts), A (4, It88, 2t-8pts), Barbarians (89-90). **ADPR:** Moseley (1987-95, 86, 11t-52pts), Worcester (1995-98, 60, 11t-55pts). Enormously powerful former England prop who joined Worcester four years ago and has been fundamental in their rise to prominence. Educated at Dunsmore CS, Rugby.

LLOYD, Stephen John (Lock)
Born Montevideo, Uruguay, 11.07.68. 6′6″, 19st. **ADPR:** Moseley (1988-95, 63, 1t-5pts), Harlequins (1995-96, 2), Worcester (1996-98, 38, 4t-20pts). Former Wales squad member and Midlands representative who has overcome a serious back injury to continue his career.

LYMAN, Neil Michael (Prop)
Born Bedford, 06.05.70. **ADPR:** Moseley (1990-93, 13), Worcester (1994-98, 42, 6t-30pts). Powerful former England U21 prop.

MILES, Peter (Lock)
Born Gloucester, 04.06.67. 6′6″, 17st 10lb. **ADPR:** Bath (1987-88, 2), Gloucester (1990-96, 14, 4t-17pts), Worcester (1996-98, 22, 4t-20pts). Useful lock who experienced the big time with Bath and Gloucester.

MITCHELL, Peter (Prop)
Born Cheltenham, 31.01.67. 6′, 17st 7lb. **ADPR:** Moseley (1989-93, 11), Waterloo (1993-94, 2), Orrell (1995-96, 14), Worcester (1996-98, 31, 3t-15pts). Has flourished since arriving back in the West Country from Orrell. A qualified chartered surveyor who works as a practice auctioneer.

MORRIS, Simon (Centre/wing)
Born Gloucester, 03.05.69. 6′, 13st. **ADPR:** Lydney (1989-90, 1t-4pts), Gloucester (1990-95, 48, 12t-55pts), Worcester (1997-98, 8, 2t-10pts). Seemed destined for great things at Gloucester before a serious knee injury intervened. Now resurrecting his career at Worcester.

PARSONS, Adrian (Centre)
Born Wolverhampton, 20.02.65. 5′10″, 14st 7lb. **ADPR:** Moseley (1987-90, 23, 2t-8pts), Worcester (1993-98, 17, 3t-15pts). Experienced centre who works as a sales executive with Berghaus.

RICHARDSON, Nigel David (Flanker)
Born Worcester, 01.02.71. 6′3″, 15st 4lb. **ADPR:** Leicester (1992-94, 6, 3t-15pts), London Irish (1996-97, 5, 1t-5pts), Worcester (1997-98, 15, 1t-5pts). Locally born and educated at King's, Worcester – Nigel is a former England U21 and Cambridge University captain.

SCOTT, Chris (Flanker)
Born 01.07.64. 5′11″, 15st 3lb. **ADPR:** Worcester (1997-98, 12, 7t-35pts). A former England Colts cap who has also featured in the full Wales squad. Former clubs include Cheltenham, Gloucester, Newport and Neath.

SMITH, Timothy John (Full-back)
Born Gloucester, 10.05.62. **ADPR:** Gloucester (1987-96, 94, 11t, 58c, 141pg, 2dg-596pts), Worcester (1996-98, 46, 12t, 72c, 48pg-348pts). Wonderfully consistent points-scorer who has taken up at Worcester where he left off at Gloucester. Underrated runner who enjoys sevens.

TISDALE, Nick (Lock)
Born Bridgenorth, 26.08.69. 6'5", 17st. **ADPR:** Worcester (1995-98, 50, 1t-5pts). Reliable lock who joined from Kidderminster.

TOMLINSON, Richard George (Centre)
Born Worcester, 25.11.71. 5'10", 13st 9lb. **ADPR:** Rugby (1992-94, 16, 1pg-3pts), Nottingham (1994-97, 16, 3t, 2c, 3pg-28pts), Worcester (1996-98, 41, 11t, 11c, 10pg-107pts). Educated at King's School, Worcester, and Loughborough University.

WYLDE, Rich (Full-back)
Born Birkenhead, 09.11.73. **ADPR:** Worcester (1992-98, 33, 6t, 4c, 5pg, 2dg-59pts). Educated at RGS Worcester and Brunel University.

REVIEW

The fairytale goes on and on with Cecil Duckworth's money and commitment off the field being matched by his team on the field. The signing of Les Cusworth as director of rugby has also proved a masterstroke. Worcester strode to the Jewson Championship and defeated Bristol in the Cup before covering themselves in glory by only losing 10-0 to Newcastle in the fifth round. It will be more testing in Premiership Two this season but there is no reason to suppose they can't move directly into Premiership One itself.

WORCESTER in Jewson One 1997-98

Aug 30	A	Liverpool St Helens	Won	42	7	B.Fenley(2T) G.Harwood(T) R.Le Bas(T) S.Lloyd(T) C.Scott(T) R.Tomlinson(2C, 2P) T.Smith(C)
Sep 7	H	Lydney	Won	30	9	N.Baxter(2T) B.Fenley(T) P.Holford(T) T.Smith(2C) R.Le Bas(2P)
13	A	Newbury	Won	28	21	R.Tomlinson(T) N.Baxter(T) G.Clark(T) R.Le Bas(2C, 3P)
20	H	Otley	Won	27	12	T.Smith(T, P) N.Baxter(T) B.Fenley(T) G.Houston(T) R.Le Bas(2C)
27	A	Rosslyn Park	Lost	3	6	R.Le Bas(P)
Oct 11	H	Wharfedale	Won	44	11	K.Hickey(3T) G.Clark(T) B.Evans(T) M.Linnett(T) T.Smith(T, 3C, P)
18	A	Harrogate	Won	26	13	B.Fenley(T) M.Linnett(T) A.Parsons(T) C.Raymond(T) D.Hughes(2C) T.Smith(C)
25	H	London Welsh	Lost	13	28	J.Jenner(T) T.Smith(C, 2P)

157

Date		Venue	Opponent	Result			Scorers
Nov 8	A	Morley		Won	63	6	J.Jenner(3T) T.Smith(T) K.Hickey(T) N.Richardson(T) M.Linnett(T) P.Holford(T) D.Hughes(T) R.Wylde(T) R.Le Bas(5C, P)
15	H	Nottingham		Won	27	0	D.Hughes(T, 2C) R.Le Bas(T, C, P) P.Mitchell(T) T.Smith(P)
22	A	Reading		Won	62	15	D.Hughes(2T) D.Ball(2T) P.Holford(2T) S.Lloyd(T) G.Clark(T) M.Linnett(T) J.Jenner(T) R.Le Bas(3C) T.Smith(3C)
Dec 13	H	Reading		Won	47	19	C.Scott(3T) R.Hilton-Jones(T) N.Baxter(T) R.Le Bas(T, 3C, 2P) J.Jenner(T)
20	H	Rugby		Won	30	16	G.Clark(T) R.Le Bas(T) S.Lloyd(T) T.Smith(5P)
27	A	Leeds		Won	15	14	T.Smith(5P)
Jan 10	A	Nottingham		Won	32	12	N.Baxter(T) R.Tomlinson(T) R.Le Bas(T) D.Hughes(T) T.Smith(3C, 2P)
17	H	Morley		Won	55	0	T.Smith(2T, 5C, P) D.Hughes(2T) B.Fenley(T) P.Holford(T) P.Miles(T) C.Raymond(T) R.Le Bas(C)
31	H	Harrogate		Won	50	3	N.Baxter(3T) J.Jenner(2T) R.Le Bas(T, 5C) R.Hilton-Jones(T) D.Hughes(T)
Feb 7	A	Wharfedale		Won	53	15	N.Baxter(3T) R.Le Bas(2T, 5C, P) M.Crane(T) P.Holford(T) R.Tomlinson(T)
14	H	Rosslyn Park		Won	57	13	N.Baxter(2T) C.Raymond(T) D.Hughes(T) R.Tomlinson(T) T.Smith(T) J.Jenner(T) P.Holford(T) R.Le Bas(7C, P)
21	A	Otley		Won	68	7	N.Baxter(6T) P.Holford(2T) J.Jenner(2T) R.Le Bas(T, 4C) D.Ball(T)
28	A	London Welsh		Won	31	22	N.Baxter(T) R.Tomlinson(T) B.Fenley(T) C.Scott(T) J.Jenner(T) R.Le Bas(3C)
Mar 7	H	Newbury		Won	41	22	P.Holford(3T) J.Jenner(2T) N.Baxter(T) R.Le Bas(4C, P)
14	A	Lydney		Won	41	12	N.Baxter(2T) S.Morris(2T) P.Holford(T) M.Linnett(T) C.Scott(T) R.Le Bas(3C)
21	H	Liverpool St Helens		Won	78	22	N.Baxter(4T) R.Myler(3T) B.Fenley(T) J.Jenner(T) C.Raymond(T) C.Scott(T) T.Smith(T) R.Le Bas(9C)
Apr 18	H	Leeds		Won	25	20	B.Fenley(T) N.Baxter(T) P.Holford(T) R.Le Bas(2C, 2P)
25	A	Rugby		Won	13	6	J.Jenner(T) R.Le Bas(C, D, P)

158

Summary of League scorers:

206 – R.Le Bas (8T, 59C, D, 15P); 145 – N.Baxter (29T); 124 – T.Smith (7T, 19C, 17P); 75 – J.Jenner (15T); 70 – P.Holford (14T); 45 – B.Fenley (9T); 44 – D.Hughes (8T, 2C); 35 – R.Tomlinson (5T, 2C, 2P), C.Scott (7T); 25 – M.Linnett (5T); 20 – C.Raymond (4T), K.Hickey (4T), G.Clark (4T); 15 – R.Myler (3T), S.Lloyd (3T), D.Ball (3T); 10 – S.Morris (2T), R.Hilton-Jones (2T); 5 – R.Wylde (T), N.Richardson (T), A.Parsons (T), P.Miles (T), G.Houston (T), G.Harwood (T), B.Evans (T), M.Crane (T).

Summary of League appearances:

25 – M.Linnett; 24 – T.Smith (+2), C.Raymond (+1), G.Clark (+2); 23 – B.Fenley (+1); 22 – R.Tomlinson, R.Le Bas; 21 – P.Holford, D.Ball (+1); 20 – D.Hughes; 19 – N.Baxter; 16 – S.Lloyd; 15 – N.Richardson (+3), P.Mitchell (+2); 14 – J.Jenner (+2); 13 – N.Tisdale (+2); 12 – C.Scott (+4); 10 – N.Lyman (+3), M.Crane (+5); 9 – R.Hilton-Jones; 8 – S.Morris (+5), G.Houston (+3); 7 – P.Miles (+5); 6 – J.Powell (+3), R.Myler, K.Hickey (+1); 5 – B.Evans; 4 – R.Wylde (+1), G.Harwood (+1); 3 – A.Parsons, J.Johal; 2 – S.Bradley, G.Blakeway (+2); 1 – S.Powell (+1), A.Martin (+1), A.Logan (+1), J.Cox (+1).

Rugby in England 1997-98

Allied Dunbar Premiership

The Allied Dunbar Premiership race in 1997-98 was notable, historically, for the changing of the old order with Newcastle and Saracens, bolstered by massive investment and high-profile recruits, eclipsing the *ancien régime*, represented by Leicester and Bath. By April it was a two-horse race, pure and simple, with Newcastle eventually taking the honours on the final Saturday of League rugby with an away win at Harlequins. The final six weeks, featuring a head-to-head fight between Newcastle and Saracens, were exciting and crowned a generally satisfactory League season, though the dreadfully structured nature of the pre-Christmas schedule resulted in a slow start.

Newcastle just deserved to take the honours, relying heavily on a wonderful durable, combative and streetwise pack and the finely tuned rugby brain of Rob Andrew at fly-half. Saracens were also good value for their runners-up spot and were denied the title only by Newcastle's excellence. Leicester, their season thrown into confusion by the sacking of Bob Dwyer, were 12 points adrift in fourth place, missing out on third by points *scored* by Bath. Elsewhere Richmond probably played the best, certainly the most entertaining rugby, and finished with six straight wins to make up for some dreadfully inconsistent form in mid-season. Gloucester could manage just two away wins, while Northampton, Wasps and Harlequins all badly underperformed. Bristol looked doomed to relegation from an early stage. London Irish, however, recovered their form and poise sufficiently in the final two months of the season to account for Rotherham in the play-offs.

Bedford were clearly the best team in Premiership Two but face a huge challenge to become competitive with the elite clubs this season, as do West Hartlepool who were also promoted. London Scottish sprang a surprise, not least on themselves, by beating Bristol in the play-offs but reacted quickly to their promotion and within weeks had announced an ambitious groundshare scheme with neighbours Harlequins. Elsewhere Rotherham continued their remarkable climb up the League structure and were by no means disgraced in their play-off games against London Irish. Orrell flattered to deceive, Moseley came perilously close to going out of existence in mid-season and Fylde, Exeter and Wakefield all struggled, though they were saved from relegation by the League's restructuring.

In Jewson One, Worcester and Leeds spent their money well and should make an immediate impact on Premiership Two, while London Welsh also responded to the professional era by matching their improvement on the pitch with much better organisation off it. Rugby, an illustrious old name, also refused to slip into decline and were good value for the fourth promotion spot.

Premiership One

	P	W	D	L	F	A	Pts
Newcastle	22	19	0	3	645	387	38
Saracens	22	18	1	3	584	396	37
Bath	22	13	0	9	575	455	26
Leicester	22	12	2	8	569	449	26
Richmond	22	12	0	10	607	499	24
Sale	22	10	2	10	605	558	22
Gloucester	22	11	1	10	512	528	21*
Northampton	22	9	1	12	493	472	19
Wasps	22	8	1	13	490	609	17
Harlequins	22	8	0	14	516	645	16
London Irish	22	6	0	16	457	673	12
Bristol	22	2	0	20	351	733	4

*Two points deducted for fielding an ineligible player

Division One play-offs (two legs): London Scottish 29, Bristol 25; Bristol 15, London Scottish 17. (London Scottish promoted to Premiership One; Bristol relegated.) Rotherham 13, London Irish 16; London Irish 26, Rotherham 14. (London Irish and Rotherham stay in their respective divisions.)

Premiership Two

	P	W	D	L	F	A	Pts
Bedford	22	20	0	2	791	365	38*
West Hartlepool	22	15	1	6	617	431	31
London Scottish	22	14	1	7	517	404	29
Rotherham	22	14	0	8	566	386	28
Orrell	22	12	0	10	533	400	24
Moseley	22	11	1	10	478	421	23
Coventry	22	11	1	10	444	532	23
Waterloo	22	11	0	11	510	525	22
Blackheath	22	8	0	14	474	621	16
Wakefield	22	6	0	16	382	556	12
Exeter	22	6	0	16	334	553	12
Fylde	22	2	0	20	258	710	4

* Two points deducted for fielding an ineligible player

Top Premiership points-scorers 1997-98: 289 Mike Rayer (Bedford); 279 Michael Lynagh (Saracens); 275 Mark Mapletoft (Gloucester); 269 Niall Woods (London Irish); 261 Lyndon Griffiths (Waterloo); 256 Simon Binns (Rotherham); 253 Gareth Rees (Wasps); 253 Joel Stransky (Leicester); 241 Steven Vile (West Hartlepool); 226 Rob Andrew (Newcastle); 224 Shane Howarth (Sale); 210 Paul Grayson (Northampton).

Top Premiership try-scorers 1997-98: 17 Dominic Chapman (Richmond), Darragh O'Mahony (Moseley), Ben Whetstone (Bedford); 16 Conan Sharman (London Scottish); 14 Tom Beim (Sale), Jason Forster (Bedford); 13 Gary Armstrong (Newcastle), Greg Austin (Rotherham), John Clarke (Blackheath).

All-time English National League records (1987-98)

Leading aggregate points:

1,292 Rob Andrew (Wasps/Newcastle) 39, 103, 90, 126, –, 29, 159, 135, 93, 292, 226
1,139 John Liley (Wakefield/Leicester/Moseley) 22, 9, 126, 110, 125, 106, 28, 99, 272, 195, 47
1,090 Andy Green (Exeter) 42, 6, 97, 92, 77, 122, 130, 32, 192, 300, –
1,027 Jon Callard (Bath) –, –, 27, –, –, 29, 178, 150, 236, 224, 183
1,004 Paul Grayson (Waterloo/Northampton) –, –, –, –, –, 126, 132, 189, 218, 129, 210
  991 Peter Rutledge (Otley) –, –, –, –, –, 121, 119, 167, 147, 287, 150
  965 Tim Smith (Gloucester/Worcester) 21, 85, 75, 75, 81, 71, 82, 24, 82, 221, 124

Leading aggregate tries:

73 Eddie Saunders (Rugby) 7, 9, 7, 7, 2, 3, 2, 7, 9, 8, 12
62 Mark Sephton (Liverpool St Helens) , –, 6, 3, 3, 8, 9, 7, 7, 11, 8
53 Jeremy Guscott (Bath) 1, 10, 4, 5, 1, 3, 2, 1, 9, 12, 5
53 Daren O'Leary (Saracens/Harlequins) –, –, –, –, –, 3, 11, 1, 14, 15, 9
52 Nick Baxter (Worcester) –, –, –, –, –, –, –, –, 5, 18, 29
51 Dave Scully (Wakefield) 6, 8, 4, 4, 3, –, 3, 2, 7, 9, 5
50 Jon Sleightholme (Wakefield/Bath/Northampton) –, –, –, –, 8, 7, 12, 2, 7, 12, 2
50 Rory Underwood (Leicester/Bedford) 1, 1, 4, 8, 9, 2, –, 3, 8, 7, 7

Jewson One

	P	W	D	L	F	A	Pts
Worcester	26	24	0	2	1001	331	48
Leeds	26	21	1	4	858	407	43
London Welsh	26	21	1	4	848	478	43
Rugby	26	21	0	5	733	405	42
Rosslyn Park	26	13	1	12	486	537	27
Nottingham	26	13	0	13	527	602	26
Newbury	26	12	2	12	639	545	24*
Reading	26	11	1	14	617	697	23
Otley	26	10	1	15	447	679	21
Wharfedale	26	8	3	15	476	684	19
Liverpool St Helens	26	8	1	17	430	767	15*
Lydney	26	5	0	21	361	575	10
Morley	26	5	0	21	372	844	10
Harrogate	26	4	1	21	463	707	9

Jewson Two (North)

	P	W	D	L	F	A	Pts
Birmingham	26	23	0	3	803	337	46
Manchester	26	21	2	3	1029	472	44
Kendal	26	18	2	6	618	357	38
Preston Grasshoppers	26	14	2	10	549	469	30
Sedgeley Park	26	14	2	10	658	592	30
Stourbridge	26	14	0	12	685	603	28
Nuneaton	26	13	0	13	453	572	26
Sandal	26	13	1	12	485	547	25*
Aspatria	26	11	0	15	524	783	22
Sheffield	26	10	2	14	552	538	20*
Walsall	26	9	1	16	539	723	19
Hinckley	26	6	1	19	429	729	13
Lichfield	26	4	1	21	365	689	9
Winnington Park	26	5	0	21	470	748	8*

Jewson Two (South)

	P	W	D	L	F	A	Pts
Camberley	26	23	1	2	803	368	47
Henley	26	22	0	4	772	384	44
Barking	26	20	0	6	762	441	40
Esher	26	18	1	7	651	448	37
Cheltenham	26	14	1	11	627	514	29
Tabard	26	14	0	12	547	532	28
North Walsham	26	12	1	13	431	373	25
Bridgwater	26	12	0	14	535	664	24
Redruth	26	10	0	16	716	580	20
Weston-super-Mare	26	10	0	16	468	651	20
Clifton	26	8	1	17	414	611	17
Havant	26	8	1	17	388	643	17
Plymouth Albion	26	6	0	20	473	756	12
Metropolitan Police	26	2	0	24	320	942	2*

* Two points deducted for fielding an ineligible player

Tetley's Bitter Cup 1997-98

Final

Saracens 48 Wasps 18 (Twickenham, 9 May 1998)

Saracens demonstrated the changing face of English club rugby with their vibrant seven-try demolition of Wasps, in a splendid showpiece occasion that added to the feel-good factor after the signing of a 'peace agreement' between the RFU and senior clubs just 24 hours earlier. Saracens' 48 points equalled the Cup final record set by Bath against Gloucester on a similarly sun-drenched day in 1990. All of which leaves Leicester and Bath – 20 prizes between them of the 24 on offer between 1984 and 1997 – toiling behind the new rulers.

Tony Diprose, the Saracens captain, recalled the Bath of eight years ago and said: 'Beforehand we set our target as matching that great display and we did it. Now we want to ensure that it's not a one-off. We want to be like Bath and Leicester and win frequent honours.' Whatever the future for Saracens they will have to face it without two of the game's finest-ever players, Michael Lynagh and Philippe Sella, both signing off in style in their last competitive appearances in a major stadium. Saracens must have known it was going to be their day when the illustrious duo were on the scoreboard within five minutes, with Sella claiming the first of seven tries and Lynagh inevitably converting.

Lynagh enjoyed a typically masterful match, organising and controlling with subtle boots and flickering hands. He made it easy for his colleagues and drove Wasps' normally secure defence to distraction. Wasps manager Nigel Melville admitted: 'He was fantastic. He's a magician. The game will be lesser without him.'

Saracens player-coach Francois Pienaar, who will be around to bid for future success, said: 'It's very gratifying to say goodbye to two legends in such style. They will always be remembered. When you get to a cup final, you have to win it. I had to prove a point to myself after being kicked out of South African rugby two years ago and the team created a wonderful performance.'

Lynagh, who was compared to a 16-year-old by Pienaar in the build-up, said: 'I thought nothing could touch winning a World Cup final with Australia at Twickenham but this is another occasion I will never forget. It was especially pleasing to have so many of the things we practise come off on a big day.'

Wasps were unrecognisable from the team which had embarked on a run of League wins late in the season to stave off the threat of relegation. Captain Lawrence Dallaglio admitted: 'Everybody in the squad made a couple of mistakes at least. Multiply that by the 19 players we used and you are up to 40 to 50 basic errors for Saracens to exploit. We are a young side and we will get better but there is almost nothing positive that we can take out of the match.'

Saracens were clear winners by the 13th minute, after Ryan Constable had followed Sella over the line and Lynagh had added a dropped goal. Gareth Rees, a survivor of the 1986 final, kicked two penalties for Wasps but Saracens' 15-6 lead was a platform for victory. By half-time, Gavin Johnson and Danny Grewcock had added further tries and Steve Ravenscroft scored the fifth, before Wasps staged a late rally with tries by Paul Volley and Shane Roiser. But Saracens finished on a high with further scores from Kyran Bracken and Richard Wallace, Lynagh ending with 13 points.

Saracens: G.Johnson; B.Daniel, P.Sella, S.Ravenscroft, R.Constable; M.Lynagh, K.Bracken; R.Grau, G.Chuter, P.Wallace, P.Johns, D.Grewcock, B.Sturnham, F.Pienaar, A. Diprose (capt).

Replacements: R.Wallace for Daniel (28), G.Botterman for Chuter (76), A.Olver for Grau (79), M.Olsen for Bracken (79).

Scorers: T: Sella, Constable, Johnson, Grewcock, Ravenscroft, Bracken, R. Wallace. C: Lynagh (5). DG: Lynagh.

Wasps: G.Rees; S.Roiser, M.Denney, R. Henderson, L.Scrase; A.King, M.Friday; D.Molloy, S.Mitchell, W.Green, M.Weedon, S.Shaw, J.Worsley, P.Volley, L.Dallaglio (capt).

Replacements: P.Sampson for Scrase (52), M.White for Worsley (54), A.Gomarsall for Friday (74), A. Black for Molloy (74).

Scorers: T: Volley, Roiser. C: Rees. PG:Rees (2).

Referee: Mr C.White.

Attendance: 65,000.

Tetley's Bitter Cup Results 1997-98

Round 1:
Aspatria 24 Stockton 13; Barking 26 Swanage & Wareham 18; Basingstoke 10
Weston-super-Mare 39; Birmingham & Solihull 22 Westleigh 10; Bridgwater 18
Metropolitan Police 30; Broadstreet 25 Walsall 21; Camberley 38 Barnstaple 16;
Cheltenham 138 Okehampton 0; Coney Hill 5 Preston Grasshoppers 16; Haywards
Heath 26 Plymouth 25; Henley 64 Cambridge 12; Hornets 28 Havant 72;
Launceston 58 Bicester 6; Lewes 12 Wimbledon 11; Lichfield 10 Manchester 28;
Longton 22 Widnes 38; Maidenhead 14 Amersham & Chiltern 36; Matson 8
Bishops Stortford 3; North Walsham 19 Esher 18; Northern 49 Derby 3; Norwich
14 Bracknell 25; Nuneaton 11 Sedgeley Park 7; Old Coventrians 13 Huddersfield
35; Olney 18 St Ives 20; Sandal 30 Chester 22; Scunthorpe 6 Doncaster 23; Selly
Oak 31 Syston 19; Sevenoaks 32 Cheshunt 13; Sheffield 38 Old Northamptonians
14; Sherborne 19 Clifton 30; St Benedict's 9 Wigton 24; Staines 35 Redruth 25;
Sunderland 8 Kendal 27; Sutton & Epsom 23 Banbury 25; Tabard 23 Harlow 0;
Taunton 34 Canterbury 12; Tynedale 32 Hinckley 8, Vagabonds 18 Old Brodleians
15; Vale of Lune 27 Ampthill 25; Whitchurch 28 Stourbridge 35; Winchester 20
Ruislip 0; Winnington Park 64 Stoke 12.

Round 2:
Aspatria 27 Widnes 18; Birmingham & Solihull 9 Otley 10; Bracknell 35 Metropolitan
Police 14; Broadstreet 41 Huddersfield 3; Cheltenham 20 Sevenoaks 18; Havant 19
Matson 10; Haywards Heath 20 Launceston 22; Henley 3 Camberley 16; Kendal 9
Harrogate 5; Lewes 10 North Walsham 42; London Welsh 65 Clifton 17; Lydney 67
Amersham & Chiltern 0; Morley 41 Selly Oak 5; Northern 5 Tynedale 22; Nottingham
20 Doncaster 24; Preston Grasshoppers 8 Manchester 33; Rugby 46 Vagabonds 0;
Sandal 12 Nuneaton 16; Sheffield 42 Vale of Lune 20; St Ives 6 Barking 53; Staines 32
Banbury 12; Stourbridge 69 Taunton 8; Tabard 0 Rosslyn Park 31;
Weston-super-Mare 17 Newbury 36; Wharfedale 35 Wigton 10; Winchester 12
Reading 26; Winnington Park 24 Liverpool St Helens 26; Worcester 28 Leeds 11.

Round 3:
Barking 13 Exeter 17; Bedford 76 Staines 15; Blackheath 32 Sandal 21; Broadstreet
15 Bracknell 21; Camberley 32 Kendal 19; Coventry 83 Sheffield 19; Doncaster 24
Tynedale 11; Fylde 48 Aspatria 5; Havant 22 Rugby 32; London Welsh 36 Waterloo
34; Lydney 3 London Scottish 45; Moseley 79 Liverpool St Helens 10; North
Walsham 11 Rosslyn Park 27; Orrell 16 Newbury 26; Otley 24 Manchester 25;
Rotherham 67 Launceston 15; Stourbridge 58 Reading 58; Wakefield 14 Morley 5;
West Hartlepool 41 Cheltenham 5; Wharfedale 8 Worcester 29.

Round 4:
Bath 24 London Scottish 23; Blackheath 31 Saracens 59; Bracknell 3 Rotherham
26; Camberley 10 Newbury 11; Coventry 14 Leicester 50; Fylde 20 Rosslyn Park 5;
London Welsh 18 Gloucester 34; Manchester 13 London Irish 36; Moseley 11 Sale
18; Newcastle 34 Exeter 10; Northampton 31 Bedford 26; Richmond 58 Doncaster
8; Rugby 26 Reading 17; Wasps 31 Harlequins 26; West Hartlepool 23 Wakefield
13; Worcester 14 Bristol 12.

Round 5:
West Hartlepool 42 Rugby 11; Northampton 30 Gloucester 11; Bath 17 Richmond
29 (aet); Worcester 0 Newcastle 10; Wasps 34 Fylde 8; Saracens 14 Leicester 13;
London Irish 27 Rotherham 14; Sale 38 Newbury 11.

Quarter-finals:
London Irish 7 Wasps 41; Northampton 17 Newcastle 7; Richmond 30 Saracens
36; West Hartlepool 21 Sale 36.

Semi-finals:
Northampton 10 Saracens 25; Wasps 15 Sale 9.

Past winners

1972 GLOUCESTER 17 Moseley 6
1973 COVENTRY 27 Bristol 15
1974 COVENTRY 26 London Scottish 6
1975 BEDFORD 28 Rosslyn Park 12
1976 GOSFORTH 23 Rosslyn Park 14
1977 GOSFORTH 27 Waterloo 11
1978 GLOUCESTER 6 Leicester 3
1979 LEICESTER 15 Moseley 12
1980 LEICESTER 21 London Irish 9
1981 LEICESTER 22 Gosforth 15
1982 GLOUCESTER 12 MOSELEY 12 (shared title)
1983 BRISTOL 28 Leicester 22
1984 BATH 10 Bristol 9
1985 BATH 24 London Welsh 15
1986 BATH 25 Wasps 17
1987 BATH 19 Wasps 12
1988 HARLEQUINS 28 Bristol 22
1989 BATH 10 Leicester 6
1990 BATH 48 Gloucester 6
1991 HARLEQUINS 25 Northampton 13 (aet)
1992 BATH 15 Harlequins 12 (aet)
1993 LEICESTER 23 Harlequins 16
1994 BATH 21 Leicester 9
1995 BATH 36 Wasps 16
1996 BATH 16 Leicester 15
1997 LEICESTER 9 Sale 3
1998 SARACENS 48 Wasps 18

Non Five Nations Internationals

New England coach Clive Woodward received the toughest possible baptism with matches on four consecutive Saturdays against Australia, South Africa and New Zealand (twice). Given the severity of that test and his declared intention of pushing young players forward into the limelight, England's record of two draws and two defeats represented a useful autumn's work. First up were Australia and a sterile 15-15 draw – probably England's least impressive performance. There was a considerable improvement seven days later at an impassioned Old Trafford, where England may have lost 25-8 to New Zealand but performed with considerably more pace and precision than against Australia. Next came South Africa and England moved smoothly into an 11-0 lead before the Springboks engaged top gear to win comfortably enough. Then came England's finest moment. Tired and battered from the gruelling schedule, they can have hardly faced the prospect of another encounter against New Zealand with relish, but they raised their game in remarkable fashion and thoroughly deserved a share of the spoils in an exciting 26-26 draw.

England 15 Australia 15 (Twickenham, 15 November 1997)

England: M.B.Perry (Bath); D.Rees (Sale), W.J.H.Greenwood (Leicester), P.R.De Glanville (Bath), A.A.Adebayo (Bath); M.J.Catt (Bath), K.P.P.Bracken (Saracens); J.Leonard (Harlequins), A.E.Long (Bath), W.R.Green (Wasps), M.O.Johnson (Leicester), G.S.Archer (Newcastle), L.B.N.Dallaglio (Wasps, capt), A.J.Diprose (Saracens), R.A.Hill (Saracens).

Replacements: P.J.Grayson (Northampton) for De Glanville (7-23), R.Cockerill (Leicester) for Long (40), A.S.Healey (Leicester) for Adebayo (65).

Scorer: PG: Catt (5).

Australia: S.Larkham (ACT); B.N.Tune (Queensland), T.J.Horan (Queensland), P.W.Howard (Queensland), J.W.Roff (ACT); E.Flatley (Queensland), G.M.Gregan (ACT); R.L.L.Harry (NSW), M.A.Foley (Queensland), A.T.Blades (NSW), J.Langford (NSW), J.A.Eales (Queensland, capt), O.Finegan (ACT), V.Ofahengaue (NSW), B.J.Robinson (ACT).

Replacements: D.J.Wilson (Queensland) for Robinson (40), A.Heath (NSW) for Blades (55).

Scorers: T: Tune, Gregan. C: Roff. PG: Roff.

Referee: A.Watson (South Africa).

England 8 New Zealand 25 (Old Trafford, 22 November 1997)

England: M.B.Perry (Bath); D.Rees (Sale), W.J.H.Greenwood (Leicester), P.R.De Glanville (Bath), A.A.Adebayo (Bath); M.J.Catt (Bath), K.P.P.Bracken (Saracens); J.Leonard (Harlequins), R.Cockerill (Leicester), D.J.Garforth (Leicester), M.O.Johnson (Leicester), G.S.Archer (Newcastle); L.B.N.Dallaglio (Wasps, capt), A.J.Diprose (Saracens), R.A.Hill (Saracens).

Replacements: N.A.Back (Leicester) for Diprose (40), A.S.Healey (Leicester) for Adebayo (55).

Scorers: T: De Glanville. PG: Catt.

New Zealand: C.M.Cullen (Manawatu); J.W.Wilson (Otago), F.E.Bunce (North Harbour), A.I.Ieremia (Wellington), J.T.Lomu (Counties); A.P.Mehrtens (Canterbury), J.W.Marshall (Canterbury, capt); C.W.Dowd (Auckland), N.J.Hewitt (Southland), O.M.Brown (Auckland), I.D.Jones (North Harbour), R.M.Brooke (Auckland), T.C.Randell (Otago), Z.V.Brooke (Auckland), J.A.Kronfeld (Otago).

Replacements: A.F.Blowers (Auckland) for Z.Brooke (52), S.J.McLeod (Waikato) for Ieremia (59), J.P.Preston (Wellington) for Wilson (81).

Scorers: T: Wilson, Jones, Randell. C: Mehrtens (2). PG: Mehrtens (2).

Referee: P.L.Marshall (Australia).

England 11 South Africa 29 (Twickenham, 29 November 1997)

England: M.B.Perry (Bath); J.Bentley (Newcastle), N.J.J.Greenstock (Wasps), W.J.H.Greenwood (Leicester), D.Rees (Sale); M.J.Catt (Bath), M.J.S.Dawson (Northampton); J.Leonard (Harlequins), R.Cockerill (Leicester), D.J.Garforth (Leicester), D.J.Grewcock (Saracens), G.S.Archer (Newcastle); L.B.N.Dallaglio (Wasps, capt), R.A.Hill (Saracens), N.A.Back (Leicester).

Replacements: P.J.Grayson (Northampton) for Catt (40), C.M.A.Sheasby (Wasps) for Hill (57), A.S.Healey (Leicester) for Bentley (65), S.D.Shaw (Wasps) for Grewcock (68).

Scorers: T: Greenstock. PG: Catt (2).

South Africa: P.C.Montgomery (W Province); J.T.Small (W Province), A.H.Snyman (N Transvaal), D.J.Muir (W Province), P.W.G.Rossouw (W Province); H.W.Honiball (Natal), W.Swanepoel (OFS); J.P.Du Randt (OFS), J.Dalton (Gauteng), A.C.Garvey (Natal), M.G.Andrews (Natal), K.Otto (N Transvaal), A.D.Aitken (W Province), G.H.Teichmann (Natal, capt), A.G.Venter (OFS).

Replacement: R.B.Skinstad (W Province) for Venter (31-37).

Scorers: T: Snyman, Swanepoel, Garvey, Andrews. C: Honiball (2), Montgomery. PG: Honiball.

Referee: C.J.Hawke (New Zealand).

England 26 New Zealand 26 (Twickenham, 6 December 1997)

England: M.B.Perry (Bath); D.Rees (Sale), W.J.H.Greenwood (Leicester), P.R.De Glanville (Bath), A.S.Healey (Leicester); P.J.Grayson (Northampton), K.P.P.Bracken (Saracens); J.Leonard (Harlequins), R.Cockerill (Leicester), D.J.Garforth (Leicester), M.O.Johnson (Leicester), G.S.Archer (Newcastle), L.B.N.Dallaglio (Wasps, capt), R.A.Hill (Saracens), N.A.Back (Leicester).

Replacements: T.R.G.Stimpson (Newcastle) for Rees (5-17) and for De Glanville (59), C.M.A.Sheasby (Wasps) for Back (20-28), M.J.S.Dawson (Northampton) for Bracken (59), M.P.Regan (Bristol) for Cockerill (64).

Scorers: T: Rees, Dallaglio, Hill. C: Grayson. PG: Grayson (3).

New Zealand: C.M.Cullen (Manawatu); J.W.Wilson (Otago), W.K.Little (North Harbour), F.E.Bunce (North Harbour), J.T.Lomu (Counties); A.P.Mehrtens (Canterbury), J.W.Marshall (Canterbury, capt); M.R.Allen (Manawatu), N.J.Hewitt (Southland), O.M.Brown (Auckland), I.D.Jones (North Harbour), R.M.Brooke (Auckland), T.C.Randell (Otago), Z.V.Brooke (Auckland), J.A.Kronfeld (Otago).

Replacements: C.C.Riechelmann (Auckland) for Kronfeld (32-34), C.J.Spencer (Auckland) for Little (65), S.J.McLeod (Waikato) for Bunce (74).

Scorers: T: Little, Mehrtens. C: Mehrtens (2). PG: Mehrtens (4).

Referee: J.M.Fleming (Scotland).

Rugby in Wales 1997-98

Welsh National Leagues

The outcome of the new-look Premiership may theoretically have been decided on the final Saturday but few people seriously doubted that Swansea were the class club side in Wales last season. Under their New Zealand-born coach John Plumtree, who learned much of his rugby in South Africa, they clinched their third Welsh Championship with a convincing 45-27 win at Pontypridd. After a slow start early in the season Swansea simply got better and better, with their strength in depth proving vital. Plumtree was never frightened to drop star names – he was widely criticised for substituting an out-of-sorts Arwel Thomas against Llanelli in October – yet nobody worked harder with the mercurial fly-half and by the end of the season Thomas was back in his pomp, heading the Premiership scoring list with 246 points. 'Winning the Premiership is a great start but it is just a start', insisted Plumtree on receiving the trophy. 'I want my players to be involved regularly in a higher status of competition.' Cardiff, generally enduring an unhappy season of dispute with the WRU, clinched second place with a dramatic last-day win over Llanelli, overcoming a 26-10 deficit despite the dismissal of Wales lock Derwyn Jones. Promising wing/centre Liam Botham grabbed two tries, a performance that convinced the England U21 selectors to take him to South Africa for the prestigious Six Nations tournament. Pontypridd, the 1996-97 champions, possibly expended too much energy and effort on their European campaign but remain a thriving club. They will miss manager Eddie Jones, who is taking over at Abercynon, but will welcome the news that Neil Jenkins is to stay at Sardis Road. At the other end of the table, nobody with any feel for the history of Welsh rugby will have enjoyed the spectacle of Newport going without a win all season.

Division One proved a romp for Caerphilly who scored 1090 points in their 30 games, losing just three. Only Aberavon and Treorchy could remotely compete with Caerphilly's pace and guile, while in an overlong season Maesteg and UWIC struggled desperately and were relegated. Once-mighty Pontypool just escaped the drop, player/coach David Bishop rolling back the years to inspire a 14-8 win over UWIC. Tredegar provided a rare ray of hope in Gwent by taking the Division Two title, while Llantrisant were deserving winners of Division Three.

Premier Division

	P	W	D	L	F	A	T*	Bonus pts	Pts
Swansea	14	11	2	1	569	263	68	11	46
Cardiff	14	10	1	3	469	297	59	9	40
Pontypridd	14	8	2	4	441	299	55	9	35
Ebbw Vale	14	8	0	6	302	375	35	4	28
Neath	14	6	1	7	351	430	41	4	23
Llanelli	14	5	2	7	370	331	44	5	22
Bridgend	14	3	2	9	276	523	33	1	12
Newport	14	0	0	14	224	484	23	2	2

* Tries scored

Leading points-scorers: 246 Arwel Thomas (Swansea); 207 Lee Jarvis (Cardiff); 157 Neil Jenkins (Pontypridd); 154 Byron Hayward (Ebbw Vale); 120 Shaun Connor (Newport); 104 Craig Warlow (Llanelli); 102 Gareth Cull (Bridgend).

Leading try-scorers: 9 Gareth Thomas (Cardiff), Richard Rees (Swansea); 8 Paul John (Pontypridd), Wayne Proctor (Llanelli); 7 Gareth Wyatt (Pontypridd), Alun Harries (Ebbw Vale), Leigh Davies (Cardiff), Lee Jarvis (Cardiff); 6 Geraint Lewis (Pontypridd), Geraint Evans (Neath), Paul Moriarty (Swansea).

Division One

	P	W	D	L	F	A	T*	Bonus pts	Pts
Caerphilly	30	27	0	3	1090	501	138	18	99
Aberavon	30	20	2	8	840	566	104	12	74
Treorchy	30	19	0	11	719	525	115	16	73
Bonymaen	30	17	0	13	656	503	86	9	60
Dunvant	30	17	1	12	723	721	87	6	58
Merthyr	29	14	4	11	690	648	87	8	54
Llandovery	30	14	0	16	710	757	88	12	54
Rumney	30	15	1	14	612	564	94	7	53
Abertillery	30	15	1	14	554	582	66	4	50
Newbridge	30	14	0	16	554	576	61	8	50
Cross Keys	29	13	1	15	646	673	75	6	46
South Wales Police	30	10	1	19	665	707	93	11	42
Blackwood	30	12	0	18	546	770	71	4	40
Pontypool	30	11	1	18	606	856	73	4	38
UWIC	30	8	0	22	655	858	86	11	35
Maesteg	30	7	0	23	531	990	60	2	23

Leading points-scorers: 393 Brett Davey (Caerphilly); 295 Mark Thomas (Dunvant); 262 Ioan Bebb (Cross Keys); 249 Jonathan Mason (Rumney); 228 Jason Williams (Newbridge); 212 Stuart Davies (Bonymaen); 205 David Lloyd (Treorchy).

Leading try-scorers: 17 Roger Bidgood (Caerphilly), Jason Riggs (Treorchy); 16 Paul Jones (Llandovery); 15 Robert Davies (Treorchy); 14 Brett Davey (Caerphilly), Paul Jones (Treorchy).

Division Two

	P	W	D	L	F	A	T*	Bonus Pts.	Pts
Tredegar	22	18	0	4	563	255	80	14	68
Tondu	22	17	1	4	524	265	73	13	65
Whitland	22	16	2	4	557	246	76	14	64
Tenby United	22	13	0	9	498	406	69	7	46
Pyle	22	10	1	11	391	426	44	6	37
Ystradgynlais	22	10	0	12	371	380	46	5	35
Narberth	22	9	1	12	404	392	49	5	33
Llanharan	22	7	3	12	368	468	50	3	27
Mountain Ash	22	8	0	14	314	511	32	0	24
Kenfig Hill	22	7	1	14	352	527	41	2	24
St Peter's	22	6	0	16	380	586	48	5	23
Abercynon	22	6	1	15	348	608	37	1	20

Leading points-scorers: 178 Matthew Chapman (Tredegar); 162 Tim Eddy (Narberth); 155 Neil Forester (Pyle); 123 Robbie Savage (Abercynon); 113 Gavin Scotcher (Tenby United); 112 Paul Williams (Tondu); 103 Stephen Pearce (Whitland); 101 David Love (Ystradgynlais).

Leading try-scorers: 15 Marc Evans (Whitland); 12 Colin Phillips (Narberth), Barry Thomas (Whitland); 11 Paul Young (Tredegar), Mark Addis (Abercynon), Chris McDonald (Narberth), Robert Phillips (Whitland), Dean Bowne (Tenby United).

Division Three

	P	W	D	L	F	A	T*	Bonus pts	Pts
Llantrisant	22	18	1	3	615	273	79	13	68
Rhymney	22	16	0	6	576	305	81	14	62
Oakdale	22	14	2	6	479	326	72	9	53
Ystrad Rhondda	22	14	0	8	446	401	65	6	48
Blaina	22	11	1	10	512	430	74	9	43
Glamorgan Wanderers	22	11	0	11	455	389	61	9	42
Felinfoel	22	12	0	10	590	531	74	5	41
Carmarthen Quins	22	10	1	11	522	398	67	8	39
Builth Wells	22	8	1	13	374	436	54	6	31
Kidwelly	22	6	0	16	332	489	51	4	22
Glynneath	22	6	0	16	326	635	41	2	20
Penarth	22	3	0	19	324	.935	38	1	10

Leading points-scorers: 235 Kevin Thomas (Felinfoel); 216 Richard Langmead (Llantrisant); 147 Craig Miller (Penarth); 130 Nick Bellamy (Glamorgan Wanderers); 117 Julien Howells (Carmarthen Quins); 110 Alistair Chambers (Carmarthen Quins).

Leading try-scorers: 15 Jamie Payne (Llantrisant); 14 Wayne Lewis (Felinfoel), Derek Wyke (Carmarthen Quins); 12 Anthony Forrest (Rhymney); 11 Jonathan Pleece (Blaina), Stuart Jarman (Rhymney).

Other honours:

Division Four: Vardre. Division 5 (East): Brynmawr. Division 5 (Central): Hirwaun. Division 5 (West): Llangennech. Division 6A (East): Abercam. Division 6A (Central): British Steel. Division 6B (Central): Cwmllynfell. Division 6B (East): Pill Harriers. Division 7A (East): Pontyclun. Division 7B (East): Pentyrch. Division 7A (Central): Maesteg Quins. Division 7B (Central): Briton Ferry. Division 7A (West): Lampeter. Division 7B (West): Bynea. East District Cup: St Peter's. Mid District Cup: Merthyr. Ben Francis Cup (Gwent): Rhymney. Tovali Cup (West Wales): Llandovery. North Wales Cup (Nant Conwy).

Leading aggregate points in eight seasons of Welsh League rugby (1990-98)

1,733 Neil Jenkins (Pontypridd) 127, 173, 203, 285, 249, 285, 254, 157
1,256 Aled Williams (Llandovery) 120, 132, 195, 176, 198, 198, 77, 160
1,138 Jonathan Mason (Rumney) 46, 16, 221, 101,138, 187, 180, 249
1,130 Byron Hayward (Ebbw Vale) 28, 121, 82, 236, 65, 205, 239, 154
  852 Adrian Davies (Cardiff) 6, –, 264, 209, 207, 166, –, –
  819 Paul Parry (Builth Wells) –, –, 222, 199, 149, 144, 105
  771 Jimmy Morris (Llanelli) 189, 161, 204, 97, 109, 11, –, –

SWALEC Cup 1997-98

Final

Llanelli 19 Ebbw Vale 12 (Ashton Gate, Bristol, 23 May 1998)

A desperately disappointing game in front of a sparse 15,000 crowd at the unfamiliar venue of Ashton Gate, Bristol, was lifted by a fairytale score from Llanelli prop Martyn Madden, who was only playing on loan from English junior club Penzance Pirates. Just three weeks earlier Madden had been sunning himself in Cornwall earning a well-deserved break, but an injury crisis at Stradey Park saw Llanelli coach Gareth Jenkins approach the Cardiff-born prop, who enjoyed a spell at Pontypool before joining Mark Ring down on the Cornish Riviera. With just two Premiership games under his belt Madden was on a hiding to nothing as he prepared for the final, but he came through with flying colours, sidestepping past two defenders and then diving past Ebbw Vale full-back Siua Taumalolo to score the winning try. Until that moment the game had been a crushing bore as Llanelli inched their way towards a record-breaking 10th SWALEC trophy. Neither side was able to impose any authority and there were so many errors that referee Clayton Thomas was unable to let the game flow. Before Madden's startling intervention it had developed into a kicking contest between Llanelli's Chris Warlow, who landed four penalties before converting Madden's try, and Byron Hayward, who despite being some way below his best, kicked three penalties and a dropped goal. Ebbw Vale's enterprising Tongan full-back Siua Taumalolo was the unanimous choice as the Lloyd Lewis Man of the Match.

Llanelli: D.Williams; W.Proctor, N.Boobyer, N.Davies, G.Evans; C.Warlow, R.Moon; D.Jones, R.McBryde (capt), M.Madden, V.Cooper, M.Voyle, C.Wyatt, H.Jenkins, I.Jones.

Replacements: M.Wintle for Boobyer (63), A.Gibbs for Wyatt (62).

Scorers: T: Madden. C: Warlow. PG: Warlow (4).

Ebbw Vale: S.Taumalolo; A.Harries, J.Hawker, J.Funnell, L.Woodward; B.Hayward, D.Llewellyn; A.Phillips, L.Phillips, M.Wilson, C.Billen, K.Feletau, R.Collins, K.Jones (capt), M.Jones.

Replacements: J.Strange for Hawker (71), S.Jones for L.Phillips (72).

Scorers: PG: Hayward (3). DG: Hayward.

Referee: Mr C .Thomas.

Round 4:
Group A: Kenfig Hill 8 Treorchy 62; Narberth 30 Wrexham 16; Pontypridd 43 Bonymaen 3; Trimsaran 0 Builth Wells 18. **Group B:** Cross Keys 67 Pontyclun 17; Ebbw Vale 57 Kidwelly 14; Gilfach Goch 5 Seven Sisters 6; Tonyrefail 24 Croesyceiliog 21. **Group C:** Beddau 14 UWIC 35; Glynneath 11 Merthyr 43; Llanelli 24 Dunvant 16; Mountain Ash 22 Neath Athletic 12. **Group D:** Cardiff 82 Abercarn 14; Carmarthen Quins 13 Llanharan 24; Newbridge 50 Abercwmboi 0; Ynysbwl 15 Treherbert 13. **Group E:** Abercynon 7 Caerphilly 44; Cwmgors 22 Porthcawl 0; Newport 58 Pwllheli 16; Tylorstown 3 South Wales Police 32. **Group F:** Cwmllynfell 13 Neath 32; Maesteg Quins 12 Llandovery 55; Morriston 16 Tredegar 17; Penygraig 29 Blaina 22. **Group G:** Aberavon 26 Bedwas 10; Blackwood 11 Maesteg 29; Garndiffaith 24 Bridgend 21; Ystradgynlais 31 Rumney 32. **Group H:** Aberavon Quins 30 Felinfoel 17; Pontypool 18 Abertillery 28; Swansea 25 Whitland 12; Tondu 26 Pyle 10.

Round 5:
Builth Wells 23 Narberth 17; Pontypridd 42 Treorchy 7; Tonyrefail 20 Ebbw Vale 60; Seven Sisters 12 Cross Keys 9 (aet); Merthyr 0 Llanelli 8; UWIC 53 Mountain Ash 29; Ynysbwl 19 Llanharan 27; Newbridge 6 Cardiff 62; South Wales Police 8 Newport 26; Cwmgors 0 Caerphilly 55; Llandovery 17 Neath 36; Penygraig 3 Tredegar 8, Garndiffaith 17 Rumney 11; Aberavon 35 Maesteg 15; Tondu 13 Swansea 54; Abertillery 15 Aberavon Quins 10.

Round 6:
Abertillery 24 Pontypridd 33; Ebbw Vale 24 Cardiff 9; Garndiffaith 19 Llanharan 14; Neath 44 Builth Wells 0; Swansea 66 Aberavon 12; Tredegar 11 Seven Sisters 15; UWIC 15 Newport 69; Llanelli 35 Caerphilly 18.

Quarter-finals:
Ebbw Vale 27 Swansea 13; Newport 29 Pontypridd 27; Seven Sisters 39 Garndiffaith 0; Llanelli 40 Neath 17.

Semi-finals:
Newport 10 Ebbw Vale 44 (Sardis Road); Llanelli 61 Seven Sisters 16 (The Gnoll).

Past Finals

	Winners		*Runners-up*		*Lloyd Lewis MOM Award*	
1972	Neath	15	Llanelli	9		
1973	Llanelli	30	Cardiff	7		
1974	Llanelli	12	Aberavon	10		
1975	Llanelli	15	Aberavon	6	Phil Bennett	(Llanelli)
1976	Llanelli	16	Swansea	4	Phil Bennett	(Llanelli)
1977	Newport	16	Cardiff	15	Ian Barnard	(Newport)
1978	Swansea	13	Newport	9	David Richards	(Swansea)
1979	Bridgend	18	Pontypridd	12	Steve Fenwick	(Bridgend)
1980	Bridgend	15	Swansea	9	Gareth Williams	(Bridgend)
1981	Cardiff	14	Bridgend	6	Rob Lakin	(Cardiff)
1982	Cardiff	12	Bridgend	12	Mark Titley	(Bridgend)
	(Cardiff win by scoring try)					
1983	Pontypool	16	Swansea	6	David Bishop	(Pontypool)
1984	Cardiff	24	Neath	19	Gareth Jones	(Neath)
1985	Llanelli	15	Cardiff	14	Gary Pearce	(Llanelli)
1986	Cardiff	28	Newport	21	Adrian Hadley	(Cardiff)
1987	Cardiff	16	Swansea	15	Anthony Clement	(Swansea)
1988	Llanelli	28	Neath	13	Jonathan Davies	(Llanelli)
1989	Neath	14	Llanelli	13	Chris Bridges	(Neath)
1990	Neath	16	Bridgend	10	Kevin Ellis	(Bridgend)
1991	Llanelli	24	Pontypool	9	Rupert Moon	(Llanelli)
1992	Llanelli	10	Swansea	7	Rupert Moon	(Llanelli)
1993	Llanelli	21	Neath	18	Gareth Llewellyn	(Neath)
1994	Cardiff	15	Llanelli	8	Andy Moore	(Cardiff)
1995	Swansea	17	Pontypridd	12	Paul Arnold	(Swansea)
1996	Pontypridd	29	Neath	22	Paul John	(Pontypridd)
1997	Cardiff	33	Swansea	26	Leigh Davies	(Cardiff)
1998	Llanelli	19	Ebbw Vale	12	Siua Taumalolo	(Ebbw Vale)

Non Five Nations Internationals

Wales' pre-Christmas international season was all about building confidence before their clash with New Zealand at Wembley on 29 November. To a degree it was successful, with a 70-21 win over Romania and a 46-12 victory over Tonga, but the step up in pace and quality against New Zealand was much too much – Wales would have benefited from stiffer opposition. Against the Romanians they ran in 11 tries at Wrexham, while they chalked up another six against Tonga. Against New Zealand their tackling was brave and committed but they were blown away in the first half by a class team on a roll. Luckily New Zealand went off the boil a little in the second half and the deserving Nigel Walker stole in for a consolation try. Possibly the best aspect of the day for Wales was the complete success of Wembley as an alternative venue – atmospheric, well-appointed and inspiring. Wales felt completely at home and their two Five Nations internationals were also wonderful 'day-trips' for their ever-loyal supporters. Wales' preparations for the Five Nations were concluded with a 23-20 win over Italy at Stradey Park, a timely reminder of just how difficult opponents the Italians might prove when they enter the Six Nations tournament in 2000.

Wales 70 Romania 21 (Wrexham, 30 August 1997)

Wales: K.A.Morgan (Pontypridd); W.T.Proctor (Llanelli), A.G.Bateman (Richmond), L.B.Davies (Cardiff), G.Thomas (Bridgend); A.C.Thomas (Swansea), P.John (Pontypridd); C.D.Loader (Swansea), B.H.Williams (Richmond), D.Young (Cardiff), S.J.Moore (Swansea), M.A.Rowley (Pontypridd), R.C.A.Appleyard (Swansea), N.Thomas (Bath), R.G.Jones (Cardiff, capt).

Replacements: L.Mustoe (Cardiff) for Young (40), N.K.Walker (Cardiff) for Proctor (66), S.M.Williams (Cardiff) for Rowley (68), L.Jarvis (Cardiff) for A.Thomas (78).

Scorers: T: Bateman (2), Davies (2), A.Thomas (2), Morgan, John, B.Williams, Walker, S.Williams. C: A.Thomas (5), Jarvis. PG: A.Thomas.

Romania: V.Maftei (Cluj); L.Colceriu (Steaua), R.S.Gontineac (Pau), G.Solomie (Timisoara), I.Rotaru (Dinamo); S.Guranescu (Dinamo), M.Iacob (Dinamo); G.Vlad (Narbonne), M.Radoi (Dinamo), A.Salageanu (Dinamo), T.E.Brinza (Narbonne, capt), M.Nedelcu (Steaua), F.Corodeanu (Steaua), E.Septar (Farul), C.S.Draguceanu (Steaua).

Replacements: P.Mitu (Steaua) for Maftei (49), C.Stan (Dinamo) for Salageanu (47), I.Ruxanda (Farul) for Septar (74).

Scorers: T: Rotaru, Draguceanu. C: Guranescu. PG: Guranescu (3).

Referee: I.Ramage (Scotland).

Wales 46 Tonga 12 (Swansea, 16 November 1997)

Wales: G.Wyatt (Pontypridd); G.Thomas (Bridgend), L.B.Davies (Cardiff), I.S.Gibbs (Swansea), N.K.Walker (Cardiff); N.R.Jenkins (Pontypridd), P.John (Pontypridd); C.D.Loader (Swansea), B.H.Williams (Richmond), S.C.John (Cardiff), S.J.Moore (Moseley), M.J.Voyle (Llanelli), R.C.A.Appleyard (Swansea), N.Thomas (Bath), R.G.Jones (Cardiff, capt).

Replacements: C.T.Anthony (Swansea) for S.John (46), R.Howley (Cardiff) for P.John (46), D.R.James (Pontypridd) for G.Thomas (70), J.M.Humphreys (Cardiff) for B.Williams (73), S.M.Williams (Cardiff) for Moore (74).

Scorers: T: G.Thomas (2), Wyatt, Davies, Walker, Anthony. C: Jenkins (2). PG: Jenkins (4).

174

Tonga: G.Tonga; D.Tiueti, F.Tatafu, P.Tanginoa, S.Faka'osi'folau; S.Taumalolo, S.M.Tuipulotu; D.Briggs (capt), V.Ma'asi, N.Ta'u, S.Latu, K.Faletau, K.Tuipulotu, H.Pohiva, T.Matakiongo.

Replacements: M.Molitika for Briggs (40), H.Lavaka for Pohiva (54), S.Hafoka for Matakiongo (58), S.Tai for Tatafu (76).

Scorers: T: Tatafu, Tai. C: Tonga.

Referee: S.Borsani (Argentina).

Wales 7 New Zealand 42 (Wembley, 29 November 1997)

Wales: K.A.Morgan (Pontypridd); G.Thomas (Bridgend), A.G.Bateman (Richmond), I.S.Gibbs (Swansea), N.K.Walker (Cardiff); N.R.Jenkins (Pontypridd), R.Howley (Cardiff); C.D.Loader (Swansea), B.H.Williams (Richmond), D.Young (Cardiff), G.O.Llewellyn (Harlequins), M.J.Voyle (Llanelli), R.C.A.Appleyard (Swansea), N.Thomas (Bath), R.G.Jones (Cardiff, capt).

Replacements: L.B.Davies (Cardiff) for Gibbs (26-35), A.C.Thomas (Swansea) for Bateman (38-40), S.M.Williams (Cardiff) for Jones (38-40) and for N.Thomas (65), J.M.Humphreys (Cardiff) for B.Williams (57), S.C.John (Cardiff) for Loader (73).

Scorers: T: Walker. C: Jenkins.

New Zealand: C.M.Cullen (Manawatu); J.W.Wilson (Otago), F.E.Bunce (North Harbour), W.K.Little (North Harbour), J.T.Lomu (Counties); A.P.Mehrtens (Canterbury), J.W.Marshall (Canterbury, capt); C.W.Dowd (Auckland), N.J.Hewitt (Southland), O.M.Brown (Auckland), R.M.Brooke (Auckland), I.D.Jones (North Harbour), T.C.Randell (Otago), Z.V.Brooke (Auckland), J.A.Kronfeld (Otago).

Replacements: S.B.T.Fitzpatrick (Auckland) for Hewitt (55), M.R.Allen (Manawatu) for Brown (58), A.F.Blowers (Auckland) for Randell (68).

Scorers: T: Cullen (3), Marshall, Randell. C: Mehrtens (4). PG: Mehrtens (2). DG: Z.Brooke.

Referee: W.J.Erickson (Australia).

Wales 23 Italy 20 (Llanelli, 7 February 1998)

Wales: N.R.Jenkins (Pontypridd); I.C.Evans (Bath), A.G.Bateman (Richmond), I.S.Gibbs (Swansea), G.Thomas (Cardiff); A.C.Thomas (Swansea), R.Howley (Cardiff, capt); A.L.P.Lewis (Cardiff), B.H.Williams (Richmond), D.Young (Cardiff), G.O.Llewellyn (Harlequins), M.J.Voyle (Llanelli), R.C.A.Appleyard (Swansea), L.S.Quinnell (Richmond), M.E.Williams (Pontypridd).

Replacements: J.M.Humphreys (Cardiff) for B.Williams (70), C.L.Charvis (Swansea) for M.Williams (70).

Scorers: T: G.Thomas, Penalty try. C: Jenkins (2). PG: Jenkins (3).

Italy: C.Pilat (Treviso); P.Vaccari (Calvisano), A.Stoica (Narbonne), L.Martin (Padova), Marcello Cuttitta (Amatori Milano); D.Dominguez (Stade Francais/CASG), A.Troncon (Treviso); Massimo Cuttitta (Harlequins), C.Orlandi (Amatori Milano), A.Castellani (L'Aquila), G.Croci (Amatori Milano), W.Cristofoletto (Treviso), M.Giovanelli (Narbonne, capt), A.Sgorlon (Treviso), J.M.Gardner (Treviso).

Scorers: T: Stoica, Sgorlon. C: Dominguez (2). PG: Dominguez (2).

Referee: S.Lander (England).

Rugby in Scotland 1997-98

SRU Tennents Premiership

Watsonians may have gone down 37-17 at Melrose in their final game of the season but the Edinburgh club were deserving winners of their first Championship in 28 years, finishing comfortably ahead of the borders club on points difference and five points clear of third-placed West of Scotland. Captained by hooker Grant McKelvey, they atoned for twice finishing runners-up in the previous three years. In a team of many talents, the biggest individual contribution came from Duncan Hodge who accumulated a massive 165 points, including a 34-point haul in their vital win over West of Scotland in the penultimate game. Scott Hastings proved a rock-solid figure at full-back, Stuart Grimes was a powerhouse at lock and New Zealand-born Cameron Mather was such an influential figure at wing forward that he was voted the Tennents player of the season and was called into Scotland's squad to tour Fiji and Australia. The joy at Watsonians' victory was possibly tinged by the thought that they will lose up to 11 players to the two Super Districts next season. Elsewhere the emerging Glasgow Hawks were the team of the season, winning Division Two at a canter and providing the basics of the Glasgow side that distinguished itself in Europe. Selkirk emerged as convincing winners of Division Three, with Aberdeen GSFP in second place.

Division 1A

	P	W	D	L	F	A	PD	Bonus pts	Pts
Watsonians	13	9	0	4	397	201	196	8	44
Melrose	13	9	0	4	331	230	101	7	43
West of Scotland	13	8	0	5	301	233	68	7	39
Currie	13	7	0	6	260	335	-75	4	32
Hawick	13	6	0	7	262	269	-7	2	26

Division 1B

	P	W	D	L	F	A	PD	Bonus pts	Pts
Boroughmuir	13	8	0	5	318	213	105	5	37
Stirling County	13	6	0	7	208	236	-28	3	27
Jed-Forest	13	5	0	8	219	388	-169	2	22
Heriot's FP	13	5	0	8	255	302	-47	1	21
Edinburgh Academicals	13	2	0	11	209	353	-144	5	13

Play-off: Heriot's FP 33 Kelso 12.

Relegated: Edinburgh Academicals.

Leading points-scorers: 165 Duncan Hodge (Watsonians); 108 Gordon Ross (Heriot's FP); 95 Campbell Aitken (Boroughmuir); 89 Chris Richards (Jed-Forest); 82 Ally Donaldson (Currie); 61 Warren Chamberlin (West of Scotland).

Leading try-scorers: 9 John Kerr (Watsonians); 8 Chris Dalgleish (Melrose); 5 Gareth Flockhart (Stirling County); 4 Duncan Hodge (Watsonians), Campbell Aitken (Boroughmuir).

Division 2A

	P	W	D	L	F	A	PD	Bonus Pts	Pts
Glasgow Hawks	13	12	0	1	521	180	341	10	58
Kelso	13	8	1	4	330	282	48	6	40
Dundee HSFP	13	7	0	6	333	270	63	9	37
Gala	13	7	0	6	301	323	-22	6	34
Kilmarnock	13	6	0	7	228	234	-6	5	29

Division 2B

	P	W	D	L	F	A	PD	Bonus pts	Pts
Kirkcaldy	13	8	0	5	365	227	138	6	38
Biggar	13	6	0	7	225	211	14	7	31
Musselburgh	13	5	2	6	213	312	-99	1	25
Peebles	13	3	1	9	173	374	-201	5	19
Preston Lodge	13	1	0	12	152	428	-276	4	8

Promoted: Glasgow Hawks

Relegated: Peebles, Preston Lodge.

Leading points-scorers: 185 Tommy Hayes (Glasgow Hawks); 118 Robbie Stewart (Kilmarnock); 102 Cliff Livingston (Musselburgh); 88 Gary Parker (Gala); 80 Derek Stark (Glasgow Hawks); 79 Denis Lavery (Biggar).

Leading try-scorers: 16 Derek Stark (Glasgow Hawks); 10 Ally Common (Glasgow Hawks); 8 Glenn Metcalfe (Glasgow Hawks), Shaun Longstaff (Dundee HSFP), Malcolm Changleng (Gala).

Division 3A

	P	W	D	L	F	A	PD	Bonus pts	Pts
Selkirk	13	11	0	2	258	135	123	4	48
Aberdeen GSFP	13	10	0	3	274	154	120	6	46
Gordonians	13	7	1	5	247	200	47	4	34
Stewart's Melville	13	7	0	6	222	279	-57	4	32
Grangemouth	13	6	0	7	300	266	34	6	30

Division 3B

	P	W	D	L	F	A	PD	Bonus pts	Pts
Glenrothes	13	8	0	5	269	166	103	5	37
Glasgow South	13	7	0	6	309	249	60	4	32
Ayr	13	5	1	7	189	190	-1	5	27
Stewartry	13	1	1	11	183	424	-241	4	10
Hillhead	13	1	1	11	151	339	-188	3	9

Promoted: Selkirk, Aberdeen GSFP

Relegated: Stewartry, Hillhead.

Other honours: Tennents National League – Division One: East Kilbride. Division Two: Annan. Division Three: Linlithgow. Division Four: Garnock. Division Five: Lochaber. Division Six: Carnoustie HSFP. Division Seven: Hamilton Academicals.

Leading points-scorers: 117 G.Blair (Selkirk); 98 J.Goldie (Glenrothes); 96 K.Oddie (Aberdeen); 93 K.Halliday (Grangemouth); 92 M.Ellis (Ayr); 62 K.Barrie (Gordonians).

Leading try-scorers: 11 J.Goldie (Glenrothes); 8 W.Gentleman (Selkirk), T.Bradley (Grangemouth); 7 A.Jackson (Glasgow South); 5 D.Hunter (Selkirk), K.Barrie (Gordonians).

SRU TENNENTS VELVET CUP 1997-98

Final

Glasgow Hawks 36 Kelso 14 (Murrayfield, 9 May 1998)

Glasgow Hawks completed a wonderful season, that included a march to the Division Two title, by outplaying Kelso to win the Tennents Velvet Cup at Murrayfield. Though not quite at their pulsating best they were much too efficient and well organised for the borders side, who had also qualified from Division Two. New Zealand-born fly-half Tommy Hayes, a Waikato man who has played World Cup rugby for the Cook Islands and now wishes to qualify for Scotland, ran the show for the Hawks, as he had done for much of the season. Hayes kicked 16 points with his normal assurance and had a hand in three of his side's four tries, which came from Ally Common (2), Derek Stark and Gordon McKay. Unfortunately the reorganisation north of the border means as many as ten of the Hawks squad will be drafted into the two Super Districts and coach Iain Russell faces a real struggle to continue his good work with his side. Kelso, though outclassed, managed tries through South African fly-half John Wearne and the versatile Iain Fairley, normally a scrum-half but playing centre on this occasion.

Glasgow Hawks: G.Metcalfe; D.Stark, C.Simmers, D.Wilson (capt), A.Common; T.Hayes, S.Simmers; G.McIllwham, C.Docherty, M.Beckham, C.Afuakwah, S.Hutton, F.Wallace, G.McKay, M.Wallace.

Replacements: C.Little for S.Simmers (49), A.Ness for McKay (71), M.Blackie for Beckham (71), K.Horton for Docherty (77), C.MacGregor for Hayes (77), M.McGrandles for C.Simmers (78).

Scorers: T: Common (2), Stark, McKay. C: Hayes (2). PG: Hayes (4).

Kelso: D.Baird; S.Ross, G.Laing, I.Fairley, C.Jackson; J.Wearne, G.Cowe; S.Murray, K.Thomson, D.Howlett, I.Fullarton, S.Laing, S.Bennet, S.Forsyth, A.Roxburgh (capt).

Replacements: S.Rowley for S.Laing (72), R.Hogarth for Murray (75).

Scorers: T: Fairley, Wearne. C: Wearne (2).

Referee: C. Muir (Langholm).

Round 3:
Alloa 3 Aberdeen GSFP 31; Berwick 7 Heriot's FP 24; Biggar 28 Hillhead/Jordanhill 15; Boroughmuir 64 Livingston 0; Corstorphine 22 Linlithgow 24; Currie 169 Allan Glens 3; Dalziel 14 Duns 13; Dundee HSFP 35 Stewart's Melville FP 8; Dunfermline 0 Kirkcaldy 5; East Kilbride 38 Stewartry 13; Falkirk 14 Strathendrick 22; Gala 60 Hawick Trades 17; Garnock 34 Hamilton Academicals 0; Glasgow Hawks 95 Cumbernauld 6; Glasgow Southern 54 RAF Lossiemouth 10; Gordonians 19 Preston

Lodge FP 11; Grangemouth 101 Dumfries 0; Haddington 0 Hawick 54; Howe of Fife 8 Stirling County 60; Hutchesons'/Aloysians 7 Annan 9; Jed-Forest 67 Lochaber 14; Kinross 5 Kelso 112; Langholm 39 Forrester FP 3; Madras College FP 3 Kilmarnock Falcons 26; Melrose 48 Glenrothes 7; Murrayfield Wanderers 18 Aberdeenshire 9; Musselburgh 82 Cumnock 0; Peebles 19 Ayr 16; St Boswells 3 Edinburgh Academicals 69; Selkirk 5 West of Scotland 39; Trinity Academicals 39 Penicuik 8; Wigtownshire 9 Watsonians 107.

Round 4:
Aberdeen GSFP 10 Glasgow Hawks 39; Biggar 0 Kilmarnock 13; East Kilbride 28 Dundee HSFP 24; Edinburgh Academicals 50 Dalziel 10; Kirkcaldy 44 Trinity Academicals 12; Hawick 27 Langholm 5; Heriot's FP 58 Annan 6; Jed-Forest 27 Garnock 5; Linlithgow 5 Boroughmuir 77; Melrose 41 Grangemouth 12; Murrayfield Wanderers 16 Kelso 32; Musselburgh 32 Currie 41; Peebles 12 Gala 30; Stirling County 27 Gordonians 14; Strathendrick 0 Watsonians 41; West of Scotland 38 Glasgow Southern 22.

Round 5:
Currie 38 Gala 13; East Kilbride 15 Hawick 28; Edinburgh Academicals 22 Watsonians 55; Heriot's FP 38 Stirling County 46; Jed-Forest 21 Glasgow Hawks 67; Kelso 10 West of Scotland 3; Kilmarnock 9 Melrose 16; Kirkcaldy 16 Boroughmuir 34.

Quarter finals:
Stirling County 14 Currie 27; Hawick 5 Boroughmuir 48; Kelso 18 Melrose 13; Watsonians 6 Glasgow Hawks 21.

Semi-finals:
Currie 17 Kelso 18; Glasgow Hawks 37 Boroughmuir 12.

Non Five Nations Internationals

Scotland's preparation for the 1998 Five Nations Championship could not have been more calamitous or disheartening. Before Christmas they were destroyed by Australia and South Africa and then, on the eve of the tournament itself, they slipped to a humiliating defeat away to Italy in Treviso. The last straw was the final straw in SRU circles and just days before the Five Nations began coach Richie Dixon resigned, to be replaced by the ever-loyal and reliable Jim Telfer. Scotland's season had started with a half-hearted performance in front of a half-empty Murrayfield, when they managed to lose 37-8 against a very ordinary Australia team. The supporters left early and 'Oh shower of Scotland' were the headlines in the Scottish press the following morning. Nobody in the Scotland camp attempted to defend their non-performance. Two weeks later the situation deteriorated further when they were humbled 68-10 by a truly outstanding South African team. Curiously, the crowd found that performance more palatable. Despite the massive scoreline there was no capitulation, Scotland were simply outclassed. And finally came a desperately poor performance against the Italians, redeemed only by a promising debut by London Scottish flanker Simon Holmes.

Scotland 8 Australia 37 (Murrayfield, 22 November 1997)

Scotland: D.W.Hodge (Watsonians); J.M.Craig (West of Scotland), A.G.Stanger (Hawick), A.V.Tait (Newcastle), K.McK.Logan (Wasps); G.P.J.Townsend (Northampton), A.D.Nicol (Bath, capt); D.I.W.Hilton (Bath), G.McKelvey (Watsonians), M.J.Stewart (Northampton), S.J.Campbell (Dundee HSFP), S.Murray (Bedford), A.J.Roxburgh (Kelso), E.W.Peters (Bath), I.R.Smith (Moseley).

Replacements: S.B.Grimes (Watsonians) for Smith (20-29) and for Roxburgh (40), G.Graham (Newcastle) for Stewart (63), C.M.Chalmers (Melrose) for Stanger (75).

Scorers: T: Murray. PG: Hodge.

Australia: S.Larkham (ACT); B.N.Tune (Queensland), T.J.Horan (Queensland), P.W.Howard (Queensland), J.W.Roff (ACT); E.Flatley (Queensland), G.M.Gregan (ACT); R.L.L.Harry (NSW), M.A.Foley (Queensland), A.T.Blades (NSW), J.Langford (NSW), J.A.Eales (Queensland, capt), O.Finegan (ACT), V.Ofahengaue (NSW), B.J.Robinson (ACT).

Replacement: D.J.Wilson (Queensland) for Robinson (40).

Scorers: T: Larkham (2), Roff, Gregan, Ofahengaue. C: Eales (3). PG: Eales (2).

Referee: T.Henning (South Africa).

Scotland 10 South Africa 68 (Murrayfield, 6 December 1997)

Scotland: R.J.S.Shepherd (Melrose); C.A.Joiner (Leicester), A.G.Stanger (Hawick), C.M.Chalmers (Melrose), D.A.Stark (Glasgow Hawks); G.P.J.Townsend (Northampton), A.D.Nicol (Bath); D.I.W.Hilton (Bath), G.C.Bulloch (West of Scotland), M.J.Stewart (Northampton), S.J.Campbell (Dundee HSFP), S.Murray (Bedford), R.I.Wainwright (Dundee HSFP, capt), E.W.Peters (Bath), I.R.Smith (Moseley).

Replacements: D.W.Hodge (Watsonians) for Stanger (20-29) and for Chalmers (51), G.Armstrong (Newcastle) for Nicol (64), P.Walton (Newcastle) for Peters (72), G.Graham (Newcastle) for Hilton (72).

Scorers: T: Stark. C: Shepherd. PG: Shepherd.

South Africa: P.C.Montgomery (W Province); J.T.Small (W Province), A.H.Snyman (N Transvaal), D.J.Muir (W Province), P.W.G.Rossouw (W Province); J.H.De Beer (OFS), W.Swanepoel (OFS); J.P.Du Randt (OFS), J.Dalton (Gauteng), A.C.Garvey (Natal), K.Otto (N Transvaal), M.G.Andrews (Natal), J.Erasmus (OFS), G.H.Teichmann (Natal, capt), A.G.Venter (OFS).

Replacements: P.F.Smith (Gauteng) for De Beer (35), J.Swart (W Province) for Small (72), W.Meyer (OFS) for Du Randt (72).

Scorers: T: Montgomery (2), Small (2), Snyman, Rossouw, Erasmus, Teichmann, Venter, Smith. C: Montgomery (8), De Beer.

Referee: P.Thomas (France).

Italy 25 Scotland 21 (Treviso, 24 January 1998)

Italy: C.Pilat (Treviso); P.Vaccari (Calvisano), A.Stoica (Narbonne), L.Martin (Padova), M.Cuttitta (Amatori Milano); D.Dominguez (Stade Francais/CASG), A.Troncon (Treviso); G.P.De Carli (Romanaise), C.Orlandi (Amatori Milano), A.Castellani (L'Aquila), G.Croci (Amatori Milano), W.Cristofoletto (Treviso), M.Giovanelli (Narbonne, capt), J.M.Gardner (Treviso), A.Sgorlon (Treviso).

Replacements: O.Arancio (Amatori Milano) for Sgorlon (78).

Scorers: T: Vaccari. C: Dominguez. PG: Dominguez (6).

Scotland: R.J.S.Shepherd (Melrose); A.G.Stanger (Hawick), A.V.Tait (Newcastle), C.M.Chalmers (Melrose), C.A.Joiner (Leicester); G.P.J.Townsend (Northampton), G.Armstrong (Newcastle); D.I.W.Hilton (Bath), G.C.Bulloch (West of Scotland), M.J.Stewart (Northampton), G.W.Weir (Newcastle), S.Murray (Bedford), R.I.Wainwright (Dundee HSFP, capt), A.J.Roxburgh (Kelso), S.D.Holmes (London Scottish).

Scorers: T: Shepherd, Tait. C: Shepherd. PG: Shepherd (3).

Referee: D.Davies (Wales).

Rugby in Ireland 1997-98

AIB League

It was a similar story of Shannon success in Ireland last season, as Limerick's premier club claimed their fourth consecutive All-Ireland title. But they had to sweat a little this time. Having won all but one of their 13 regular-season League matches and left Limerick neighbours Garryowen and Young Munster trailing by five clear points, they then had to participate in the newly introduced League play-offs to claim the title outright. Motivation was a big problem, having to all intents and purposes already won the League, but Tony Foley's squad stirred themselves again. First they accounted for St Mary's 28-21 in the semi-final, Andrew Thompson kicking immaculately to land seven penalties and a conversion, and then they defeated Garryowen 15-9 in a typically tight final at Lansdowne Road. The title was theirs. Foley, Eddie Halvey and Alan Quinlan were always influential performers in the backrow, Michael Galwey reliable as ever at lock, while in the backs New Zealander Rhys Ellison was a huge influence. Elsewhere Garryowen and Young Munster were always competitive and St Mary's continued to play an exciting brand of rugby, witness their total of 409 points. Clontarf confounded the critics and comfortably survived – flourished even – in the top flight but Old Belvedere and Old Crescent struggled throughout.

The story in Division Two revolved totally around the heartening success of Connacht's two representatives – Galwegians and Buccaneers – which provides tangible evidence of the rugby resurgence in the Province. Galwegians, with Eric Elwood at the helm, were runaway unbeaten winners of the League and Buccaneers dramatically claimed a second promotion spot by defeating Dungannon in the play-offs. Buccaneers had seemingly squandered their chance in the first leg when they lost 17-11 to the Ulster side, their first home reverse of the season, but inspired by former Ireland internationals Noel Mannion and Brian Rigney and powerful New Zealander Mark McConnell they pulled off a remarkable 27-10 win at Dungannon. Much credit must also go to coach Eddie Sullivan, who was unfortunately not able to see his side's finest moment as he was away coaching the USA national side. In Division Three Portadown were the class act, though Ballynahinch, with Ireland flanker Andy Ward leading by example, pressed them hard. Division Four went to County Carlow.

Division One

	P	W	D	L	F	A	Pts
Shannon	13	12	0	1	367	142	24
Garryowen	13	9	1	3	361	224	19
Young Munster	13	9	1	3	244	176	19
St Mary's College	13	9	0	4	409	274	18
Cork Constitution	13	8	0	5	289	217	16
Ballymena	13	7	0	6	344	287	14
Clontarf	13	7	0	6	276	267	14
Terenure College	13	5	1	7	241	263	11
Lansdowne	13	4	2	7	264	328	10
Blackrock College	13	4	1	8	249	326	9
Dungannon	13	4	0	9	240	309	8
Dolphin	13	3	2	8	227	345	8
Old Crescent	13	4	0	9	165	298	8
Old Belvedere	13	2	0	11	208	428	4

Championship Play-offs
Semi-finals: Shannon 28, St Mary's College 21; Garryowen 24, Young Munster 10.
Final (at Lansdowne Road): Shannon 15, Garryowen 9.
Division One Play-offs (two legs):
Buccaneers 11, Dungannon 17. Dungannon 10, Buccaneers 27. Buccaneers promoted to Division One, Dungannon relegated.

Division Two

	P	W	D	L	F	A	Pts
Galwegians	13	13	0	0	336	164	26
Buccaneers	12	11	0	1	311	102	22
Sunday's Well	13	7	2	4	252	227	16
City of Derry	13	8	0	5	277	255	16
UC Cork	13	6	1	6	204	282	13
Skerries	13	6	0	7	248	224	12
DLS Palmerston	12	6	0	6	258	246	12
Old Wesley	13	5	1	7	256	248	11
Greystones	13	5	1	7	204	212	11
Bective Rangers	13	5	1	7	210	233	11
Malone	13	5	0	8	210	255	10
Wanderers	12	5	0	7	200	252	10
Monkstown	12	2	0	10	184	314	4
Instonians	13	2	0	11	205	341	4

Division Three

	P	W	D	L	F	A	Pts
Portadown	10	10	0	0	217	106	20
Ballynahinch	10	8	0	2	283	125	16
Highfield	10	7	0	3	170	87	14
UC Dublin	9	7	0	2	186	105	14
Bohemians	10	6	0	4	194	165	12
N of Ireland	10	5	0	5	190	158	10
Galway	10	4	0	6	178	214	8
Dublin Univ	9	3	0	6	142	189	6
Collegians	10	2	1	7	130	229	5
Suttonians	10	1	1	8	153	254	3
Queen's Belfast	10	0	0	10	128	339	0

Division Three play-offs (two legs):
Richmond 15, Collegians 8; Collegians 10, Richmond 15. Richmond promoted to Division Three, Collegians relegated.

Division Four

	P	W	D	L	F	A	Pts
County Carlow	9	8	0	1	284	56	16
Richmond	9	7	1	1	171	113	15
Bangor	9	5	1	3	177	144	11
Ballina	9	5	0	4	169	128	10
Waterpark	9	5	0	4	131	155	10
Omagh Academicals	9	4	0	5	137	147	8
Ards	9	4	0	5	109	158	8
CIYMS	9	3	1	5	122	204	7
Sligo	9	2	1	6	111	147	5
Creggs	9	0	0	9	89	248	0

Division Four play-off:
Midleton 30, Sligo 7 (at Portadown). Midleton promoted to Division Four, Sligo relegated.

Guinness Interprovincial Championship 1997-98

	P	W	D	L	F	A	Pts
Leinster	3	2	0	1	61	46	4
Munster	3	2	0	1	56	43	4
Ulster	3	1	0	2	64	65	2
Connacht	3	1	0	2	42	69	2

Results: Leinster 26 Ulster 25; Connacht 9 Munster 29; Connacht 27 Ulster 17; Munster 15 Leinster 12; Ulster 22 Munster 12; Leinster 23 Connacht 6.

Past Championships

1946 Ulster	1965 Munster
1947 Munster	1966 Ulster-Munster
1948 Leinster	1967 Ulster
1949 Leinster	1968 Munster
1950 Ulster	1969 Ulster
1951 Ulster	1970 Ulster
1952 Munster	1971 Leinster
1953 Ulster	1972 Leinster-Munster-Ulster
1954 Leinster-Munster	1973 Munster
1955 Ulster-Connacht	1974 Ulster
1956 Leinster-Ulster-Connacht	1975 Leinster-Ulster-Munster
1957 Munster	1976 Ulster
1958 Leinster	1977 Leinster-Munster-Ulster
1959 Munster	1978 Munster
1960 Leinster	1979 Leinster
1961 Leinster	1980 Leinster
1962 Munster	1981 Leinster
1963 Leinster	1982 Leinster-Ulster-Munster
1964 Leinster	1983 Leinster-Ulster-Munster

1984 Ulster	1992 Ulster
1985 Ulster	1993 Ulster
1986 Ulster	1994 Ulster
1987 Ulster	1995 Munster
1988 Ulster	1996 Leinster
1989 Ulster	1997 Munster
1990 Ulster	1998 Leinster
1991 Ulster	

Branch competitions 1997-98

LEINSTER

Heineken Senior Cup: Lansdowne
Kitty O'Shea Championship: Lansdowne
Smithwicks Provincial Cup: Naas
Heineken Junior League: St Mary's College
AIB Qualifying League: Naas
Coca Cola Senior Schools Cup: Clongowes Wood
Coca Cola Junior Schools Cup: Blackrock College

ULSTER

First Trust Bank Senior Cup: Dungannon
Famous Grouse Senior League: Ballymena
Phoenix Gas Junior Cup: Ballymena
Phoenix Gas Qualifying League: Banbridge
Smithwicks Provincial Towns Cup: Coleraine
Renault Schools Cup: Royal Belfast Academical Institute
Renault Schools Shield: Regent House

MUNSTER

Carling Senior Cup: Shannon
Carling Development League: Cork Constitution
Carling Junior Cup: Midleton
Carling Junior League: Midleton
Coca Cola Senior Schools Cup: Christian Brothers Cork
Coca Cola Junior Schools Cup: St Munchin's College

CONNACHT

Smithwicks Senior Cup: Corinthians
Senior League: Buccaneers
Xerox Junior Cup: Corinthians
Xerox Junior League: Westport
AIB Qualifying League: Moniviea
Statoil Senior Cup: Garbally College
Statoil Junior Cup: Garbally College

Non Five Nations Internationals

Ireland's international season started with a chastening 63-15 home defeat against the All Blacks, who probably saved their best performance on tour for Lansdowne Road. Remarkably Ireland looked in contention for much of the first half when Keith Wood scored two tries, but a Justin Marshall try just before half-time was the killer blow and after the break New Zealand pulled ahead in unstoppable style. It was awesome to watch, and though Ireland were thoroughly outplayed their mood was positive afterwards. This, to a certain extent, was carried forward to Ireland's next game when they produced a workmanlike performance to beat a disappointing Canada side 33-11. There were five Irish tries through Kevin Nowlan (2), Kevin Maggs, Conor McGuinness and Victor Costello, but any confidence Ireland took from their display was blown away three weeks later when they slipped to a disappointing 37-22 defeat against Italy, being outscored three tries to one in Bologna.

Ireland 15 New Zealand 63 (Lansdowne Road 15 November 1997)

Ireland: K.W.Nowlan (St Mary's College); D.A.Hickie (St Mary's College), R.A.J.Henderson (Wasps), C.M.McCall (London Irish), J.P.J.McWeeney (St Mary's College); E.P.Elwood (Galway), C.D.McGuinness (St Mary's College); N.J.Popplewell (Newcastle), K.G.M.Wood (Harlequins, capt), P.S.Wallace (Saracens), P.S.Johns (Saracens), M.E.O'Kelly (London Irish), E.O.Halvey (Shannon), E.R.P.Miller (Leicester), K.Dawson (London Irish).

Replacements: R.P.Nesdale (Newcastle) for Wood (40), K.M.Maggs (Bristol) for McWeeney (60), D.J.Erskine (Sale) for Halvey (60), B.T.O'Meara (Cork Constitution) for McGuinness (73).

Scorers: T: Wood (2). C: Elwood. PG: Elwood.

New Zealand: C.M.Cullen (Manawatu); J.W.Wilson (Otago), F.E.Bunce (North Harbour), A.I.Ieremia (Wellington), G.M.Osborne (North Harbour); A.P.Mehrtens (Canterbury), J.W.Marshall (Canterbury, capt); C.W.Dowd (Auckland), N.J.Hewitt (Southland), O.M.Brown (Auckland), I.D.Jones (North Harbour), R.M.Brooke (Auckland), T.C.Randell (Otago), Z.V.Brooke (Auckland), A.F.Blowers (Auckland).

Replacements: C.C.Riechelmann (Auckland) for R.Brooke (51), J.A.Kronfeld (Otago) for Blowers (60), J.P.Preston (Wellington) for Mehrtens (75), S.J.McLeod (Wellington) for Bunce (65).

Scorers: T: Wilson (2), Osborne (2), Ieremia, Mehrtens, Marshall. C: Mehrtens (5). PG: Mehrtens (6).

Referee: A.J.Spreadbury (England).

Ireland 33 Canada 11 (Lansdowne Road 30 November 1997)

Ireland: K.W.Nowlan (St Mary's College); D.A.Hickie (St Mary's College), R.A.J.Henderson (Wasps), C.M.McCall (London Irish), K.M.Maggs (Bristol); E.P.Elwood (Galway), C.D.McGuinness (St Mary's College); N.J.Popplewell (Newcastle, capt), R.P.Nesdale (Newcastle), P.S.Wallace (Saracens), P.S.Johns (Saracens), M.E.O'Kelly (London Irish), D.J.Erskine (Sale), V.C.P.Costello (St Mary's College), K.Dawson (London Irish).

Replacements: R.Corrigan (Greystones) for Popplewell (69), E.O.Halvey (Shannon) for Dawson (73).

Scorers: T: Nowlan (2), Maggs, McGuinness, Costello. C: Elwood. PG: Elwood (2).

Canada: D.S.Stewart (Harlequins); J.Pagano (Yeomen), D.C.Lougheed (Balmy Beach), R.Toews (Meraloma), W.Stanley (Blackheath); G.L.Rees (Wasps, capt), J.D.Graf (UBCOB); R.G.A.Snow (Newport), M.E.Cardinal (James Bay), R.A.R.Bice (Vancouver RC), J.Tait (Cardiff), M.B.James (Perpignan), M.Schmid (Rotherham), A.J.Charron (Moseley), J.R.Hutchinson (IBM Japan).

Replacements: A.Healy (James Bay) for Tait (53), E.A.Evans (IBM Japan) for Bice (63), C.J.McKenzie (Burnaby Lake) for Schmid (71).

Scorers: T: Cardinal. PG: Rees (2).

Referee: A.Giacomel (Italy).

Italy 37 Ireland 22 (Bologna, 20 December 1997)

Italy: C.Pilat (Treviso); P.Vaccari (Calvisano), A.Stoica (Narbonne), M.Dallan (Treviso), Marcello Cuttitta (Amatori Milano); D.Dominguez (Stade Francais/CASG), A.Troncon (Treviso); Massimo Cuttitta (Harlequins), C.Orlandi (Amatori Milano), A.Castellani (L'Aquila), G.Croci (Amatori Milano), C.Checchinato (Treviso), M.Giovanelli (Narbonne, capt), A.Sgorlon (Treviso), J.M.Gardner (Treviso).

Replacements: O.Arancio (Amatori Milano) for Giovanelli (20-24) and for Gardner (28-30), W.Cristofoletto (Treviso) for Checchinato (80).

Scorers: T: Pilat, Stoica, Dominguez. C: Dominguez (2). PG: Dominguez (6).

Ireland: K.W.Nowlan (St Mary's College); D.A.Hickie (St Mary's College), K.M.Maggs (Bristol), C.M.McCall (London Irish), D.W.O'Mahony (Moseley); D.G.Humphreys (London Irish), N.A.Hogan (London Irish); R.Corrigan (Greystones), K.G.M.Wood (Harlequins, capt), P.M.N.Clohessy (Young Munster), P.S.Johns (Saracens), M.E.O'Kelly (London Irish), D.J.Erskine (Sale), E.R.P.Miller (Leicester), D.O'Grady (Sale).

Replacements: E.P.Elwood (Galway) for Humphreys (63), A.T.H.Clarke (Northampton) for Wood (72), V.C.P.Costello (St Mary's College) for Erskine (77).

Scorers: T: O'Mahony. C: Elwood. PG: Humphreys (4), Elwood.

Referee: D.Mene (France).

HEINEKEN EUROPEAN CUP 1997-98

It wasn't a classic but the third Heineken European Cup final, played in front of a capacity 36,500 crowd at the Stade Lescure in Bordeaux, provided a fitting climax to a dramatic season of European rugby, on and off the field. Bath, badly affected by injuries all season and seemingly out of sorts going into the final after losing at home to Richmond in the Tetley's Bitter Cup the previous week, again demonstrated that they should never be written off when the stakes are highest. Early in the second half they were nine points down and apparently on the ropes as Brive laid siege to their line but at seven consecutive scrums Andy Nicol's side refused to buckle. Having survived the onslaught they moved upfield, Jon Callard scored a try which he converted himself and then kicked two penalties, the second and decisive shot at goal coming 80 seconds into injury time. Even then Christophe Lamaison, who had kicked five penalties to go alongside Alain Penaud's dropped goal, had an opportunity to clinch the game but fired wide. Bath, bolstered by their travelling army of 7,000 fans, took the trophy to which they had always aspired.

The politics of the English clubs' mass withdrawal from the 1998-99 competition in January have been much discussed but in pure rugby terms a number of points need to be made. Firstly all clubs, but especially the English, were under a misapprehension if they felt that European Cup rugby could provide the financial foundation for professional rugby – even among our footballing friends only Manchester United make serious money out of Europe. The Heineken Cup should be seen as the icing on the cake – an exciting and colourful diversion from the bread and butter of Premiership rugby. England and France probably do deserve a bigger representation than the Celtic countries and in a competition so dominated by their clubs, they also deserve a bigger say in the running of the tournament. Having said that, the novelty and surprise value of Cup rugby should never be dispensed with. New, possibly lesser, opponents should not be discouraged. Clubs from all the major rugby-playing countries in Europe should be represented, or at least be given the chance of qualifying.

Final

Bath 19 Brive 18 (Stade Lescure, Bordeaux, 31 January 1998)

Bath: J.Callard; I.Evans, P.de Glanville, J.Guscott, A.Adebayo; M.Catt, A.Nicol (capt); D.Hilton, M.Regan, V.Ubogu, M.Haag, N.Redman, N.Thomas, R.Webster, D.Lyle.

Replacements: R.Earnshaw for Thomas (71), F.Mendez for Regan (78).

Scorers: T: Callard. C: Callard. P: Callard (4).

Brive: A.Penaud; J.Carrat, C.Lamaison, D.Venditti, S.Carrat; L.Arbizu, P.Carbonneau (capt); D.Casadei, L.Travers, R.Crespy, E.Alegret, Y.Manhes, L.van der Linden, O.Magne, F.Duboisset.

Replacements: D.Laperne for Crespy (50), R.Sonnes for Duboisset (71), S.Viars for S.Carrat (76).

Scorers: P: Lamaison (5). DG: Penaud.

Referee: J.Fleming (Scotland).

Semi-finals

France provided three of the four semi-finalists, so the onus was on Bath to ensure a non-French interest in the final. A packed crowd at the Rec – another 10,000 tickets could have been sold – made for a great atmosphere and Bath produced a thoroughly professional performance to ensure that Pau's dangerous runners were not unleashed. The home pack generally controlled proceedings with a try from a rejuvenated Victor Ubogu and the goal-kicking of Jon Callard heralding a narrow but uneventful victory. Pau were on their best behaviour and perhaps, not coincidentally, a little devil had gone out of their back play. Their only try was a consolation effort by France wing Philippe Bernat-Salles.

There was much more drama the following day at the Stade Toulouse, where 27,500 colourful fans crowded into the half-completed stadium for Toulouse's clash with Brive. A bright start by Brive ended with a shoulder injury to Olivier Magne, incurred when scoring a try, and for the remainder of regular time Toulouse and their mighty pack controlled the game. Going into the final minute they led 16-11 when Brive moved the ball thrillingly for Sebastien Carrat to score close to the posts. Incredibly Christophe Lamaison missed the conversion and extra time followed. Fittingly two extra-time penalties from the France centre, the last two minutes from time, enabled Brive to tie 22-22 and progress on a 2-1 try countback.

Bath 20 Pau 14 (The Recreation Ground, Bath, 20 December 1997)

Bath: J.Callard; I.Evans, P.de Glanville, M.Perry, A.Adebayo; M.Catt, A.Nicol (capt); K.Yates, M.Regan, V.Ubogu, G.Llanes, N.Redman, N.Thomas, R.Webster, D.Lyle.

Replacements: E.Peters for Lyle (82), R.Butland for de Glanville (43-51).

Scorers: T: Ubogu. C: Callard (5).

Pau: N.Brusque; P.Bernat-Salles, D.Dantiacq, F.Leloir, Y.Martin; D.Aucagne, F.Torossian; P.Triep-Capdevielle, J.Rey, J-M.Gonzalez, A.Lagouarde, T.Cleda, S.Keith, N.Bacque, F.Rolles.

Replacements: S.Vignol for Rolles (55), T.Mentieres for Cleda (64), S.Bria for Triep-Capdevielle (71).

Scorers: T: Bernat-Salles. Pens: Aucagne (3).

Referee: D.Bevan (Wales).

Toulouse 22 Brive 22 (aet, Brive win 2-1 on try count) (Stade Toulouse, 21 December 1997)

Toulouse: S.Ougier; E.Ntamack, P.Bondouy, Y.Delaigue, P.Lapoutge; C.Deylaud, J.Cazalbou; C.Califano, P.Soula, F.Tournaire, H.Miorin, F.Pelous, D.Lacroix, C.Labit, S.Dispagne.

Replacements: F.Bellot for Pelous (57), N.Martin for Deylaud (95), X.Garbajosa for Lapoutge (107), J-L.Jordana for Tournaire (90), N.Spanghero for Lacroix (108).

Scorers: T: Bondouy. C: Delaigue. PG: Deylaud (2), Delaigue (2).

Brive: A.Penaud; J.Carrat, C.Lamaison, D.Venditti, S.Carrat; L.Arbizu, P.Carbonneau (capt); D.Casadei, L.Travers, D.Laperne, E.Alegret, Y.Manhes, L.van der Linden, O.Magne, F.Duboisset.

Replacements: L.Mallier for Magne (20), R.Sonnes for Duboisset (40), L.Arbo for S.Carrat (95), O.Gouaillard for van der Linden (107), J-C.Vicard for Travers (78).

Scorers: T: Magne, S.Carrat. C: Lamaison (4).

Referee: D.McHugh (Ireland).

Quarter-finals

Toulouse, the 1996 Heineken Cup champions, produced the performance of the quarter-finals with a 51-10 demolition of Harlequins, a display that marked them out as favourites for the 1998 tournament. Working off the command and authority of their superb pack, the Toulousians claimed six tries and threatened many more. By the final whistle Harlequins were reduced to admiring spectators. Back in Britain, Bath manufactured their most convincing display in a long while to defeat Cardiff 32-21 and avenge their quarter-final defeat of the previous season. The action on Sunday featured two Anglo/French encounters, both deservedly going France's way. Down in Pau the home side completely outplayed Leicester who should have had no complaints about the 35-18 scoreline – coach Bob Dwyer, however, launched an astonishing tirade against the referee and Pau afterwards. At Loftus Road, Wasps' European dreams came crashing down when they were outscored three tries to none by a thoroughly competent Brive side who never allowed a hint of an upset.

Toulouse 51 Harlequins 10 (Stade de Toulouse, 8 November 1997)

Toulouse: S.Ougier; E.Ntamack, R.Paillat, P.Bondouy, P. Lapoutge; Y.Delaigue, J.Cazalbou; C.Califano, P.Soula, F.Tournaire, H.Miorin, F.Pelous, D.Lacroix, C.Labit, S.Dispagne.

Replacements: F.Belot for Miorin (55), M.Marfaing for Ntamack (55), J-L.Jordana for Tournaire (62), N.Begue for Soula (71), N.Martin for Paillat (69), J.Tilloles for Cazalbou (66).

Scorers: T: Ntamack, Lapoutge, Bondouy (2), Dispagne, D.Lacroix. C: Ougier (2), Delaigue. PG: Ougier (5).

Harlequins: J.Williams; D.O'Leary, W.Carling, J.Ngauamo, T.Tollett; T.Lacroix, H.Harries; A.Ozdemir, K.Wood (capt), J.Leonard, G.Llewellyn, L.Gross, R.Jenkins, L.Cabannes, B.Davison.

Replacements: D.Rouse for Ozdemir (55), N.Walshe for Harries (55), J.Keyter for O'Leary (77).

Scorers: T: Lacroix. C: Lacroix. PG: Lacroix.

Referee: D.Bevan (Wales).

Bath 32 Cardiff 21 (The Recreation Ground, Bath, 8 November 1997)

Bath: J.Callard; I.Evans, P.de Glanville, M.Perry, A.Adebayo; M.Catt, A.Nicol (capt); K.Yates, A.Long, V.Ubogu, G.Llanes, N.Redman, N.Thomas, E.Peters, D.Lyle.

Replacement: R.Webster for Peters (62).

Scorers: T: de Glanville, Ubogu, Lyle. C: Callard. PG: Callard (5).

Cardiff: J.Thomas; C.Morgan, L.Davies, M.Hall, N.Walker; L.Jarvis, R.Howley; A.Lewis, J.Humphreys (capt), D.Young, J.Tait, D.Jones, G.Kacala, G.Jones, S.Williams.

Replacements: S.John for Lewis (47), L.Mustoe for Young (70), J.Ringer for Jones (70).

Scorers: T: Davies (2). C: Jarvis. PG: Jarvis (3).

Referee: D.Mene (France).

Pau 35 Leicester 18 (Stade de Hameau, 9 November 1997)

Pau: N. Brusque; P.Bernat-Salles, D.Dantiacq, F.Leloir, Y.Martin; D.Aucagne, F.Torossian; P.Triep-Capdevielle, J.Rey (capt), J-M.Gonzalez, T.Cleda, T.Mentieres, S.Keith, N.Bacque, F.Rolles.

Replacements: S.Vignolo for Keith (53), S.Bria for Capdevielle (63), A.Lagouarde for Mentieres (69).

Scorers: T: Cleda, Leloir, Bernat-Salles, Brusque. C: Aucagne (3). PG: Aucagne (3).

Leicester: M.Horak; A.Healey, W.Greenwood, S.Potter, L.Lloyd; J.Stransky, W.Serevi; G.Rowntree, R.Cockerill, D.Garforth, M.Johnson (capt), D.Richards, M.Corry, N.Back, E.Miller.

Replacements: J.Wells for Richards (63), P.Freshwater for Garforth (75-77).

Scorers: T: Back, Serevi. C: Stransky. PG: Stransky (2).

Referee: Mr D.Davies (Wales).

Wasps 18 Brive 25 (Loftus Road, 9 November 1997)

Wasps: G.Rees; S.Roiser, N.Greenstock, R.Henderson, K.Logan; A.King, M.Wood; D.Molloy, S.Mitchell, W.Green, D.Cronin, A.Reed, L.Dallaglio (capt), P.Volley, C.Sheasby.

Replacements: D.Macer for Mitchell (82), S.Shaw for Cronin (57), P.Dunston for Green (21-25).

Scorers: PG: Rees (6).

Brive: S.Viars; J.Carrat, C.Lamaison, D.Venditti, S.Carrat; P.Carbonneau (capt), S.Bonnet; D.Casadei, L.Travers, R.Crespy, E.Alegret, Y.Manhes, L.van der Linden, O.Magne, F.Duboisset.

Replacements: P.Bomati for Viars (33), R.Sonnes for Duboisset (40), L.Mallier for van der Linden (59), O.Gouaillard for Casadei (71), L.Arbo for Bonnet (78), D.Laperne for Crespy (60).

Scorers: T: S.Carrat, van der Linden, J.Carrat. C: Lamaison (2). PG: Lamaison (2).

Referee: C.Muir (Scotland).

Pool stages

The pool stages, though occasionally lacking in genuine quality, were nothing if not entertaining and controversial, particularly the latter. The nadir was undoubtedly reached over the weekend of September 13-14 which featured two bitter Franco/Welsh clashes. Pau's home game against Llanelli was an ugly affair from start to finish with Frederic Torossian's head-butt the most notable illegality – there were plenty to choose from. The following day an otherwise breathtaking game between Brive and Pontypridd was marred by a savage first-half brawl featuring the majority of the players which resulted in the dismissal of Dale McIntosh and Lionel Mallier. Worse was to follow much later that evening when three Pontypridd players – McIntosh, Phil John and Andre Barnard – were arrested following a bar-room brawl with some of the Brive players. Pontypridd and Brive were both fined £30,000, with £15,000 suspended, for the on-the-field violence while Pau and Llanelli were fined £20,000 with £10,000 suspended.

Back on the rugby pitches of Europe, Pool A was very much a two-horse race between Toulouse and Leicester, with Leicester's defeat at Leinster ultimately condemning them to second place. Their two clashes with Toulouse were both minor classics, the Tigers' 22-17 win at Sept Deniers representing their best performance of the entire season. With Waisale Serevi at fly-half they then outplayed Toulouse for much of the return game at Welford Road, but lost concentration at the end and slipped to a 23-22 defeat.

Wasps emerged from Pool B with the only 100 per cent record, Swansea coming closest to toppling them when they lost 29-28 at Loftus Road. Glasgow emerged from the pack to finish second, the powerful running of James Craig and Derek Stark and the kicking of Tommy Hayes being the highlight of their pool games.

Pool C featured a high-intensity clash between Bath, Brive and Pontypridd with Bath's consistency seeing them take the pool, by one point, from Brive. Poor Scottish Borders suffered bravely, conceding 222 points in their six games, more than any other side. Harlequins started well and then stuttered before squeezing through on points difference to take Pool D from Cardiff while Pau claimed the winners' spot in Pool E from Llanelli, also on points difference.

Pool A

	P	W	D	L	F	A	Pts	Diff
Toulouse	6	5	0	1	200	121	10	+79
Leicester	6	4	0	2	163	117	8	+46
Leinster	6	2	0	4	137	167	4	-30
Milan	6	1	0	5	111	206	2	-95

Results: Leinster 25 Toulouse 34; Leicester 26 Milan 10; Leinster 16 Leicester 9; Milan 14 Toulouse 19; Milan 33 Leinster 32; Toulouse 17 Leicester 22; Toulouse 69 Milan 19; Leicester 47 Leinster 22; Leicester 22 Toulouse 23; Leinster 23 Milan 6; Toulouse 38 Leinster 19; Milan 29 Leicester 37.

Pool B

	P	W	D	L	F	A	Pts	Diff
Wasps	6	6	0	0	243	104	12	+139
Glasgow	6	3	0	3	132	167	6	-35
Swansea	6	2	0	4	157	161	4	-4
Ulster	6	1	0	5	95	195	2	-100

Results: Swansea 25 Wasps 31; Ulster 12 Glasgow 18; Swansea 33 Ulster 16; Glasgow 22 Wasps 46; Glasgow 35 Swansea 21; Wasps 56 Ulster 3; Ulster 28 Swansea 20; Wasps 43 Glasgow 5; Ulster 21 Wasps 38; Swansea 30 Glasgow 22; Glasgow 30 Ulster 15; Wasps 29 Swansea 28.

Pool C

	P	W	D	L	F	A	Pts	Diff
Bath	6	5	0	1	141	119	10	+22
Brive	6	4	1	1	210	146	9	+64
Pontypridd	6	2	1	3	154	147	5	+7
Borders	6	0	0	6	129	222	0	-93

Results: Brive 56 Borders 18; Pontypridd 15 Bath 21; Brive 32 Pontypridd 31; Borders 17 Bath 31; Bath 27 Brive 25; Borders 16 Pontypridd 23; Bath 27 Borders 23; Pontypridd 29 Brive 29; Pontypridd 46 Borders 26; Brive 29 Bath 12; Bath 23 Pontypridd 10; Borders 29 Brive 39.

Pool D

	P	W	D	L	F	A	Pts	Diff
Harlequins	6	4	0	2	198	141	8	+57
Cardiff	6	4	0	2	184	146	8	+38
Munster	6	2	0	4	141	180	4	−39
Bourgoin	6	2	0	4	93	149	4	−56

Results: Bourgoin 26 Cardiff 25; Harlequins 48 Munster 40; Harlequins 45 Bourgoin 7; Cardiff 43 Munster 23; Munster 17 Bourgoin 15; Cardiff 21 Harlequins 28; Munster 32 Cardiff 37; Bourgoin 18 Harlequins 30; Bourgoin 21 Munster 6; Harlequins 31 Cardiff 32; Cardiff 26 Bourgoin 6; Munster 23 Harlequins 16.

Pool E

	P	W	D	L	F	A	Pts	Diff
Pau	6	4	0	2	203	89	8	+114
Llanelli	6	4	0	2	144	142	8	+2
Treviso	6	2	0	4	146	162	4	−16
Caledonia	6	2	0	4	89	189	4	−100

Results: Treviso 18 Pau 19; Caledonia 18 Llanelli 23; Pau 44 Llanelli 12; Caledonia 17 Treviso 9; Llanelli 39 Treviso 18; Pau 50 Caledonia 8; Treviso 52 Caledonia 6; Llanelli 14 Pau 10; Treviso 42 Llanelli 25; Caledonia 30 Pau 24; Llanelli 31 Caledonia 10; Pau 56 Treviso 7.

Quarter-final play-offs: Brive 25 Pontypridd 20; Leicester 90 Glasgow 19; Cardiff 24 Llanelli 20.

Leading points-scorers: 134 L.Jarvis (Cardiff); 129 J.Callard (Bath); 111 C.Lamaison (Brive); 106 G.Rees (Wasps), J.Stransky (Leicester); 91 T.Lacroix (Harlequins); 84 T.Hayes (Glasgow); 81 D.Aucagne (Pau); 79 N.Jenkins (Pontypridd); 72 A.McGowan (Leinster); 66 S.Ougier (Toulouse); 65 S.Laing (Ulster).

Leading try-scorers: 7 X.Garbajosa (Toulouse), J.Carrat, S.Viars (both Brive), K.Logan (Wasps), W.Greenwood (Leicester); 5 P.Bondouy (Toulouse), D.James (Pontypridd), M.Horak (Leicester), J.Williams (Harlequins); 4 F.Rolles, N.Bacque (both Pau), R.Paillat (Toulouse), R.Moon (Llanelli), J.Craig, T.Hayes (both Glasgow), L.Davies (Cardiff), S.Rosier, N.Greenstock (both Wasps), L.Belligoi (Harlequins), J.Lacey (Munster), J.McWeeney (Leinster), M.Perziano, M.Dallan (both Treviso).

Suspensions: G.Grespan (Treviso) 60 days; D.McIntosh (Pontypridd) 30 days; L.Mallier (Brive) 30 days; T.Rees (Cardiff) 90 days.

Heineken European Cup records 1995-98

Highest score: 90. Leicester 90 Glasgow 19.
Biggest winning margin: 78. Benetton Treviso 86 Farul Constanta 8.
Most points in a match: 113. Pau 85 Scottish Borders 28.
Most points by a player: 35. Joel Stransky (Leicester v Glasgow).
Most tries in a match: 17. Pau 13 Borders 4; Leicester 14 Glasgow 3.
Most tries by one team: 14. Leicester v Glasgow.

Most tries in match by one player: 4. Sebastien Carrat (Brive v Neath); Mike Catt (Bath v Treviso); Benjamin Lhande (Pau v Borders); Michael Horak (Leicester v Glasgow).
Leading points-scorer overall: 193. Lee Jarvis (Pontypridd/Cardiff).
Leading try-scorer: 12. Sebastien Carrat (Brive).
Biggest crowds: Pool stage: 11,000 (Toulouse v Leicester 1997-98); Quarter/semi-finals: 26,000 (Toulouse v Brive 1997-78); Final: 41,664 (Brive v Leicester 1996-97).

Heineken European Cup Final 1997

Brive 28 Leicester 9 (Cardiff Arms Park, 25 January 1997)

Brive: S.Viars; G.Fabre, C.Lamaison, D.Venditi, S.Carrat; A.Penaud (capt), P.Carbonneau; D.Casadei, L.Travers, R.Crespy, E.Allegret, G.Ross, L.van der Linden, G.Kacala, F.Duboisset.

Replacements: T.Labrousse for Duboisset (49), A.Rees for Allegret (69), R.Pailat for Penaud (70), E.Bouti for Casadei (71), Y.Domi for van der Linden (79).

Scorers: T: Carrat (2), Viars, Fabre. C: Lamaison. PG: Lamaison. DG: Lamaison.

Leicester: J.Liley; S.Hackney, W.Greenwood, S.Potter, R.Underwood; R.Liley, A.Healey; G.Rowntree, R.Cockerill, D.Garforth, M.Johnson, M.Poole, J.Wells, N.Back, D.Richards.

Replacements: P.Freshwater for Garforth (16-20), E.Miller for Richards (67), L.Lloyd for Underwood (74).

Scorers: PG: R.Liley (3).

Referee: Mr D.Bevan (Wales).

Heineken European Cup Final 1996

Cardiff 18 Toulouse 21 (aet) (Cardiff Arms Park, 7 January 1996)

Cardiff: M.Rayer; S.Ford, M.Hall, M.Ring, S.Hill; A.Davies, A.Moore; A.Lewis, J.Humphreys, L.Mustoe, D.Jones, J.Wakeford, E.Lewis, H.Taylor (capt), O.Williams.

Replacements: J.Davies for Ring (40), N.Walker for Ford (90).

Scorers: PG: A.Davies (6).

Toulouse: S.Ougier; E.Ntamack (capt), P.Carbonneau, T.Castaignede, D.Berty; C.Deylaud, J.Cazalbou; C.Califano, P.Soula, C.Portolan, H.Miorin, F.Belot, D.Lacroix, S.Dispagne, H.Manent.

Replacements: R.Castel for Lacroix (57), H.Mola for Berty (70), E.Artiguste for Castaignede (93).

Scorers: T: Castaignede, Cazalbou. C: Deylaud. PG: Deylaud (2). DG: Castaignede.

Referee: D.McHugh (Ireland).

European Conference Final 1997-98

Colomiers 43 Agen 5 (Stade Toulouse, 1 February 1998)

Colomiers became the second winners of the European Conference when they swept Agen aside in exciting fashion at Stade Toulouse. The Toulouse-based club scored seven breathtaking tries as Agen, normally renowned for their defensive qualities, were totally outplayed. Colomiers, under the captaincy of France captain Jean-Luc Sadourny, were undoubtedly the class team of the tournament, qualifying with a 100 per cent record from a group including Richmond, Bridgend and Grenoble. In the quarter-finals they defeated Montferrand 23-13, before a 19-13 semi-final win over Stade Francais.

Colomiers: J-L.Sadourny (capt); M.Biboulet, S.Roque, J.Sieurac, D.Dal Pos; M.Carre, F.Galthie; J-P.Beyssen, Y.Bru, P.Pages, J-P.Revaillier, J-M.Loreni, B.de Giusti, H.Manent, S.Peysson.

Replacements: P.Tabacco for Manent (40), D.Skrela for Dal Pos (40), C.Barrau for Roque (55), S.Milhas for Sadourny (57), J-P.Beyssen for Pages (75).

Scorers: T: de Giusti (2), Biboulet, Roque, Sieurac, Galthie, Bru. C: Carre (4).

Agen: C.Heymans; J-C.Cistacq, O.Campan, J.Mateo, J-F.Mateo; G.Bouic, D.Tastet; E.Rodriguez, M.Dal Maso, P.Piacentini, N.Mekkaoui, C.Porcu, P.Benetton (capt), J.Troader, S.Bohn.

Replacements: G.Sudre for Tastet (40), S.Prosper for Bouic (40), S.Terle for Piacentini (62), J.Mateo for Heymans (70).

Scorers: T: Porcu.

Referee: E.Morrison (England).

Leading points-scorers: 108 L.Labit (Colomiers); C.Reigt (Stade Français); 102 T.Stimpson (Newcastle); 96 E.Elwood (Connacht); 90 T.Castaignede (Castres); 80 G.Cull (Bridgend); 78 G.Merceron (Montferrand); 76 M.Mapletoft (Gloucester); 75 J-F.Bouche (La Rochelle), N.Woods (London Irish); 74 G.Bouic (Agen); 73 J.Valls (Narbonne); 71 D.Hodge (Edinburgh).

Leading try-scorers: 8 E.Bolobolo (Stade Francais), D.Bory (Montferrand), M.Biboulet (Colomiers); 6 T.Stimpson, V.Tuigamala (both Newcastle), J-V.Bertrand (Montpellier), M.Moore (Sale), C.Heymans (Agen); 5 J-F.Mateo (Agen), J.Sieurac (Colomiers), S.Peysson (Colomiers), P.Lam (Newcastle), C.Dominici (Stade Francais), J.Machacek (Newport), M.Dawson (Northampton).

Heineken Cup Timetable of Trouble 1997-98

September 13:
Violence mars Pool E clash between Pau and Llanelli – home scrum-half Frederic Torossian caught on camera head-butting Scarlets centre Neil Boobyer.

September 14:
Pontypridd's Dale McIntosh and Brive forward Lionel Mallier sent off and banned for one month following violent Pool C match in France.

September 15:
Three Pontypridd players – McIntosh, Phil John and Andre Barnard – placed under police investigation following an alleged incident at Le Bar Toulzac in Brive.

September 23:
Pontypridd and Brive each fined £30,000 – £15,000 suspended – for the on-pitch brawl.

September 23:
Harlequins cite Cardiff lock Tony Rees for allegedly stamping on their Welsh international Gareth Llewellyn in group game at the Arms Park.

September 30:
Pau and Llanelli each fined £20,000 – £10,000 suspended – but Llanelli say they will not pay up.

October 1:
Tony Rees banned for 90 days by tournament director Roger Pickering following Harlequins' citing.

October 14:
McIntosh cleared of disrepute charge after making a thumbs-up gesture to the crowd when he was sent off in Brive.

October 27:
Pontypridd refused legal exemption certificate allowing McIntosh, John and Barnard to revisit Brive for quarter-final play-off.

November 8:
French referee Didier Mene jostled and allegedly assaulted by supporters following quarter-final between Bath and Cardiff.

January 7:
Top English clubs announce blanket withdrawal from next season's Heineken Cup and European Conference in protest at fixture scheduling.

NB: At the time of publication a format for the 1998-99 Heineken European Cup had not been finalised.

Five Nations Championship 1998

There are those who dismissed the 1998 Five Nations Championship as a predictable procession, but that would cruelly underestimate France's achievement in claiming back-to-back Grand Slams for the first time in their illustrious history. That they completed the task in utterly memorable fashion by destroying Wales 51-0 at Wembley was entirely fitting – a timely reminder that France, on their day, are well capable of challenging the southern hemisphere superpowers in the 1999 World Cup.

Their march to victory in the Five Nations came after a calamitous performance against South Africa in December when they were humbled 52-10 at the Parc des Princes. Coach Jean-Claude Skrela cleared out many of the old guard that day – Laurent Cabannes, Thierry Lacroix, Philippe Saint-Andre, Olivier Merle, Abdelatif Benazzi – but thereafter remained steadfastly loyal to his squad.

France cleared the toughest hurdle first, defeating England 24-17, a victory that was considerably easier than the margin would suggest. Next came a sensational 51-16 win over Scotland at Murrayfield when Olivier Magne sparkled at openside wing forward as France ran in seven tries. Their one dip in form and attitude came against Ireland in Paris when they made the mistake of not showing sufficient respect to their opponents and were lucky to escape with an 18-16 win. Such a lesson will stay with captain Raphael Ibanez and his team for years to come.

England, under Clive Woodward, bounced back from defeat in Paris to post a record 60-26 score over Wales at Twickenham, but this was followed with comfortable but less impressive wins, over Scotland and Ireland. Throughout the season Leicester flanker Neil Back was a constant source of excellence, captain Lawrence Dallaglio was rarely far from the action, Will Greenwood forged a promising centre partnership with Jeremy Guscott and Garath Archer was generally impressive. But the front row remains a worry, as does the lack of cover at wing, full-back and fly-half.

Curiously for a side that suffered a whitewash, Ireland emerged with some credit, deserving to beat France and performing bravely against England. They should have beaten Scotland but were well below par against Wales. Scotland's coach Richie Dixon resigned on the eve of the tournament so Jim Telfer could do little but content himself with damage limitation but Wales must be grievously worried that they conceded 111 points in the two games that counted, against England and France. They suffered badly from injuries and the retirement of Ieuan Evans but their biggest concern remains the lack of a competitive international pack.

The experiment of Sunday rugby – largely driven by the demands of TV – was only a limited success. Many fans experienced travel difficulties and the atmosphere at Murrayfield was definitely muted compared with previous Calcutta Cup games, though that may be something to do with Scotland's declining fortunes. France's win over Wales at Wembley on the final Sunday provided a splendid finale, however, and rounded the tournament off nicely after England's win over Ireland the previous day.

An unreserved success was France's new 80,000 capacity Stade de France, a magnificent, atmospheric and spectator-friendly stadium. Finally, the coming Five Nations will be the last before Italy are admitted, a welcome and timely addition to the world's oldest international tournament.

FINAL TABLE

	P	W	D	L	F	A	Pts
France	4	4	0	0	144	49	8
England	4	3	0	1	146	87	6
Wales	4	2	0	2	75	145	4
Scotland	4	1	0	3	66	120	2
Ireland	4	0	0	4	70	100	0

Top Points-scorers

	T	C	P	DG	Pts
Paul Grayson (England)	1	14	10	1	66
Christophe Lamaison (France)		9	7		39
Eric Elwood (Ireland)		4	7		29
Neil Jenkins (Wales)	1	6	4		29
Craig Chalmers (Scotland)		1	8		26
Philippe Bernat-Salles (France)	4				20
Thomas Castaignede (France)	1	3	1	1	17
Allan Bateman (Wales)	3				15
Denis Hickie (Ireland)	3				15
Jean-Luc Sadourny (France)	2			1	13
David Humphreys (Ireland)		1	2	1	11
Arwel Thomas (Wales)		1	3		11
Neil Back (England)	2				10
Matt Dawson (England)	2				10
Xavier Garbajosa (France)	2				10
Austin Healey (England)	2				10
Marc Lievremont (France)	2				10
David Rees (England)	2				10
Tony Stanger (Scotland)	2				10
Rowen Shepherd (Scotland)			2		6
Olivier Brouzet (France)	1				5
Kyran Bracken (England)	1				5
Christian Califano (France)	1				5
Philippe Carbonneau (France)	1				5
Mike Catt (England)	1				5
Richard Cockerill (England)	1				5
Victor Costello (England)	1				5
Damien Cronin (Scotland)	1				5
Lawrence Dallaglio (England)	1				5
Phil de Glanville (England)	1				5
Christophe Dominici (France)	1				5
Fabien Galthie (France)	1				5
Scott Gibbs (Wales)	1				5
Stephane Glas (France)	1				5
Will Greenwood (England)	1				5
Raphael Ibanez (France)	1				5
Thomas Lievremont (France)	1				5
Shaun Longstaff (Scotland)	1				5
Kevin Morgan (Wales)	1				5
Matt Perry (England)	1				5
Wayne Proctor (Wales)	1				5
Alan Tait (Scotland)	1				5
Gareth Thomas (Wales)	1				5
Gregor Townsend (Scotland)	1				5
Andy Ward (Ireland)	1				5
Derrick Lee (Scotland)		2			4

IRELAND 16 SCOTLAND 17 (Lansdowne Road, Dublin, 7 February 1998)

Scotland scraped a precious victory just nine days after coach Richie Dixon 'resigned' in a mediocre game containing precious little excitement. Ireland played the quality rugby and did more than enough to win but blew their chances with a baffling, mindless display in the final 20 minutes. 'I don't know whose tactics they were but they were nothing to do with me,' said Ireland coach Brian Ashton famously after the game. Within a fortnight Ashton had resigned, despairing of ever effecting a transformation in Ireland's fortunes. Scotland were lucky but also undeniably brave, given the circumstances of their arrival in Dublin after autumn thrashings at the hands of Australia and South Africa and a humiliating defeat in Italy. Both sides scored first-half tries – Ireland a penalty try from a five-yard scrum, Scotland a fine effort from Alan Tait – but Ireland led 16-11 going into the final quarter when they squandered a series of six scrums on the Scotland line. They then conceded two needless penalties in front of their posts and spent much of the closing minutes kicking the ball aimlessly into touch. Scotland clung on to record an incredible 10th consecutive Five Nations victory over Ireland, their 11th win on the trot if you include their 1991 World Cup triumph at Murrayfield. There was much celebrating in Dublin for the Scots though London Scottish full-back Derrick Lee, who won his first cap as a 78th-minute replacement for Rowen Shepherd, received a nasty shock on the Monday when he presented himself at the Exiles office at the Recreation Ground, Richmond, to collect a £10,000 bonus for becoming a senior international. After examination of the small print it became evident he had to either start the game or appear for at least 10 minutes as a substitute. Lee had to wait another fortnight, when he started against France, before pocketing the cheque.

Ireland: C.O'Shea (London Irish); R.Wallace (Saracens), K.Maggs (Bristol), M.McCall (London Irish), D.Hickie (St Mary's); D.Humphreys (London Irish), B.O'Meara (Cork Constitution); R.Corrigan (Greystones), K.Wood (Harlequins, capt), P.Wallace (Saracens), P.Johns (Saracens), M.O'Kelly (London Irish), D.Corkery (Bristol), K.Dawson (London Irish), E.Miller (Leicester).

Replacements: N.Popplewell (Newcastle) for Wallace (60-62); V.Costello (St Mary's) for Dawson (66).

Scorers: T: Pen try. C: Humphreys. PG: Humphreys (2). DG: Humphreys.

Scotland: R.Shepherd (Melrose); C.Joiner (Leicester), A.Tait (Newcastle), G.Townsend (Northampton), K.Logan (Wasps); C.Chalmers (Melrose), G.Armstrong (Newcastle, capt); G.Graham (Newcastle), G.Bulloch (West of Scotland), M.Stewart (Northampton), D.Cronin (Wasps), G.Weir (Newcastle), R.Wainwright (Dundee HSFP), S.Holmes (London Scottish), P.Walton (Newcastle).

Replacements: D.Hilton (Bath) for Graham (60); S.Grimes (Watsonians) for Cronin (64); D.Lee (London Scottish) for Shepherd (78).

Scorers: T: Tait. PG: Shepherd (2), Chalmers (2).

Referee: A.Watson (South Africa).

FRANCE 24 ENGLAND 17 (Stade de France, Paris, 7 February 1998)

A record crowd for a rugby match in France – 80,000 – crammed into the sparkling new Stade de France to watch France record their fourth consecutive win over England, a run dating back to their World Cup play-off game in Pretoria in 1995. It was also England's sixth consecutive game without a victory, their poorest run since 1971-72. Forward dominance was at the heart of France's win, especially the formidable front row of Christian Califano, new captain Raphael Ibanez and Franck Tournaire who gave their opposite numbers a miserable time. England defended well after a shaky start to remain competitive but coach Clive Woodward was left with plenty to think about as England's Grand Slam aspirations disappeared. France moved effortlessly into a 12-3 lead with well taken tries by Philippe Bernat-Salles and Christophe Dominici and could have scored three more by half-time but for over-elaboration and determined English tackling. England rallied after the break through Paul Grayson's goal-kicking and a try by Neil Back but France replied with two Christophe Lamaison penalties and dropped goals by Thomas Castaignede and Jean-Luc Sadourny. France's victory was all the more remarkable considering that they had been humiliated in their previous international, losing 52-10 to South Africa. That defeat hit at the very heart of the French psyche but they recovered magnificently, due in no small measure to the inspired choice of the pugnacious Dax hooker Ibanez as captain – Ibanez had led France to the World Students Cup in South Africa in 1996. Two days after the game France asked England to study a video of Leonard allegedly stamping on Thomas Lievremont but England saw nothing wrong with the incident and declined to take any disciplinary measures.

France: J-L.Sadourny (Colomiers); P.Bernat-Salles (Pau), C.Lamaison (Brive), S.Glas (Bourgoin), C.Dominici (Stade Français); T.Castaignede (Castres), P.Carbonneau (Brive); C.Califano (Toulouse), R.Ibanez (Dax, capt), F.Tournaire (Toulouse), O.Brouzet (Begles-Bordeaux), F.Pelous (Toulouse), P.Benetton (Agen), O.Magne (Brive), T.Lievremont (Perpignan).

Replacements: M.Lievremont (Stade Français) for Benetton (15); T.Cleda (Pau) for T.Lievremont (54).

Scorers: T: Bernat-Salles, Dominici. C: Lamaison. PG: Lamaison (2). DG: Castaignede, Sadourny.

England: M.Catt (Bath); D.Rees (Sale), J.Guscott (Bath), W.Greenwood (Leicester), A.Healey (Leicester); P.Grayson (Northampton), K.Bracken (Saracens); J.Leonard (Harlequins), M.Regan (Bath), D.Garforth (Leicester), M.Johnson (Leicester), G.Archer (Newcastle), L.Dallaglio (Wasps, capt), N.Back (Leicester), R.Hill (Saracens).

Replacement: D.West (Leicester) for Regan (70).

Scorers: T: Back. PG: Grayson (4).

Referee: D.McHugh (Ireland).

ENGLAND 60 WALES 26 (Twickenham, 21 February 1998)

England responded to the disappointment of defeat in Paris by producing a record-breaking performance in a remarkable victory at Twickenham. Their total of 60 points equalled their highest ever – against Japan in 1987 and Canada in 1994 – while the match aggregate of 86 points was the highest in the Five Nations. It was England's fifth consecutive win over Wales, their best run since the 1880s, the third highest number of points conceded by Wales, behind their 63-6 defeat against Australia in 1991 and their 96-13 humiliation against South Africa in June 1998. Curiously a dismal afternoon for Wales started brightly with two tries from Allan Bateman guiding them into a 12-3 lead. Then, 15 minutes before half-time, England hit a purple patch scoring 21 points in seven minutes and by the break had built an impregnable 34-12 lead. David Rees, Neil Back, Kyran Bracken and captain Lawrence Dallaglio all scored before half-time, while in the second half Rees added a second before Austin Healey, Will Greenwood and Matt Dawson completed the rout. Wales, completely outplayed up front, still had enough talent in their back division to claim tries through Gareth Thomas and Scott Gibbs. Rarely has a side scored four tries at Twickenham, which was some consolation, but never have Wales been so completely outplayed by the oldest of enemies. 'Eventually we will become a great side,' said Dallaglio afterwards. 'But we have a long way to go. Our first try did not come until the 28th minute, by which time we had conceded two. We can get much better.' After the game, debutant Phil Vickery was cited for punching and initially suspended for a month, but his suspension was later quashed on appeal.

England: M.Perry (Bath); D.Rees (Sale), W.Greenwood (Leicester), J.Guscott (Bath), A.Healey (Leicester); P.Grayson (Northampton), K.Bracken (Saracens); J.Leonard (Harlequins), R.Cockerill (Leicester), P.Vickery (Gloucester), M.Johnson (Leicester), G.Archer (Newcastle), L.Dallaglio (Wasps, capt), N.Back (Leicester), R.Hill (Saracens).

Replacements: D.Garforth (Leicester) for Vickery (56); D.Grewcock (Saracens) for Johnson (56); A.Diprose (Saracens) for Hill (56); M.Catt (Bath) for Grayson (70); M.Dawson (Northampton) for Bracken (70); P.de Glanville (Bath) for Greenwood (70).

Scorers: T: Rees (2), Greenwood, Healey, Bracken, Dawson, Back, Dallaglio. C: Grayson (7). PG: Grayson (2).

Wales: N.Jenkins (Pontypridd); G.Thomas (Cardiff), A.Bateman (Richmond), S.Gibbs (Swansea), N.Walker (Cardiff); A.Thomas (Swansea), R.Howley (Cardiff, capt); A.Lewis (Cardiff), B.Williams (Richmond), D.Young (Cardiff), G.Llewellyn (Harlequins), M.Voyle (Llanelli), C.Charvis (Swansea), M.Williams (Pontypridd), S.Quinnell (Richmond).

Replacements: W.Proctor (Llanelli) for Walker (4); R.Appleyard (Swansea) for Quinnell (50); J.Humphreys (Cardiff) for B.Williams (64); L.Davies (Cardiff) for Bateman (64); C.Stephens (Bridgend) for Voyle (74); L.Mustoe (Cardiff) for Lewis (76).

Scorers: T: Bateman (2), G.Thomas, Gibbs. C: Jenkins (3).

Referee: C.Hawke (New Zealand).

SCOTLAND 16 FRANCE 51 (Murrayfield, 21 February 1998)

France, arriving in Edinburgh with the unimpressive record of just one win at Murrayfield in the previous 20 years, laid that particular bogey to rest with an exhilarating victory, outscoring a brave but limited Scotland side seven tries to one. All this was achieved despite completely going off the boil for twenty minutes in the second half when the French could scarcely string a couple of passes together. For much of the game they were superb however, especially flankers Olivier Magne and Marc Lievremont. Scotland actually played better in defeat than when winning against Ireland, but simply could not resist the French. The Scots went into a 6-0 lead with two penalties from Craig Chalmers, but quickly conceded two tries to Lievremont, with the blindside flanker showing the pace of a centre to claim his second. Chalmers and Lamaison swapped penalties but France put the issue beyond doubt with a fine try by Philippe Bernat-Salles. After the break Califano and Bernat-Salles quickly added tries as France threatened to run riot, but Scotland managed to hang in as the French lost concentration. Tony Stanger, playing his 50th game, celebrated with a breakaway try after Castaignede had squandered possession, but France finally rallied in the final ten minutes with a deserved try for tireless scrum-half Philippe Carbonneau and a well-worked score for Castaignede, who had also taken over kicking duties when Lamaison was replaced at half-time. 'It's absolutely illogical that this gap should be opening up,' mused the experienced Rob Wainwright afterwards. 'It's only a couple of years since Scotland beat France twice and lost narrowly in the World Cup in Pretoria. We have got a good number of professionals playing rugby with top clubs – that should at least put us on a par with them.' Not on this occasion it didn't.

Scotland: D.Lee (London Scottish); A.Stanger (Hawick), A.Tait (Newcastle), G.Townsend (Northampton), K.Logan (Wasps); C.Chalmers (Melrose), G.Armstrong (Newcastle, capt); D.Hilton (Bath), G.Bulloch (West of Scotland), M.Stewart (Northampton), D.Cronin (Wasps), G.Weir (Newcastle), R.Wainwright (Dundee HSFP), S.Holmes (London Scottish), P.Walton (Newcastle).

Replacements: S.Grimes (Watsonians) for Cronin (20); G.Graham (Newcastle) for Hilton (65); A.Roxburgh (Kelso) for Watson (65); S.Longstaff for Chalmers (78).

Scorers: T: Stanger. C: Chalmers. PG: Chalmers (3).

France: J-L.Sadourny (Colomiers); P.Bernat-Salles (Pau), C.Lamaison (Brive), S.Glas (Bourgoin), C.Dominici (Stade Français); T.Castaignede (Castres), P.Carbonneau (Brive); C.Califano (Toulouse), R.Ibanez (Dax, capt), F.Tournaire (Toulouse), O.Brouzet (Begles-Bordeaux), F.Pelous (Toulouse), M.Lievremont (Stade Français), O.Magne (Brive), T.Lievremont (Perpignan).

Replacements: D.Aucange (Pau) for Lamaison (40); P.Benetton (Agen) for T.Lievremont (79); C.Soulette (Beziers) for Tournaire (78); T.Cleda (Pau) for Pelous (80).

Scorers: T: M.Lievremont (2), Bernat-Salles (2), Califano, Castaignede, Carbonneau. C: Lamaison (2), Castaignede (3). PG: Lamaison, Castaignede.

Referee: P.O'Brien (New Zealand).

FRANCE 18 IRELAND 16 (Stade de France, Paris, 7 March 1998)

Ireland, under new coach Warren Gatland, confounded all the critics by producing a superlative performance at the Stade de France that should have resulted in a deserved victory for the 33-1 outsiders, playing their first game since the shock resignation of Brian Ashton. In the words of Keith Wood, who enjoyed an outstanding game before going off injured, Ireland 'went back to basics' and did what they were good at. They tackled, harried and drove forward with real passion and in scrum-half Conor McGuinness had the man of the match. The backrow of Victor Costello, debutant New Zealander Andy Ward and a rejuvenated David Corkery were outstanding, eclipsing their highly rated opponents. Despite being denied a legitimate try in the first half when Jean-Luc Sadourny made a mess of touching down a kick through and Paul Wallace pounced, Ireland built a 13-3 half-time lead with two penalties from Eric Elwood, who also converted Denis Hickie's exciting breakaway try when he intercepted Christophe Lamaison's pass. Better still, they went into a 16-6 lead with a third Elwood penalty but France hit back with a well worked score for Philippe Bernat-Salles, though the final pass from Sadourny was forward. Captain Raphael Ibanez then burrowed over for a try, but Ireland finished much the stronger with a series of sharp breaks by McGuinness and a fine free-flowing movement which resulted in Maggs just spilling the ball on the line. The game ended with Costello surging dangerously forward, with the No 8 just being unable to find a supporting player. This was a defeat that seemed like victory – certainly from the stands – but that was little consolation for an Ireland side who for the second consecutive game had outplayed their opponents only to finish as losers.

France: J-L.Sadourny (Colomiers); P.Bernat-Salles (Pau), C.Lamaison (Brive), S.Glas (Bourgoin), X.Garbajosa (Toulouse); T.Castaignede (Castres), P.Carbonneau (Brive); C.Califano (Toulouse), R.Ibanez (Dax, capt), F.Tournaire (Toulouse), O.Brouzet (Begles-Bordeaux), F.Pelous (Toulouse), M.Lievremont (Stade Français), O.Magne (Brive), T.Lievremont (Perpignan).

Replacements: P.Benetton (Agen) for M.Lievremont (53); C.Soulette (Beziers) for Tournaire (65); T.Cleda (Pau) for Pelous (71).

Scorers: T: Bernat-Salles, Ibanez. C: Lamaison. PG: Lamaison (2).

Ireland: C.O'Shea (London Irish); R.Wallace (Saracens), R.Henderson (Wasps), K.Maggs (Bristol), D.Hickie (St Mary's); E.Elwood (Galwegians), C.McGuinness (St Mary's); R.Corrigan (Greystones), K.Wood (Harlequins, capt), P.Wallace (Saracens), P.Johns (Saracens), M.O'Kelly (London Irish), D.Corkery (Bristol), Λ.Ward (Ballynahinch), V.Costello (St Mary's).

Replacements: R.Nesdale (Newcastle) for Wood (58); N.Popplewell (Newcastle) for Corrigan (58); P.Clohessy (Young Munster) for Wallace (64); M.Galwey (Shannon) for Johns (64).

Scorers: T: Hickie. C: Elwood. PG: Elwood (3).

Referee: J.Fleming (Scotland).

WALES 19 SCOTLAND 13 (Wembley, 7 March 1998)

A spirited return to action from two Celtic nations after severe drubbings at the hands of England and France in the previous round provided fine entertainment for a 75,000 crowd at Wembley, Wales' temporary home from home while their new Millennium Stadium is built in Cardiff. Scotland started in sensational fashion, Gregor Townsend rounding off a 75-metre move to score in the sixth minute. Craig Chalmers and Neil Jenkins swapped penalties before the latter went off injured and Scotland seemed to move ahead decisively with a short-range try from Cronin but crucially, replacement fly-half Arwel Thomas clawed back two penalties in the 39th and 44th minutes of a protracted first half. Scotland were left ruminating on a number of missed chances and they continued to create try-scoring opportunities after the break but alas lacked the killer instinct. Wales, aware that coach Kevin Bowring's job was probably on the line, were nothing if not dogged and could always rely on the excellence of Scott Gibbs and Allan Bateman in midfield. They pulled ahead three minutes after the break with a try from Wayne Proctor after Wales had seized on a mistake by replacement full-back Rowen Shepherd to move forward. They won the subsequent line-out and after good work in midfield, Proctor squeezed in. Arwel Thomas clinched the issue with a conversion and penalty. Though occasionally scrappy there was much to admire, especially the play of Wales full-back Kevin Morgan, Bateman, Robert Howley and rapidly developing No 8 Colin Charvis. For Scotland Gregor Townsend was dangerous again, New Zealand-reared wing Shaun Longstaff looked to the manor born, Derrick Lee threatened before getting injured and the backrow emerged with honours even after a hectic afternoon of confrontation.

Wales: K.Morgan (Pontypridd); W.Proctor (Llanelli), A.Bateman (Richmond), S.Gibbs (Swansea), G.Thomas (Cardiff); N.Jenkins (Pontypridd), R.Howley (Cardiff, capt); A. Lewis (Cardiff), G.Jenkins (Swansea), D.Young (Cardiff), M.Voyle (Llanelli), A.Moore (Swansea), R.Appleyard (Swansea), K.Jones (Ebbw Vale), C.Charvis (Swansea).

Replacements: A.Thomas (Swansea) for Jenkins (18); S.Quinnell (Richmond) for Appleyard (58); J.Humphreys (Cardiff) for Jenkins (69).

Scorers: T: Proctor. C: Thomas. PG: Jenkins, Thomas (3).

Scotland: D.Lee (London Scottish); T.Stanger (Hawick), G.Townsend (Northampton), A.Tait (Newcastle), S.Longstaff (Dundee HSFP); C.Chalmers (Melrose), G.Armstrong (Newcastle, capt); D.Hilton (Bath), G.Bulloch (West of

Scotland), M.Stewart (Northampton), D.Cronin (Wasps), G.Weir (Newcastle), R.Wainwright (Dundee HSFP), A.Roxburgh (Kelso), E.Peters (Bath).

Replacements: R.Shepherd (Melrose) for Lee (29); S.Grimes (Watsonians) for Cronin (50); G.Graham (Newcastle) for Stewart (65).

Scorers: T: Townsend, Cronin. PG: Chalmers.

Referee: J.Dume (France).

IRELAND 21 WALES 30 (Lansdowne Road, 21 March 1998)

After the heroics of Paris, Irish hopes were high going into this game but, as so often has been the case, they crashed disappointingly under the burden of expectation. Ireland, it seems, have to be massive underdogs before they can begin to perform. For Wales victory ended a depressing run of four consecutive defeats against Ireland and was achieved without the considerable services of centre Scott Gibbs who withdrew with a shoulder problem – the powerful Leigh Davies proved an excellent replacement, underlining his own considerable potential. The Welsh build-up had also been marked by the announcement of former captain Ieuan Evans's retirement from the international scene. Ireland started where they left off in Paris with the forwards in command as early tries for Andy Ward and the hugely improved Victor Costello saw them build a 12-3 lead, but an opportunist score from Allan Bateman kick-started the Welsh effort and from then on they looked the more dangerous team when in possession. Kevin Morgan scored a sparkling try in the game's best moment and Neil Jenkins, who has never lost in Dublin, clinched victory with a try in the 80th minute after a powerful surge from replacement Stuart Davies. Jenkins, back in his preferred position of fly-half, contributed 20 points with his usual quiet efficiency. Ireland did not lack for effort and individuals continued to perform – Malcolm O'Kelly, Costello and Rob Henderson – but collectively they lacked direction and precision. Too often they pressed forward dangerously only to panic and lose discipline when presented with try-scoring opportunities. If Warren Gatland had not previously appreciated the magnitude of the task he faced, he did after this performance.

Ireland: C.Clarke (Terenure College); R.Wallace (Saracens), K.Maggs (Bristol), R.Henderson (Wasps), D.Hickie (St Mary's); E.Elwood (Galwegians), C.McGuinness (St Mary's); R.Corrigan (Greystones), K.Wood (Harlequins, capt), P.Wallace (Saracens), P.Johns (Saracens), M.O'Kelly (London Irish), D.Corkery (Bristol), A.Ward (Ballynahinch), V.Costello (St Mary's).

Replacements: P.Clohessy (Young Munster) for Wallace (58); R.Nesdale (Newcastle) for Wood (58); E.Miller (Leicester) for Ward (64).

Scorers: T: Ward, Costello. C: Elwood. PG: Elwood (3).

Wales: K.Morgan (Pontypridd); W.Proctor (Llanelli), A.Bateman (Richmond), L.Davies (Cardiff), G.Thomas (Cardiff); N.Jenkins (Pontypridd), R.Howley (Cardiff, capt); A.Lewis (Cardiff), G.Jenkins (Swansea), D.Young (Cardiff), M.Voyle (Llanelli), A.Moore (Swansea), R.Appleyard (Swansea), K.Jones (Ebbw Vale), C.Charvis (Swansea).

Replacements: J.Humphreys (Cardiff) for Jenkins (60); S.Davies (Swansea) for Jones (60); L.Mustoe (Cardiff) for Young (71).

Scorers: T: Bateman, Morgan, Jenkins. C: Jenkins (3). PG: Jenkins (3).

Referee: E.Morrison (England).

SCOTLAND 20 ENGLAND 34 (Murrayfield, 22 March 1998)

England, while never hitting the heights, recorded their ninth consecutive victory over the Scots in the first Five Nations game to be staged on a Sunday, an experiment that met with mixed reactions. England arrived with Newcastle captain Dean Ryan among their ranks, the abrasive No 8 making his first international appearance since playing against Canada in 1992. Club colleague Johnny Wilkinson, just 18, was also included on the bench. Scotland, whose A side had completed their grand slam on the previous Friday evening, produced their best performance of the season and with better finishing could have led at half-time. Instead the score was level at 6-6 and England predictably took charge after the break. A prolonged siege of the Scottish line resulted in a penalty try before Matt Dawson, starting the game because of Kyran Bracken's shoulder injury, darted over for a well-taken second. Scotland then lost concentration altogether and gifted a try to Healey after a mix-up in midfield. Paul Grayson, enjoying a fine game at fly-half, completed the England score with an excellent individual try but Scotland hit back in spirited fashion with two late tries which owed much to the powerful running and slick passing of openside flanker Adam Roxburgh. Tony Stanger finished off a sweeping move to equal the immortal Ian Smith's record of 24 international tries for Scotland and finally New Zealand-born wing Shaun Longstaff touched down. Scotland's brave finish at least gave them hope as they contemplated a summer tour of Australia. One win in the Five Nations might not be much to shout about but given their traumas either side of Christmas it could have been much worse.

Scotland: D.Lee (London Scottish); T.Stanger (Hawick), A.Tait (Newcastle), G.Townsend (Northampton), S.Longstaff (Dundee HSFP); C.Chalmers (Melrose), G.Armstrong (Newcastle, capt); D.Hilton (Bath), G.Bulloch (West of Scotland), P.Burnell (London Scottish), D.Cronin (Wasps), G.Weir (Newcastle), R.Wainwright (Dundee HSFP), A.Roxburgh (Kelso), E.Peters (Bath).

Replacements: S.Grimes (Watsonians) for Cronin (52); C.Murray (Hawick) for Chalmers (72).

Scorers: T: Stanger, Longstaff. C: Lee (2). PG: Chalmers (2).

England: M.Perry (Bath); A.Healey, W.Greenwood (both Leicester), J.Guscott, A.Adebayo (both Bath); P.Grayson, M.Dawson (both Northampton); J.Leonard (Harlequins), R.Cockerill, D.Garforth, M.Johnson (all Leicester), G.Archer (Newcastle), L.Dallaglio (Wasps, capt), N.Back (Leicester), D.Ryan (Newcastle).

Replacements: T.Diprose (Saracens) for Ryan (68); P.de Glanville (Bath) for Healey (71); D.Grewcock (Saracens) for Johnson (74); D.West (Leicester) for Cockerill (83).

Scorers: T: Pen try, Dawson, Healey, Grayson. C: Grayson (4). PG: Grayson. DG: Grayson.

Referee: C.Thomas (Wales).

ENGLAND 35 IRELAND 17 (Twickenham, 4 April 1998)

England claimed a fourth consecutive Triple Crown to equal the Welsh record of the mid-70s but although they played well sporadically, this was a fairly low-key end to a winter of eight international games. First-half tries from Matt Perry, his first in a senior international, Richard Cockerill and Mike Catt, playing on the wing, ensured victory but Ireland were in no mood to roll over and provided fierce opposition after the break. Indeed the Irish pack achieved parity throughout and gave England a painful lesson in how to ruck, too many white-shirted forwards being content to lie on the ball and prevent quick release. Ireland scored two tries through quicksilver wing Denis Hickie, the second after a delightful inside flick from Elwood, but

England regrouped enough for substitute de Glanville to score a fourth try and the reliable boot of Paul Grayson provided further insurance against an upset. Victory was slightly marred on the final whistle when captain Lawrence Dallaglio refused to shake the hand of David Corkery, though they did swap shirts in the dressing room afterwards. Corkery, at his abrasive best/worst throughout the game, had complained of English arrogance before the match and immediately upset England with his rather childlike antics when confronting Martin Johnson at the first ruck, a display of petulance which saw a penalty for Ireland reversed and Matt Perry sweep in for the first England try from the subsequent scrum. For England Neil Back enjoyed another wonderful game to underline his position as their best player of the season, while Martin Johnson showed a welcome return to top form. For Ireland Victor Costello, Malcolm O'Kelly and Paul Wallace were again outstanding but their deficiencies behind the scrum remain as obvious as ever.

England: M.Perry; M.Catt (both Bath), W.Greenwood (Leicester), J.Guscott (Bath), A.Healey (Leicester); P.Grayson, M.Dawson (both Northampton); J.Leonard (Harlequins), R.Cockerill, D.Garforth, M.Johnson (all Leicester), G.Archer (Newcastle), L.Dallaglio (Wasps, capt), N.Back (Leicester), A.Diprose (Saracens).

Replacements: P.de Glanville (Bath) for Greenwood (53); D.Grewcock (Saracens) for Archer (53); J.Wilkinson (Newcastle) for Catt (78).

Scorers: T: Perry, Cockerill, Catt, de Glanville. C: Grayson (3). PG: Grayson (3).

Ireland: C.Clarke (Terenure College); R.Wallace (Saracens), K.Maggs (Bristol), M.McCall (London Irish), D.Hickie (St Mary's); E.Elwood (Galwegians), C.McGuinness (St Mary's); R.Corrigan (Greystones), K.Wood (Harlequins, capt), P.Wallace, P.Johns (both Saracens), M.O'Kelly (London Irish), D.Corkery (Bristol), A.Ward (Ballynahinch), V.Costello (St Mary's).

Replacements: K.Keane (Garryowen) for McCall (46); D.Humphreys (London Irish) for Clarke (70).

Scorers: T: Hickie (2). C: Elwood (2). PG: Elwood.

Referee: D.Bevan (Wales).

WALES 0 FRANCE 51 (Wembley, 5 April 1998)

France claimed a back-to-back Grand Slam for the first time in their history with a glorious display of running rugby at Wembley that left Wales chasing shadows. Their 51-0 victory was the biggest winning margin in Five Nations history and provided reassuring evidence that at least one northern hemisphere side is likely to mount a serious challenge for the 1999 World Cup. After performing badly against Ireland, coach Jean-Claude Skrela shrewdly kept faith with exactly the same starting 15, using their determination to redeem themselves as a motivating factor. Everybody wanted to play, so much so that prop Franck Tournaire underwent eight hours of dental surgery the previous Sunday after having four teeth knocked out in a club game against Montferrand. France had the game won within 25 minutes after an opening burst of two tries from Jean-Luc Sadourny and a third from reliable No 8 Thomas Lievremont. Thereafter it was a case of desperate defence from Wales as France threatened to run riot with further tries for Xavier Garbajosa (2), Stephane Glas and replacement Fabien Galthie. Nor did France lose concentration in defence, on the contrary they were adamant that Wales should not cross their line and it is possibly that focus, as much as their traditional attacking skills, that gives them real hope for the future. Wales were outclassed, especially in midfield where their preparations had been badly disrupted by a neck injury to Scott Gibbs and the withdrawal of Allan Bateman, whose young daughter was seriously ill with an eye complaint. Ironically the much-criticised Wales pack produced one of their better performances – they certainly surprised France in the scrum – but France are a team of many talents who simply chose, on this occasion, to utilise them elsewhere. They were worthy champions and marvellous entertainment value.

Wales: K.Morgan (Pontypridd); W.Proctor (Llanelli), L.Davies (Cardiff), N.Boobyer (Llanelli), G.Thomas (Cardiff); N.Jenkins (Pontypridd), R.Howley (Cardiff, capt); A.Lewis (Cardiff), G.Jenkins (Swansea), D.Young (Cardiff), M.Voyle (Llanelli), A.Moore (Swansea), R.Appleyard (Swansea), C.Charvis (Swansea), S.Davies (Swansea).

Replacements: L.Mustoe (Cardiff) for Lewis (45); J.Humphreys (Cardiff) for Jenkins (55); D.James (Pontypridd) for Boobyer (55).

France: J-L.Sadourny (Colomiers); P.Bernat-Salles (Pau), C.Lamaison (Brive), S.Glas (Bourgoin), X.Garbajosa (Toulouse); T.Castaignede (Castres), P.Carbonneau (Brive); C.Califano (Toulouse), R.Ibanez (Dax, capt), F.Tournaire (Toulouse), O.Brouzet (Begles-Bordeaux), F.Pelous (Toulouse), M.Lievremont (Stade Français), O.Magne (Brive), T.Lievremont (Perpignan).

Replacements: P.Benetton (Agen) for T.Lievremont (67); D.Aucagne (Pau) for Castaignede (67); F.Galthie (Colomiers) for Carbonneau (67); M.Dal Maso (Agen) for Ibanez (67); J-M.Aue (Castres) for Lamaison (77), T.Cleda (Pau) for Brouzet (81).

Scorers: T: Sadourny (2), T.Lievremont, Glas, Garbajosa (2), Galthie. C: Lamaison (5). PG: Lamaison (2).

Referee: P. Marshall (Australia).

Five Nations Championship

Winners, Triple Crowns and Grand Slams

CHAMPIONS		WHITEWASH
1883	England†	Ireland
1884	England†	Ireland
1885	Not completed	
1886	England and Scotland	
1887	Scotland	
1888	Ireland, Scotland, Wales	
1889	Scotland	
1890	England and Scotland	
1891	Scotland†	Ireland
1892	England†	
1893	Wales†	
1894	Ireland†	
1895	Scotland†	Ireland
1896	Ireland	
1897	Not completed	
1898	Not completed	
1899	Ireland†	England
1900	Wales†	
1901	Scotland†	England
1902	Wales†	Scotland
1903	Scotland†	England
1904	Scotland	
1905	Wales†	England
1906	Ireland and Wales	
1907	Scotland†	
1908	Wales*	
1909	Wales*	
1910	England	France
1911	Wales*	Scotland
1912	England and Ireland	France
1913	England*	France
1914	England*	France, Scotland
1915-19	World War 1	
1920	England, Scotland, Wales	Ireland
1921	England*	
1922	Wales	

CHAMPIONS		WHITEWASH
1923	England*	
1924	England*	France
1925	Scotland*	France
1926	Ireland and Scotland	France
1927	Ireland and Scotland	
1928	England*	
1929	Scotland	France
1930	England	
1931	Wales	
1932	England, Ireland, Wales	
1933	Scotland†	
1934	England†	
1935	Ireland	
1936	Wales	
1937	England†	
1938	Scotland†	
1939	England, Ireland, Wales	
1940-46	World War 2	
1947	England and Wales	Scotland
1948	Ireland*	
1949	Ireland†	
1950	Wales*	
1951	Ireland	
1952	Wales*	Scotland
1953	England	Scotland
1954	England†, Wales, France	Scotland
1955	France, Wales	
1956	Wales	
1957	England*	France
1958	England	
1959	France	
1960	England†, France	Ireland
1961	France	
1962	France	
1963	England	
1964	Scotland, Wales	
1965	Wales†	
1966	Wales	
1967	France	
1968	France*	Scotland
1969	Wales†	

208

1970	France, Wales	
1971	Wales*	
1972	Not completed	England
1973	Five-way tie	
1974	Ireland	
1975	Wales	
1976	Wales*	England
1977	France*	Ireland
1978	Wales*	Scotland
1979	Wales†	
1980	England†	
1981	France*	Ireland
1982	Ireland†	
1983	France, Ireland	
1984	Scotland*	Ireland
1985	Ireland†	Scotland
1986	France, Scotland	Ireland
1987	France*	
1988	France, Wales	
1989	France	
1990	Scotland*	Wales
1991	England*	
1992	England*	Ireland
1993	France	
1994	Wales	
1995	England*	Wales
1996	England†	
1997	France*	
1998	France*	Ireland

*Denotes Grand Slam
†Denotes Triple Crown

Notes: Whitewash is losing all Championship games in a season. The tournament became Five Nations contest when France joined in 1910. Reverted to Four Nations from 1932-39 when France were banned because players were paid at club level. England did not compete in 1888 and 1889, declining membership of the new International Rugby Board. Disputes marred uncompleted Championships in 1885, 1897 and 1898. In 1972 Scotland and Wales refused to play in Dublin because of violence in Ulster. The trophy was first awarded in 1993. Wales won the 1994 title on tie-break. Until 1993 teams level on points shared title.

OTHER TEST MATCHES

(From 1 July 1997 to 4 July 1998)

Bledisloe Cup

05/07/1997 New Zealand 30 Australia 13 (Christchurch)

New Zealand: C.M.Cullen (Manawatu); J.W.Wilson (Otago), F.E.Bunce (North Harbour), L.Stensness (Auckland), T.J.F.Umaga (Wellington); C.J.Spencer (Auckland), J.W.Marshall (Canterbury); C.W.Dowd (Auckland), S.B.T.Fitzpatrick (Auckland, capt), O.M.Brown (Auckland), I.D.Jones (North Harbour), R.M.Brooke (Auckland), T.C.Randell (Otago), Z.V.Brooke (Auckland), J.A.Kronfeld (Otago).

Replacements: A.I.Ieremia (Wellington) for Umaga (68), C.C.Riechelmann (Auckland) for Z.Brooke (68), M.P.Carter (Auckland) for Kronfeld (77).

Scorers: T: Z.Brooke (2), Kronfeld (2). C: Spencer (2). PG: Spencer (2).

Australia: S.Larkham (ACT); B.N.Tune (Queensland), D.J.Herbert (Queensland), P.W.Howard (Queensland), J.W.Roff (ACT); T.J.Horan (Queensland), G.M.Gregan (ACT), R.L.L.Harry (NSW), M.E.Caputo (ACT), E.J.A.McKenzie (ACT), M.Cockbain (Queensland), J.A.Eales (Queensland, capt), B.J.Robinson (ACT), T.Coker (ACT), D.J.Wilson (Queensland).

Replacements: D.T.Manu (NSW) for Coker (40-60), J.Holbeck (ACT) for Howard (54), M.Hardy (ACT) for Roff (68), M.A.Foley (Queensland) for Caputo (68).

Scorers: T: Horan. C: Eales. PG: Eales (2).

Referee: E.F.Morrison (England).

Tri Nations

19/07/1997 South Africa 32 New Zealand 35 (Johannesburg)

South Africa: R.G.Bennett (Border); A.H.Snyman (N Transvaal), P.C.Montgomery (W Province), D.Van Schalkwyk (N Transvaal), P.W.G.Rossouw (W Province); J.H.De Beer (OFS), J.H.Van Der Westhuizen (N Transvaal); J.P.Du Randt (OFS), A.E.Drotske (OFS), M.H.Hurter (N Transvaal), M.G.Andrews (Natal), K.Otto (N Transvaal), R.J.Kruger (N Transvaal), G.H.Teichmann (Natal, capt), A.G.Venter (OFS).

Replacements: J.T.Small (W Province) for Bennett (41), F.J.Van Heerden (W Province) for Andrews (66), D.F.Theron (Griqualand West) for Du Randt (67), H.W.Honiball (Natal) for Montgomery (72).

Scorers: T: Bennett, Drotske. C: De Beer (2). PG: De Beer (4). DG: De Beer (2).

New Zealand: C.M.Cullen (Manawatu); J.W.Wilson (Otago), F.E.Bunce (North Harbour), L.Stensness (Auckland), T.J.F.Umaga (Wellington); O.M.Brown (Auckland), J.W.Marshall (Canterbury); O.M.Brown (Auckland), S.B.T.Fitzpatrick (Auckland, capt), C.W.Dowd (Auckland), I.D.Jones (North Harbour), R.M.Brooke (Auckland), T.C.Randell (Otago), Z.V.Brooke (Auckland), J.A.Kronfeld (Otago).

Replacements: A.I.Ieremia (Wellington) for Umaga (28), N.J.Hewitt (Southland) for Fitzpatrick (48).

Scorers: T: Bunce (2), Wilson, Spencer. C: Spencer (3). PG: Spencer (3).

Referee: P.L.Marshall (Australia).

26/07/1997 Australia 18 New Zealand 33 (Melbourne)

Australia: M.Burke (NSW); B.N.Tune (Queensland), J.S.Little (Queensland), J.Holbeck (ACT), J.W.Roff (ACT); T.J.Horan (Queensland), G.M.Gregan (ACT); R.L.L.Harry (NSW), M.A.Foley (Queensland), A.Heath (NSW), G.J.Morgan (Queensland), J.A.Eales (Queensland, capt), D.T.Manu (NSW), M.C.Brial (NSW), B.J.Robinson (ACT).

Replacements: T.Coker (ACT) for Brial (34), S.Larkham (ACT) for Horan (40), D.J.Wilson (Queensland) for Robinson (61), S.J.Payne (NSW) for Burke (78).

Scorers: T: Little, Gregan. C: Burke. PG: Burke (2).

New Zealand: C.M.Cullen (Manawatu); J.W.Wilson (Otago), F.E.Bunce (North Harbour), A.I.Ieremia (Wellington), G.M.Osborne (North Harbour); C.J.Spencer (Auckland), J.W.Marshall (Canterbury); O.M.Brown (Auckland), S.B.T.Fitzpatrick (Auckland, capt), C.W.Dowd (Auckland), I.D.Jones (North Harbour), R.M.Brooke (Auckland), T.C.Randell (Otago), Z.V.Brooke (Auckland), J.A.Kronfeld (Otago).

Replacement: A.R.Cashmore (Auckland) for Wilson (40).

Scorers: T: Cullen, Wilson, Bunce. C: Spencer (3). PG: Spencer (4).

Referee: E.F.Morrison (England).

02/08/1997 Australia 32 South Africa 20 (Brisbane)

Australia: S.Larkham (ACT); B.N.Tune (Queensland), J.S.Little (Queensland), J.Holbeck (ACT), J.W.Roff (ACT); D.J.Knox (NSW), G.M.Gregan (ACT); A.Heath (NSW), M.A.Foley (Queensland), R.L.L.Harry (NSW), O.Finegan (ACT), J.A.Eales (Queensland, capt), M.Cockbain (Queensland), D.T.Manu (NSW), D.J.Wilson (Queensland).

Replacements: T.Coker (ACT) for Cockbain (57), B.J.Robinson (ACT) for Manu (60), A.T.Blades (NSW) for Heath (73), Heath for Harry (79).

Scorers: T: Tune (2), Larkham, Manu. C: Knox (3). PG: Knox (2).

South Africa: R.G.Bennett (Border); A.H.Snyman (N Transvaal), P.C.Montgomery (W Province), D.Van Schalkwyk (N Transvaal), P.W.G.Rossouw (W Province); J.H.De Beer (OFS), J.H.Van Der Westhuizen (N Transvaal); J.P.Du Randt (OFS), A.E.Drotske (OFS), D.F.Theron (Griqualand West), K.Otto (N Transvaal), M.G.Andrews (Natal), R.J.Kruger (N Transvaal), G.H.Teichmann (Natal, capt), A.G.Venter (OFS).

Replacements: J.T.Small (W Province) for Snyman (50), A.C.Garvey (Natal) for Du Randt (63), H.W.Honiball (Natal) for Van Schalkwyk (83).

Scorers: T: De Beer, Du Randt, Andrews. C: De Beer. PG: De Beer.

Referee: C.J.Hawke (New Zealand).

09/08/1997 New Zealand 55 South Africa 35 (Auckland)

New Zealand: C.M.Cullen (Manawatu); J.W.Wilson (Otago), F.E.Bunce (North Harbour), A.I.Ieremia (Wellington), T.J.F.Umaga (Wellington); C.J.Spencer (Auckland), J.W.Marshall (Canterbury); C.W.Dowd (Auckland), S.B.T.Fitzpatrick (Auckland, capt), O.M.Brown (Auckland), I.D.Jones (North Harbour), R.M.Brooke (Auckland), T.C.Randell (Otago), Z.V.Brooke (Auckland), J.A.Kronfeld (Otago).

Replacements: C.C.Riechelmann (Auckland) for Z.Brooke (58-64), A.P.Mehrtens (Canterbury) for Spencer (58-64), M.R.Allen (Taranaki) for Dowd (74).

Scorers: T: Cullen (2), Ieremia, Umaga, Spencer, Marshall, Randell. C: Spencer (4). PG: Spencer (4).

South Africa: R.G.Bennett (Border); J.T.Small (W Province), P.C.Montgomery (W Province), H.W.Honiball (Natal), A.H.Snyman (N Transvaal); J.H.De Beer (OFS), J.H.Van Der Westhuizen (N Transvaal); J.P.Du Randt (OFS), J.Dalton (Gauteng), M.H.Hurter (N Transvaal), K.Otto (N Transvaal), M.G.Andrews (Natal), R.J.Kruger (N Transvaal), G.H.Teichmann (Natal, capt), A.G.Venter (OFS).

Replacements: F.J.Van Heerden (W Province) for Kruger (12), A.E.Drotske (OFS) for Otto (58), P.W.G.Rossouw (W Province) for De Beer (69), D.F.Theron (Griqualand West) for Hurter (76).

Scorers: T: Montgomery, Van Der Westhuizen, Kruger, Teichmann, Rossouw. C: Honiball (2). C: De Beer (3).

Referee: W.D.Bevan (Wales).

16/08/1997 New Zealand 36 Australia 24 (Dunedin)

New Zealand: C.M.Cullen (Manawatu); J.W.Wilson (Otago), F.E.Bunce (North Harbour), A.I.Ieremia (Wellington), G.M.Osborne (North Harbour); C.J.Spencer (Auckland), J.W.Marshall (Canterbury); C.W.Dowd (Auckland), S.B.T.Fitzpatrick (Auckland, capt), O.M.Brown (Auckland), R.M.Brooke (Auckland), I.D.Jones (North Harbour), T.C.Randell (Otago), Z.V.Brooke (Auckland), J.A.Kronfeld (Otago).

Replacements: O.F.J.Tonu'u (Auckland) for Marshall (64), M.R.Allen (Taranaki) for Jones (75).

Scorers: T: Cullen, Marshall, Randell. C: Spencer (3). PG: Spencer (5).

Australia: S.Larkham (ACT); B.N.Tune (Queensland), J.S.Little (Queensland), J.Holbeck (ACT), J.W.Roff (ACT); D.J.Knox (NSW), G.M.Gregan (ACT); R.L.L.Harry (NSW), M.A.Foley (Queensland), A.T.Blades (NSW), O.Finegan (ACT), J.Langford (ACT), F.S.Finau (NSW), T.Coker (ACT), D.J.Wilson (Queensland, capt).

Replacements: B.J.Robinson (ACT) for Langford (64), M.Hardy (ACT) for Roff (69).

Scorers: T: Larkham (2), Tune, Roff. C: Knox (2).

Referee: J.Dume (France).

23/08/1997 South Africa 61 Australia 22 (Pretoria)

South Africa: A.J.Joubert (Natal); J.T.Small (W Province), P.C.Montgomery (W Province), H.W.Honiball (Natal), A.H.Snyman (N Transvaal); J.H.De Beer (OFS), J.H.Van Der Westhuizen (N Transvaal); J.P.Du Randt (OFS), J.Dalton (Gauteng),

M.H.Hurter (N Transvaal), J.J.Strydom (Gauteng), M.G.Andrews (Natal), W.G.Brosnihan (OFS), G.H.Teichmann (Natal, capt), J.Erasmus (OFS).

Replacements: P.W.G.Rossouw (W Province) for Snyman (28), S.Bekker (N Transvaal) for Teichmann (52-55), W.W.Els (OFS) for Strydom (68), W.Swanepoel (OFS) for Small (84).

Scorers: T: Montgomery (2), De Beer, Dalton, Andrews, Brosnihan, Erasmus, Rossouw. C: De Beer (6). PG: De Beer (3).

Australia: S.Larkham (ACT); B.N.Tune (Queensland), J.S.Little (Queensland), J.Holbeck (ACT), J.W.Roff (ACT); D.J.Knox (NSW), G.M.Gregan (ACT); R.L.L.Harry (NSW), M.A.Foley (Queensland), A.T.Blades (NSW), O.Finegan (ACT), J.Langford (ACT), M.Cockbain (Queensland), T.Coker (ACT), D.J.Wilson (Queensland, capt).

Replacements: B.J.Robinson (ACT) for Coker (56), T.Kefu (Queensland) for Cockbain (78). Sent off: Holbeck (70).

Scorers: T: Little, Roff, Knox. C: Knox (2). PG: Knox.

Referee: P.D.O'Brien (New Zealand).

Other Tests

05/07/1997 US Eagles 20 Wales 30 (Wilmington, 1st Test)

US Eagles: C.G.Morrow (Aspen); V.N.Anitoni (San Mateo), T.Z.Takau (Aspen), M.A.Scharrenberg (Reading), B.Hightower (Aspen); M.Alexander (Denver B), A.Bachelet (Reading); C.Lippert (OMBAC), T.W.Billups (Harlequins), R.P.Lehner (Hamilton), D.Hodges (OMBAC), L.Gross (Harlequins), J.Walker (Aspen), D.J.Lyle (Bath, capt), J.P.Wilkerson (Pontypridd).

Replacements: A.Saulala (San Mateo) for Scharrenberg (40), S.Allen (OMBAC) for Wilkerson (40), M.McLeod (OMBAC) for Lyle (51), M.Stanaway (OMBAC) for Lippert (58), K.Shuman (Penn State) for Morrow (75).

Scorers: T: Anitoni, Takau. C: Alexander (2). PG: Alexander (2).

Wales: K.A.Morgan (Pontypridd); W.T.Proctor (Llanelli), L.B.Davies (Cardiff), G.Thomas (Bridgend), N.K.Walker (Cardiff); A.C.Thomas (Swansea), P.John (Pontypridd); C.D.Loader (Swansea), G.R.Jenkins (Swansea), L.Mustoe (Cardiff), G.O.Llewellyn (Harlequins), M.J.Voyle (Llanelli), A.Gibbs (Llanelli), S.M.Williams (Neath), R.G.Jones (Cardiff, capt).

Replacements: C.T.Anthony (Swansea) for Loader (75), N.Thomas (Bath) for Williams (75).

Scorers: T: Walker, A.Thomas (2), Jones. C: A.Thomas (2). PG: A.Thomas (2).

Referee: K.W.McCartney (Scotland).

12/07/1997 US Eagles 23 Wales 28 (San Francisco, 2nd Test)

US Eagles: C.G.Morrow (Aspen); V.N.Anitoni (San Mateo), T.Z.Takau (Aspen), M.A.Scharrenberg (Reading), B.Hightower (Aspen); M.Alexander (Denver B), A.Bachelet (Reading); C.Lippert (OMBAC), T.W.Billups (Harlequins), R.P.Lehner (Hamilton), L.Gross (Harlequins), D.Hodges (OMBAC), D.J.Lyle (Bath, capt), J.Walker (Aspen), J.P.Wilkerson (Pontypridd).

Replacements: S.Allen (OMBAC) for Billups (53), S.Yungling (OMBAC) for Wilkerson (48), M.K.Sika (Rhinos) for Hightower (78), A.Saulala (San Mateo) for Takau (75).

Scorers: T: Anitoni, Walker. C: Alexander (2). PG: Alexander (3).

Wales: K.A.Morgan (Pontypridd); W.T.Proctor (Llanelli), L.B.Davies (Cardiff), G.Thomas (Bridgend), N.K.Walker (Cardiff); A.C.Thomas (Swansea), P.John (Pontypridd); I.M.Buckett (Swansea), R.C.McBryde (Llanelli), L.Mustoe (Cardiff), G.O.Llewellyn (Harlequins), M.J.Voyle (Llanelli), A.Gibbs (Llanelli), N.Thomas (Bath), R.G.Jones (Cardiff, capt).

Replacements: S.M.Williams (Neath) for Jones (41), C.T.Anthony (Swansea) for Buckett (77).

Scorers: T: Proctor (3), A.Thomas. C: A.Thomas. PG: A.Thomas (2).

Referee: C.Muir (Scotland).

19/07/1997 Canada 25 Wales 28 (Toronto)

Canada: R.P.Ross (James Bay); W.Stanley (Cats), D.C.Lougheed (Balmy Beach), S.Bryan (Balmy Beach), D.S.Stewart (UBC); G.L.Rees (Wasps, capt), J.D.Graf (Bridgend); E.A.Evans (IBM Japan), K.Morgan (Ajax W), R.G.A.Snow (Newport), J.Tait (Varries), M.B.James (Perpignan), A.J.Charron (Moseley), M.Schmid (Abbotsford), J.R.Hutchinson (IBM Japan).

Replacements: M.E.Cardinal (James Bay) for Morgan (41), R.Bice (Vancouver RC) for Evans (54).

Scorers: T: Schmid (2), Ross. C: Rees (2). PG: Rees. DG: Ross.

Wales: K.A.Morgan (Pontypridd); W.T.Proctor (Llanelli), L.B.Davies (Cardiff), G.Thomas (Bridgend), N.K.Walker (Cardiff); A.C.Thomas (Swansea), P.John (Pontypridd, capt); I.M.Buckett (Swansea), G.R.Jenkins (Swansea), L.Mustoe (Cardiff), S.J.Moore (Swansea), M.J.Voyle (Llanelli), A.Gibbs (Llanelli), S.M.Williams (Neath), R.C.A.Appleyard (Swansea).

Replacements: N.Thomas (Bath) for Gibbs (63), C.T.Anthony (Swansea) for Buckett (70).

Scorers: T: Proctor, Davies, G.Thomas. C: A.Thomas (2). PG: A.Thomas (3).

Referee: S.Borsani (Argentina).

12/07/1997 Australia 25 England 6 (Sydney)

Australia: M.Burke (NSW); B.N.Tune (Queensland), J.S.Little (Queensland), J.Holbeck (ACT), J.W.Roff (ACT); T.J.Horan (Queensland), G.M.Gregan (ACT); C.D.Blades (NSW), M.A.Foley (Queensland), E.J.A.McKenzie (ACT), G.J.Morgan (Queensland), J.A.Eales (Queensland, capt), D.T.Manu (NSW), T.Coker (ACT), B.J.Robinson (ACT).

Replacements: D.J.Wilson (Queensland) for Coker (75), A.T.Blades (NSW) for McKenzie (66).

Scorers: T: Burke, Tune, Horan, Gregan. C: Burke. PG: Eales.

England: T.R.G.Stimpson (Newcastle); J.Bentley (Newcastle), P.R.De Glanville (Bath, capt), N.J.J.Greenstock (Wasps), N.D.Beal (Northampton); M.J.Catt (Bath), M.J.S.Dawson (Northampton); C.G.Rowntree (Leicester), M.P.Regan (Bristol), D.J.Garforth (Leicester), N.C.Redman (Bath), S.D.Shaw (Wasps), L.B.N.Dallaglio (Wasps), T.A.K.Rodber (Northampton), R.A.Hill (Saracens).

Replacements: A.S.Healey (Leicester) for Dawson (41), B.B.Clarke (Richmond) for Hill (69).

Scorers: PG: Stimpson. DG: Catt.

Referee: P.D.O'Brien (New Zealand).

18/10/1997 France 30 Italy 19 (Auch)

France: J-L.Sadourny (Colomiers); L.Leflamand (Bourgoin-Jallieu), C.Lamaison (Brive), T.Castaignede (Castres), P.Saint-Andre (Gloucester, capt); T.Lacroix (Harlequins), F.Galthie (Colomiers); C.Califano (Toulouse), M.Dal Maso (Agen), F.Tournaire (Toulouse), O.Brouzet (Begles-Bordeaux), O.Merle (Montferrand), A.Benazzi (Agen), F.Pelous (Toulouse), L.Cabannes (Harlequins).

Replacements: J.Cazalbou (Toulouse) for Galthie (31), S.Glas (Bourgoin-Jallieu) for Castaignede (39), O.Magne (Brive) for Merle (53), P.Benetton (Agen) for Cabannes (68), R.Ibanez (Dax) for Dal Maso (81).

Scorers: T: Saint-Andre, Califano. C: Lamaison. PG: Lamaison (6).

Italy: M.Ravazzolo (Amatori Milano); P.Vaccari (Calvisano), A.Stoica (Narbonne), I.Francescato (Treviso), Marcello Cuttitta (Amatori Milano); D.Dominguez (Stade Francais/CASG), A.Troncon (Treviso); Massimo Cuttitta (Harlequins), C.Orlandi (Amatori Milano), F.Properzi-Curti (Amatori Milano), G.Croci (Amatori Milano), W.Cristofoletto (Treviso), M.Giovanelli (Narbonne, capt), C.Checchinato (Treviso), A.Sgorlon (Treviso).

Replacements: L.Martin (Padova) for Stoica (29), C.Caione (L'Aquila) for Cristofoletto (59).

Scorers: T: Vaccari. C: Dominguez. PG: Dominguez (3). DG: Dominguez.

Referee: S.Borsani (Argentina).

22/10/1997 France 39 Romania 3 (Lourdes)

France: J-L.Sadourny (Colomiers); P.Bondouy (Toulouse), C.Lamaison (Brive), S.Glas (Bourgoin-Jallieu), P.Saint-Andre (Gloucester, capt); T.Lacroix (Harlequins), J.Cazalbou (Toulouse); F.Tournaire (Toulouse), R.Ibanez (Dax), C.Soulette (Beziers), O.Merle (Montferrand), F.Pelous (Toulouse), N.Bacque (Pau), P.Benetton (Agen), O.Magne (Brive).

Replacements: N.Brusque (Pau) for Sadourny (40), D.Aucagne (Pau) for Lacroix (50), A.Benazzi (Agen) for Pelous (50), P.Mignoni (Beziers) for Cazalbou (65), C.Califano (Toulouse) for Tournaire (65).

Scorers: T: Saint-Andre, Tournaire, Merle, Benazzi, pen try. C: Lamaison (4). PG: Lamaison (2).

Romania: V.Maftei (Cluj); L.Colceriu (Steaua), G.Solomie (Timisoara), R.S.Gontineac (Pau), I.Rotaru (Dinamo); I.Tofan (Steaua), C.Dragnea (Petrosani); E.Niculae (Romans), M.Radoi (Dinamo), G.Vlad (Narbonne), S.Ciorascu (Auch), T.E.Brinza (Narbonne, capt), A.Girbu (Oyonnax), O.Slusariuc (Dinamo), C.S.Draguceanu (Steaua).

Replacements: V.Nedelcu (Dinamo) for Slusariuc (11), D.Talaba (Farul) for Colceriu (40), M.Iacob (Dinamo) for Rotaru (70), A.Salageanu (Dinamo) for Niculae (78).

Scorers: PG: Tofan.

Referee: S.Borsani (Argentina).

26/10/1997 France 32 Argentina 27 (Tarbes)

France: J-L.Sadourny (Colomiers); L.Leflamand (Bourgoin), C.Lamaison (Brive), S.Glas (Bourgoin), P.Saint-Andre (Gloucester, capt); T.Lacroix (Harlequins), J.Cazalbou (Toulouse); C.Califano (Toulouse), M.Dal Maso (Agen), F.Tournaire (Toulouse), O.Brouzet (Begles-Bordeaux), F.Pelous (Toulouse), P.Benetton (Agen), A.Benazzi (Agen), L.Cabannes (Harlequins).

Replacements: P.Mignoni (Beziers) for Cabannes (45-53), O.Magne (Brive) for Benetton (65).

Scorers: T: Leflamand, Califano, Dal Maso, Benazzi. C: Lamaison, Lacroix (2). PG: Lacroix (2).

Argentina: E.Jurado (Jockey Club); D.Albanese (San Isidro), F.A.Turnes (Banco Nacional), E.Simone (Liceo Naval), F.Soler (Tala); L.Arbizu (Brive), A.Pichot (Richmond); M.Reggiardo (Castres), M.Ledesma Arocena (Curupayti), O.J.Hasan Jalil (Wellington), P.L.Sporleder (Curupayti, capt), G.A.Llanes (Bath), R.A.Martin (Richmond), P.J.Camerlinckx (Buena Vista), M.A.Ruiz (Cuyo).

Replacements: M.Scelzo (Hipo) for Hasan Jalil (54), A.Allub (Jockey Club) for Llanes (58), R.Travaglini (San Isidro) for Camerlinckx (79). Sent off: Travaglini (81).

Scorers: T: Simone, Sporleder, Martin. C: Arbizu (3). PG: Arbizu. DG: Arbizu.

Referee: A.Giacomel (Italy).

01/11/1997 Argentina 15 Australia 23 (Buenos Aires, 1st Test)

Argentina: E.Jurado (Jockey Club); D.Albanese (San Isidro), E.Simone (Liceo Naval), F.A.Turnes (Banco Nacional), D.Giannantonio (Tala); L.Arbizu (Brive), A.Pichot (Richmond); R.D.Grau (Liceo Naval), M.Ledesma Arocena (Curupayti), M.Reggiardo (Castres), P.L.Sporleder (Curupayti, capt), A.Allub (Jockey Club), R.A.Martin (Richmond), M.A.Ruiz (Cuyo), P.J.Camerlinckx (Buena Vista).

Replacement: M.Scelzo (Hipo) for Ledesma (65).

Scorer: PG: Giannantonio (5).

Australia: S.Larkham (ACT); B.N.Tune (Queensland), T.J.Horan (Queensland), P.W.Howard (Queensland), J.W.Roff (ACT); D.J.Knox (NSW), G.M.Gregan (ACT); R.L.L.Harry (NSW), M.A.Foley (Queensland), A.T.Blades (NSW), W.W.Waugh (NSW), J.A.Eales (Queensland, capt), O.Finegan (ACT), T.Coker (ACT), B.J.Robinson (ACT).

Replacements: V.Ofahengaue (NSW) for Finegan (40-60) and for Coker (75), M.Hardy (ACT) for Larkham (78).

Scorers: T: Finegan. PG: Knox (6).

Referee: H.A.Smith (Ireland).

08/11/1997 Argentina 18 Australia 16 (Buenos Aires, 2nd Test)

Argentina: E.Jurado (Jockey Club); D.Albanese (San Isidro), E.Simone (Liceo Naval), F.A.Turnes (Banco Nacional), D.Giannantonio (Tala); L.Arbizu (Brive), A.Pichot (Richmond); R.D.Grau (Liceo Naval), M.Ledesma Arocena (Curupayti), M.Reggiardo (Castres), P.L.Sporleder (Curupayti, capt), A.Allub (Jockey Club), R.A.Martin (Richmond), M.A.Ruiz (Cuyo), P.J.Camerlinckx (Buena Vista).

Replacement: O.J.Hasan Jalil (Wellington) for Reggiardo (57).

Scorers: T: Pichot, Martin. C: Giannantonio. PG: Giannantonio (2).

Australia: S.Larkham (ACT); B.N.Tune (Queensland), T.J.Horan (Queensland), P.W.Howard (Queensland), J.W.Roff (ACT); D.J.Knox (NSW), G.M.Gregan (ACT); R.L.L.Harry (NSW), M.A.Foley (Queensland), A.T.Blades (NSW), W.W.Waugh (NSW), J.A.Eales (Queensland, capt), O.Finegan (ACT), T.Coker (ACT), B.J.Robinson (ACT).

Replacement: V.Ofahengaue (NSW) for Coker (59).

Scorers: T: Tune, Finegan. PG: Knox (2).

Referee: D.T.M.McHugh (Ireland).

08/11/1997 Italy 31 South Africa 62 (Bologna)

Italy: J.Pertile (Rugby Roma); P.Vaccari (Calvisano), A.Stoica (Narbonne), I.Francescato (Treviso), Marcello Cuttitta (Amatori Milano); D.Dominguez (Stade Francais/CASG), A.Troncon (Treviso); Massimo Cuttitta (Harlequins), C.Orlandi (Amatori Milano), F.Properzi-Curti (Amatori Milano), C.Checchinato (Treviso), G.Croci (Amatori Milano), M.Giovanelli (Narbonne, capt), J.M.Gardner (Treviso), A.Sgorlon (Treviso).

Replacements: W.Cristofoletto (Treviso) for Checchinato (56), M.Ravazzolo (Amatori Milano) for Pertile (51), F.Mazzariol (Rugby Roma) for Ravazzolo (80).

Scorers: T: Vaccari, Francescato, Gardner. C: Dominguez (2). PG: Dominguez (4).

South Africa: J.Swart (W Province); J.T.Small (W Province), A.H.Snyman (N Transvaal), D.J.Muir (W Province), P.W.G.Rossouw (W Province); H.W.Honiball (Natal), J.H.Van Der Westhuizen (N Transvaal); J.P.Du Randt (OFS), J.Dalton (Gauteng), A.C.Garvey (Natal), K.Otto (N Transvaal), M.G.Andrews (Natal), J.Erasmus (OFS), G.H.Teichmann (Natal, capt), A.G.Venter (OFS).

Scorers: T: Small (2), Rossouw (2), Erasmus (2), Swart, Muir, Du Randt. C: Honiball (7). PG: Honiball.

Referee: P.Deluca (Argentina).

15/11/1997 France 32 South Africa 36 (Lyon, 1st Test)

France: J-L.Sadourny (Colomiers); L.Leflamand (Bourgoin-Jallieu), S.Glas (Bourgoin-Jallieu), C.Lamaison (Brive), P.Saint-Andre (Gloucester, capt); T.Lacroix (Harlequins), F.Galthie (Colomiers); C.Califano (Toulouse), M.Dal Maso (Agen), F.Tournaire (Toulouse), F.Pelous (Toulouse), O.Brouzet (Begles-Bordeaux), P.Benetton (Agen), A.Benazzi (Agen), L.Cabannes (Harlequins).

Replacement: O.Merle (Montferrand) for Pelous (50).

Scorers: T: Glas, Califano, Merle. C: Lamaison. PG: Lamaison (5).

South Africa: P.C.Montgomery (W Province); J.T.Small (W Province), A.H.Snyman (N Transvaal), D.J.Muir (W Province), P.W.G.Rossouw (W Province); H.W.Honiball (Natal), J.H.Van Der Westhuizen (N Transvaal); J.P.Du Randt (OFS), J.Dalton (Gauteng), A.C.Garvey (Natal), M.G.Andrews (Natal), K.Otto (N Transvaal), J.Erasmus (OFS), G.H.Teichmann (Natal, capt), A.G.Venter (OFS).

Replacement: W.Swanepoel (OFS) for Van Der Westhuizen (78).

Scorers: T: Montgomery, Small, Muir, Rossouw, Dalton. C: Honiball (4). PG: Honiball.

Referee: W.D.Bevan (Wales).

22/11/1997 France 10 South Africa 52 (Parc des Princes, 2nd Test)

France: J-L.Sadourny (Colomiers); D.Venditti (Brive), C.Lamaison (Brive), S.Glas (Bourgoin), P.Saint-Andre (Gloucester, capt); T.Lacroix (Harlequins), F.Galthie (Colomiers); C.Califano (Toulouse), M.Dal Maso (Agen), F.Tournaire (Toulouse), O.Merle (Montferrand), O.Brouzet (Begles-Bordeaux), P.Benetton (Agen), A.Benazzi (Agen), L.Cabannes (Harlequins).

Replacements: F.Pelous (Toulouse) for Merle (45), L.Leflamand (Bourgoin) for Venditti (47), J.Cazalbou (Toulouse) for Galthie (53), R.Ibanez (Dax) for Dal Maso (55), D.Aucagne (Pau) for Cazalbou (68-69), D.Casadei (Brive) for Saint-Andre (75).

Scorers: T: Ibanez. C: Lamaison. PG: Lamaison.

South Africa: P.C.Montgomery (W Province); J.T.Small (W Province), A.H.Snyman (N Transvaal), D.J.Muir (W Province), P.W.G.Rossouw (W Province); H.W.Honiball (Natal), W.Swanepoel (OFS); J.P.Du Randt (OFS), J.Dalton (Gauteng), A.C.Garvey (Natal), M.G.Andrews (Natal), K.Otto (N Transvaal), A.G.Venter (OFS), G.H.Teichmann (Natal, capt), J.Erasmus (OFS).

Replacements: A.D.Aitken (W Province) for Erasmus (48), J.H.De Beer (OFS) for Rossouw (79).

Scorers: T: Rossouw (4), Snyman, Honiball, Teichmann. C: Honiball (7). PG: Honiball.

Referee: P.D.O'Brien (New Zealand).

26/05/1998 Fiji 51 Scotland 26 (Suva)

Fiji: J.Waqa; A.Tuilevu, S.C.Sorovaki (capt), M.Nakauta, F.Lasagavibau; N.Little, S.Rabaka; J.Veitayaki, I.Rasila, M.Taga, E.Katalau, S.V.Raiwalui, A.Naevo, A.Mocelutu, M.Tamanitoakula.

Replacements: W.T.Serevi for Little (50), S.Saumaisue for Naevo (50), I.Tawake for Mocelutu (62).

Scorers: T: Lasagavibau (3), Waqa, Tuilevu, Veitayaki, Naevo. C: Serevi (4), Little. PG: Little, Serevi.

Scotland: D.J.Lee (London Scottish); H.R.Gilmour (Heriot's FP), C.A.Murray (Hawick), I.C.Jardine (Stirling Co), S.L.Longstaff (Dundee HSFP); G.P.J.Townsend (Brive), B.W.Redpath (Melrose); G.R.McIlwham (Glasgow Hawks), G.C.Bulloch (West of Scotland), M.C.Proudfoot (Melrose), S.Murray (Bedford), S.B.Grimes (Watsonians), R.I.Wainwright (Dundee HSFP, capt), E.W.Peters (Bath), A.J.Roxburgh (Kelso).

Replacements: R.J.S.Shepherd (Melrose) for Jardine (22-23), M.J.Stewart (Northampton) for Proudfoot (65), S.J.Campbell (Dundee HSFP) for S.Murray (70).

Scorers: T: Gilmour, Bulloch. C: Lee (2). PG: Lee (4).

Referee: P.Honiss (New Zealand).

06/06/1998 Australia 76 England 0 (Brisbane)

Australia: M.Burke (NSW); B.N.Tune (Queensland), D.J.Herbert (Queensland), T.J.Horan (Queensland), J.W.Roff (ACT); S.Larkham (ACT), G.M.Gregan (ACT); R.L.L.Harry (NSW), P.N.Kearns (NSW), A.T.Blades (NSW), T.M.Bowman (NSW), J.A.Eales (Queensland, capt), M.Cockbain (Queensland), T.Kefu (Queensland), D.J.Wilson (Queensland).

Replacements: O.Finegan (ACT) for Cockbain (44), V.Ofahengaue (NSW) for Kefu (50), D.J.Crowley (Queensland) for Harry (61), J.S.Little (Queensland) for Burke (66).

Scorers: T: Tune (3), Larkham (3), Horan (2), Burke, Gregan, Kefu. C: Burke (4), Larkham (2). PG: Burke (3).

England: T.R.G.Stimpson (Leicester); S.Brown (Richmond), M.B.Perry (Bath), S.C.W.Ravenscroft (Saracens), A.S.Healey (Leicester); J.Wilkinson (Newcastle), S.Benton (Gloucester); C.G.Rowntree (Leicester), R.Cockerill (Leicester), P.J.Vickery (Gloucester), D.J.Grewcock (Saracens), G.S.Archer (Newcastle), B.Sturnham (Saracens), A.J.Diprose (Saracens, capt), R.J.Pool-Jones (Stade Francais/CASG).

Replacements: S.Potter (Leicester) for Ravenscroft (26-34), B.B.Clarke (Richmond) for Pool-Jones (26-40), D.Chapman (Richmond) for Stimpson (66).

Referee: A.Watson (South Africa).

06/06/1998 Zimbabwe 11 Wales 49 (Harare)

Zimbabwe: V.Olonga; G.Campbell, J.Ewing, B.French, R.Karimazondo; K.C.Tsimba, R.Bekker; G.M.Snyder, W.Barratt, G.Stewart, B.W.Catterall, S.Landman, L.Greeff, B.N.Dawson (capt), M.Mwerenga.

Replacements: D.A.Walters for Karimazondo (49), D.O.Trivella for Tsimba (60), N.Nortje for Bekker (70), I.Neilson for Barratt (72).

Scorers: T: Bekker. PG: Tsimba (2).

Wales: D.Weatherley (Swansea); R.Rees (Swansea), M.Taylor (Swansea), D.R.James (Pontypridd), W.T.Proctor (Llanelli); A.C.Thomas (Swansea), R.Howley (Cardiff, capt); D.Morris (Neath), G.R.Jenkins (Swansea), J.D.Davies (Richmond), M.A.Jones (Ebbw Vale), A.P.Moore (Swansea), N.Thomas (Bath), L.S.Quinnell (Richmond), M.E.Williams (Pontypridd).

Replacements: J.Funnell (Ebbw Vale) for Taylor (27), B.I.Hayward (Ebbw Vale) for Weatherley (31), B.H.Williams (Richmond) for Jenkins (56), C.L.Charvis (Swansea) for Quinnell (56), C.P.Wyatt (Llanelli) for Jones (71), P.John (Pontypridd) for Howley (78).

Scorers: T: Hayward (3), Rees (2), Thomas (2), Proctor. C: Thomas (3). PG: Thomas.

Referee: J.Meuwesen (Namibia).

13/06/1998 Australia 45 Scotland 3 (Sydney, 1st Test)

Australia: M.Burke (NSW); B.N.Tune (Queensland), D.J.Herbert (Queensland), T.J.Horan (Queensland), J.W.Roff (ACT); S.Larkham (ACT), G.M.Gregan (ACT); R.L.L.Harry (NSW), P.N.Kearns (NSW), A.T.Blades (NSW), T.M.Bowman (NSW), J.A.Eales (Queensland, capt), M.Cockbain (Queensland), T.Kefu (Queensland), D.J.Wilson (Queensland).

Replacements: O.Finegan (ACT) for Cockbain (36-54), V.Ofahengaue (NSW) for Kefu (50), D.J.Crowley (Queensland) for Harry (67), J.Paul (ACT) for Kearns (72).

Scorers: T: Tune (2), Burke, Horan, Wilson. C: Burke (4). PG: Burke (4).

Scotland: G.H.Metcalfe (Glasgow Hawks); D.J.Lee (London Scottish), C.A.Murray (Hawick), R.J.S.Shepherd (Melrose), S.L.Longstaff (Dundee HSFP); G.P.J.Townsend (Brive), B.W.Redpath (Melrose); D.I.W.Hilton (Bath), G.C.Bulloch (West of Scotland), M.C.Proudfoot (Melrose), S.Murray (Bedford), S.B.Grimes (Watsonians), R.I.Wainwright (Dundee HSFP, capt), E.W.Peters (Bath), G.L.Simpson (Kirkcaldy).

Replacements: K.D.McKenzie (Stirling Co) for Bulloch (40), A.J.Roxburgh (Kelso) for Simpson (76).

Scorer: PG: Lee.

Referee: A.Watson (South Africa).

13/06/1998 South Africa 37 Ireland 13 (Bloemfontein, 1st Test)

South Africa: P.C.Montgomery (W Province); S.Terblanche (Boland), A.H.Snyman (N Transvaal), P.G.Muller (Natal), P.W.G.Rossouw (W Province); G.S.Du Toit (Griqualand West), J.H.Van Der Westhuizen (N Transvaal); A-H.Le Roux (OFS), J.Dalton (Gauteng), A.C.Garvey (Natal), K.Otto (N Transvaal), M.G.Andrews (Natal), J.Erasmus (OFS), G.H.Teichmann (Natal, capt), A.G.Venter (OFS).

Replacement: P.F.Smith (Gauteng) for Du Toit (6-15).

Scorers: T: Terblanche (4), Andrews. C: Du Toit (3). PG: Du Toit (2).

Ireland: C.M.P.O'Shea (London Irish); J.P.Bishop (London Irish), K.M.Maggs (Bristol), C.M.McCall (London Irish), D.A.Hickie (St Mary's College); E.P.Elwood (Lansdowne), C.D.McGuinness (St Mary's College); J.M.Fitzpatrick (London Irish), K.G.M.Wood (Harlequins), P.S.Wallace (Saracens), M.E.O'Kelly (London Irish), P.S.Johns (Saracens, capt), D.O'Cuinneagain (Sale), V.C.P.Costello (St Mary's College), A.J.Ward (Ballynahinch).

Replacements: R.A.J.Henderson (Wasps) for Hickie (69), T.Brennan (Bective R) for Costello (70), G.M.Fulcher (London Irish) for Johns (73).

Scorers: T: Bishop. C: Elwood. PG: Elwood (2).

Referee: E.F.Morrison (England).

13/06/1998 Argentina 18 France 35 (Buenos Aires, 1st Test)

Argentina: E.Jurado (Jockey Club); D.L.Albanese (San Isidro), E.Simone (Liceo Naval), J.Orengo (Rosario), F.Soler (Tala); L.Arbizu (Brive, capt), A.Pichot (Richmond); R.D.Grau (Saracens), F.E.Mendez (Bath), M.Reggiardo (Castres), A.Allub (Jockey Club), G.A.Llanes (Bath), R.A.Martin (Richmond), F.Rossi (Rosario), M.A.Ruiz (Mendosa).

Replacements: S.Phelan (CASI) for Martin (41), C.I.Fernandez Lobbe (Liceo Naval) for Allub (41), O.J.Hasan Jalil (ACT) for Grau (41), D.Giannantonio (Tala) for Jurado (54), M.Ledesma Arocena (Curupayti) for Mendez (70).

Scorers: T: Orengo, Soler. C: Arbizu. PG: Arbizu (2).

France: A.Gomes (Stade Francais/CASG); P.Bernat-Salles (Pau), F.Comba (Stade Francais/CASG), S.Glas (Bourgoin-Jallieu), C.Dominici (Stade Francais/CASG); T.Castaignede (Castres), P.Carbonneau (Brive); C.Soulette (Beziers), R.Ibanez

(Perpignan, capt), F.Tournaire (Toulouse), O.Brouzet (Begles-Bordeaux), F.Pelous (Toulouse), M.Lievremont (Stade Francais/CASG), T.Lievremont (Perpignan), O.Magne (Brive).

Replacements: M.Dal Maso (Agen) for Ibanez (38-46), P.Benetton (Agen) for Magne (54), S.De Besombes (Perpignan) for Tournaire (75), T.Cleda (Pau) for Pelous (78).

Scorers: T: M.Lievremont (2), Dominici, Castaignede, Dal Maso. C: Castaignede (5).

Referee: S.Walsh (New Zealand).

20/06/1998 New Zealand 64 England 22 (Dunedin, 1st Test)

New Zealand: C.M.Cullen (Wellington); J.W.Wilson (Otago), M.A.Mayerhofler (Canterbury), W.K.Little (North Harbour), J.T.Lomu (Counties); A.P.Mehrtens (Canterbury), O.F.J.Tonu'u (Auckland); O.M.Brown (Auckland), A.D.Oliver (Otago), C.W.Dowd (Auckland), I.D.Jones (North Harbour), R.M.Brooke (Auckland), M.N.Jones (Auckland), T.C.Randell (Otago, capt), J.A.Kronfeld (Otago).

Replacements: T.J.Blackadder (Canterbury) for M.Jones (20), M.D.Robinson (North Harbour) for Tonu'u (62).

Scorers: T: Cullen (2), Wilson (2), Randell (2), Mayerhofler, Lomu, Kronfeld. C: Mehrtens (5). PG: Mehrtens (3).

England: M.B.Perry (Bath); T.R.G.Stimpson (Leicester), N.D.Beal (Northampton), J.Lewsey (Bristol), A.S.Healey (Leicester); J.Wilkinson (Newcastle), M.J.S.Dawson (Northampton, capt); C.G.Rowntree (Leicester), R.Cockerill (Leicester), P.J.Vickery (Gloucester), G.S.Archer (Newcastle), D.J.Grewcock (Saracens), B.B.Clarke (Richmond), S.O.Ojomoh (Bath), P.H.Sanderson (Sale).

Replacements: W.R.Green (Wasps) for Rowntree (10-17) and for Vickery (57), B.Sturnham (Saracens) for Ojomoh (34-57), T.D.Beim (Sale) for Wilkinson (41), P.B.T.Greening (Gloucester) for Cockerill (57), D.Sims (Gloucester) for Archer (77).

Scorers: T: Dawson, Cockerill, Beim. C: Stimpson (2). PG: Stimpson.

Referee: W.Erickson (Australia).

20/06/1998 South Africa 33 Ireland 0 (Pretoria, 2nd Test)

South Africa: P.C.Montgomery (W Province); S.Terblanche (Boland), A.H.Snyman (N Transvaal), P.G.Muller (Natal), P.W.G.Rossouw (W Province); P.F.Smith (Gauteng), J.H.Van Der Westhuizen (N Transvaal); A-H.Le Roux (OFS), J.Dalton (Gauteng), A.C.Garvey (Natal), K.Otto (N Transvaal), M.G.Andrews (Natal), J.Erasmus (OFS), G.H.Teichmann (Natal, capt), A.G.Venter (OFS).

Replacements: McN.Hendricks (Boland) for Terblanche (44), R.Kempson (Natal) for Le Roux (55), A.E.Drotsk (OFS) for Dalton (61), A.D.Aitken (W Province) for Erasmus (74), W.Swanepoel (OFS) for Van Der Westhuizen (74).

Scorers: T: Rossouw, Van Der Westhuizen, Dalton, Erasmus, Teichmann. C: Montgomery (4).

Ireland: C.M.P.O'Shea (London Irish); J.P.Bishop (London Irish), K.M.Maggs (Bristol), C.M.McCall (London Irish), D.A.Hickie (St Mary's College); E.P.Elwood (Lansdowne), C.D.McGuinness (St Mary's College); J.M.Fitzpatrick (London

Irish), K.G.M.Wood (Harlequins), P.S.Wallace (Saracens), M.E.O'Kelly (London Irish), P.S.Johns (Saracens, capt), D.O'Cuinneagain (Sale), V.C.P.Costello (St Mary's College), A.J.Ward (Ballynahinch).

Replacements: D.G.Humphreys (London Irish) for Elwood (20-24, 38-40 and 53), R.A.J.Henderson (Wasps) for Hickie (41), T.Brennan (Bective R) for Costello (55), P.M.N.Clohessy (Young Munster) for Fitzpatrick (61).

Referee: J.Dume (France).

20/06/1998 Australia 33 Scotland 11 (Brisbane, 2nd Test)

Australia: M.Burke (NSW); B.N.Tune (Queensland), D.J.Herbert (Queensland), T.J.Horan (Queensland), J.W.Roff (ACT); S.Larkham (ACT), G.M.Gregan (ACT); R.L.L.Harry (NSW), P.N.Kearns (NSW), A.T.Blades (NSW), T.M.Bowman (NSW), J.A.Eales (Queensland, capt), M.Cockbain (Queensland), T.Kefu (Queensland), D.J.Wilson (Queensland).

Replacements: O.Finegan (ACT) for Cockbain (23-31 and 72), V.Ofahengaue (NSW) for Kefu (40), D.J.Crowley (Queensland) for Blades (59), J.S.Little (Queensland) for Tune (61), N.Grey (NSW) for Horan (76).

Scorers: T: Tune, Larkham, Ofahengaue, Grey. C: Burke (2). PG: Burke (3).

Scotland: G.H.Metcalfe (Glasgow Hawks); D.J.Lee (London Scottish), C.A.Murray (Hawick), R.J.S.Shepherd (Melrose), S.L.Longstaff (Dundee HSFP); G.P.J.Townsend (Brive), B.W.Redpath (Melrose); D.I.W.Hilton (Bath), K.D.McKenzie (Stirling Co), M.C.Proudfoot (Melrose), S.Murray (Bedford), S.B.Grimes (Watsonians), R.I.Wainwright (Dundee HSFP, capt), G.L.Simpson (Kirkcaldy), E.W.Peters (Bath).

Replacements: C.A.Joiner (Leicester) for C.Murray (59), G.R.McIlwham (Glasgow Hawks) for Hilton (61), D.W.Hodge (Watsonians) for Metcalfe (66), S.J.Campbell (Dundee HSFP) for Grimes (70), A.J.Roxburgh (Kelso) for Simpson (76).

Scorers: T: Hodge. PG: Lee (2).

Referee: B.Campsall (England).

20/06/1998 Argentina 12 France 37 (Buenos Aires, 2nd Test)

Argentina: D.Giannantonio (Tala); D.L.Albanese (San Isidro), E.Simone (Liceo Naval), J.Orengo (Rosario), F.Soler (Tala); L.Arbizu (Brive), A.Pichot (Richmond); M.Reggiardo (Castres), M.Ledesma Arocena (Curupayti), O.J.Hasan Jalil (ACT), A.Allub (Jockey Club), P.L.Sporleder (Curupayti, capt), S.Phelan (CASI), C.I.Fernandez Lobbe (Liceo Naval), R.A.Martin (Richmond).

Replacements: F.E.Mendez (Bath) for Reggiardo (52), M.A.Ruiz (Mendosa) for Martin (52), M.Scelzo (Hindu) for Hasan Jalil (57), G.Quesada (Hindu) for Arbizu (temp).

Scorer: PG: Arbizu (3). DG: Arbizu.

France: A.Gomes (Stade Francais/CASG); P.Bernat-Salles (Pau), F.Comba (Stade Francais/CASG), S.Glas (Bourgoin-Jallieu), C.Dominici (Stade Francais/CASG); T.Castaignede (Castres), P.Carbonneau (Brive); C.Soulette (Beziers), R.Ibanez (Perpignan, capt), F.Tournaire (Toulouse), O.Brouzet (Begles-Bordeaux), F.Pelous (Toulouse), M.Lievremont (Stade Francais/CASG), T.Lievremont (Perpignan), O.Magne (Brive).

Replacements: X.Garbajosa (Toulouse) for Bernat-Salles (21), P.Benetton (Agen) for Magne (43), D.Aucagne (Pau) for Castaignede (79).

Scorers: T: Soulette (2), Dominici, Brouzet, Garbajosa. C: Castaignede (3). PG: Castaignede (2).

Referee: P.Honiss (New Zealand).

27/06/1998 New Zealand 40 England 10 (Auckland, 2nd Test)

New Zealand: C.M.Cullen (Wellington); J.W.Wilson (Otago), C.S.Ralph (Auckland), M.A.Mayerhofler (Canterbury), J.T.Lomu (Counties); A.P.Mehrtens (Canterbury), O.F.J.Tonu'u (Auckland); C.W.Dowd (Auckland), A.D.Oliver (Otago), O.M.Brown (Auckland), I.D.Jones (North Harbour), R.M.Brooke (Auckland), T.J.Blackadder (Canterbury), T.C.Randell (Otago, capt), J.A.Kronfeld (Otago).

Replacements: C.H.Hoeft (Otago) for Dowd (7-8) and for Hewitt (70), C.J.Spencer (Auckland) for Mayerhofler (40), N.J.Hewitt (Southland) for Oliver (40-51), M.P.Carter (Auckland) for Blackadder (49), I.Maka (Otago) for Jones (53), J.Vidiri (Counties) for Lomu (60).

Scorers: T: Wilson (2), Mayerhofler, Randell, Vidiri, Maka. C: Mehrtens (2), Spencer (3).

England: M.B.Perry (Bath); T.D.Beim (Sale), N.D.Beal (Northampton), J.J.N.Baxendell (Sale), A.S.Healey (Leicester); J.Lewsey (Bristol), M.J.S.Dawson (Northampton, capt); C.G.Rowntree (Leicester), R.Cockerill (Leicester), P.J.Vickery (Gloucester), R.J.Fidler (Gloucester), D.Sims (Gloucester), B.B.Clarke (Richmond), A.J.Diprose (Saracens), P.H.Sanderson (Sale).

Replacements: B.Sturnham (Saracens) for Sanderson (18-20), T.R.G.Stimpson (Leicester) for Beal (36), S.C.W.Ravenscroft (Saracens) for Healey (69), P.B.T.Greening (Gloucester) for Cockerill (74).

Scorer: T: Dawson. C: Dawson. PG: Dawson.

Referee: P.Marshall (Australia).

27/06/1998 South Africa 96 Wales 13 (Pretoria)

South Africa: P.C.Montgomery (W Province); S.Terblanche (Boland), A.H.Snyman (N Transvaal), P.G.Muller (Natal), P.W.G.Rossouw (W Province); P.F.Smith (Gauteng), J.H.Van Der Westhuizen (N Transvaal); R.Kempson (Natal), J.Dalton (Gauteng), A.C.Garvey (Natal), K.Otto (N Transvaal), M.G.Andrews (Natal), J.Erasmus (OFS), G.H.Teichmann (Natal, capt), A.G.Venter (OFS).

Replacements: R.B.Skinstad (W Province) for Andrews (42), H.W.Honiball (Natal) for Muller (44), W.Swanepoel (OFS) for Van Der Westhuizen (44), McN.Hendricks (Boland) for Terblanche (49), A.D.Aitken (W Province) for Teichmann (61), A-H.Le Roux (OFS) for Garvey (66), A.E.Drotske (OFS) for Dalton (75).

Scorers: T: Rossouw (3), Montgomery (2), Terblanche (2), Venter (2), Smith, Van Der Westhuizen, Otto, Erasmus, Skinstad, Hendricks. C: Montgomery (9). PG: Montgomery.

Wales: B.I.Hayward (Ebbw Vale); D.R.James (Pontypridd), M.Taylor (Swansea), J.Funnell (Ebbw Vale), G.R.Evans (Llanelli); A.C.Thomas (Swansea), P.John (Pontypridd); M.Griffiths (Pontypridd), B.H.Williams (Richmond), J.D.Davies (Richmond), I.Gough (Newport), A.P.Moore (Swansea), N.Thomas (Bath), C.L.Charvis (Swansea), P.K.B.Jones (Ebbw Vale, capt).

Replacements: C.P.Wyatt (Llanelli) for K.Jones (40), D.J.Williams (Llanelli) for Hayward (48), S.M.Jones (Llanelli) for Funnell (50), D.Morris (Neath) for Davies

(60), G.R.Jenkins (Swansea) for B.Williams (66), G.P.Lewis (Pontypridd) for Charvis (71), D.Llewellyn (Ebbw Vale) for John (79).

Scorer: T: Thomas. C: Thomas. PG: Thomas (2).

Referee: P.O'Brien (New Zealand).

27/06/1998 Fiji 9 France 34 (Suva)

Fiji: J.Waqa; A.Tuilevu, S.C.Sorovaki (capt), M.Nakauta, F.Lasagavibau; N.Little, S.Rauluni; J.Veitayaki, I.Rasila, M.Taga, S.V.Raiwalui, E.Katalau, A.Naevo, T.Tabua, S.Saumaisue.

Replacements: J.Uluinayau for Tuilevu (48), W.T.Serevi for Little (62), I.Tawake for Tabua (66), V.Cavubati for Taga (45), M.Tamanitoakula for Saumaisue (68-73).

Scorer: PG: Little (3).

France: A.Gomes (Stade Francais/CASG); P.Bernat-Salles (Pau), F.Comba (Stade Francais/CASG), S.Glas (Bourgoin-Jallieu), X.Garbajosa (Toulouse); T.Castaignede (Castres), P.Carbonneau (Brive); C.Soulette (Beziers), R.Ibanez (Perpignan, capt), F.Tournaire (Toulouse), O.Brouzet (Begles-Bordeaux), F.Pelous (Toulouse), M.Lievremont (Stade Francais/CASG), T.Lievremont (Perpignan), O.Magne (Brive).

Replacements: T.Cleda (Pau) for Pelous (45), P.Benetton (Agen) for T.Lievremont (63), S.De Besombes (Perpignan) for Soulette (67), J.Marlu (Montferrand) for Garbajosa (68), D.Aucagne (Pau) for Glas (75), F.Galthi (Colomiers) for Carbonneau (75), M.Dal Maso (Agen) for Ibanez (75).

Scorers: T: Gomes, Bernat-Salles, T.Lievremont, Aucagne. C: Castaignede (4). PG: Castaignede. DG: Castaignede.

Referee: A.Cole (Australia).

04/07/1998 South Africa 18 England 0 (Cape Town)

South Africa: P.C.Montgomery (W Province); S.Terblanche (Boland), A.H.Snyman (N Transvaal), P.G.Muller (Natal), P.W.G.Rossouw (W Province); H.W.Honiball (Natal), J.H.Van Der Westhuizen (N Transvaal); R.Kempson (Natal), J.Dalton (Gauteng), A.C.Garvey (Natal), K.Otto (N Transvaal), M.G.Andrews (Natal), J.Erasmus (OFS), G.H.Teichmann (Natal, capt), A.G.Venter (OFS).

Replacements: R.B.Skinstad (W Province) for Otto (9-19), A-H.Le Roux (OFS) for Kempson (75).

Scorers: T: Terblanche, Van Der Westhuizen. C: Montgomery. PG: Montgomery (2).

England: M.B.Perry (Bath); S.Brown (Richmond), N.D.Beal (Northampton), J.J.N.Baxendell (Sale), P.C.Sampson (Wasps); J.Lewsey (Bristol), M.J.S.Dawson (Northampton, capt); C.G.Rowntree (Leicester), R.Cockerill (Leicester), P.J.Vickery (Gloucester), R.J.Fidler (Gloucester), D.Sims (Gloucester), B.B.Clarke (Richmond), A.J.Diprose (Saracens), P.H.Sanderson (Sale).

Replacement: T.R.G.Stimpson (Leicester) for Sampson (55).

Referee: C.J.Hawke (New Zealand).

A Internationals

26/08/1997 Wales A 36 Romania 21 (Pontypridd)

Wales A: L.Davies (Swansea); G.Wyatt (Pontypridd), D.R.James (Pontypridd), J.Lewis (Pontypridd), N.K.Walker (Cardiff); M.Lewis (Bridgend), R.G.Jones (Swansea); I.M.Buckett (Swansea), R.C.McBryde (Llanelli), C.T.Anthony (Swansea), G.O.Llewellyn (Harlequins, capt), N.Watkins (Neath), A.Gibbs (Llanelli), M.E.Williams (Pontypridd), C.Wyatt (Llanelli).

Replacements: D.Case (Neath) for Davies (64), M.Lloyd (Pontypridd) for Watkins (73).

Scorers: T: Wyatt (2), M.Williams (2), Llewellyn. C: Davies. PG: Davies (3).

Romania: V.Maftei (Cluj); I.Rotaru (Dinamo), R.S.Gontineac (Pau), G.Solomie (Timisoara), L.Colceriu (Steaua); S.Guranescu (Dinamo), M.Iacob (Dinamo); D.Nicolae (Romans), M.Radoi (Dinamo), A.Salageanu (Dinamo), C.Branescu (Farul), V.Nedelcu (Dinamo), F.Corodeanu (Steaua), E.Septar (Farul), O.Slusariuc (Dinamo).

Replacements: P.Mitu (Steaua) for Maftei (8), G.Vlad (Narbonne) for Nicolae (37), T.E.Brinza (Narbonne) for Branescu (53), C.Stan (Dinamo) for Salageanu (53), I.Ruxanda (Farul) for Slusariuc (74).

Scorers: T: Solomie (2), Gontineac. C: Guranescu (3).

Referee: C.White (England).

11/11/1997 Wales A 8 New Zealand 51 (Cardiff)

Wales A: M.J.Back (Swansea); G.Thomas (Bridgend), N.Boobyer (Llanelli), J.Lewis (Pontypridd), D.R.James (Pontypridd); B.Hayward (Ebbw Vale), A.P.Moore (Richmond); I.M.Buckett (Swansea), J.Jenkins (Swansea), C.T.Anthony (Swansea), G.O.Llewellyn (Harlequins, capt), C.Stephens (Bridgend), M.Spiller (Pontypridd), M.E.Williams (Pontypridd), C.Wyatt (Llanelli).

Replacements: L.Jarvis (Cardiff) for G.Thomas (45), N.Eynon (Pontypridd) for Buckett (47), D.Thomas (Swansea) for Wyatt (67), W.S.Roy (Pontypridd) for Stephens (78), H.Harries (Harlequins) for Hayward (78).

Scorers: T: James. PG: Hayward.

New Zealand: T.J.Miller (Waikato); T.J.F.Umaga (Wellington), S.J.McLeod (Waikato), W.K.Little (North Harbour), J.T.Lomu (Counties); C.J.Spencer (Auckland), M.D.Robinson (North Harbour); M.R.Allen (Manawatu), A.D.Oliver (Otago), C.K.Barrell (Canterbury), C.C.Riechelmann (Auckland), M.S.B.Cooksley (Waikato), T.J.Blackadder (Canterbury, capt), M.P.Carter (Auckland), S.D.Surridge (Canterbury).

Replacements: A.R.Hopa (Waikato) for Riechelmann (63), G.L.Slater (Taranaki) for Barrell (69).

Scorers: T: McLeod (2), Carter, Lomu, Miller, Oliver, Robinson. C: Spencer (5). PG: Spencer (2).

Referee: J.Pearson (England).

18/11/1997 France A 21 South Africa 7 (Toulon)

France A: N.Brusque (Pau); P.Bondouy (Toulouse), F.Leloir (Pau), J-M.Aue (Castres), D.Bory (Montferrand); B.Bellot (Perpignan), P.Mignoni (Beziers); C.Soulette (Beziers), Y.Bru (Colomiers), R.Crespy (Brive), H.Miorin (Toulouse), T.Cleda (Pau), N.Bacque (Pau), T.Lievremont (Perpignan, capt), P.Tabacco (Colomiers).

Replacement: P.Escalle (Castres) for Brusque (40).

Scorers: T: Bondouy, Cleda. C: Bellot. PG: Bellot (3).

South Africa: G.M.Delport (Gauteng); B.Paulse (W Province), J.W.Gillingham (Gauteng), P.F.Smith (Gauteng), McN.Hendricks (Boland); J.C.Wessels (Griqualand West), D.J.Van Zyl (Mpumalanga); A-H.Le Roux (OFS), D.Santon (Boland), D.F.Theron (Griqualand West), W.W.Basson (N Transvaal), W.W.Els (OFS), A.D.Aitken (W Province, capt), W.G.Brosnihan (OFS), R.B.Skinstad (W Province).

Replacements: A.E.Drotske (OFS) for Santon (26), A.G.Venter (OFS) for Basson (8-21).

Scorer: T: Smith. C: Smith.

Referee: H.A.Smith (Ireland).

26/11/1997 Ireland A 26 Canada 10 (Ravenhill)

Ireland A: C.P.Clarke (Terenure College); D.W.O'Mahony (Moseley), P.Duignan (Galway), M.Lynch (Young Munster), J.P.J.McWeeney (St Mary's College); P.A.Burke (Bristol), B.Free (Saracens); J.M.Fitzpatrick (London Irish), W.J.M.Mulcahy (Skerries), P.M.N.Clohessy (Young Munster), G.M.Fulcher (London Irish, capt), B.Cusack (Bath), S.D.Corkery (Bristol), A.Quinlan (Shannon), S.Easterby (Leeds).

Replacements: G.Easterby (Rotherham) for Free (40), J.P.Bishop (London Irish) for McWeeney (69-72).

Scorers: T: O'Mahony, Clohessy. C: Burke (2). PG: Burke (4).

Canada: J.Pagano (Yeomen); C.D.Smith (Meraloma), C.Robertson (Montreal Wanderers), R.Toews (Meraloma), D.C.Lougheed (Balmy Beach); R.P.Ross (Cardiff), R.Card (Oak Bay Castaways); E.A.Evans (IBM Japan), K.Morgan (Ajax Wanderers), J.Thiel (Bayside), A.Healy (James Bay), G.Rowlands (Saskatchewan), J.R.Hutchinson (IBM Japan), C.J.McKenzie (Burnaby Lake, capt), R.Robson (James Bay AA).

Replacements: J.D.Graf (UBCOB) for Card (55), A.J.Charron (Moseley) for Robson (57), M.B.James (Perpignan) for Rowlands (60), W.Stanley (Blackheath) for Lougheed (66).

Scorer: T: Ross. C: Ross. PG: Ross.

Referee: C.White (England)

02/12/1997 England A 19 New Zealand 30 (Leicester)

England A: T.R.G.Stimpson (Newcastle); S.Brown (Richmond), S.Potter (Leicester), M.C.Allen (Northampton), A.A.Adebayo (Bath); R.de V.Butland (Bath), S.Benton (Gloucester); C.G.Rowntree (Leicester), M.P.Regan (Bath), P.J.Vickery (Gloucester), D.Sims (Gloucester), R.Fidler (Gloucester), R.H.J.Jenkins (Harlequins), B.B.Clarke (Richmond, capt), P.H.Sanderson (Sale).

Replacements: V.E.Ubogu (Bath) for Vickery (57), R.Winters (Bedford) for Jenkins (65), M.S.Mapletoft (Gloucester) for Butland (71).

Scorers: T: Benton. C: Stimpson. PG: Stimpson (4).

New Zealand: T.J.Miller (Waikato); T.J.F.Umaga (Wellington), A.I.Ieremia (Wellington), S.J.McLeod (Waikato), G.M.Osborne (North Harbour); C.J.Spencer (Auckland), M.D.Robinson (North Harbour); M.R.Allen (Manawatu), A.D.Oliver (Otago), G.L.Slater (Taranaki), M.S.B.Cooksley (Counties), C.C.Riechelmann (Auckland), M.P.Carter (Auckland), S.D.Surridge (Canterbury), T.J.Blackadder (Canterbury, capt).

Replacements: J.P.Preston (Wellington) for Robinson (29), A.F.Blowers (Auckland) for Carter (40), A.R.Hopa (Waikato) for Cooksley (72).

Scorers: T: McLeod, Oliver, Riechelmann, Umaga. C: Spencer (2). PG: Spencer, Preston.

Referee: A.Lewis (Wales).

06/02/1998 Ireland A 9 Scotland A 11 (Donnybrook)

Ireland A: K.W.Nowlan (St Mary's College); J.Cunningham (Ballymena), K.Keane (Garryowen), M.Lynch (Young Munster), D.W.O'Mahony (Moseley); P.A.Burke (Bristol, capt), S.Bell (Dungannon); J.M.Fitzpatrick (London Irish), A.T.H.Clarke (Northampton), G.Walsh (Garryowen), M.J.Galwey (Shannon), B.Cusack (Bath), A.Quinlan (Shannon), D.J.Erskine (Sale), D.O'Grady (Sale).

Replacements: G.Longwell (Ballymena) for Cusack (76), D.Wallace (Garryowen) for Quinlan (76).

Scorer: PG: Burke (3).

Scotland A: H.R.Gilmour (Heriot's); S.L.Longstaff (Dundee HSFP), A.G.Shiel (Melrose), J.McLaren (Stirling Co), J.A.Kerr (Watsonians); D.W.Hodge (Watsonians), B.W.Redpath (Melrose, capt); P.H.Wright (West of Scotland), K.D.McKenzie (Stirling Co), W.Anderson (Kirkcaldy), S.Murray (Bedford), A.Lucking (Currie), E.W.Peters (Bath), T.C.Pountney (Northampton), S.J.Reid (Boroughmuir).

Replacements: S.J.Brotherstone (Melrose) for McKenzie (73), G.McIlwham (Glasgow Hawks) for Anderson (73).

Scorers: T: Longstaff. PG: Hodge (2).

Referee: N.Williams (Wales).

06/02/1998 France A 32 England A 17 (Tours)

France A: R.Dourthe (Dax); M.Biboulet (Colomiers), S.Roque (Colomiers), J-M.Aue (Castres), D.Bory (Montferrand); B.Bellot (Perpignan), C.Laussucq (Stade Francais/CASG); P.Collazo (Begles-Bordeaux), P.Bru (Colomiers), J-M.Gonzales (Pau), Y.Manhes (Brive), F.Belot (Toulouse), M.Raynaud (Narbonne, capt), P.Raschi (Bourgoin-Jallieu), R.Castel (Beziers).

Replacements: S.Marconnet (Stade Francais/CASG) for Collazo (58), T.Mentieres (Pau) for Manhes (69).

Scorers: T: Laussucq (2), Collazo, Raynaud. C: Bellot (3). PG: Bellot (2).

England A: C.Catling (Gloucester); B.G.W.Johnson (Gloucester), N.J.J.Greenstock (Wasps), M.C.Allen (Northampton), D.Chapman (Richmond); M.S.Mapletoft (Gloucester), A.C.T.Gomarsall (Wasps); D.Molloy (Wasps), G.Chuter (Saracens),

V.E.Ubogu (Bath), R.Fidler (Gloucester), S.D.Shaw (Wasps), M.E.Corry (Leicester), B.B.Clarke (Richmond), R.H.J.Jenkins (Harlequins).

Replacements: S.C.W.Ravenscroft (Saracens) for Catling (68), C.Gillies (Richmond) for Fidler (70).

Scorers: T: Chuter. PG: Mapletoft (4).

Referee: C.Muir (Scotland).

20/02/1998 England A 22 Wales A 41 (Leicester)

England A: C.Catling (Gloucester); B.G.W.Johnson (Gloucester), J.J.N.Baxendell (Sale), M.C.Allen (Northampton), A.A.Adebayo (Bath); M.S.Mapletoft (Gloucester), A.C.T.Gomarsall (Wasps); V.E.Ubogu (Bath), G.Chuter (Saracens), W.R.Green (Wasps), C.Gillies (Richmond), S.D.Shaw (Wasps), R.H.J.Jenkins (Harlequins), B.B.Clarke (Richmond, capt), P.H.Sanderson (Sale).

Replacements: R.Winters (Bedford) for Clarke (56-62), N.J.J.Greenstock (Wasps) for Allen (73).

Scorers: T: Ubogu. C: Mapletoft. PG: Mapletoft (4). DG: Mapletoft.

Wales A: K.A.Morgan (Pontypridd); G.Wyatt (Pontypridd), M.Taylor (Swansea), J.Lewis (Pontypridd), D.R.James (Pontypridd); B.Hayward (Ebbw Vale), A.P.Moore (Richmond); A.Griffiths (Pontypridd), G.R.Jenkins (Swansea), C.T.Anthony (Swansea), W.S.Roy (Pontypridd), A.P.Moore (Swansea), M.Lloyd (Pontypridd), C.Wyatt (Llanelli), P.K.B.Jones (Ebbw Vale, capt).

Replacements: I.Boobyer (Neath) for Lloyd (64), V.Cooper (Llanelli) for Wyatt (59-66) and for Roy (70).

Scorers: T: James, Hayward, Moore (Richmond), Jenkins. C: Hayward (3). PG: Hayward (5).

Referee: E.Murray (Scotland).

20/02/1998 Scotland A 24 France A 20 (Goldenacre)

Scotland A: H.R.Gilmour (Heriot's); C.A.Joiner (Leicester), C.A.Murray (Hawick), I.C.Jardine (Stirling Co), J.A.Kerr (Watsonians); D.W.Hodge (Watsonians), B.W.Redpath (Melrose, capt); P.H.Wright (West of Scotland), S.J.Brotherstone (Melrose), W.Anderson (Kirkcaldy), S.Murray (Bedford), R.Metcalfe (Newcastle), E.W.Peters (Bath), S.J.Reid (Boroughmuir), T.C.Pountney (Northampton).

Replacements: D.Officer (Currie) for Jardine (42), G.McIlwham (Glasgow Hawks) for Wright (60).

Scorers: T: Gilmour, Hodge. C: Hodge. PG: Hodge (4).

France A: R.Dourthe (Dax); M.Biboulet (Colomiers), J-M.Aue (Castres), J.Sieurac (Colomiers), F.Schisano (Narbonne); M.Carre (Colomiers), A.Hueber (Toulon); P.Collazo (Begles-Bordeaux), M.De Rougemont (Toulon), J-M.Gonzales (Pau), F.Belot (Toulouse), Y.Manhes (Brive), M.Raynaud (Narbonne, capt), P.Raschi (Bourgoin), B.De Giusti (Colomiers).

Replacements: R.Castel (Beziers) for De Giusti (40), C.Porcu (Agen) for Manhes (40).

Scorers: T: Sieurac, Hueber, Raschi. C: Dourthe. PG: Dourthe.

Referee: H.A.Smith (Ireland).

06/03/1998 France A 30 Ireland A 30 (Quimper)

France A: N.Brusque (Pau); M.Biboulet (Colomiers), L.Lafforgue (Begles-Bordeaux), J.Sieurac (Colomiers), S.Roque (Colomiers); B.Bellot (Perpignan), S.Castaignede (Montferrand); M.De Rougemont (Toulon), W.Taofifenua (Grenoble), J-M.Gonzales (Pau), Y.Manhes (Brive), F.Belot (Toulouse, capt), B.De Giusti (Colomiers), E.Gouloumet (Biarritz Stade), L.Mallier (Grenoble).

Replacements: P.Bondouy (Narbonne) for Biboulet (57), P.Colazzo (Begles-Bordeaux) for Taofifenua (71), C.Dongieu (Begles-Bordeaux) for Manhes (79).

Scorers: T: Bellot (2), Biboulet, Gonzales. C: Bellot (2). PG: Bellot (2).

Ireland A: K.W.Nowlan (St Mary's College); J.P.J.McWeeney (St Mary's College), K.Keane (Garryowen), M.Murphy (Galway), D.W.O'Mahony (Moseley); P.A.Burke (Bristol, capt), S.C.McIvor (Garryowen); J.M.Fitzpatrick (London Irish), A.T.H.Clarke (Northampton), G.Walsh (Garryowen), G.M.Fulcher (London Irish), G.Longwell (Ballymena), E.O.Halvey (Shannon), D.Wallace (Garryowen), D.J.Erskine (Sale).

Scorers: T: McWeeney, Longwell. C: Burke. PG: Burke (6).

Referee: A.Davies (Wales).

06/03/1998 Wales A 10 Scotland A 18 (Newport)

Wales A: W.J.L.Thomas (Cardiff); G.Wyatt (Pontypridd), J.Lewis (Pontypridd), N.Boobyer (Llanelli), D.R.James (Pontypridd); B.Hayward (Ebbw Vale), A.P.Moore (Richmond, capt); A.Griffiths (Pontypridd), B.H.Williams (Richmond), C.T.Anthony (Swansea), G.O.Llewellyn (Harlequins), C.Stephens (Bridgend), M.Lloyd (Pontypridd), C.Wyatt (Llanelli), M.E.Williams (Pontypridd).

Replacements: I.Boobyer (Neath) for Lloyd (54), R.C.McBryde (Llanelli) for B.Williams (62).

Scorers: T: Lloyd. C: Hayward. PG: Hayward.

Scotland A: H.R.Gilmour (Heriot's); K.McK.Logan (Wasps), D.Officer (Currie), J.McLaren (Stirling Co), J.A.Kerr (Watsonians); D.W.Hodge (Watsonians), G.G.Burns (Watsonians); P.H.Wright (West of Scotland), S.J.Brotherstone (Melrose), W.Anderson (Kirkcaldy), S.Murray (Bedford), R.Metcalfe (Newcastle), P.Walton (Newcastle), S.J.Reid (Boroughmuir, capt), G.N.Flockhart (Stirling Co).

Replacements: G.Metcalfe (Glasgow Hawks) for McLaren (64), C.Mather (Watsonians) for Walton (78), G.McIlwham (Glasgow Hawks) for Wright (69), G.Perrett (West of Scotland) for Metcalfe (2-17).

Scorers: T: Logan, Brotherstone. C: Hodge. PG: Hodge (2).

Referee: P.Thomas (France).

20/03/1998 Ireland A 27 Wales A 42 (Limerick)

Ireland A: K.W.Nowlan (St Mary's College); J.P.J.McWeeney (St Mary's College), K.Keane (Garryowen), M.Murphy (Galway), D.W.O'Mahony (Moseley); P.A.Burke (Bristol, capt), S.C.McIvor (Garryowen); J.M.Fitzpatrick (London Irish), A.T.H.Clarke (Northampton), G.Walsh (Garryowen), G.M.Fulcher (London Irish), G.Longwell (Ballymena), E.O.Halvey (Shannon), D.Wallace (Garryowen), K.Dawson (London Irish).

Replacements: M.Lynch (Young Munster) for Burke (54), B.Jackman (Clontarf) for Clarke (62), G.Leslie (Dungannon) for Walsh (71), B.Cusack (Bath) for Longwell (71), D.J.Erskine (Sale) for Fulcher (79).

Scorers: T: McWeeney, Burke, McIvor. C: Burke (2), Keane. PG: Burke (2).

Wales A: W.J.L.Thomas (Cardiff); G.Wyatt (Pontypridd), D.R.James (Pontypridd), J.Lewis (Pontypridd), R.Rees (Swansea); A.C.Thomas (Swansea), A.P.Moore (Richmond, capt); A.Griffiths (Pontypridd), R.C.McBryde (Llanelli), C.T.Anthony (Swansea), G.O.Llewellyn (Harlequins), C.Stephens (Bridgend), M.Lloyd (Pontypridd), C.Wyatt (Llanelli), M.E.Williams (Pontypridd).

Replacements: D.Weatherley (Swansea) for W.Thomas (31), C.Warlow (Llanelli) for G.Wyatt (74), I.Boobyer (Neath) for C.Wyatt (77), N.Eynon (Pontypridd) for Williams (83).

Scorers: T: Weatherley (2), A.Thomas, Moore, C.Wyatt. C: A.Thomas (4), PG: A.Thomas (3).

Referee: J.Gastou (France).

20/03/1998 Scotland A 42 England A 14 (Inverleith)

Scotland A: R.J.S.Shepherd (Melrose); G.Metcalfe (Glasgow Hawks), D.Officer (Currie), B.R.S.Eriksson (London Scottish), J.A.Kerr (Watsonians); D.W.Hodge (Watsonians), G.G.Burns (Watsonians); G.McIlwham (Glasgow Hawks), S.J.Brotherstone (Melrose), W.Anderson (Kirkcaldy), S.Murray (Bedford), R.Metcalfe (Newcastle), P.Walton (Newcastle), S.J.Reid (Boroughmuir, capt), G.N.Flockhart (Stirling Co).

Replacements: M.Proudfoot (Melrose) for Anderson (54), C.Mather (Watsonians) for Walton (54).

Scorers: T: Officer (2), Kerr, Hodge, Reid, pen try. C: Hodge (3). PG: Hodge (2).

England A: C.Catling (Gloucester); B.G.W.Johnson (Gloucester), N.J.J.Greenstock (Wasps), M.C.Allen (Northampton), D.Chapman (Richmond); R.de V.Butland (Bath), P.C.Richards (London Irish); D.M.Barnes (Newcastle), M.P.Regan (Bath), V.E.Ubogu (Bath), C.Gillies (Richmond), R.Fidler (Gloucester), R.Winters (Bedford), B.B.Clarke (Richmond, capt), P.H.Sanderson (Sale).

Replacements: M.Shaw (Newcastle) for Allen (37), R.H.J.Jenkins (Harlequins) for Sanderson (54), J.Lewsey (Bristol) for Butland (69), C.Harrison (Orrell) for Richards (69), J.A.H.Mallett (Bath) for Ubogu (69), G.Chuter (Saracens) for Catling (74).

Scorers: T: Chapman. PG: Butland (3).

Referee: G.Borreani (France).

03/04/1998 Wales A 18 France A 27 (Bridgend)

Wales A: W.J.L.Thomas (Cardiff); S.D.Hill (Cardiff), J.Lewis (Pontypridd), M.Taylor (Swansea), R.Rees (Swansea); A.C.Thomas (Swansea), A.P.Moore (Richmond, capt); A.Griffiths (Pontypridd), R.C.McBryde (Llanelli), C.T.Anthony (Swansea), C.Stephens (Bridgend), G.O.Llewellyn (Harlequins), M.Lloyd (Pontypridd), C.Wyatt (Llanelli), I.Boobyer (Neath).

Replacements: D.Thomas (Swansea) for Boobyer (50), D.Llewellyn (Ebbw Vale) for Lewis (67), D.Weatherley (Swansea) for Moore (70), I.Gough (Newport) for Stephens (70).

Scorers: T: Wyatt, D.Thomas. C: A.Thomas. PG: A.Thomas (2).

France A: P.Fauthoux (Begles-Bordeaux); C.Heymans (Agen), J-C.Cistacq (Agen), D.Plana (Perpignan), P.Bondouy (Narbonne); B.Bellot (Perpignan), C.Laussucq (Stade Français); P.Colazzo (Begles-Bordeaux), M.De Rougemont (Toulon), J-M.Gonzales (Pau), F.Belot (Toulouse, capt), J.Daude (Bourgoin), M.Raynaud (Narbonne), E.Goulmoumet (Biarritz Stade), G.Combes (Aurillac).

Replacements: G.Sudre (Agen) for Laussucq (60), L.Mallier (Brive) for Combes (58), D.Barrier (Montferrand) for Goulmoumet (70), S.De Besombes (Perpignan) for Colazzo (58).

Scorers: T: Fauthoux, Plana, pen try. C: Bellot (3). PG: Bellot (2).

Referee: I.Ramage (Scotland).

03/04/1998 England A 40 Ireland A 30 (Richmond)

England A: T.R.G.Stimpson (Newcastle); S.Brown (Richmond), P.Mensah (Harlequins), S.C.W.Ravenscroft (Saracens), D.Chapman (Richmond); J.Lewsey (Bristol), P.C.Richards (London Irish); D.M.Barnes (Newcastle), P.B.T.Greening (Gloucester), J.A.H.Mallett (Bath), R.Fidler (Gloucester), C.Gillies (Richmond), R.H.J.Jenkins (Harlequins, capt), B.Sturnham (Saracens), R.J.Hutton (Richmond).

Replacements: M.Cornwell (Gloucester) for Gillies (65), W.R.Green (Wasps) for Mallett (69), A.Bennett (Saracens) for Jenkins (69), A.D.King (Wasps) for Stimpson (75), G.Chuter (Saracens) for Greening (77), M.C.Allen (Northampton) for Hutton (78).

Scorers: T: Brown, Mensah, Lewsey, Fidler, Gillies, Sturnham. C: Stimpson (2). PG: Stimpson (2).

Ireland A: S.McDowell (Ballymena); J.P.J.McWeeney (St Mary's College), M.Murphy (Galway), N.K.P.Woods (London Irish), P.Duignan (Galway); B.Everitt (Garryowen), S.C.McIvor (Garryowen); J.M.Fitzpatrick (London Irish), B.Jackman (Clontarf), G.Walsh (Garryowen), B.Cusack (Bath), G.M.Fulcher (London Irish, capt), T.Brennan (Bective R), D.O'Cuinneagain (Sale), K.Dawson (London Irish).

Replacements: M.A.McDermott (Shannon) for Jackman (26), A.G.Foley (Shannon) for Dawson (65), D.J.Crotty (Garryowen) for McWeeney (68), S.Leahy (Garryowen) for Fulcher (77).

Scorers: T: McWeeney, Murphy, Everitt. C: Woods (3). PG: Woods (3).

Referee: G.Morandin (Italy).

Rugby World Cup 1999

By the time the two finalists run out onto pitch at the new Millennium Stadium in Cardiff on 6 November next year the RWC99 tournament will have been running for three years, a time span that will have encompassed 178 matches. The third biggest sporting event in the world, behind football's World Cup and the Olympics, RWC99 kicked off in Riga back on 26 September 1996 when Latvia defeated Norway 44-6 at the old University Stadium. Since then the RWC flag has been seen fluttering the world over – the Cook Islands, Moldova, Barbados, Tunisia, Sri Lanka, Tahiti, Uruguay, Kenya and all points west. The competition's main purpose during these early stages was to give all the developing rugby nations something to focus their efforts on and attract local commercial concerns to offer long-term financial support. As the shake-up got under way all manner of stories unfolded. Frano Botica, a World Cup medallist with New Zealand in 1987, returned to the land of his father to play for Croatia, along with a number of first-generation New Zealanders such as Pau's combative flanker Scott Keith. Then there was plucky Andorra beating favourites Sweden in their group and feeling encouraged to appoint their first professional player as a result. In the Pacific, the tiny Cook Islands showed up well before running into the might of Fiji and Tonga, while Chile, where the game is really taking a hold at junior level, nearly pipped Uruguay for the fourth spot in the Americas qualifying tournament in Buenos Aires this summer. The European seeding tournaments will be held at Huddersfield, Lansdowne Road and Murrayfield in November and December 1998 with England playing Italy and Holland, while Ireland will meet Romania and surprise qualifiers Georgia. Scotland, meanwhile, will entertain Spain and Portugal.

Rugby World Cup Qualifying rounds

EUROPE

Round A, Pool 1
Ukraine 60 Yugoslavia 0 (Kiev); Austria 3 Yugoslavia 0 (w/o); Switzerland 0 Ukraine 30 (Nyon); Israel 15 Austria 3 (Tel Aviv); Israel 9 Switzerland 9 (Tel Aviv); Yugoslavia 8 Israel 0 (Belgrade); Austria 6 Ukraine 36 (Vienna); Yugoslavia 10 Israel 7 (Belgrade); Ukraine 51 Israel 15 (Odessa); Switzerland 31 Austria 3 (Basle). Pool winners: Ukraine.

Round A, Pool 2
Latvia 44 Norway 6 (Riga); Bulgaria 6 Moldova 14 (Sofia); Norway 7 Croatia 43 (Oslo); Moldova 3 Latvia 8 (Chisinau); Bulgaria 31 Croatia 46 (Sofia); Moldova 31 Norway 7 (Chisinau); Latvia 89 Bulgaria 0 (Riga); Croatia 60 Moldova 5 (Split); Croatia 43 Latvia 24 (Makarska); Norway 22 Bulgaria 7 (Oslo). Pool winners: Croatia.

Round A, Pool 3
Lithuania 26 Luxembourg 3 (Vilnius); Andorra 54 Lithuania 24 (Andorra La Vella); Sweden 39 Hungary 17 (Vanersborg); Luxembourg 3 Hungary 12 (Cessange); Andorra 21 Sweden 20 (Andorra La Vella); Luxembourg 16 Andorra 30 (Luxembourg); Sweden 48 Luxembourg 5 (Karlskrona); Lithuania 17 Sweden 84 (Plunge); Hungary 16 Lithuania 3 (Budapest); Hungary 5 Andorra 34 (Budapest). Pool winners: Andorra.

Round B, Pool 1
Georgia 29 Croatia 15 (Tbilisi); Denmark 8 Georgia 19 (Copenhagen); Croatia 23 Russia 16 (Makarska); Italy 102 Denmark 3 (Brescia), Italy 31 Georgia 14

(L'Aquila); Russia 18 Italy 48 (Krasnoiarsk); Russia 45 Denmark 9 (Penza); Denmark 6 Croatia 40 (Aalborg); Georgia 12 Russia 6 (Tbilisi); Croatia 27 Italy 39 (Makarska).

Round B, Pool 2
Belgium 13 Romania 83 (Brussels); Ukraine 45 Belgium 5 (Kiev); Netherlands 49 Poland 7 (Amsterdam); Netherlands 35 Ukraine 13 (Amsterdam); Poland 30 Belgium 10 (Gdynia); Belgium 16 Netherlands 19 (Brussels); Romania 42 Netherlands 3 (Bucharest); Romania 74 Poland 13 (Bucharest); Poland 8 Ukraine 18 (Gdansk); Ukraine 17 Romania 39 (Kharkov).

Round B, Pool 3
Czech Republic 45 Andorra 20 (Prague); Andorra 11 Germany 56 (Andorra La Vella); Germany 31 Czech Republic 17 (Hanover); Andorra 3 Spain 62 (Andorra la Vella); Spain 39 Czech Republic 8 (Santander); Portugal 30 Germany 6 (Lisbon); Czech Republic 10 Portugal 15 (Prague); Germany 9 Spain 24 (Heidelberg); Spain 33 Portugal 22 (Madrid); Portugal 53 Andorra 11 (Lousa).

PACIFIC

Round A
Cook Islands 22 Papua New Guinea 19 (Rarotonga); Papua New Guinea 92 Tahiti 6 (Port Moresby); Tahiti 0 Cook Islands 40 (Papeete). Pool winners: Cook Islands.

Round B
Fiji 20 Tonga 10 (Suva); Cook Islands 7 Fiji 53 (Raratonga); Tonga 68 Cook Islands 12 (Nuku'Alofa). Pool winners: Fiji. Tonga also progress to Round C.

ASIA

Round A
Singapore 11 Thailand 16 (Singapore); Thailand 15 Sri Lanka 30 (Bangkok); Sri Lanka 18 Singapore 15 (Kuala Lumpur). Pool winners: Sri Lanka.

Round B
Malaysia 15 Sri Lanka 37 (Kuala Lumpur); Chinese Taipei 51 Malaysia 13 (Taiwan); Sri Lanka 29 Chinese Taipei 34 (Bangkok). Pool winners: Chinese Taipei.

AFRICA

Round A
Arabian Gulf 53 Botswana 13 (Bahrain); Zambia 30 Arabian Gulf 44 (Ndola); Botswana 13 Zambia 20 (Jwaneng). Pool winners: Arabian Gulf.

Round B
Kenya 37 Arabian Gulf 18 (Nairobi); Arabian Gulf 12 Tunisia 11 (Bahrain); Tunisia 52 Kenya 5 (Tunis). Pool winners: Tunisia.

Round C
Zimbabwe 43 Tunisia 9 (Bulawayo) Tunisia 20 Namibia 17 (Tunis); Namibia 32 Zimbabwe 26 (Windhoek). Namibia and Zimbabwe progress to Africa play-off.

AMERICAS

Round A, Pool 1
Trinidad & Tobago 41 Brazil 0 (Port of Spain); Brazil bt Guyana (w/o); Trinidad & Tobago bt Guyana (w/o). Pool winners: Trinidad & Tobago.

Round A, Pool 2
Bahamas 3 Bermuda 24 (Nassau); Barbados 23 Bahamas 37 (Bridgetown); Bermuda 52 Barbados 3 (Hamilton). Pool winners: Bermuda.

Round B
Trinidad & Tobago 6 Chile 35 (Port of Spain); Bermuda 52 Trinidad & Tobago 6 (Hamilton); Chile 65 Bermuda 8 (Santiago). Pool winners: Chile.

Round C
Chile 54 Paraguay 6 (Santiago); Uruguay 20 Chile 14 (Punta del Este); Paraguay 3 Uruguay 43 (Asuncion). Pool winners: Uruguay.

Qualifying groups:

Americas (Buenos Aires): 15 August Argentina v USA, Canada v Uruguay; 19 August Canada v USA, Argentina v Uruguay; 23 August USA v Uruguay, Argentina v Canada.

Africas (Casablanca): 12 September Morocco v Zimbabwe, Cote D'Ivoire v Namibia; 16 September Cote D'Ivoire v Zimbabwe, Morocco v Namibia; 19 September Zimbabwe v Namibia, Cote D'Ivoire v Morocco.

Pacific (Sydney, Canberra, Brisbane): 18 September (Sydney) Australia v Fiji, Western Samoa v Tonga; 22 September (Canberra) Australia v Tonga, Fiji v Western Samoa; 26 September (Brisbane) Australia v Western Samoa, Tonga v Fiji.

Asia (Singapore): 24 October Japan v Korea, Hong Kong v Chinese Taipei; 27 October Japan v Chinese Taipei, Hong Kong v Korea; 31 October Korea v Chinese Taipei, Japan v Hong Kong.

Europe (Huddersfield, Dublin, Edinburgh): (Huddersfield) 14 November England v Netherlands, 18 November Italy v Netherlands, 22 November England v Italy; (Dublin) 14 November Ireland v Georgia, 18 November Georgia v Romania, 22 Novemebr Ireland v Romania; (Murrayfield) 28 November Scotland v Portugal, 2 December Portugal v Spain, 5 December Scotland v Spain.

RWC Women's World Cup

New Zealand, with the full financial and logistical backing of the New Zealand Rugby Union, took the women's game onto a different plane during a glorious two-week exhibition of rugby at the third Women's World Cup at the Dutch National Rugby Centre in Amsterdam. During the course of five games they amassed 344 points and conceded just three tries, completing their masterclass by defeating USA 44-12 in the final.

Women's rugby the New Zealand way is played with pace, skill and athleticism. They have attracted the top female athletes from the country – netball, softball, lacrosse, hockey – and moulded them into a stylish, graceful side around which the women's game worldwide can develop. Individually there were many players to admire: prolific wing Vanessa Cootes who has scored a staggering 35 tries in 9 Tests, razor-sharp full-back Tammi Wilson, fly-half Anna Richards, No 8 Rochelle Martin and flanker Melodie Robinson who is a former Miss Canterbury. Possibly the pick of the bunch was Annaleah Rush, a hugely skilful centre and formidable competitor.

Only England and USA, the finalists in 1994, were capable of living with the All Blacks and it was England's misfortune to meet them at the semi-final stage, when the 44-11 scoreline did scant justice to their efforts in freakish 90-degree temperatures. The disparity between the world's top teams was emphasised when England defeated Canada 81-15 in the 3rd-4th place play-off game.

Though the big three are disappearing into the distance, the general standard has also risen remarkably since 1994. The pace is quicker, the tackles more ferocious and the skill levels noticeably higher, especially in the kicking department. Spain epitomised this and were cruelly denied a chance of challenging for the plate trophy by an unlucky defeat against Australia, courtesy of a last-minute penalty decision. Undeterred, the Spanish clinched 7th place with a 22-9 win over France.

Kazakhstan were possibly the surprise team of the tournament, defeating Sweden, Wales and Ireland (twice) to claim the Bowl final. In fly-half and captain Alfia Tamaeva they possessed one of the most naturally gifted players on view, an individual who could have stepped into the New Zealand squad and still shone. How a young student in the largely desert state of Kazakhstan could have picked up such skills almost defies belief, but is one of the reasons rugby can seriously hope, one day, to become a truly worldwide game.

The International Rugby Board clearly think so and are to be congratulated for contributing close on £500,000 to the organisation of the competition. Women's rugby is here to stay and if nurtured will benefit the game in general.

New Zealand: T.Wilson; V.Cootes, A.Rush, S.Shortland, L.Wall; A.Richards, M.Hirovanaa; T.Waters, F.Palmer (capt), R.Sheck, F.King, F.Richards, M.Robinson, D.White, R.Martin.

Scorers: T: Cootes (5), Wall, Palmer, Sheck. C: Rush (2).

USA: J.Crawford; K.McFarren, P.Jervey, A.Westerman, K.Cyganik; J.Bergmann, L.Rowe; M.Ottens, S.Boyle, A.Sorensen, N.Fit, A.Williams, K.Kim, D.Schnapp, B.Bond.

Scorers: T: Crawford, Schnapp. C: Bergmann.

Referee: E.Morrison (RFU).

Results

Round 1:
Canada 16 Netherlands 7; Spain 38 Wales 18; New Zealand 134 Germany 6;
France 23 Kazakhstan 6; USA 84 Russia 0; England 75 Sweden 0; Australia 21
Ireland 0; Scotland 37 Italy 8.

Round 2:
England 72 Canada 6; Netherlands 44 Sweden 0; USA 38 Spain 16; Wales 83
Russia 7; New Zealand 76 Scotland 0; Italy 34 Germany 5; France 10 Australia 8;
Kazakhstan 12 Ireland 6.

Quarter-finals:
Cup: USA 25 Scotland 10; Canada 9 France 7; England 30 Australia 13; New
Zealand 46 Spain 3. Shield/Plate/Bowl: Italy 51 Russia 7; Kazakhstan 47 Sweden 5;
Ireland 21 Netherlands 18; Wales 55 Germany 12.

Semi-finals:
Cup: England 11 New Zealand 44; USA 46 Canada 6. Plate: Australia 17 Spain 15;
Scotland 27 France 7. Bowl: Kazakhstan 18 Wales 13; Ireland 20 Italy 5.
Shield: Netherlands 61 Russia 0; Germany 20 Sweden 18.

Plate Final:
Australia 25 Scotland 15.

Bowl Final:
Kazakhstan 26 Ireland 10.

Shield Final:
Netherlands 67 Germany 3.

Final placings:
1 New Zealand; 2 USA; 3 England; 4 Canada; 5 Australia; 6 Scotland; 7 Spain; 8
France; 9 Kazakhstan; 10 Ireland; 11 Wales; 12 Italy; 13 Netherlands; 14 Germany;
15 Sweden; 16 Russia.

IRB/FIRA World Youth Championship

Ireland, improving out of all recognition as the tournament progressed, silenced a partisan 9,000 crowd at the Sept Deniers Stadium in Toulouse to emerge as surprise winners of the IRB/FIRA World Youth (U19) Championship by defeating France 18-0. Ireland's victory was based on superlative defence and a willingness to counter-attack whenever possible. They built up a 10-0 half-time lead after centre Brian O'Driscoll kicked a penalty and converted fly-half Patrick Wallace's try. After the break Wallace, whose half-back partnership with London Irish scrum-half Kieran Campbell was the key to Ireland's success, dropped a goal and the result was put beyond doubt when wing Darragh Holt scored a late try.

Though New Zealand, Australia and England declined to enter nobody can argue Ireland enjoyed an easy passage. After defeating USA 47-13 in their opening match they overturned a 17-point deficit to draw 17-17 with South Africa in their final pool game. They 'lost' the penalty shoot-out 4-3 but South Africa were later disqualified as one of their kickers had played no part in the game. In their semi-final Ireland met favourites Argentina, winners of seven of the last ten tournaments, and won 18-3 to progress into the final. Next year's tournament will be held in Wales as part of the build up to RWC99.

Tournament details:

Pool A
Argentina 34 Russia 15; Uruguay 13 Romania 10; France 55 Japan 19; Italy 20 Spain 10; Canada 23 Wales 19; Chile 7 Scotland 3; Ireland 47 USA 13; South Africa 93 Poland 3; Argentina 51 Uruguay 3; Romania 42 Russia 5; France 37 Italy 8; Japan 15 Spain 7; Canada 19 Chile 16; Wales 20 Scotland 7; Ireland 17 South Africa 17; Poland 17 USA 11; Ireland 18 Argentina 3; France 53 Canada 6; South Africa 71 Uruguay 10; Italy 23 Chile 3; Romania 27 Poland 9; Wales 39 Japan 10; Russia 27 USA 17; Scotland 56 Spain 10.

Final:
Ireland 18 France 0. *3/4th play-off*: Argentina 68 Canada 0; *5/6th*: South Africa 52 Italy 15; *7/8th*: Chile 14 Uruguay 13; *9/10th*: Wales 34 Romania 19; *11/12th*: Japan 47 Poland 7; *13/14th*: Scotland 45 Russia 5; *15/16th*: Spain 51 USA 8.

Pool B
Portugal 17 Paraguay 6; Czech Republic 28 Holland 3; Georgia 7 Germany 3; Belgium 15 Morocco 5; Portugal 28 Belgium 9; Georgia 21 Czech Republic 6; Paraguay 15 Morocco 10; Germany 29 Holland 7.

Standings:
17/18th: Georgia 25 Portugal 7; 19/20th: Czech Republic 27 Belgium 21; 21/22nd: Germany 20 Paraguay 3; 23/24th: Morocco 45 Holland 5.

Pool C
Rep of China 15 Sweden 6; Ukraine 26 Croatia 11; Ivory Coast 51 Bulgaria 3; Brazil 20 Andorra 5; Rep of China 13 Brazil 0; Ukraine 31 Ivory Coast 5; Andorra 15 Sweden 10; Croatia 65 Bulgaria 6.

Standings:
25/26th: Ukraine 20 Rep of China 15; 27/28th: Brazil 55 Ivory Coast 3; 29/30th: Croatia 62 Andorra 0; 31/32nd: Sweden 36 Bulgaria 15.

Varsity Match 1997

Cambridge University 29 Oxford University 17 (Twickenham, 9 December 1997)

Cambridge confidently claimed their fourth consecutive victory in one of the better Varsity matches in recent years when, for once, the overriding fear of defeat did not seem to inhibit the contestants. Perhaps all concerned had been inspired by the events of three days before at Twickenham when England and New Zealand had fought out that 26-26 classic. Cambridge made a blistering start and were 14-0 up after the opening quarter with tries from veteran second row and veterinary student Richard Bramley, who was driven over from a line-out, and wing Nick Walne who scooted over after good interplay following a quick tapped penalty. Thereafter Oxford, with former Ireland captain Niall Hogan to the forefront, got their act together and the final hour was keenly contested, much to the enjoyment of a 70,000 crowd watching the 116th meeting between the sides. David Kelaher missed two simple penalty kicks for Oxford before finally locating the target but Cambridge went further ahead after the break with a try from Mark Denney. Back came Oxford with tries for backrow forward Kevin Spicer and wing Nick Booth but Cambridge finished with a flourish, full-back Paul Surridge joining a rolling maul to finally claim the score. 'He'll be fined for that', joked Cambridge coach Tony Rodgers who considered this the best of the four winning performances since 1994. 'Before the game we had been marked down as good in the backs and poor in the forwards. Wrongly so. Today it was good to show that we can mix both styles.'

Oxford University: R.Maher (St Ignatius Coll, Sydney, and University, capt); N.Booth (Lytham St Anne's HS and Worcester), N.Larsen (Hilton Coll, Durban, and Lincoln), B.Rudge (St Edward's Coll, Liverpool, and Keble), R.Pollock (Diocesan Coll, Cape Town, and Keble); T.Jensen (St Edward's Coll, Canberra, and St Anne's), N.Hogan (Terenure Coll, Dublin, and Merton); R.Lehner (Jesuit HS, Sacramento, and St Anne's), M.Collard (King's School, Sydney, and St Anne's), A.Reuben (Solihull School and University), T.Eisenhauer (St Ignatius Coll, Sydney, and St Anne's), A.Roberts (Ampleforth and New), M.Orsler (King's, Canterbury, and Christchurch), D.Kelaher (St Joseph's Coll, Sydney, and St Cross), K.Spicer (Clongowes Wood Coll, Dublin, and St Anne's).

Replacements: G.Lewis (Cheadle Hulme Sch and St Anne's) for Pollock (32), S.van Reenen (Paul Roos Gymnasium, Cape Town, and St Anne's) for Roberts (40), C.Lavin (King Edward's, Lytham, and St Edmund Hall) for Kelaher (83).

Scorers: T: Spicer, Booth. C: Kelaher (2). PG: Kelaher.

Cambridge University: P.Surridge (St Kentigern Coll, NZ, and Hughes Hall); N.Walne (Caerleon CS and St Catharine's), M.Robinson (Opunake HS, NZ, and Hughes Hall), M.Denney (Bedford Modern and St Edmund's), N.Hill (St Ignatius Coll, Sydney, and St Edmunds); R.Ashforth (Bradford GS and Peterhouse), R.Elliott (Durham Sch and St Edmund's); G.Reynolds (Cheshunt Sch and St Edmund's), T.Murphy (St Joseph's, Brisbane, and St Edmund's, capt), M.Foulds (Christ Coll, Canterbury, and Sidney Sussex), R.Bramley (QEGS, Wakefield and St Edmund's), A.Craig (Tauranga Coll, NZ, and Hughes Hall), M.Hyde (St Ignatius Coll, Sydney, and St Edmund's), H.Whitford (The Leys School and Homerton), J.Cocks (Newington Coll, Sydney, and St Edmund's).

Replacements: A.Goldsmith (Oundle and Homerton) for Surridge (80), G.Williams (Hinchingbrook School and Homerton) for Hill (83).

Scorers: T: Bramley, Walne, Denney, Surridge. C: Surridge (3). PG: Surridge.

Referee: B.Campsall (Yorkshire).

Cambridge lead the series 55-48 with 13 matches drawn.

Middlesex and Hong Kong Sevens

Barbarians retained their Middlesex Sevens title at Twickenham with a hard-fought 36-28 victory over Leicester in the final. The select Barbarians side took control after just 30 seconds and never looked like losing, despite a late Tigers rally. Paniela Quaqua grabbed a hat-trick in just five minutes as Leicester were sent reeling by wave after wave of Barbarian attacks. A penalty try and a Tim Barlow score enabled Leicester to salvage some pride but for the Barbarians, victory was never in doubt. Gareth Flockhart and Dave Scully grabbed tries to assure a second successive title.

Both finalists had looked impressive in qualifying. Leicester breezed past Nottingham and London Broncos without breaking sweat and were comfortably the better team in a tough semi-final win over a strong-looking Saracens. The Barbarians also looked powerful in the early stages and with a strong contingent of sevens specialists from World Cup-winning Fiji, always looked like reaching the final.

London Welsh did put up a brave fight in the first round, only to be denied by two late tries by Glasgow's speed merchant Derek Stark. However, Harlequins presented little opposition in the second round and a 38-17 victory set up a fascinating semi-final clash with Kenya, who were making their first appearance at the home of rugby and delighting the Twickenham crowd with their free-flowing game. They claimed the scalps of Chichester and Gloucester before being overrun by the Barbarians just 20 minutes short of a fairytale debut final appearance.

Middlesex Charity Sevens, Twickenham. *1st rd*: Saracens 31 Rosslyn Park 12; Sale 0 Wasps 33; Leicester 35 Nottingham 7; Reading 12 Emerging London Broncos 38; Kenya 24 Chichester Institute of H.E. 5; Gloucester 26 London Nigerians 10; Harlequins 26 Northampton 14; London Welsh 19 The Barbarians 24. *2nd rd*: Saracens 26 Wasps 21; Leicester 31 Emerging London Broncos 0; Kenya 33 Gloucester 7; Harlequins 17 The Barbarians 38. *Semi-finals*: Saracens 14 Leicester 26; Kenya 14 The Barbarians 33. *Final*: Leicester 28 The Barbarians 36.

Middlesex Sevens Past Winners

1926	Harlequins	1949	Heriot's FP
1927	Harlequins	1950	Rosslyn Park
1928	Harlequins	1951	Richmond II
1929	Harlequins	1952	Wasps
1930	London Welsh	1953	Richmond
1931	London Welsh	1954	Rosslyn Park
1932	Blackheath	1955	Richmond
1933	Harlequins	1956	London Welsh
1934	Barbarians	1957	St Luke's College
1935	Harlequins	1958	Blackheath
1936	Sale	1959	Loughborough College
1937	London Scottish	1960	London Scottish
1938	Metropolitan Police	1961	London Scottish
1939	Cardiff	1962	London Scottish
1940	St Mary's Hospital	1963	London Scottish
1941	Cambridge University	1964	Loughborough College
1942	St Mary's Hospital	1965	London Scottish
1943	St Mary's Hospital	1966	Loughborough College
1944	St Mary's Hospital	1967	Harlequins
1945	Nottinghamshire	1968	London Welsh
1946	St Mary's Hospital	1969	St Luke's College
1947	Rosslyn Park	1970	Loughborough College
1948	Wasps	1971	London Welsh

1972	London Welsh	1986	Harlequins
1973	London Welsh	1987	Harlequins
1974	Richmond	1988	Harlequins
1975	Richmond	1989	Harlequins
1976	Loughborough College	1990	Harlequins
1977	Richmond	1991	London Scottish
1978	Harlequins	1992	Western Samoa
1979	Richmond	1993	Wasps
1980	Richmond	1994	Bath
1981	Rosslyn Park	1995	Leicester
1982	Stewart's Melville FP	1996	Wigan RL
1983	Richmond	1997	Barbarians
1984	London Welsh	1998	Barbarians
1985	Wasps		

Hong Kong Sevens

The 1998 Hong Kong Sevens were always going to prove among the most testing in the tournament's history, with the Colony's takeover by China and the growing demands on players worldwide threatening to challenge its pre-eminence. The financial problems of the Far East's Tiger economies also had a role to play, prospective sponsors Peregrine Investments going into receivership just two months before the tournament – the Hong Kong Rugby Union are to be congratulated on moving quickly to secure another blue-chip sponsor, Credit Suisse First Boston. Overall attendances were down – entirely because the number of travelling fans from Britain and Australasia was down by 50 per cent – but the sale of local tickets actually increased, which was encouraging.

On the field nothing changed. Fiji, New Zealand and Western Samoa remained the teams to beat and eventually it was Fiji, led by Waisale Serevi and with the powerful Marika Vunibaka scoring two long-range tries on the wing, who triumphed in the final beating old rivals Western Samoa 28-19. It was an upbeat ending to a disappointing season for Serevi who struggled to command a first-team place at Leicester. New Zealand, with an unusually inexperienced squad, lost 24-17 to the Fijians in the semi-final, while Chester Williams' Springbok side were outclassed 45-7 by Western Samoa.

Championship: *Quarter-finals*: Western Samoa 52 Canada 0; France 19 South Africa 24; Australia 7 Fiji 21; Argentina 7 New Zealand 19. *Semi-finals*: Western Samoa 45 South Africa 7; Fiji 24 New Zealand 17. *Final*: Western Samoa 19 Fiji 28.

Plate: *Quarter-finals*: Korea 24 United States 19; Netherlands 12 Spain 14; Tonga 12 Papua New Guinea 19; Japan 27 Hong Kong 21. *Semi-finals*: Korea 40 Spain 0; Papua New Guinea 26 Japan 12. *Final*: Korea 40 Papua New Guinea 14.

Bowl: *Quarter-finals*: Morocco 29 China 5; Malaysia 26 Singapore 17; Thailand 17 Chinese Taipei 19; Sri Lanka 14 Zimbabwe 36. *Semi-finals*: Morocco 17 Malaysia 10; Chinese Taipei 18 Zimbabwe 7. *Final*: Morocco 31 Chinese Taipei 14.

Hong Kong Sevens Winners

1976	Cantabrians	Plate:	Hong Kong
1977	Fiji	Plate:	Tonga
1978	Fiji	Plate:	Fiji
1979	Australia	Plate:	Papua New Guinea
1980	Fiji	Plate:	Japan
1981	Barbarians	Plate:	Tonga

1982	Australia	Plate:	Korea		
1983	Australia	Plate:	Korea		
1984	Fiji	Plate:	Australia	Bowl:	Sri Lanka
1985	Australia	Plate:	Tonga	Bowl:	Hong Kong
1986	New Zealand	Plate:	USA	Bowl:	Papua New Guinea
1987	New Zealand	Plate:	Fr Barbarians	Bowl:	Hong Kong
1988	Australia	Plate:	USA	Bowl:	Taipei
1989	New Zealand	Plate:	Tonga	Bowl:	Netherlands
1990	Fiji	Plate:	Hong Kong	Bowl:	West Germany
1991	Fiji	Plate:	Argentina	Bowl:	Korea
1992	Fiji	Plate:	Hong Kong	Bowl:	Romania
1993	Western Samoa	Plate:	Tonga	Bowl:	Romania
1994	New Zealand	Plate:	Korea	Bowl:	Hong Kong
1995	New Zealand	Plate:	Canada	Bowl:	Hong Kong
1996	New Zealand	Plate:	France	Bowl:	Japan
1997	No competition				
1998	Fiji	Plate:	Korea	Bowl:	Morocco

Principal Fixtures 1998-99

At the time of going to press, with negotiations concerning the British league ongoing, only the first five weeks of the Allied Dunbar Premiership One season had, unofficially, been released. In addition, ERC Cup and Shield fixtures had yet to be confirmed.

Saturday 15 August

IRU – INTERPROVINCIAL
Connacht v Munster
Leinster v Ulster

Saturday 22 August

IRU – INTERPROVINCIAL
Connacht v Ulster
Munster v Leinster

Saturday 29 August

WRU – LEAGUE
Premier Division
Bridgend v Swansea
Caerphilly v Pontypridd
Cardiff v Neath
Llanelli v Ebbw Vale
Division One
Blackwood v Cross Keys
Dunvant v Aberavon
Llandovery v Bonymaen
Pontypool v Merthyr
Rumney v Newport
South Wales Police v Newbridge
Tredegar v Tondu
Treorchy v Abertillery

IRU – INTERPROVINCIAL
Leinster v Connacht

Saturday 5 September

ALLIED DUNBAR ONE
Bath v Wasps
Gloucester v London Irish
Leicester v Harlequins
London Scottish v Sale
Richmond v Newcastle
Saracens v Northampton

ALLIED DUNBAR TWO
Exeter v Bristol
Fylde v Orrell
Leeds v London Welsh
Moseley v Wakefield
Rugby v Blackheath
Waterloo v Rotherham
Worcester v Coventry

TETLEY'S BITTER CUP
Preliminary Round

SRU – TENNENTS LEAGUE
Premiership One
Currie v Boroughmuir
Glasgow Hawks v Heriot's FP
Jed-Forest v West of Scotland
Stirling County v Hawick
Watsonians v Melrose
Premiership Two
Dundee HSFP v Kelso
Edinburgh Academicals v Musselburgh
Gala v Aberdeen GSFP
Kilmarnock Falcons v Kirkcaldy
Selkirk v Biggar

WRU – LEAGUE
Premier Division
Ebbw Vale v Bridgend
Neath v Caerphilly
Pontypridd v Llanelli
Swansea v Cardiff
Division One
Aberavon v Treorchy
Bonymaen v Pontypool
Cross Keys v Llandovery
Merthyr v Tredegar
Newbridge v Abertillery
Newport v Blackwood
South Wales Police v Rumney
Tondu v Dunvant

IRU – INTERPROVINCIAL
Ulster v Munster

Sunday 6 September

ALLIED DUNBAR ONE
Saracens v Northampton

Tuesday 8 September

WRU – LEAGUE
Premier Division
Bridgend v Pontypridd
Cardiff v Caerphilly
Llanelli v Neath
Swansea v Ebbw Vale

Saturday 12 September

ALLIED DUNBAR ONE
London Scottish v Leicester
Newcastle v Bath
Northampton v Harlequins
Richmond v Gloucester
Sale v Bedford
West Hartlepool v London Irish

ALLIED DUNBAR TWO
Blackheath v London Welsh
Bristol v Fylde
Coventry v Waterloo
Moseley v Leeds
Orrell v Rugby
Rotherham v Exeter
Wakefield v Worcester

SRU – TENNENTS LEAGUE
Premiership One
Boroughmuir v Stirling County
Hawick v Glasgow Hawks
Heriot's FP v Jed-Forest
Melrose v Currie
West of Scotland v Watsonians
Premiership Two
Aberdeen GSFP v Dundee HSFP
Biggar v Gala
Kelso v Edinburgh Academicals
Kirkcaldy v Selkirk
Musselburgh v Kilmarnock Falcons

SRU SCOTTISH CUP
1st Round

WRU – LEAGUE
Premier Division
Caerphilly v Llanelli
Ebbw Vale v Cardiff

Neath v Bridgend
Pontypridd v Swansea
Division One
Abertillery v Aberavon
Blackwood v South Wales Police
Dunvant v Merthyr
Llandovery v Newport
Pontypool v Cross Keys
Rumney v Newbridge
Tredegar v Bonymaen
Treorchy v Tondu

IRU – INTERPROVINCIAL
Munster v Connacht
Ulster v Leinster

Saturday 19 September

ALLIED DUNBAR ONE
Bath v Richmond
Bedford v London Scottish
Gloucester v West Hartlepool
Leicester v Northampton
London Irish v Wasps
Saracens v Sale

ALLIED DUNBAR TWO
Exeter v Coventry
Fylde v Rotherham
Leeds v Blackheath
London Welsh v Orrell
Rugby v Bristol
Waterloo v Wakefield
Worcester v Moseley

TETLEY'S BITTER CUP
1st Round

SRU – TENNENTS LEAGUE
Premiership One
Currie v Stirling County
Glasgow Hawks v Boroughmuir
Jed-Forest v Hawick
Melrose v West of Scotland
Watsonians v Heriot's FP
Premiership Two
Dundee HSFP v Biggar
Edinburgh Academicals v Aberdeen
  GSFP
Kilmarnock Falcons v Kelso
Kirkcaldy v Musselburgh
Selkirk v Gala

WRU – LEAGUE
Division One
Bonymaen v Dunvant
Cross Keys v Tredegar
Merthyr v Treorchy
Newbridge v Aberavon
Newport v Pontypool
Rumney v Blackwood
South Wales Police v Llandovery
Tondu v Abertillery

Sunday 20 September

ALLIED DUNBAR ONE
Saracens v Sale

Tuesday 22 September

WRU – LEAGUE
Division One
Aberavon v Tondu
Abertillery v Merthyr
Blackwood v Newbridge
Dunvant v Cross Keys
Llandovery v Rumney
Pontypool v South Wales Police
Tredegar v Newport
Treorchy v Bonymaen

Saturday 26 September

ALLIED DUNBAR ONE
Bath v Gloucester
Bedford v Leicester
London Scottish v Saracens
Newcastle v London Irish
Sale v Harlequins
Wasps v West Hartlepool

ALLIED DUNBAR TWO
Bristol v London Welsh
Coventry v Fylde
Moseley v Waterloo
Orrell v Blackheath
Rotherham v Rugby
Wakefield v Exeter
Worcester v Leeds

SRU – TENNENTS LEAGUE
Premiership One
Boroughmuir v Jed-Forest
Hawick v Watsonians

Heriot's FP v Melrose
Stirling County v Glasgow Hawks
West of Scotland v Currie
Premiership Two
Aberdeen GSFP v Kilmarnock Falcons
Biggar v Edinburgh Academicals
Gala v Dundee HSFP
Kelso v Kirkcaldy
Musselburgh v Selkirk

WRU – LEAGUE
Division One
Blackwood v Llandovery
Bonymaen v Abertillery
Cross Keys v Treorchy
Merthyr v Aberavon
Newbridge v Tondu
Newport v Dunvant
Rumney v Pontypool
Tredegar v South Wales Police

WRU SWALEC CUP
1st Round

Saturday 3 October

ALLIED DUNBAR ONE
Gloucester v Wasps
Harlequins v London Scottish
London Irish v Richmond
Northampton v Sale
West Hartlepool v Newcastle

ALLIED DUNBAR TWO
Blackheath v Bristol
Exeter v Moseley
Fylde v Wakefield
Leeds v Orrell
London Welsh v Rotherham
Rugby v Coventry
Waterloo v Worcester

SRU – TENNENTS LEAGUE
Premiership One
Currie v Glasgow Hawks
Jed-Forest v Stirling County
Melrose v Hawick
Watsonians v Boroughmuir
West of Scotland v Heriot's FP
Premiership Two
Edinburgh Academicals v Gala
Kilmarnock Falcons v Biggar
Kirkcaldy v Aberdeen GSFP
Musselburgh v Kelso

Selkirk v Dundee HSFP

WRU – LEAGUE
Premier Division
Bridgend v Caerphilly
Ebbw Vale v Pontypridd
Llanelli v Cardiff
Swansea v Neath
Division One
Aberavon v Bonymaen
Abertillery v Cross Keys
Dunvant v South Wales Police
Newbridge v Llandovery
Pontypool v Blackwood
Tondu v Merthyr
Tredegar v Rumney
Treorchy v Newport

IRU – INTERPROVINCIAL
Connacht v Leinster
Munster v Ulster

Sunday 4 October

ALLIED DUNBAR ONE
Saracens v Bedford

Saturday 10 October

ALLIED DUNBAR TWO
Bristol v Orrell
Coventry v London Welsh
Moseley v Fylde
Rotherham v Blackheath
Wakefield v Rugby
Waterloo v Leeds
Worcester v Exeter

SRU – TENNENTS LEAGUE
Premiership One
Boroughmuir v Melrose
Glasgow Hawks v Jed-Forest
Hawick v West of Scotland
Heriot's FP v Currie
Stirling County v Watsonians
Premiership Two
Aberdeen GSFP v Musselburgh
Biggar v Kirkcaldy
Dundee HSFP v Edinburgh
    Academicals
Gala v Kilmarnock Falcons
Kelso v Selkirk

SRU SCOTTISH CUP
2nd Round

WRU – LEAGUE
Division One
Abertillery v Newport
Blackwood v Tredegar
Bonymaen v Tondu
Cross Keys v Aberavon
Llandovery v Pontypool
Merthyr v Newbridge
Rumney v Dunvant
South Wales Police v Treorchy

Saturday 17 October

ALLIED DUNBAR TWO
Blackheath v Coventry
Exeter v Waterloo
Fylde v Worcester
Leeds v Bristol
London Welsh v Wakefield
Orrell v Rotherham
Rugby v Moseley

TETLEY'S BITTER CUP
2nd Round

SRU – TENNENTS LEAGUE
Premiership One
Currie v Jed-Forest
Heriot's FP v Hawick
Melrose v Stirling County
Watsonians v Glasgow Hawks
West of Scotland v Boroughmuir
Premiership Two
Kelso v Aberdeen GSFP
Kilmarnock Falcons v Dundee HSFP
Kirkcaldy v Gala
Musselburgh v Biggar
Selkirk v Edinburgh Academicals

WRU – LEAGUE
Division One
Aberavon v Newport
Abertillery v South Wales Police
Dunvant v Blackwood
Llandovery v Tredegar
Merthyr v Bonymaen
Newbridge v Pontypool
Tondu v Cross Keys
Treorchy v Rumney

Saturday 24 October

ALLIED DUNBAR TWO
Coventry v Orrell
Exeter v Leeds
Moseley v London Welsh
Rotherham v Bristol
Wakefield v Blackheath
Waterloo v Fylde
Worcester v Rugby

SRU – TENNENTS LEAGUE
Premiership One
Boroughmuir v Heriot's FP
Currie v Hawick
Glasgow Hawks v Melrose
Jed-Forest v Watsonians
Stirling County v West of Scotland
Premiership Two
Biggar v Kelso
Dundee HSFP v Kirkcaldy
Edinburgh Academicals v Kilmarnock
   Falcons
Gala v Musselburgh
Selkirk v Aberdeen GSFP

WRU – LEAGUE
Premier Division
Caerphilly v Swansea
Cardiff v Pontypridd
Llanelli v Bridgend
Neath v Ebbw Vale
Division One
Blackwood v Treorchy
Bonymaen v Newbridge
Cross Keys v Merthyr
Llandovery v Dunvant
Newport v Tondu
Pontypool v Tredegar
Rumney v Abertillery
South Wales Police v Aberavon

WRU SWALEC CUP
2nd Round

IRU – INTERPROVINCIAL
Leinster v Munster
Ulster v Connacht

Tuesday 27 October

WRU – LEAGUE
Division One
Aberavon v Rumney
Abertillery v Blackwood

Bonymaen v Cross Keys
Dunvant v Pontypool
Merthyr v Newport
Newbridge v Tredegar
Tondu v South Wales Police
Treorchy v Llandovery

Saturday 31 October

ALLIED DUNBAR TWO
Blackheath v Moseley
Bristol v Coventry
Fylde v Exeter
Leeds v Rotherham
London Welsh v Worcester
Orrell v Wakefield
Rugby v Waterloo

SRU – TENNENTS LEAGUE
Premiership One
Hawick v Boroughmuir
Heriot's FP v Stirling County
Melrose v Jed-Forest
Watsonians v Currie
West of Scotland v Glasgow Hawks
Premiership Two
Aberdeen GSFP v Biggar
Kelso v Gala
Kilmarnock Falcons v Selkirk
Kirkcaldy v Edinburgh Academicals
Musselburgh v Dundee HSFP

Saturday 7 November

ALLIED DUNBAR TWO
Blackheath v Moseley
Bristol v Coventry
Fylde v Exeter
Leeds v Rotherham
London Welsh v Worcester
Orrell v Wakefield
Rugby v Waterloo

SRU – TENNENTS LEAGUE
Premiership One
Boroughmuir v Currie
Hawick v Stirling County
Heriot's FP v Glasgow Hawks
Melrose v Watsonians
West of Scotland v Jed-Forest
Premiership Two
Aberdeen GSFP v Gala
Biggar v Selkirk

Kelso v Dundee HSFP
Kirkcaldy v Kilmarnock Falcons
Musselburgh v Edinburgh Academicals

WRU – LEAGUE
Division One
Blackwood v Aberavon
Cross Keys v Newbridge
Llandovery v Abertillery
Newport v Bonymaen
Pontypool v Treorchy
Rumney v Tondu
South Wales Police v Merthyr
Tredegar v Dunvant

Tuesday 10 November

Glasgow Caledonians v South Africa

Wednesday 11 November

Edinburgh Reivers v N Z Maori

Saturday 14 November

ENGLAND v NETHERLANDS,
  Huddersfield

IRELAND v GEORGIA, Dublin

SCOTLAND v NZ MAORI,
  Murrayfield

WALES v SOUTH AFRICA, Wembley

Sunday 15 November

SRU SCOTTISH CUP
3rd Round

Tuesday 17 November

Edinburgh Reivers v South Africa

Wednesday 18 November

GEORGIA v ROMANIA, Dublin

ITALY v NETHERLANDS,
  Huddersfield
Glasgow Caledonians v NZ Maori

Saturday 21 November

SCOTLAND v SOUTH AFRICA,
  Murrayfield

WALES v ARGENTINA, TBC

ALLIED DUNBAR TWO
Blackheath v Waterloo
Bristol v Moseley
Leeds v Coventry
London Welsh v Exeter
Orrell v Worcester
Rotherham v Wakefield
Rugby v Fylde

WRU – LEAGUE
Division One
Aberavon v Pontypool
Abertillery v Tredegar
Bonymaen v Rumney
Cross Keys v South Wales Police
Merthyr v Blackwood
Newbridge v Newport
Tondu v Llandovery
Treorchy v Dunvant

Sunday 22 November

ENGLAND v ITALY, Huddersfield

IRELAND v ROMANIA, Dublin

Tuesday 24 November

Glasgow Caledonians v Canterbury

Friday 27 November

Edinburgh Reivers v Canterbury

Saturday 28 November

ENGLAND v AUSTRALIA,
  Twickenham

IRELAND v SOUTH AFRICA, Dublin

SCOTLAND v PORTUGAL,
  Murrayfield

WRU – LEAGUE
Premier Division
Bridgend v Cardiff
Ebbw Vale v Caerphilly

Pontypridd v Neath
Swansea v Llanelli
Division One
Blackwood v Tondu
Dunvant v Newbridge
Llandovery v Aberavon
Newport v Cross Keys
Pontypool v Abertillery
Rumney v Merthyr
South Wales Police v Bonymaen
Tredegar v Treorchy

WRU SWALEC CUP
3rd Round

Sunday 29 November

SRU SCOTTISH CUP
4th Round

Tuesday 1 December

WRU – LEAGUE
Premier Division
Ebbw Vale v Llanelli
Neath v Cardiff
Pontypridd v Caerphilly
Swansea v Bridgend

Wednesday 2 December

PORTUGAL v SPAIN, Murrayfield

Saturday 5 December

**ENGLAND v SOUTH AFRICA,
  Twickenham**

SCOTLAND v SPAIN, Murrayfield

IRU – AIB LEAGUE
Division One
Ballymena v Shannon
Blackrock College v Terenure College
Buccaneers v Galwegians
Garryowen v Clontarf
Lansdowne v Cork Constitution
Young Munster v St Mary's College
Division Two
Bective Rangers v Portadown
Dungannon v Greystones
Old Belvedere v Old Wesley
Old Crescent v City of Derry

Skerries v Dolphin
Sunday's Well v Ballynahinch
UC Cork v Malone
Wanderers v DLS Palmerston

WRU – LEAGUE
Premier Division
Bridgend v Ebbw Vale
Caerphilly v Neath
Cardiff v Swansea
Llanelli v Pontypridd
Division One
Aberavon v Tredegar
Blackwood v Bonymaen
Dunvant v Abertillery
Llandovery v Merthyr
Pontypool v Tondu
Rumney v Cross Keys
South Wales Police v Newport
Treorchy v Newbridge

Tuesday 8 December

BOWRING BOWL
Oxford Univ v Cambridge Univ,
  Twickenham

Saturday 12 December

ALLIED DUNBAR TWO
Exeter v Blackheath
London Welsh v Fylde
Moseley v Rotherham
Rugby v Leeds
Wakefield v Coventry
Waterloo v Orrell
Worcester v Bristol

IRU – AIB LEAGUE
Division One
Clontarf v Buccaneers
Cork Constitution v Ballymena
Galwegians v Blackrock College
Shannon v Garryowen
St Mary's College v Lansdowne
Terenure College v Young Munster
Division Two
Ballynahinch v Dungannon
City of Derry v Sunday's Well
DLS Palmerston v Bective Rangers
Dolphin v Old Crescent
Greystones v Old Belvedere
Malone v Wanderers

Old Wesley v Skerries
Portadown v UC Cork

SRU – TENNENTS LEAGUE
Premiership One
Currie v Melrose
Glasgow Hawks v Hawick
Jed-Forest v Heriot's FP
Stirling County v Boroughmuir
Watsonians v West of Scotland
Premiership Two
Dundee HSFP v Aberdeen GSFP
Edinburgh Academicals v Kelso
Gala v Biggar
Kilmarnock Falcons v Musselburgh
Selkirk v Kirkcaldy

WRU – LEAGUE
Division One
Aberavon v Dunvant
Abertillery v Treorchy
Bonymaen v Llandovery
Cross Keys v Blackwood
Merthyr v Pontypool
Newbridge v South Wales Police
Newport v Rumney
Tondu v Tredegar

Saturday 19 December

ALLIED DUNBAR TWO
Blackheath v Fylde
Bristol v Waterloo
Coventry v Moseley
Leeds v Wakefield
London Welsh v Rugby
Orrell v Exeter
Rotherham v Worcester

IRU – AIB LEAGUE
Division One
Ballymena v St Mary's College
Blackrock College v Shannon
Buccaneers v Terenure College
Garryowen v Galwegians
Lansdowne v Clontarf
Young Munster v Cork Constitution
Division Two
Ballynahinch v City of Derry
Bective Rangers v Wanderers
Dolphin v Old Wesley
Dungannon v Portadown
Old Belvedere v Malone
Skerries v Greystones

UC Cork v DLS Palmerston

SRU – TENNENTS LEAGUE
Premiership One
Boroughmuir v Glasgow Hawks
Hawick v Jed-Forest
Heriot's FP v Watsonians
Stirling County v Currie
West of Scotland v Melrose
Premiership Two
Aberdeen GSFP v Edinburgh
    Academicals
Biggar v Dundee HSFP
Gala v Selkirk
Kelso v Kilmarnock Falcons
Musselburgh v Kirkcaldy

WRU SWALEC CUP
4th Round

Sunday 20 December

IRU – AIB LEAGUE
Division Two
Sunday's Well v Old Crescent

Saturday 26 December

IRU – AIB LEAGUE
Division Two
Dungannon v Malone
Old Wesley v Wanderers

WRU – LEAGUE
Premier Division
Caerphilly v Cardiff
Ebbw Vale v Swansea
Neath v Llanelli
Pontypridd v Bridgend
Division One
Abertillery v Newbridge
Blackwood v Newport
Dunvant v Tondu
Llandovery v Cross Keys
Pontypool v Bonymaen
Rumney v South Wales Police
Tredegar v Merthyr
Treorchy v Aberavon

Saturday 2 January

ALLIED DUNBAR TWO
Coventry v Leeds
Exeter v London Welsh
Fylde v Rugby
Moseley v Bristol
Wakefield v Rotherham
Waterloo v Blackheath
Worcester v Orrell

IRU – AIB LEAGUE
Division One
Clontarf v Ballymena
Cork Constitution v Blackrock College
Galwegians v Young Munster
Shannon v Buccaneers
St Mary's College v Garryowen
Terenure College v Lansdowne
Division Two
City of Derry v UC Cork
DLS Palmerston v Dungannon
Greystones v Dolphin
Malone v Skerries
Old Crescent v Old Wesley
Portadown v Ballynahinch
Sunday's Well v Bective Rangers
Wanderers v Old Belvedere

WRU – LEAGUE
Premier Division
Bridgend v Neath
Cardiff v Ebbw Vale
Llanelli v Caerphilly
Swansea v Pontypridd
Division One
Aberavon v Abertillery
Bonymaen v Tredegar
Cross Keys v Pontypool
Merthyr v Dunvant
Newbridge v Rumney
Newport v Llandovery
South Wales Police v Blackwood
Tondu v Treorchy

Saturday 9 January

TETLEY'S BITTER CUP
4th Round

IRU – AIB LEAGUE
Division One
Ballymena v Terenure College
Blackrock College v Clontarf

Buccaneers v St Mary's College
Garryowen v Cork Constitution
Lansdowne v Galwegians
Division Two
Ballynahinch v Malone
Bective Rangers v Old Crescent
Dolphin v Wanderers
Dungannon v City of Derry
Old Belvedere v DLS Palmerston
Skerries v Portadown
UC Cork v Sunday's Well

SRU SCOTTISH CUP
5th Round

WRU – LEAGUE
Division One
Aberavon v Newbridge
Abertillery v Tondu
Blackwood v Rumney
Dunvant v Bonymaen
Llandovery v South Wales Police
Pontypool v Newport
Tredegar v Cross Keys
Treorchy v Merthyr

Sunday 10 January

IRU – AIB LEAGUE
Division One
Young Munster v Shannon
Division Two
Old Wesley v Greystones

Saturday 16 January

ALLIED DUNBAR TWO
Blackheath v Worcester
Bristol v Wakefield
Leeds v Fylde
London Welsh v Waterloo
Orrell v Moseley
Rotherham v Coventry
Rugby v Exeter

IRU – AIB LEAGUE
Division One
Clontarf v Young Munster
Cork Constitution v Buccaneers
Galwegians v Ballymena
Shannon v Lansdowne
St Mary's College v Blackrock College
Terenure College v Garryowen

Division Two
Bective Rangers v UC Cork
City of Derry v Old Belvedere
DLS Palmerston v Skerries
Malone v Old Wesley
Old Crescent v Ballynahinch
Portadown v Dolphin
Sunday's Well v Dungannon
Wanderers v Greystones

SRU – TENNENTS LEAGUE
Premiership One
Currie v West of Scotland
Glasgow Hawks v Stirling County
Jed-Forest v Boroughmuir
Melrose v Heriot's FP
Watsonians v Hawick
Premiership Two
Dundee HSFP v Gala
Edinburgh Academicals v Biggar
Kilmarnock Falcons v Aberdeen GSFP
Kirkcaldy v Kelso
Selkirk v Musselburgh

WRU – LEAGUE
Division One
Bonymaen v Treorchy
Cross Keys v Dunvant
Merthyr v Abertillery
Newbridge v Blackwood
Newport v Tredegar
Rumney v Llandovery
South Wales Police v Pontypool
Tondu v Aberavon

Saturday 23 January

ALLIED DUNBAR TWO
Coventry v Bristol
Exeter v Fylde
Moseley v Blackheath
Rotherham v Leeds
Wakefield v Orrell
Waterloo v Rugby
Worcester v London Welsh

IRU – AIB LEAGUE
Division One
Buccaneers v Garryowen
Clontarf v St Mary's College
Cork Constitution v Galwegians
Lansdowne v Blackrock College
Shannon v Terenure College
Young Munster v Ballymena

Division Two
Ballynahinch v Bective Rangers
Dolphin v DLS Palmerston
Dungannon v Wanderers
Greystones v Malone
Old Belvedere v Sunday's Well
Old Crescent v UC Cork
Old Wesley v Portadown
Skerries v City of Derry

SRU – TENNENTS LEAGUE
Premiership One
Boroughmuir v Watsonians
Glasgow Hawks v Currie
Hawick v Melrose
Heriot's FP v West of Scotland
Stirling County v Jed-Forest
Premiership Two
Aberdeen GSFP v Kirkcaldy
Biggar v Kilmarnock Falcons
Dundee HSFP v Selkirk
Gala v Edinburgh Academicals
Kelso v Musselburgh

Saturday 30 January

TETLEY'S BITTER CUP
5th Round

IRU – AIB LEAGUE
Division Two
Ballynahinch v Dolphin
Bective Rangers v Old Belvedere
City of Derry v Wanderers
DLS Palmerston v Old Wesley
Malone v Old Crescent
Portadown v Greystones
Sunday's Well v Skerries
UC Cork v Dungannon

SRU – TENNENTS LEAGUE
Premiership One
Currie v Heriot's FP
Jed-Forest v Glasgow Hawks
Melrose v Boroughmuir
Watsonians v Stirling County
West of Scotland v Hawick
Premiership Two
Edinburgh Academicals v Dundee
 HSFP
Kilmarnock Falcons v Gala
Kirkcaldy v Biggar
Musselburgh v Aberdeen GSFP
Selkirk v Kelso

WRU – LEAGUE
Division One
Aberavon v Merthyr
Abertillery v Bonymaen
Dunvant v Newport
Llandovery v Blackwood
Pontypool v Rumney
South Wales Police v Tredegar
Tondu v Newbridge
Treorchy v Cross Keys

WRU SWALEC CUP
5th Round

Tuesday 2 February

WRU – LEAGUE
Division One
Blackwood v Pontypool
Bonymaen v Aberavon
Cross Keys v Abertillery
Llandovery v Newbridge
Merthyr v Tondu
Newport v Treorchy
Rumney v Tredegar
South Wales Police v Dunvant

Saturday 6 February

IRELAND v FRANCE, Dublin

SCOTLAND v WALES, Murrayfield

ALLIED DUNBAR TWO
Blackheath v Wakefield
Bristol v Rotherham
Fylde v Waterloo
Leeds v Exeter
London Welsh v Moseley
Orrell v Coventry
Rugby v Worcester

Saturday 13 February

ALLIED DUNBAR TWO
Bristol v Leeds
Coventry v Blackheath
Moseley v Rugby
Rotherham v Orrell
Wakefield v London Welsh
Waterloo v Exeter
Worcester v Fylde

IRU – AIB LEAGUE
Division One
Ballymena v Buccaneers
Blackrock College v Young Munster
Galwegians v Clontarf
Garryowen v Lansdowne
St Mary's College v Shannon
Terenure College v Cork Constitution
Division Two
Dolphin v Sunday's Well
Greystones v DLS Palmerston
Malone v Portadown
Old Belvedere v Ballynahinch
Old Crescent v Dungannon
Old Wesley v City of Derry
Skerries v Bective Rangers
Wanderers v UC Cork

SRU SCOTTISH CUP
Quarter-finals

WRU – LEAGUE
Premier Division
Caerphilly v Bridgend
Cardiff v Llanelli
Neath v Swansea
Pontypridd v Ebbw Vale
Division One
Aberavon v Cross Keys
Dunvant v Rumney
Newbridge v Merthyr
Newport v Abertillery
Pontypool v Llandovery
Tondu v Bonymaen
Tredegar v Blackwood
Treorchy v South Wales Police

Saturday 20 February

**ENGLAND v SCOTLAND,
Twickenham**

WALES v IRELAND, Wembley

Saturday 27 February

ALLIED DUNBAR TWO
Blackheath v Rotherham
Exeter v Worcester
Fylde v Moseley
Leeds v Waterloo
London Welsh v Coventry
Orrell v Bristol

Rugby v Wakefield

TETLEY'S BITTER CUP
Quarter-finals

IRU – AIB LEAGUE
Division One
Ballymena v Garryowen
Blackrock College v Buccaneers
Clontarf v Shannon
Cork Constitution v St Mary's College
Terenure College v Galwegians
Young Munster v Lansdowne
Division Two
Bective Rangers v Dolphin
City of Derry v Greystones
DLS Palmerston v Malone
Dungannon v Old Belvedere
Portadown v Old Crescent
Skerries v Wanderers
Sunday's Well v Old Wesley
UC Cork v Ballynahinch

SRU – TENNENTS LEAGUE
Premiership One
Boroughmuir v West of Scotland
Glasgow Hawks v Watsonians
Hawick v Heriot's FP
Jed-Forest v Currie
Stirling County v Melrose
Premiership Two
Aberdeen GSFP v Kelso
Biggar v Musselburgh
Dundee HSFP v Kilmarnock Falcons
Edinburgh Academicals v Selkirk
Gala v Kirkcaldy

WRU SWALEC CUP
6th Round

Saturday 6 March

IRELAND v ENGLAND, Dublin

FRANCE v WALES, Paris

SCOTLAND v ITALY, Murrayfield

Saturday 13 March

ALLIED DUNBAR TWO
Bristol v Blackheath
Coventry v Rugby
Moseley v Exeter
Orrell v Leeds

Rotherham v London Welsh
Wakefield v Fylde
Worcester v Waterloo

IRU – AIB LEAGUE
Division One
Buccaneers v Young Munster
Clontarf v Cork Constitution
Garryowen v Blackrock College
Lansdowne v Ballymena
Shannon v Galwegians
St Mary's College v Terenure College
Division Two
Ballyhahinch v DLS Palmerston
Bective Rangers v Greystones
Dolphin v Dungannon
Malone v Sunday's Well
Old Belvedere v Skerries
Portadown v City of Derry
UC Cork v Old Wesley
Wanderers v Old Crescent

SRU – TENNENTS LEAGUE
Premiership One
Hawick v Currie
Heriot's FP v Boroughmuir
Melrose v Glasgow Hawks
Watsonians v Jed-Forest
West of Scotland v Stirling County
Premiership Two
Aberdeen GSFP v Selkirk
Kelso v Biggar
Kilmarnock Falcons v Edinburgh
   Academicals
Kirkcaldy v Dundee HSFP
Musselburgh v Gala

WRU – LEAGUE
Premier Division
Bridgend v Llanelli
Ebbw Vale v Neath
Pontypridd v Cardiff
Swansea v Caerphilly
Division One
Blackwood v Dunvant
Bonymaen v Merthyr
Cross Keys v Tondu
Newport v Aberavon
Pontypool v Newbridge
Rumney v Treorchy
South Wales Police v Abertillery
Tredegar v Llandovery

Saturday 20 March

ENGLAND v FRANCE, Twickenham

ITALY v WALES, TBC

SCOTLAND v IRELAND, Murrayfield

Tuesday 23 March

WRU – LEAGUE
Division One
Aberavon v South Wales Police
Abertillery v Rumney
Dunvant v Llandovery
Merthyr v Cross Keys
Newbridge v Bonymaen
Tondu v Newport
Tredegar v Pontypool
Treorchy v Blackwood

Saturday 27 March

ALLIED DUNBAR TWO
Blackheath v Orrell
Exeter v Wakefield
Fylde v Coventry
Leeds v Worcester
London Welsh v Bristol
Rugby v Rotherham
Waterloo v Moseley

IRU – AIB LEAGUE
Division One
Blackrock College v Ballymena
Buccaneers v Lansdowne
Cork Constitution v Shannon
Galwegians v St Mary's College
Terenure College v Clontarf
Young Munster v Garryowen
Division Two
Ballynahinch v Wanderers
DLS Palmerston v City of Derry
Greystones v UC Cork
Malone v Bective Rangers
Old Crescent v Skerries
Old Wesley v Dungannon
Sunday's Well v Portadown

SRU – TENNENTS LEAGUE
Premiership One
Boroughmuir v Hawick
Currie v Watsonians

Glasgow Hawks v West of Scotland
Jed-Forest v Melrose
Stirling County v Heriot's FP
Premiership Two
Biggar v Aberdeen GSFP
Dundee HSFP v Musselburgh
Edinburgh Academicals v Kirkcaldy
Gala v Kelso
Selkirk v Kilmarnock Falcons

WRU – LEAGUE
Division One
Blackwood v Abertillery
Cross Keys v Bonymaen
Llandovery v Treorchy
Newport v Merthyr
Pontypool v Dunvant
Rumney v Aberavon
South Wales Police v Tondu
Tredegar v Newbridge

WRU SWALEC CUP
Quarter-finals

Sunday 28 March

IRU – AIB LEAGUE
Division Two
Dolphin v Old Belvedere

Saturday 3 April

ALLIED DUNBAR TWO
Blackheath v Leeds
Bristol v Rugby
Coventry v Exeter
Moseley v Worcester
Orrell v London Welsh
Rotherham v Fylde
Wakefield v Waterloo

TETLEY'S BITTER CUP
Semi-finals

IRU – AIB LEAGUE
Division Two
City of Derry v Dolphin
Dungannon v Bective Rangers
Old Belvedere v UC Cork
Old Crescent v Greystones
Skerries v Ballynahinch
Sunday's Well v DLS Palmerston
Wanderers v Portadown